CLI : Command line inter[...]

Class A   0   0 — 127
"   B   10   128 — 191
"   C   110   192 — 223

{ 128 64 32 16 8 4 2 1

ISO

| USer |
| APPlication |
| Presentation |
| Session |
| TransPort |
| Network |
| Data-link |
| PHysical |

Personal Identification Information (PII)
Network Adress Translator (NAT)

In the router distance is mesure in
HOPS => How many routers (switch) do I Have to go through?

How ~~many~~ does the router know How to get to a
destination?   ① static Routers
                 ② use routing protocol
                    { distance vector
                    { link state

RIP => Router Information
                      Protocol

ARP => address Resolution protocol

In an adress 171.16.251.0
The 0 represent The Subnet name
The broadcast adress is 255.

Routers and Routing Basics

CCNA 2 Companion Guide

Wendell Odom

Rick McDonald

Cisco Press

800 East 96th Street

Indianapolis, Indiana 46240 USA

Routers and Routing Basics

CCNA 2 Companion Guide

Wendell Odom

Rick McDonald

Copyright© 2007 Cisco Systems, Inc.

Published by:
Cisco Press
800 East 96th Street
Indianapolis, IN 46240 USA

Printed in the United States of America

Seventeenth Printing September 2014

Library of Congress Cataloging-in-Publication Number: 2005934966

ISBN: 1-58713-166-8

Trademark Acknowledgments

Warning and Disclaimer

Publisher
Paul Boger

Cisco Representative
Anthony Wolfenden

Cisco Press Program Manager
Jeff Brady

Executive Editor
Mary Beth Ray

Production Manager
Patrick Kanouse

Development Editor
Dayna Isley

Senior Project Editor
San Dee Phillips

Copy Editor
Bill McManus

Technical Editors
Stephen Kalman
William Salice

Book and Cover Designer
Louisa Adair

Composition
Mark Shirar

Indexer
Tim Wright

Proofreader
Gayle Johnson

Feedback Information

At Cisco Press, our goal is to create in-depth technical books of the highest quality and value. Each book is crafted with care and precision, undergoing rigorous development that involves the unique expertise of members from the professional technical community.

Readers' feedback is a natural continuation of this process. If you have any comments regarding how we could improve the quality of this book, or otherwise alter it to better suit your needs, you can contact us through e-mail at feedback@ciscopress.com. Please make sure to include the book title and ISBN in your message.

We greatly appreciate your assistance.

Corporate Headquarters
Cisco Systems, Inc.
170 West Tasman Drive
San Jose, CA 95134-1706
USA
www.cisco.com
Tel: 408 526-4000
 800 553-NETS (6387)
Fax: 408 526-4100

European Headquarters
Cisco Systems International BV
Haarlerbergpark
Haarlerbergweg 13-19
1101 CH Amsterdam
The Netherlands
www-europe.cisco.com
Tel: 31 0 20 357 1000
Fax: 31 0 20 357 1100

Americas Headquarters
Cisco Systems, Inc.
170 West Tasman Drive
San Jose, CA 95134-1706
USA
www.cisco.com
Tel: 408 526-7660
Fax: 408 527-0883

Asia Pacific Headquarters
Cisco Systems, Inc.
Capital Tower
168 Robinson Road
#22-01 to #29-01
Singapore 068912
www.cisco.com
Tel: +65 6317 7777
Fax: +65 6317 7799

Cisco Systems has more than 200 offices in the following countries and regions. Addresses, phone numbers, and fax numbers are listed on the
Cisco.com Web site at www.cisco.com/go/offices.

Argentina • Australia • Austria • Belgium • Brazil • Bulgaria • Canada • Chile • China PRC • Colombia • Costa Rica • Croatia • Czech Republic
Denmark • Dubai, UAE • Finland • France • Germany • Greece • Hong Kong SAR • Hungary • India • Indonesia • Ireland • Israel • Italy
Japan • Korea • Luxembourg • Malaysia • Mexico • The Netherlands • New Zealand • Norway • Peru • Philippines • Poland • Portugal
Puerto Rico • Romania • Russia • Saudi Arabia • Scotland • Singapore • Slovakia • Slovenia • South Africa • Spain • Sweden
Switzerland • Taiwan • Thailand • Turkey • Ukraine • United Kingdom • United States • Venezuela • Vietnam • Zimbabwe

About the Authors

Wendell Odom, **CCIE No. 1624**, is a senior instructor with Skyline Advanced Technology Services (http://www.skyline-ats.com), where he teaches the QOS, CCIE, MPLS, and CCNA courses. Wendell has worked in the networking arena for over 20 years, with jobs in pre- and post-sales technical consulting, teaching, and course development. He has authored several Cisco Press books, including the best-selling *CCNA INTRO Exam Certification Guide* and *CCNA ICND Exam Certification Guide*, as well as the *QoS Exam Certification Guide*, *Computer Networking First-Step*, *CCIE Routing and Switching Official Exam Certification Guide*, Second Edition, and *Networking Basics CCNA 1 Companion Guide*.

Rick McDonald teaches computer and networking courses at the University of Alaska Southeast in Ketchikan, Alaska. He holds a BA in English and an MA in educational technology from Gonzaga University in Spokane, Washington. After several years in the airline industry, he returned to full-time teaching. Rick started in the Cisco Networking Academy Program in North Carolina, where he taught CCNA and CCNP courses and was a CCNA Instructor Trainer. In addition, Rick has written CCNP study guides for the Academy program and was a technical editor for *CCNA 3 and 4 Companion Guide*, Third Edition (Cisco Press). His current project is developing methods for delivering hands-on training via distance in Alaska using web conferencing and NETLAB tools. Rick enjoys travel and hiking with his wife, Becky, and his sons, Greg, Paul, and Sam.

About the Technical Reviewers

Stephen Kalman is a data security trainer. He is the author of *Web Security Field Guide* (Cisco Press) and the technical editor of more than 20 books, courses, and computer-based training (CBT) titles. In addition to those responsibilities, Stephen runs a consulting company, Esquire Micro Consultants, which specializes in network security assessments and forensics. Stephen holds CISSP, CEH, CHFI, CCNA, CCSA (Checkpoint), A+, Network+, and Security+ certifications. He is also a member of the New York State Bar.

William Salice is the Director of Education for ECPI College of Technology in Virginia Beach, Virginia. He has worked with network infrastructures for nine years and has taught the Cisco Networking Academy Program curriculum for four years. William holds CCNA, CCAI, MCSE, NET+, A+, CFOI, CFOT, and Senior CET certifications. He loves networking, teaching, and his son Julian.

Acknowledgments

From Wendell Odom:

Rick McDonald certainly deserves the most credit for helping this book be more than just a technology book, by helping make sure that it meets the unique needs of the Cisco Networking Academies. Rick helped tremendously with keeping the book focused and determining when more info was better and, more importantly, when more info was probably too much. Rick, thanks so much for helping shape this book.

Thanks to the technical editors for their work providing feedback and suggestions about the manuscript. I will take full blame for any remaining errors in the book, but both technical editors helped limit those errors, while helping me change and emphasize certain points. Steve Kalman edited yet another of my books, doing his usual wonderful job and stopping me from spreading an urban legend! (Thanks for that one especially, Steve!) Bill Salice did a nice job verifying accuracy and helping us meet the audience level based on his experience with the Cisco Networking Academy Program. Thanks to both of you.

Mary Beth Ray hooked Rick and me together to work on this book. She also worked with us through some scheduling issues, particularly when at one point we were juggling the schedules of four separate book project schedules. Thanks, MB, for making the schedule work so that I could do two of the new *Companion Guides*, not just one!

Dayna Isley got to sift through all the messiness of the first draft (again, two in a row now), and she seemingly remained incredibly sane through the process. It's so helpful to have such a sharp mind and a very nice person guiding the manuscript through the many little details of what's required with these books. Thanks, Dayna!

Patrick Kanouse's production team did the usual wonderful job, taking my broken sentences and figures and making me look good, again. Thanks to Bill McManus for all the detailed copyediting, and especially for tolerating my whining when I wanted things my way rather than the correct way. Thanks (yet again) to San Dee Phillips for keeping things light, even when it came down to requests like "Can you review these 100 pages by 3 p.m.?—and make changes—and let me see them again by 3 p.m.?" (And yes, to all the production crew at CP, the double quotes are here on purpose!)

The schedule for writing and revising this book, and *Networking Basics CCNA 1 Companion Guide*, was essentially compressed into a total of 7–8 months. My wife, Kris, and daughter, Hannah, were incredibly understanding during this time. Here's to changing "normal" from a life where I'm working incessantly to "normal" being/having around hubby/daddy for evenings and weekends. Thanks for helping get us through! And finally, thanks to my Savior Jesus Christ, without whom all this effort and work is meaningless.

From Rick McDonald:

You may be familiar with the saying "If you like sausage with your breakfast and have a respect for the law, you should never watch either one being made." There were times in the beginning of this process that I felt the same way about textbooks. Now, however, I stand in awe of the level of cooperation and support required to produce a book of this nature, and I am grateful for the support and patience given to me by Wendell Odom, Mary Beth Ray, Dayna Isley, and the technical reviewers, Stephen Kalman and William Salice.

Wendell is the best kind of technical resource, because he is willing and able to parse the nuances of IP as well as suffer the speed bumps we encountered with grace and aplomb. It has been a true privilege to benefit from his vast technical and publishing experience. I am convinced that the only thing bigger than his knowledge is his heart. Through the many hours of conversation and the countless e-mails, one thing that stands out is Wendell's concern that students have the best available when they use this book, and I think that concern has been met. Wendell, it has been both an adventure and a pleasure, and I thank you for it.

Mary Beth Ray has been the steady hand guiding me through the procedural maze and providing support on numerous levels. Whenever I needed a voice of calm assurance or an esoteric resource, she always answered the call. Thank you for doing it all so well and for bringing me to the table with Wendell.

Dayna, Stephen, and William amazed me with the things they could see and that I could miss. If there are errors or conceptual vagaries in this book, they are mine and certainly not from them. Thank you for all the time and effort to make this a resource that will enhance the learning experience for many students.

Of course, many people who have encouraged me along the way deserve a long-overdue note of thanks. To Celese Ward at CPCC, who enticed me into the Cisco Academy so long ago, and to Cathy LeCompte at the University of Alaska Southeast in Ketchikan, whose support and encouragement have been vital, I thank you for your patience and support.

Dedications

For Mike M. and Mike Z., our leaders at Skyline ATS. This book—and several others, for that matter—would've never happened without your generosity, flexibility, and kindheartedness. Thanks from the bottom of my heart.

—Wendell Odom

For my wife, Becky. Without her patience and support, my involvement in this project would not have been possible. Thank you.

—Rick McDonald

Contents at a Glance

Contents

Icons Used in This Book

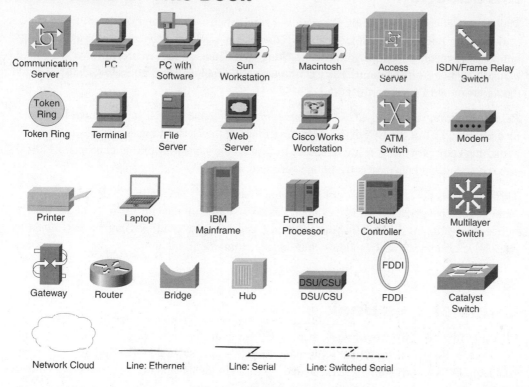

Command Syntax Conventions

The conventions used to present command syntax in this book are the same conventions used in the *Cisco IOS Command Reference*:

- **Bold** indicates commands and keywords that are entered literally as shown. In actual configuration examples and output (not general command syntax), bold indicates commands that the user manually inputs (such as a **show** command).

- *Italic* indicates arguments for which you supply actual values.

- Vertical bars (|) separate alternative, mutually exclusive elements.

- Square brackets, [ ], indicate an optional element.

- Braces, { }, indicate a required choice.

- Braces within brackets, [{ }], indicate a required choice within an optional element.

Introduction

The Cisco Networking Academy Program is a comprehensive e-learning program that provides students with Internet technology skills. A Networking Academy delivers web-based content, online assessment, student performance tracking, and hands-on labs to prepare students for industry-standard certifications. The CCNA curriculum includes four courses oriented around the topics on the CCNA certification.

Routers and Routing Basics CCNA 2 Companion Guide is the official supplemental textbook to be used with v3.1 of the CCNA 2 online curriculum of the Networking Academy. As a text-book, this book provides a ready reference to explain the same networking concepts, technologies, protocols, and devices as the online curriculum.

This book goes beyond previous editions of the Cisco Press *Companion Guides* by providing many alternative explanations and examples as compared with the course. You can use the online curriculum as directed by your instructor, and then also use this *Companion Guide*'s alternative examples to help solidify your understanding of all the topics.

Goals of This Book

First and foremost, by providing a fresh, complementary perspective of the online content, this book helps you learn all the required materials of the second course in the Networking Academy CCNA curriculum. As a secondary goal, individuals who do not always have Internet access can use this text as a mobile replacement for the online curriculum. In those cases, you can read the appropriate sections of this book, as directed by your instructor, and learn the same material that appears in the online curriculum. Another secondary goal of this book is to serve as your offline study material to help prepare you for the CCNA exam.

Audience for This Book

This book's main audience is anyone taking the second CCNA course of the Networking Academy curriculum. Many Networking Academies use this textbook as a required tool in the course, while other Networking Academies recommend the *Companion Guides* as an additional source of study and practice materials.

This book's secondary audience includes people taking CCNA-related classes from professional training organizations and anyone wanting to read and learn about computer-networking basics.

Book Features

All the features of this book are either new or improved to facilitate your full understanding of the course material. The educational features focus on supporting topic coverage, readability, and practice of the course material.

Topic Coverage

The following features give you a thorough overview of the topics covered in each chapter so that you can make constructive use of your study time. Also see the upcoming section "A Word About the Scope of Topics in This Book."

- **Objectives**—Listed at the beginning of each chapter, the objectives reference the *core* concepts covered in the chapter. The objectives match the objectives stated in the corresponding modules of the online curriculum; however, the question format in this *Companion Guide* encourages you to think about finding the answers as you read the chapter.

- *NEW* **Additional Topics of Interest**—Several chapters of this book contain topics that cover more details about previous topics or related topics that are less important to the chapter's primary focus. The list at the beginning of the chapter lets you know that additional coverage can be found on the accompanying CD-ROM.

- *NEW* **How To**—When this book covers a set of steps that you need to perform for certain tasks, it lists the steps as a how-to list. When you are studying, the How To icon helps you easily refer to this feature as you skim through the book.

- **Notes, Tips, Cautions, and Warnings**—Short sidebars listed in the margins of the page point out interesting facts, time-saving methods, and important safety issues.

- **Chapter Summaries**—At the end of each chapter is a summary of the chapter's key concepts. It provides a synopsis of the chapter and serves as a study aid.

Readability

The authors have completely rewritten the material so that it has a more conversational tone that follows a consistent and accessible reading level. In addition, the following features have been updated to assist your understanding of the networking vocabulary:

- *NEW* **Key Terms**—Each chapter begins with a list of key terms, along with a page-number reference from the chapter. The terms are listed in the order in which they are explained in the chapter. This handy reference allows you to find a term, flip to the page where the term appears, and see the term used in context. The Glossary defines all the key terms.

- *NEW* **Glossary**—This book contains an all-new Glossary with more than 400 terms. The Glossary defines not only the key terms from the chapters, but also terms you might find helpful in working toward your CCNA certification.

Practice

Practice makes perfect. This new *Companion Guide* offers you ample opportunities to put what you learn into practice. You will find the following features valuable and effective in reinforcing the instruction you receive:

- *NEW* **Check Your Understanding questions and answer key**—Updated review questions are presented at the end of each chapter as a self-assessment tool. These questions match the style of questions you see on the online course assessments. Appendix A, "Answers to Check Your Understanding and Challenge Questions," provides an answer key to all the questions and includes an explanation of each answer.

- *NEW* **Challenge Questions and Activities**—Additional, and more challenging, review questions and activities are presented at the end of most chapters. These questions are purposefully designed to be similar to the more complex styles of questions you might see on the CCNA exam. This section might also include activities to help prepare you for the exams. Appendix A provides the answers.

- *NEW* **Packet Tracer activities**—This book contains many activities to work with the Cisco Packet Tracer tool. Packet Tracer allows you to create networks, simulate how packets flow in the network, and use basic testing tools to determine whether the network would work. Version 3.2 of Packet Tracer is included on the accompanying CD-ROM. The various Packet Tracer configuration files referred to throughout this book are accessible via ciscopress.com after you register your book. When you see this icon, you can use Packet Tracer with the listed configuration to perform a task suggested in this book.

- **Lab references**—This icon notes good places to stop and perform the related labs from the online curriculum. The supplementary book *Routers and Routing Basics CCNA 2 Labs and Study Guide* by Cisco Press (ISBN: 1-58713-167-6) contains all the labs from the curriculum plus additional challenge labs and study guide material.

A Word About the Scope of Topics in This Book

The CCNA 2 v3.1 course covers a lot of material in a single course. However, because the curriculum is taught in a range of different instructional settings—from high schools to universities—instructors choose what to cover to ensure their students' success.

This book's authors help instructors make these choices by prioritizing certain topics and putting less emphasis on other topics. This separation is based on directives from the Cisco Networking Academy Program and instructor feedback in various academic settings. Rest assured that the full scope of the course topics in the curriculum is covered in this *Companion Guide*, either in the main text or on the accompanying CD-ROM.

The "Objectives" section in each chapter highlights the core topics that are covered in the main text. The section "Additional Topics of Interest," included at the beginning of some chapters, lists material that is important for networkers to understand in the world today but that is not necessarily associated with the core course objectives. This additional material is found on the CD-ROM.

In addition, the authors have addressed a need for more information about real-world networks beyond the online course. So, this *Companion Guide* offers various examples and perspectives on networks in the real world and additional topics of interest to make you a better networker. We encourage you to take advantage of all the material, and yet we realize that you and your instructor have limited time to deliver and learn this material. We hope the segregation of the information helps you be more productive in focusing your time.

How This Book Is Organized

This book covers the major topic headings in the same sequence as the online curriculum for the CCNA 2 Cisco Networking Academy Program course. The online curriculum has 11 modules for CCNA 2, so this book has 11 chapters with the same names and numbers as the online course modules.

To make it easier to use this book as a companion to the course, inside each chapter, the major topic headings correspond to the major sections of the online course modules. However, this *Companion Guide* presents many topics in a slightly different order under each major heading. Additionally, the book typically uses different examples from the course and covers many topics in slightly greater depth than the online curriculum. As a result, students get more detailed explanations, a second set of examples, and different sequences of individual topics, all to aid the learning process. This new design, based on research into the needs of the Networking Academies, helps typical students lock in their understanding of all the course topics.

You can also use this book as an independent study source without being in a CCNA 2 class by reading the chapters in order.

Chapters and Topics

The book has 11 chapters, two appendixes, and a Glossary. Chapters 1 through 11 match the 11 modules of the online curriculum in number, name, and topics covered, as described in this list:

- **Chapter 1, "WANs and Routers,"** introduces the concepts related to WAN links, which typically connect to routers to allow communications between remote sites. This chapter also introduces some of a router's components, in particular the physical interfaces and management ports on routers.

- **Chapter 2, "Introduction to Routers,"** focuses on router software, particularly how to access and use a router's command-line interface (CLI). It also covers the router initialization (boot) process.

- **Chapter 3, "Configuring a Router,"** shows the process by which an engineer can tell the router what to do by adding configuration commands to the router. The chapter covers a wide variety of configuration commands as a side effect of the discussions about the configuration process. It also explains the methods and reasons for needing to document the router configurations in a network.

- **Chapter 4, "Learning About Other Devices,"** focuses on four tools that an engineer can use to learn about the devices in a network: Cisco Discovery Protocol (CDP), telnet, ping, and traceroute.

- **Chapter 5, "Managing Cisco IOS Software,"** explains how a router chooses the operating system (OS) to load when the router boots. That OS may be Cisco IOS software, or it may be another special-purpose OS used when doing some special maintenance tasks. This chapter also explains how to copy files into and out of a router, including the files that hold the IOS.

- **Chapter 6, "Routing and Routing Protocols,"** is the first of two chapters devoted to how routers forward (route) packets and how routers learn the routes they need to know to successfully route packets. This chapter explains the concepts of connected routes, static routes, and using a dynamic routing protocol to learn routes.

- **Chapter 7, "Distance Vector Routing Protocols,"** covers the theory behind one major class of routing protocols—distance vector routing protocols. The chapter goes on to describe the Routing Information Protocol (RIP), which is the oldest of the IP routing protocols that are included in the Cisco Networking Academy Program curriculum.

- **Chapter 8, "TCP/IP Suite Error and Control Messages,"** briefly explains how the Internet Control Message Protocol (ICMP) defines a set of messages that routers use to test and control the process of routing and delivering packets.

- **Chapter 9, "Basic Router Troubleshooting,"** covers a wide variety of topics, many of which have already been covered in the *Networking Basics CCNA 1 Companion Guide* or in early chapters of this book. However, this chapter organizes the coverage based on how to troubleshoot problems in a network, reviewing how routing works and filling in some of the missing details. It also defines several troubleshooting methods and suggests the best ways to approach isolating the root cause of networking problems so that the problems can be solved.

- **Chapter 10, "Intermediate TCP/IP,"** examines Transmission Control Protocol (TCP) and User Datagram Protocol (UDP), which are the two transport layer protocols in the TCP/IP model.

- **Chapter 11, "Access Control Lists,"** concludes the core chapters of this book by examining the two higher layers of the TCP/IP networking model, explaining how routers can examine packets as they pass through the router, with the router deciding whether to allow the packet to be forwarded as normal or to discard it.

This book also includes the following:

- **Appendix A, "Answers to Check Your Understanding and Challenge Questions,"** provides the answers to the Check Your Understanding questions that you find at the end of each chapter. It also includes answers for the Challenge Questions and Activities that conclude most chapters.

- **Appendix B, "Binary/Decimal Conversion Chart,"** provides a table with decimal numbers 0 through 255 and their 8-bit binary equivalents. This chart can be useful when practicing subnetting.

- The **Glossary** provides a compiled list of all the key terms that appear throughout this book. The Glossary also defines other networking terms that you might find useful as you work toward your CCNA certification.

About the CD-ROM

The CD-ROM included with this book provides many useful tools:

- **Interactive media activities**—These are activities from the online course that visually demonstrate some of the topics in the course. These tools can be particularly useful when your Networking Academy does not have the same cable or hardware or when you use this book for self-study.

- **Packet Tracer v3.2**—Included on the CD-ROM is the full version of Packet Tracer v3.2. Note that the configuration files this book references are available on this book's website (http://www.ciscopress.com/title/1587131668). These files cover v3.2 and any subsequent releases of Packet Tracer. These configuration files match some of the examples from this book, as indicated by the icon, so you can load the configuration and watch the flow of packets in the same network.

- **Additional topics of interest**—Several chapters include a list at their beginning to let you know that the CD-ROM provides supplemental coverage of additional topics. The topics are beneficial to your becoming a well-rounded networker. (The free Adobe Acrobat Reader is needed to view these PDF files.)

About the Cisco Press Website for This Book

Cisco Press provides additional content that you can access by registering your individual book at the ciscopress.com website. Becoming a member and registering is free, and you then gain access to the following items and more:

- All the Packet Tracer configuration files referred to within this *Companion Guide*

- Exclusive deals on other resources from Cisco Press

To register this book, go to http://www.ciscopress.com/bookstore/register.asp and enter this book's ISBN, which is located on the back cover. You will then be prompted to log in or join ciscopress.com to continue registration. After you register this book, you will see a link to the supplementary content listed on your My Registered Books page.

About the CCNA Exam

The computing world has many different certifications available. Some of these certifications are sponsored by vendors and others by consortiums of different vendors. Regardless of the sponsor of the certifications, most IT professionals today recognize the need to become certified to prove their skills, prepare for new job searches, and learn new skills while at their existing job.

Over the years, the Cisco certification program has had a tremendous amount of success. The CCNA certification has become the most popular networking certification. Also, the CCIE certification has won numerous awards as the most prestigious certification in the computing industry. With well over 70 percent market share in the enterprise router and switch marketplace, having Cisco-specific certifications on your resume is a great way to increase your chances of landing a new job, getting a promotion, or looking more qualified when representing your company on a consulting job.

How to Obtain Your CCNA Certification

Cisco Systems requires that you take one of two paths to get your CCNA certification. You can either take a single comprehensive exam or take two exams—with each exam covering a subset of the CCNA exam topics. Table I-1 lists these exams.

Table I-1   CCNA Exam Names and Numbers

Name	Exam	Comment
INTRO exam	640-821	Maps to Cisco Networking Academy Program CCNA 1 and 2
ICND exam	640-811	Maps to Cisco Networking Academy Program CCNA 3 and 4
CCNA exam	640-801	Covers all four courses

So, you could take the first two courses in the Academy Program, do some extra preparation for the exam, and take the INTRO exam. Then you could take courses 3 and 4, prepare for the ICND exam, and break up your study. Alternatively, you could take the CCNA exam at the end of all four courses.

How to Prepare to Pass the CCNA Exam(s)

The Cisco Networking Academy Program CCNA curriculum helps prepare you for CCNA certification by covering a superset of the topics on the CCNA exam. The four courses of the online curriculum, and the corresponding Cisco Press *Companion Guides*, cover many more introductory topics than the topics required for CCNA. The reason for this is that the curriculum is intended as a very first course in computing, not just networking. So, if you successfully complete all four semesters in the CCNA curriculum, you will learn the topics covered on the CCNA exam.

However, taking the CCNA curriculum does not mean that you will automatically pass the CCNA exam. In fact, Cisco purposefully attempts to make the CCNA exam questions prove that you know the material well by making you apply the concepts. In fact, the CCNA exam questions tend to be a fair amount more involved than the Cisco Networking Academy Program CCNA assessment questions. (For a deeper perspective on this point, refer to http://www.ciscopress.com/articles/article.asp?p=393075.) So, if you know all the concepts from the CCNA curriculum and *Companion Guides*, you have most of the factual knowledge you need for the exam. However, the exam requires that you apply that knowledge to different scenarios. So, many CCNA students need to study further to pass the exam(s).

Many resources exist to help you in your exam preparation. Some of these resources are books from Cisco Press, and some are other online resources. The following list details some of the key tools:

- *CCNA Official Exam Certification Library with CD*, **Second Edition (ISBN 1-58720-169-0), by Wendell Odom**—This two-book library covers the CCNA materials in more depth, with a large (more than 300) question bank of exam-realistic questions and many other tools to help in your study including 30 minutes of visual instruction on CD-ROM.

- *Cisco CCNA Network Simulator* **(ISBN 1-58720-131-3), by Boson Software, Inc.**—This software tool is a router/switch/network simulator that you can use to practice hands-on skills on Cisco routers and switches without having a real lab available.

- **Cisco CCNA Prep Center (http://www.cisco.com/go/prepcenter)**—A free online resource from Cisco Systems. (You need a Cisco.com account to access this site, but registration is free.) It has discussion boards, interviews with experts, sample questions, and other resources to aid in your CCNA exam preparation.

Don't forget to register your copy of this book at ciscopress.com to get special offers on these items. To do so, go to http://www.ciscopress.com/bookstore/register.asp and follow the instructions.

What's on the CCNA Exams

As with any test, everyone wants to know what's on the exam. Thankfully, Cisco Systems publishes a list of exam topics for each exam to give candidates a better idea of what's on the exam. Unfortunately, those exam topics do not provide as much detail as most people want to see. However, the exam topics are a good starting point. To see the exam topics for the CCNA exams, follow these steps:

Step 1   Go to http://www.cisco.com/go/ccna.

Step 2   Click the text for the exam about which you want more information.

Step 3   In the next window, click the **Exam Topics** link.

Beyond that, the Cisco Networking Academy Program CCNA curriculum covers what is arguably a superset of the CCNA exam topics. However, the topics included in the printed chapters of the book are all fair game on the CCNA exams.

Some topics are certainly more important than others for the exams—topics that many people already know are more important. This book includes many important topics for the exam. In particular, the topics of routing, routing protocols, and ACLs are certainly very important. Additionally, because the Cisco CCNA exams ask questions that use a router simulator, you should practice and become very comfortable with moving around in the router CLI, issuing commands, and interpreting the command output, as covered in many chapters of this book.

Note that with a typical CCNA exam having only 45–55 questions, your individual exam annot possibly cover all the topics in the CCNA curriculum.

CHAPTER 1

WANs and Routers

Objectives

Upon completion of this chapter, you should be able to answer the following questions:

- Which four groups of industry professionals create the rules and standards that allow wide-area networks (WANs) to work together?

- How do WANs and LANs differ?

- What is the main purpose of a LAN?

- Why were WANs developed?

- What are three types of WAN connections (encapsulations)?

- Where do WANs and LANs operate on the OSI model?

- What devices are used in LANs? In WANs?

- Why is a LAN faster than a WAN?

- How do routers work in LANs and WANs?

- What are the main components of a router, and what tasks do they perform?

- What are the most common interface connections on routers, and how are they used?

- What are six types of serial encapsulations used on routers?

- What kinds of cables are used to connect routers to other routers on serial and Ethernet links?

Key Terms

This chapter uses the following key terms. You can find the definitions in the Glossary:

router   page 3

default gateway   page 3

wide-area network (WAN)   page 5

point-to-point WAN link   page 6

leased line   page 6

telephone company (telco)   page 6

channel service unit/data service unit (CSU/DSU)
  page 6

serial cables   page 7

customer premises equipment (CPE)   page 7

data circuit-terminating equipment (DCE)   page 7

data terminal equipment (DTE)   page 8

clocking   page 8

synchronization   page 8

serial links   page 8

serial interfaces   page 8

International Organization for Standardization (ISO)
  page 9

Internet Engineering Task Force (IETF)   page 9

Electronic Industries Alliance (EIA)   page 9

continues

continued

This chapter begins the Cisco Networking Academy Program's CCNA 2 curriculum. The CCNA 2 course and book focus almost entirely on routers—what they are, what they are capable of doing, how to tell them specifically what to do, and how to find out if they are doing their jobs correctly.

This chapter introduces routers, focusing on how routers forward packets between different LANs by using wide-area networks (WANs). The first section of this chapter begins with a review of the basics of how routers route IP packets. As the chapter continues, the text takes a closer look at the WAN links used by routers to forward packets. The second major section of this chapter then moves the focus to the physical components of an internetwork with routers and WAN links, taking a look at the internal and external components of routers, and some details about how to connect cables to routers.

Introduction to Routing Over WANs

The most important function of a *router* is simply put:

> Routers route packets.

This one seemingly simple statement summarizes the most important function of a router—namely, the routing, or forwarding, of IP packets. Although Chapter 10, "Routing Fundamentals and Subnets," of *Networking Basics CCNA 1 Companion Guide* (and the corresponding module of the Networking Basics CCNA 1 online curriculum) covered IP routing in some detail, a brief review of routing is helpful as you begin to learn more about router hardware and software.

From the perspective of the OSI network layer—Layer 3—hosts (computers) and routers work together to deliver packets from one host to another. To do so, the host that creates the packet sends the packet to a nearby router. That router might send the packet to a second router, with that second router forwarding the packet to a third router, and so on, until the packet is delivered to a router that is connected to the same LAN as the destination computer. That last router then sends the packet to the final destination. Figure 1-1 shows just such an example, with the web server on the left sending a packet back to the PC on the right.

Figure 1-1 shows three main steps, all from the perspective of the Internet Protocol (IP):

1. The web server needs to send a packet to the computer on the right (172.16.3.3), so the web server sends the packet to its *default gateway* router—namely, R1.

2. R1 decides to forward the packet to R2 next, based on R1's routing table.

3. R2's routing table shows that 172.16.3.3 should be on a subnet directly connected to R2, so R2 knows to send the packet directly to the destination (172.16.3.3).

Figure 1-1   IP Routing, from a Layer 3 Perspective

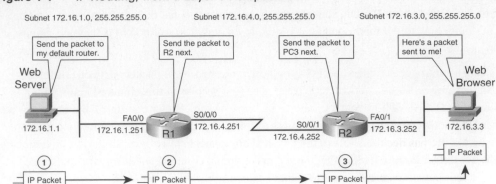

This description focuses on the OSI Layer 3 (network layer) details of how hosts and routers forward packets in an IP network. However, both the hosts and the routers must also be aware of how to use Layer 1 and Layer 2 standards and protocols to send the packets over the various types of physical networks. For example, Figure 1-2 and the descriptions that follow it explain some of the Layer 2 details of the process. Specifically, the example shows the data-link headers and trailers, along with the encapsulation process.

Figure 1-2   IP Routing, Including Layer 2 Encapsulation and De-encapsulation

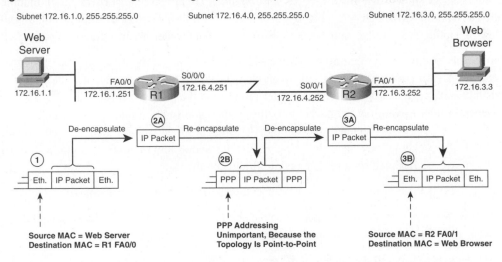

Figure 1-2 focuses on how the hosts and routers need to encapsulate the packet before sending anything over the LAN and WAN links. Hosts and routers must use data-link protocols, such as Ethernet on the LAN and Point-to-Point Protocol (PPP) on WAN links, to forward the packets over the physical links. To use the data links, a router encapsulates the packet into a data-link frame by putting the packet between a data-link header and trailer. The receiving router removes, or de-encapsulates, the packet. Figure 1-2 shows the same three steps as Figure 1-1, but focuses on the encapsulation and de-encapsulation process at Layer 2:

1. The web server encapsulates the IP packet in an Ethernet frame to send the packet to its default gateway (R1).

2. R1 processes and routes the packet as follows:

    A. R1 de-encapsulates the packet by extracting the packet from the received Ethernet frame.

    B. After R1 has decided to forward the packet out interface S0/0/0, R1 must encapsulate the packet in the correct data-link frame for that link—in this case, a PPP frame.

3. R1 processes and routes the packet as follows:

    A. R2 de-encapsulates (removes) the IP packet from the PPP frame.

    B. After R2 knows that it needs to forward the packet over an Ethernet LAN out interface Fa0/0, R2 encapsulates the IP packet in a new Ethernet frame before sending the data over the Ethernet on the right.

Routers must use OSI Layer 1, 2, and 3 standards and protocols to perform one of the most basic functions of routers: the end-to-end routing of packets across an internetwork. The explanations of Figure 1-1 describe some of the Layer 3 logic, while the explanations of Figure 1-2 describe some of the OSI Layer 2 logic. The routing process includes many other small details, including physical layer details.

 Packet Tracer configuration file NA02-0102 uses a configuration that mostly matches Figure 1-2. Simulation scenario 1 shows the packet flow shown in the figure.

This first major section of the chapter describes some of the more important basic features of how routers can be used to create a *wide-area network (WAN)*. First, this section describes how to create WAN links between two remote sites, and then it shows how to create the equivalent of a WAN link in a lab, which allows engineers to test WAN concepts for the cost of a few inexpensive cables. This section goes on to cover a little more information about routing over WANs and router WAN hardware.

Connecting Routers to WAN Links

Many network diagrams purposefully ignore the physical details of how a router connects to a WAN link. For example, Figure 1-1 and Figure 1-2 show a lightning-bolt line between R1 and R2, meaning that a point-to-point WAN link exists, but the cabling details are unimportant to the discussion for those diagrams. This section takes a closer look at WAN links, particularly the cabling and devices that connect to a router to create a WAN link.

This chapter focuses on the simplest type of WAN link, called a ***point-to-point WAN link***. A point-to-point WAN link, also called a ***leased line***, leased circuit, or WAN link, connects two devices over a WAN. Leased lines give the devices on each end (typically routers) the ability to send data to each other at the same time. Leased lines are also permanently installed, meaning that the devices can send data to each other at any time.

To create a point-to-point WAN link, a company must use the services of a ***telephone company (telco)*** or other company that sells WAN services. To install a new leased line, a company must order the leased line from a telco or other company that sells such services. The order form for the leased line lists the street address of each site, the exact location inside the building to which the telco should install its cables, and the speed at which the leased line should run. The telco then can physically install cables into the buildings, to the correct floor and room, to provide a physical link over which bits can be sent between the two devices.

Additionally, the telco requires a special type of networking device to be attached to the end of the leased line. This device, called a ***channel service unit/data service unit (CSU/DSU)***, helps protect the telco's equipment electrically and provides many other functions to make the leased line work.

Note

You can think of LANs as using cables that you own, and WAN links as using cables that you lease or rent.

The following list outlines the steps a network engineer could use to install a point-to-point WAN link:

Step 1   Order the leased line from a telco or other company that sells such services.

Step 2   Order a router and a CSU/DSU for each of the two sites.

Step 3   Physically install the router and CSU/DSU at each site.

Step 4   Connect the router and CSU/DSU to the line from the telco, at each site.

Figure 1-3 shows the resulting leased line.

Figure 1-3   WAN Link Showing the Serial Cables, CSU/DSUs, and Telco

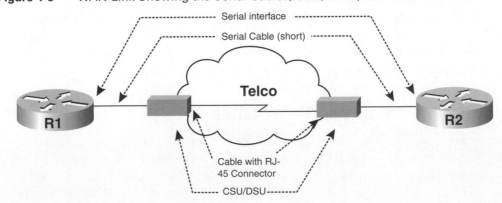

Figure 1-3 shows many of the details of a WAN link. The figure shows two *serial cables*, whose job is to connect a router's serial interface to a CSU/DSU. The leased line from the telco acts as if it were a single cable, with two twisted pairs: one for transmission in each direction. However, the telco does not actually run a cable between the two routers, but instead uses other technology that is beyond the scope of this book and the related course. So, the telco cloud and lightning-bolt line represent the fact that the details are hidden and unimportant for this discussion.

Figure 1-3 cannot really show the length of the cables very well. The serial cables are typically very short, usually less than 50 feet in length, and often only a few feet in length. The router and CSU/DSU at each site typically sit in the same room, often next to each other. However, the line from the telco may be a few miles long, or it may be thousands of miles long, depending on the distance between the sites.

This book often uses the term telco to refer to any company that sells WAN services, but many other terms can be used as well. For example, up until the early 1980s, the United States used a single large monopoly telco (AT&T), but then the U.S. Department of Justice decided to break up that monopoly to increase competition. As a result, some of the old parts of AT&T that provided local telephone services became separate companies, with these companies often being called regional Bell operating companies (RBOC). (The "Bell" in the name refers to Alexander Graham Bell, who both invented the telephone and started the company that became AT&T.) Over time, telcos came to be known by the more generic name of *service provider*. In some parts of the world, telcos are called Post, Telephone, and Telegraph (PTT) companies, with a single government-controlled company providing postal services and telephone services throughout a single country. Regardless of which term you use, these companies provide services such as the point-to-point WAN link shown in Figure 1-3.

The routers and CSU/DSUs in Figure 1-3 are collectively referred to by the telco as *customer premises equipment (CPE)*, because from the telco's perspective, the router and CSU/DSU are equipment that sits at the telco customer's site.

Next, the text takes a closer look at two more detailed topics related to WAN links. The first, clocking and synchronization, is very important to how WAN links work. Following that, a few of the more important WAN standards are covered.

WAN Clocking on DTE and DCE Devices

The routers and CSU/DSUs in a typical leased line play the role of either data circuit-terminating equipment (DCE) or data terminal equipment (DTE). In normal circumstances, the router acts as the DTE, and the CSU/DSU as the DCE, which are defined as follows:

- *Data circuit-terminating equipment (DCE)*—A device that connects to the leased line provided by the telco. The term *circuit-terminating* refers to the fact that a leased line is sometimes called a data circuit, or simply a circuit, and the CSU/DSU sits at the end of the circuit. The DCE also provides clocking to the DTE.

Note

Cisco Systems gives its customers the option to buy router serial interfaces either with or without built-in CSU/DSUs. Interfaces with built-in CSU/DSUs connect the telco's cable directly to the router, with no need for an external CSU/DSU or serial cable.

Note

Some networking texts use the term *data communications equipment* to mean the same thing as data circuit-terminating equipment.

■ *Data terminal equipment (DTE)*—A device that sends data over a circuit. Routers act as DTEs because they send IP packets, encapsulated in data-link frames, over WAN links. DTEs also expect to receive clocking from the DCE.

The definitions of DCE and DTE both bring up the topic of *clocking*, which is also known as *synchronization*. The *serial links* used between two routers typically use synchronous communication, which means that both routers on the ends of the leased line must use the exact same speed for sending and receiving bits. Building hardware that uses the exact same speed is expensive, because creating clocks that run at the exact same speed is expensive. For example, if you go to the store and buy two wristwatches, and let them run for a few months, it would not be surprising if one watch runs a few seconds faster than the other watch. The same kind of thing happens with networking devices. With WAN links, the clocks need to match exactly, so the two routers synchronize their clocks continually to make sure their clocks run at the same speed.

For example, assume that a leased line has been installed, and the line should run at a speed of 64 Kbps. The routers need to send a new bit every 1/64,000th of a second. To do that, the routers have a chip that acts as a clock. However, one router's clock may run a little slower or faster than the other router's clock. Synchronization, or clocking, is a method by which the routers are made to adjust their clock rates continually so that they both run at the same speed.

To synchronize the clocks on the *serial interfaces* of both routers on the ends of a serial link, a couple of things must happen. First, the telco uses a clock, typically an atomic clock, which is a precise method of keeping time. The CSU/DSUs can adjust their internal clocks based on the electrical signals coming over the leased line from the telco. Then, the CSU/DSUs, acting as DCE, provide a clocking signal to the routers (acting as DTEs) over the serial cables. The routers then adjust their clocks so that they continuously run at the same speed. It is like the scene in spy movies where all the spies synchronize their wristwatches to the same time before starting some amazing timed-to-the-second trickery. On a WAN link, the synchronization occurs continually, based on one master clock source inside the telco.

Now that you have seen the basics of WAN link cabling, the next section looks at some of the standards bodies and standards that define more of the details about how different WAN links work.

WAN Standards

The term *WAN* refers to Layer 1 and Layer 2 standards from many organizations. The reasons for the large variety of standards are varied. WANs have existed for more than 50 years, predating LAN standards by a few decades. Similar to how computers keep getting faster and cheaper, the speed of WANs has continually improved, while the cost per kbps has decreased. Each new advance in speed and technology has required a new set of standards. To make all this work, over a long period of time, a large number of WAN standards have been created.

Today, most WAN standards are created by one of many standards bodies listed in Table 1-1. Regardless of their reason for existence, these organizations play a role in the development of WAN standards, oftentimes sharing or referring to standards from other organizations.

Table 1-1   Popular WAN Standards Organizations

Standards Body	General Purpose
International Organization for Standardization (ISO)	An international standards body composed of delegates from each equally participating country. It develops a very wide range of international standards.
Internet Engineering Task Force (IETF)	An open international networking organization that develops the protocols of the TCP/IP networking model.
Electronic Industries Alliance (EIA)	A trade association that works closely with the Telecommunications Industry Association (TIA) on cabling standards.
International Telecommunication Union (ITU)	An international standards organization, under the control of the United Nations, for the purpose of developing world-wide telecommunications standards.

Unlike Ethernet LAN standards, which define both Layer 1 and Layer 2 details, most WAN standards focus on either Layer 1 or Layer 2. For example, on the leased line shown in Figure 1-1 and Figure 1-2, the *Point-to-Point Protocol (PPP)* data link layer protocol, defined by IETF, can be used. Alternatively, ITU's *High-Level Data Link Control (HDLC)* protocol can be used. Other WAN data link layer protocols, such as *Frame Relay*, allow more than two routers to connect to a WAN and communicate with each other, unlike leased lines, which allow only two routers to communicate. However, none of these standards defines the physical layer details of transmitting bits over a WAN link.

At Layer 1, the leased lines shown in Figure 1-1 and Figure 1-2 could be T1 lines, as used in North America, or E1 lines, as used in Europe. Or, instead of leased lines, those lines could use a switched service standard such as *Integrated Services Digital Network (ISDN)*, which allows a temporary point-to-point link to be created by doing the equivalent of making a phone call.

Table 1-2 lists some of the more popular standards used at Layer 1 and Layer 2 for WANs. The names shown in the table are the commonly used names for the WAN standards rather than the formal names, because most people do not use the formal names.

Note

Table 1-2 is included for reference, but you do not need to memorize the details listed. The CCNA 4 course covers the more commonly used standards in more detail.

Table 1-2   Popular WAN Standards at Layers 1 and 2

Layer 1 Standards	Layer 2 Standards
EIA/TIA-232	HDLC
EIA/TIA-449	Frame Relay
V.24	PPP
V.35	Synchronous Data Link Control (SDLC)
X.21	Serial Line Internet Protocol (SLIP)
G.703	X.25
EIA-530	Asynchronous Transfer Mode (ATM)
ISDN	Link Access Procedure, Balanced (LAPB)
T1, T3, E1, and E3	Link Access Procedure on the D channel (LAPD)
xDSL	Link Access Procedure Frame (LAPF)
SONET (OC-3, OC-12, OC-48, OC-192)	

Although the number of different standards may be a bit overwhelming at first glance, you can learn most of the details of how routers use WANs by working with simple point-to-point leased lines, so most of the rest of the book uses leased lines in its examples.

Creating Inexpensive Leased Lines in a Lab

Leased lines and other WAN services that connect two sites cost money. Typically, the telcos and other WAN service providers charge a fee to install a new leased line, and then they charge a monthly charge for use of the line as well. In fact, the "leased" part of the term "leased line" comes from the fact that the pricing works much like a lease on a car or an apartment, with some small fee up front and an ongoing monthly fee as well.

Two routers can be made to think they have a leased line between them—without having an actual leased line from the telco—as long as the routers sit relatively close to each other. For example, when building a lab to use for this course, the routers typically sit in the same room. To install the equivalent of a WAN leased line between two routers' serial interfaces, without having to pay any money to a telco, you can follow these steps:

Step 1   Buy two routers, each with a serial interface.

Step 2   For one router, buy a serial *DTE cable*. The connector on one end of the cable should be connected to one of the router's serial interfaces.

Step 3   For the other router, buy a serial *DCE cable*. The connector on one end of the cable should connect to the second router's serial interface.

Step 4   Connect the DTE and DCE cables together. The DTE cable has a male connector, and the DCE cable has a female connector. (When purchasing the cables, make sure that both the DTE and DCE cables have the same type of connector so that they will connect to each other.)

Step 5   Enable clocking on the router that is connected to the DCE cable so that the router takes the place of the telco and CSU/DSU by providing clocking to the other router.

Figure 1-4 shows an example of how to connect the DCE and DTE cables to create a WAN link. Such links, called *back-to-back* WAN links due to the connection of the two cables together, are widely popular. Most networking labs used for network testing before deploying a new site, and most labs used for teaching classes, use these back-to-back WAN links.

Figure 1-4   Router as DCE: Back-to-Back Serial Links

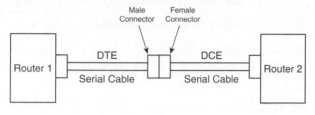

For two cables to connect correctly, one cable must use a male connector (the DTE cable) and the other must use a female connector (the DCE cable). Figure 1-5 shows a picture of the ends of two V.35 serial cables, one a DTE cable with a male connector, and the other a DCE cable with a female connector. V.35 is one of the more popular types of connectors for serial cables.

Figure 1-5   V.35 DTE and DCE Cable Connectors

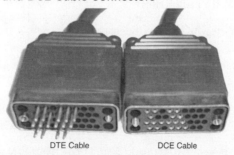

Besides ordering and installing the correct cables, you must configure one router to provide clocking, as mentioned in Step 5 of the process. If there is no telco, and no CSU/DSUs, the routers do not have any device that provides the clocking and synchronization function. Conveniently, you can make one of the router serial interfaces supply that clocking by using the **clock rate** command. The router serial interface that acts as the DCE (the router serial interface that is cabled to the DCE cable) can provide the clocking function.

Note

Unlike the cables shown in Figure 1-5, DTE and DCE cables from most cable suppliers have the word "DTE" or "DCE" printed on them to help identify the cable as a DTE or DCE cable.

Note

Any of a router's serial interfaces can provide clocking, as shown in Figure 1-4.

Overview of Routing Over WANs

Any time you see a drawing of a network that uses routers, the routers seem to always be connected to at least one WAN. Why is that? Well, routers route packets based on Layer 3, oftentimes routing based on the IP protocol. The IP protocol, being a network layer protocol, was purposefully designed to allow packets to be forwarded over most any type of physical network. So, routers can connect to Ethernet LANs, Token Ring LANs, point-to-point WANs, Frame Relay WANs, cable networks, DSL lines, dialed lines using modems, ISDN, and most any kind of physical network that people will create in the future. In short, routers are designed to give network engineers a wide variety of options for the types of physical networks used, with routers being able to route packets over any and every type of media.

The beginning of this chapter reviewed the basics of one of the most important functions of routers: the routing of packets from one host (computer) to another. The following list summarizes some of the key functions performed by routers:

- **Routing**—The process of forwarding packets, as reviewed in Figure 1-1 and Figure 1-2.

- **Path selection**—When multiple possible routes to reach a subnet exist, routers must choose the best route or path over which to reach the subnet. This process can be referred to as path determination or *path selection*.

- **Dynamic and static routes**—Routers may learn or select routes either dynamically, using routing protocols, or statically, with the engineer configuring the routers with routing information.

- **Logical addressing**—Routers rely on the logical addressing defined by Layer 3 protocols. Layer 3 addressing (for example, IP addressing) allows addresses to be grouped for easier routing, which aids the process of end-to-end packet delivery by routers.

Path selection is one of the more interesting features of routers. When a router learns about multiple paths to reach a particular subnet, the router must pick the best route, typically based on the routing protocol *metric* for each router.

Figure 1-6 shows an example in which router R1 learns two possible routes, one from router R2 and one from router R3. The routers use the RIP routing protocol to advertise routes in this case, with RIP using hop count as the metric. The figure shows the process of how R1 learns a route to reach subnet 172.16.3.0/24, as follows:

1. R2 advertises a route to reach 172.16.3.0/24, using routing protocol messages sent out both of its serial interfaces. The advertisements list a metric of 1 in each case.

2. After learning about the metric 1 route to 172.16.3.0/24 from R2, R3 then advertises about the same route in a routing protocol message sent to R1, but with a metric of 2.

3. As a result, R1 has learned of two routes to reach 172.16.3.0, but the route learned from R2 has the lower metric, so R1 chooses that route.

4. R1 adds a route for 172.16.3.0/24 to its IP routing table— a route referencing router R2 as the next-hop router to which packets should be forwarded.

Figure 1-6   Redundant Routes Learned by R1 in a WAN

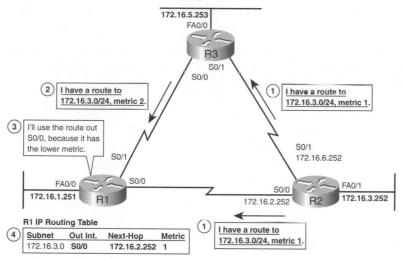

Both R1 and R3 could have been configured with the static routes shown in their respective routing tables, or they could have learned the routes using a dynamic routing protocol. With statically configured routes, the router does not need to use a routing protocol to learn about the routes in the network.

Packet Tracer configuration file NA02-0106 shows an internetwork that closely matches Figure 1-6. By clicking a router icon in real-time mode, you can see the routing table on that router.

Router Hardware and Software Components

Routers have to do a lot of work, including forwarding potentially large numbers of packets per second and performing many important overhead functions such as learning and maintaining good IP routes. For example, a router in the core of a large enterprise network might route hundreds of thousands of packets per second, and a router in the core of the Internet might route millions of packets per second. To do that work, a router has many of the same components as a PC. In fact, a router is actually a computer that is designed for the specialized purpose of routing packets. In contrast, PCs are general-purpose computers, designed to perform many different tasks.

Each router has some hardware and software that essentially work just like a typical PC. Like PCs, each router has a central processing unit (CPU), *random-access memory (RAM)*, and read-only memory (ROM). For example, R1 in Figure 1-6 may receive a packet whose destination is 172.16.3.2, which is an address in subnet 172.16.3.0. To forward the packet, the router needs to look at its routing table, which is stored in RAM. To make the decision about which route to use, R1 needs to process the packet, which involves comparing the destination IP address with R1's routing table—work that can be done by the CPU. The router's ROM holds some of the basic diagnostic software that runs when the router is first powered on.

The logic used to route packets is a part of the router's operating system, which on Cisco routers is called *Cisco IOS*. (*IOS* is short for Internetwork Operating System.) Cisco IOS is software that includes all the specialized features needed by routers, including routing protocols, basic routing logic, and support for allowing network engineers to log in to the router.

Additionally, just like PCs have network interface cards (NIC), routers have physical network interfaces. Because routers are designed to connect to many different kinds of physical networks, routers have a large variety of types of network interfaces. For example, in Figure 1-6, R1 has one Fast Ethernet interface, labeled Fa0/0, and two serial interfaces, labeled S0/0 and S0/1.

Routers also have a few important types of memory that are not typically used on PCs. Unlike PCs, routers typically do not have a disk drive. Instead, routers use the following two different types of memory that can permanently store data:

- *Nonvolatile RAM (NVRAM)*—Where the router stores its configuration, including its IP addresses and masks, the routing protocol to use, and other related information.

- *Flash memory*—Where the router stores the OS (Cisco IOS) and other files.

Table 1-3 summarizes these components of routers. The section "Internal Router Components" on the next page covers a little more detail about these and other components of routers. Also, Chapters 2, 3, and 5 cover in more depth the features supported by NVRAM, RAM, and flash memory.

Table 1-3   Overview of the Main Use of Router Internal Hardware Components

Internal Component	Characteristics
Random-access memory (RAM)	▪ Stores routing tables ▪ Holds ARP cache ▪ Performs packet buffering ▪ Provides temporary memory for a router's configuration file while the router is powered on ▪ Loses content when a router is powered down or restarted
NVRAM	▪ Stores the backup/startup configuration file for the router ▪ Retains content when the router is powered down or restarted
Read-only memory (ROM)	▪ Maintains instructions for power-on self test (POST) diagnostics ▪ Requires replacing pluggable chips on the motherboard for software upgrades ▪ Stores bootstrap program and basic operating system software

Table 1-3   Overview of the Main Use of Router Internal Hardware Components   *(continued)*

Internal Component	Characteristics
Flash memory	• Holds the Cisco IOS software image • Allows software to be updated without removing and replacing chips on the processor • Retains content when a router is powered down or restarted • Can store multiple versions of Cisco IOS software • Is a type of electrically erasable programmable read-only memory (EEPROM)
Interfaces	• Physical network connection through which packets enter and exit a router • Located on the motherboard or on a separate interface module

Router Components and Cabling

The main purpose of a router is to route packets. To do so, a router must have physical interfaces with which to connect to physical networks. Internally, a router must be able to receive the bits on one interface, process the received bits, store the bits in memory, move the bits to the outbound interface, and send the bits. The router also needs to support some method for humans to examine how the router is working, and to tell the router any important parameters it should be using when routing packets. This second major section of this chapter covers the details of the internal and external components of routers that support all these functions.

Internal Router Components

You may work with routers on a regular basis and never have to look at all the electronics inside the router. In fact, to work with routers at a general level, you really only need to know the basic facts about router internals that have already been covered, such as that NVRAM holds the configuration, that flash memory holds the Cisco IOS software, and that the router has a CPU and RAM that it uses when processing packets. However, to work with routers at a more detailed level (and to achieve certification), you need to understand more about the internal components.

Each model of router has the same general types of hardware components, but, depending on the model, those components are located at different places inside the router. To show just one example, Figure 1-7 shows a picture of the inside of a Cisco 2600 series router. The figure views the router with the top cover removed, looking down into the router.

Note

The online curriculum includes an Interactive Media Activity that shows a color image of Figure 1-7.

Note

Figure 1-7 and Figure 1-8 give you some perspectives of the internals of a Cisco router. The specific location of a particular feature is not very important. Table 1-4 that follows the figures lists the more important details.

Figure 1-7   Inside of a Cisco 2600 Router

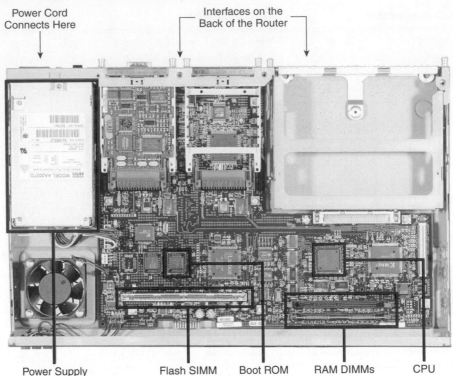

Figure 1-7 shows some of the main components, most of which are on the motherboard of the router. The RAM is typically composed of chips attached to a small removable circuit board, called a dual in-line memory module (DIMM). Flash memory also consists of chips on a circuit board, using a similar type of technology called a single in-line memory module (SIMM). ROM is often called boot ROM, because when any computer is first turned on, the computer "boots" itself up to a working state. A router uses the software in boot ROM to boot itself into a working state.

Whereas Figure 1-7 shows a picture of the inside of a Cisco 2600 series router, Figure 1-8 shows a logic diagram of how some of the internal components work together. Like Figure 1-7, the actual location of the components in Figure 1-8 is not very important, but the figure provides some perspectives on how the components may be connected.

Figure 1-8 shows a lot of words inside small boxes, with lines connecting the boxes. The words inside the boxes represent different components inside the router, with the lines representing the *buses*. Computers use buses to move data internally, much like cities use buses to move people around the city. In this particular logic diagram, the memory is shown on the left, and the interfaces on the right. The CPU chip is shown in the text box labeled M68030, which is a CPU chip made by the Motorola corporation. Although the details in operation are not important, it is important to see that the router's different internal components—the different types of memory, the CPU, and the interfaces—are all connected via buses. The buses then allow the router to move bits around internally.

Figure 1-8   Logic Diagram of the Internal Components of a Cisco 2600 Series Router

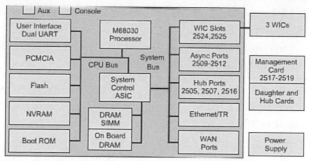

From a practical perspective, knowing the function of a router's main internal components is more important than knowing the locations of the physical components inside a particular model of router. Table 1-4 lists internal components and includes comments about how each is used.

Table 1-4   Key Internal Router Components

Component	Description
CPU	Executes the operating system's instructions. Among these functions are system initialization, routing functions, and network interface control.
RAM	Used to store the Cisco IOS software and the working memory that it needs. This includes the routing table, running configurations, and packet queues, which hold packets until the interface can be used to forward the packet. The contents of RAM are lost when the router loses power.
Flash memory	Used to store a full Cisco IOS software image. In most routers a copy of the Cisco IOS software image is transferred to RAM from flash memory during the boot process. Physically, flash memory consists of SIMMs or PCMCIA cards, which can be upgraded to increase the amount of flash memory. Flash memory does not lose its contents when the router loses power.
NVRAM	NVRAM is used to store the startup configuration. As described in Chapter 2, "Introduction to Routers," a router copies the startup configuration from NVRAM into RAM when the router is initialized and uses the running configuration in RAM for normal router operation. NVRAM retains its contents when the router loses power.

Table 1-4   Key Internal Router Components   *(continued)*

Component	Description
Buses	Buses provide a physical means for the router to move bits between the router's different components. Most routers contain a system bus and a CPU bus. The system bus is used to communicate between the CPU and the interfaces; for example, this bus transfers the packets to and from the interfaces. The CPU uses the CPU bus to access router storage devices, such as NVRAM and flash memory.
ROM	Holds the bootstrap program, the ROM monitor software, and optionally a scaled-down version of the Cisco IOS software. (Chapter 2 covers these types of software.) ROM is not erasable, and can be upgraded only by replacing the ROM chips, but ROM does retain its contents when the router loses power.
Power supply	Converts the voltage and current of a standard power source to the voltage and current required by the devices in the router. The power supplies may be internal or external to the router chassis (the metal box that holds the router's components), and some routers have multiple power supplies for redundancy.

To see the internal router components of Figure 1-7, you must use a screwdriver to take the metal cover off the router. Typically, you do not need to open the router unless you are upgrading memory—for example, when adding or replacing a flash memory SIMM. However, some components do need to be accessed on a somewhat regular basis, so Cisco makes those components available as physical connectors that are easily accessed from the back of a router. These physical connectors fall into two major categories—interfaces and management ports—and are covered in the remainder of this chapter.

External Router Interfaces

Although the term *interface* may seem generic, when speaking of Cisco routers, the term interface has a very specific meaning. In particular, interface refers to a physical connector on the router whose intended purpose is to receive and forward packets. These interfaces consist of a socket or jack into which a cable can be easily connected. The interfaces are not inside the router, but outside, typically in the back of the router. Figure 1-9 shows a picture of the back of a Cisco 2600 series router, with several LAN and WAN interfaces shown.

Routers support a wide variety of different types of interfaces because routers need to be able to forward packets over many kinds of physical networks. For example, some routers may have serial interfaces, DSL interfaces, ISDN, cable TV, or other types of WAN interfaces, and the list goes on. Figure 1-9 shows a typical router, with some LAN interfaces and some WAN interfaces. The left side of the figure shows the interfaces, with the bottom-left showing two 10/100

Fast Ethernet interfaces with RJ-45 jacks. The upper part of the figure shows three serial interfaces. The two serial interfaces on the left use a connector called a *smart serial interface*, which is smaller than the DB-60 connector on the right.

Figure 1-9   Interfaces on a Cisco 2600 Series Router

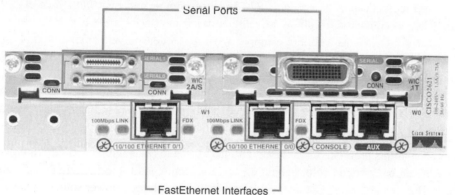

Note

The 10/100 Ethernet interfaces shown in Figure 1-9 have many similarities to a PC 10/100 NIC. The connectors are the familiar RJ-45 jacks, and they use the same Layer 1 and Layer 2 Ethernet standards.

Note

The CCNA 2 online curriculum references two Interactive Media Activities that show an interactive PhotoZoom of a router model and the router's interfaces.

To be useful, most router interfaces need to be connected to a cable. (The notable exception to that rule is a wireless interface, which uses an antenna instead of a cable.) The next two sections examine cabling for both LANs and WANs.

Cabling Ethernet LAN Interfaces

In most cases, the LAN cabling required for a router's Ethernet LAN interfaces is very straightforward. Many router Ethernet, Fast Ethernet, and Gigabit Ethernet interfaces come with RJ-45 jacks that support unshielded twisted-pair (UTP) cabling, as was covered extensively in the Networking Basics CCNA 1 course. For these interfaces, the only possibly tricky part is to remember that as far as Ethernet UTP cabling pinouts are concerned, routers act like PCs. (This is just another example of the similarities between a PC Ethernet NIC and a router Ethernet interface.) So, routers use a straight-through cable to connect to a switch, just as a straight-through cable should be used to connect a PC NIC to a switch. Figure 1-10 shows an example.

Figure 1-10   Interfaces on a Cisco 2600 Series Router

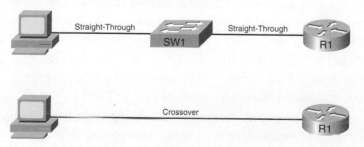

Note

The lab topology recommended for use with many of the labs from the online curriculum uses a router connected via a crossover cable to a PC, as shown in Figure 1-10.

The bottom half of Figure 1-10 shows another common choice for router LAN cabling used in labs. When creating a network in a lab, often only one PC is needed on the LAN connected to a router. In such cases, the router can be cabled directly to that one PC, creating an Ethernet segment with the router and the PC. To make it work, an Ethernet crossover cable must be used.

Connecting Ethernet cables to a router's RJ-45 jacks is simple and easy, but a little extra care must be taken as compared to cabling PCs. Other router interfaces, such as non-Ethernet interfaces, use an RJ-45 jack as well. For example, most router console and auxiliary ports use an RJ-45 jack (see Figure 1-9 for an example). Also, routers' ISDN Basic Rate Interface (BRI) interfaces use a jack called an RJ-48 jack, which is the exact same size and shape as an RJ-45 jack, so an Ethernet cable with an RJ-45 connector can be plugged into a BRI interface. Also, some router serial interfaces have a built-in CSU/DSU; in those cases, the physical interface is again an RJ-48 jack.

To help combat this problem, Cisco labels all interfaces and ports with a text description and uses a different background color behind the text for each type of interface. Table 1-5 lists the interfaces that can accept a cable with an RJ-45 connector, along with the color codes used on the back of the router.

Table 1-5   Router Interfaces and Ports into Which an RJ-45 Connector Fits

Interface or Port	Type of Jack	Background Color
Ethernet	RJ-45	Yellow
Console port	RJ-45	Light blue
Auxiliary port	RJ-45	Black
BRI with S/T interface	RJ-48C	Orange
BRI with U interface	RJ-49C	Orange
T1/E1 with built-in CSU/DSU	RJ-48C	Light green

Caution

In some cases, connecting the wrong equipment to the wrong router interface or port can damage the equipment.

Whereas the figures in this book are black and white, the online curriculum has several color pictures that show the color schemes listed in Table 1-5. Memorizing the colors in the table is probably not all that important, but it is useful to look for the colors when looking at routers in the lab or when looking at the online curriculum. Also note that cables supplied by Cisco also match this color scheme, making it a little easier to make sure you use the right cable on the right interfaces.

 Lab 1.2.6   Connecting Router LAN Interfaces

In this activity, you identify the Ethernet and Fast Ethernet interfaces on the router. You then identify and locate the proper cables to connect the router. Finally, you use the cables to connect the router and computer to a hub or switch.

Cabling WAN Interfaces for Leased Lines

As mentioned earlier, in the section "Connecting Routers to WAN Links," around Figure 1-3, a single WAN leased line connects two sites, and two sites only. The equipment at each site consists of a router with a serial interface, and a CSU/DSU. Together, the equipment at a single site is called the customer premises equipment (CPE), which is a term using the telco's perspective, because this equipment sits at the telco customer's site, not at the telco's site.

Figure 1-3 earlier in the chapter shows the general concept of how each router connects via a serial cable to the CSU/DSU, with the CSU/DSU then connecting to the leased line installed by the telco. As a reminder, Figure 1-11 shows the cabling between the router and an external CSU/DSU, showing the shapes of several of the more popular connectors used on serial cables to connect to the CSU/DSUs.

Figure 1-11   Serial Cables

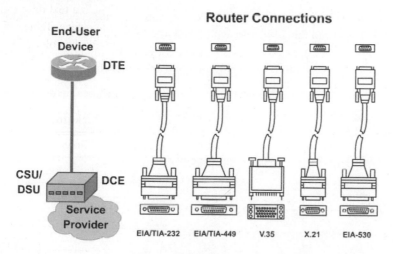

Even from Figure 1-11, you can see that many different types of serial cables exist. Picking the right serial cable requires more thought than does picking the right Ethernet UTP cable. Network engineers must consider three main points when ordering serial cables:

- The serial cable must have a connector that matches the type of serial connector on the router. Routers support several styles of serial interface connectors, with the most popular being the smart serial connector and DB-60 connectors shown in Figure 1-9.

- The serial cable's other end must have a connector that matches the connector on the CSU/DSU that will be used. Even more standards exist for these connectors, with five different styles shown in Figure 1-11.

- Serial cables typically use one of two different pinouts, based on whether the router is acting as DTE or DCE. The engineer must determine the role of the router (typically DTE), and then choose a DTE cable or DCE cable.

Note

If the router has an internal CSU/DSU built in to the serial interface, the interface has an RJ-48 jack. In this case, an external CSU/DSU is not needed, and the cable from the phone company connects directly to the router.

(Note that the online curriculum includes a similar list, but with one additional step, which points out that the cables must have the correct gender [male or female]. However, by making sure that you correctly choose either a DTE or DCE cable, you coincidentally ensure that you are using the right connector gender.)

Lab 1.2.7   Connecting WAN Interfaces

In this activity, you identify the serial interfaces on the router. You then identify and locate the proper cables to interconnect the routers. Finally, you use the cables to connect the routers.

Cabling Other Types of WANs

As mentioned earlier in the "WAN Standards" section, this book uses point-to-point leased lines for WAN links to keep things simple, with the WAN Technologies CCNA 4 course covering more details about other types of WANs. However, it is useful to know a little about two other general types of WANs: *circuit switching* and *packet switching*.

A single point-to-point leased line allows two routers to communicate with each other. Circuit switching and packet switching, however, allow more than two routers to communicate. For example, Figure 1-12 shows a typical circuit-switched WAN, with three routers.

Figure 1-12   Circuit-Switched WAN Using Modems

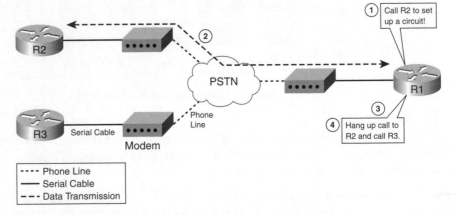

Note

The right side of the photo in Figure 1-17, shown later in this chapter, shows an external modem.

Note

ISDN is also a circuit-switched standard, but the technical details, as covered in the CCNA 4 curriculum, are very different from those for modems.

Figure 1-12 shows a circuit-switched WAN using phone lines and routers with asynchronous serial interfaces. The routers' *asynchronous serial interfaces* connect to *external modems* using short serial cables like those shown in Figure 1-11. The modem then connects to the phone line from the phone company.

To send data over a circuit-switched WAN, a router creates the equivalent of a phone call to one other router. While the phone call is active, the two routers send packets to each other. Figure 1-12 shows two routers with asynchronous serial interfaces, external modems, and a phone line connected to each of the three modems in the figure. The following process matches that shown in Figure 1-12:

1. Router R1 places a phone call to router R2, creating a circuit between R1 and R2.

2. R1 and R2 exchange packets over the circuit.

3. When R1 has finished sending all the data it wants to send, R1 does the equivalent of hanging up the phone by terminating the call.

4. R1 can then call R3 to send data.

The term *circuit switching* is actually very descriptive in this case. Using telco terminology, the word **circuit** refers to the transmission path between two phones during a phone call. So, routers such as R1 set up a circuit to another router such as R2 to send data back and forth. Those same routers can switch between circuits to different sites, sending to one remote site at a time.

The term *packet switching* is also very descriptive, because a router can change, or switch, the interfaces out which it forwards data for each different packet. Instead of having to do the equivalent of calling and hanging up the phone to each site when sending a packet, the router stays permanently connected to a **packet-switched network (PSN)**. The PSN forwards the packets sent by the router based on an address inside the packet. The router can send multiple packets into the PSN, each with different addresses. The PSN in turn forwards the packets to the correct destinations. As a result, the routers can stay connected to the PSN, and not have to create and tear down circuits—a much more efficient process for the routers.

Figure 1-13 shows a sample of how a Frame Relay network works. Frame Relay is one type of packet-switching technology, with X.25 and Asynchronous Transfer Mode (ATM) being two others.

Figure 1-13   Packet-Switched WAN Example: Frame Relay

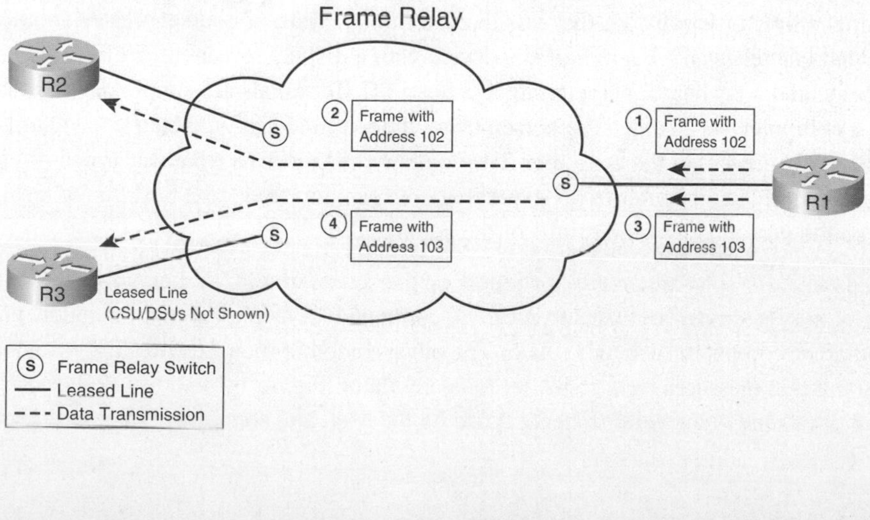

In a Frame Relay network, each router essentially has a leased line connecting it to a device, called a Frame Relay switch, in the Frame Relay network. Once connected, routers can send Frame Relay frames, placing a Frame Relay address in the header. The Frame Relay address tells the Frame Relay network which remote router needs to receive the frame. The process steps shown in Figure 1-13 are explained by the following list:

1. R1 sends a frame with address 102 to the Frame Relay network.

2. The switches in the Frame Relay network know that address 102 means that the frame should be sent to router R2, so the switches forward the frame correctly.

3. R1 now needs to send data to R3, so R1 sends a frame into the Frame Relay network, this time with address 103 in the frame header.

4. The switches in the Frame Relay network know that address 103 means that the frame should be sent to router R3, so the switches forward the frame correctly.

A router's interfaces are used to forward packets over WAN packet-switched services, such as the network in Figure 1-13, and over other types of WAN and LAN links. For example, routers use serial interfaces to connect to the Frame Relay service in Figure 1-13. The next section looks at another type of physical connector on routers, called management ports, and how they are used to log in to, configure, and troubleshoot a router.

Router Management Ports

When talking about routers, the term *interface* specifically refers to physical connectors used for the purpose of forwarding packets. In contrast, the term **port** refers to a physical connector used for managing and controlling a router.

Most routers have two management ports: the **console port** and the **auxiliary port (aux port)**. (Some routers do not have aux ports.) Both ports are meant to allow a terminal, or more likely a PC with a **terminal emulator**, to log in to the router to issue commands on the router. These commands may be used to troubleshoot problems or to configure the router to tell it how to act.

A terminal emulator is software that acts like a terminal. That, of course, creates another question—what is a terminal? A *terminal* is a device with a display screen, much like one used with a PC today, and a keyboard, but a terminal is not a PC. Terminals are simple devices that connect to a computer via a cable. The person using the terminal can type on the keyboard, and the terminal sends the text to the computer. The computer responds to what was typed—typically a command to tell the computer to do something—by sending some text back to the terminal screen so the person knows the results of the command.

Terminal emulator software creates a window on the screen of a PC. When you use that window, any text you type on the keyboard (typically a command) is displayed in the window and sent to some other computer, such as a router. The other computer then executes the command and sends some text messages back to the terminal emulator. Figure 1-14 shows such an example, with the command **show version** being typed by the user, and some text being returned from a routcr. Note that the figure shows the results, with the **show version** command sitting near the top of the window.

Note

It is unlikely that you would use a terminal to access a router today, because terminals are no longer commonly sold.

Figure 1-14   Using a Terminal Emulator and a Router

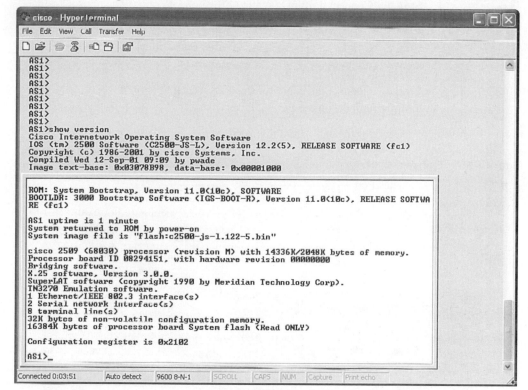

To use a terminal emulator to send commands to a router, you can connect the PC to the router's console port or aux port, or use Telnet. The next two sections show how to connect to the console and aux ports. To connect using Telnet, the emulator can be told to use Telnet to connect to a given IP address or hostname, and the PC uses its connection to an IP network, typically through its NIC, to connect to the router.

Cabling and Accessing a Router Console Port

To successfully log in to a router via its console, you must install the correct cabling and then configure the terminal emulator correctly. The trickiest part of the cabling is that the terminal emulator typically uses a PC serial port to communicate with the router. (A PC's serial port is often referred to as a *COM port*, which is short for serial communications port.) The serial port is oftentimes either a nine-pin connector, called a *DB-9 connector*, or a *Universal Serial Bus (USB) connector*. The console cable supplied by Cisco—a *rollover cable*—typically has RJ-45 connectors on the ends. So, you have to make sure that you have a small piece of hardware called a converter that attaches to the end of the RJ-45 rollover cable, providing either a DB-9 or USB connector as needed.

After you have the right cables and connector converters available, however, the process is relatively simple. You can use the following steps to correctly install the cabling, with the details related to the PC serial port at Step 2:

Step 1 Connect a rollover cable to the console port. (The console port is typically an RJ-45 jack, and the rollover cable also has RJ-45 connectors.)

Step 2 Connect a converter to the other end of the rollover cable to match the type of connector on the PC's serial port.

Step 3 Connect the cable (or the converter that is on the end of the cable) to the serial port on the PC.

Figure 1-15 shows a picture of the cabling components.

Figure 1-15 Console Cabling

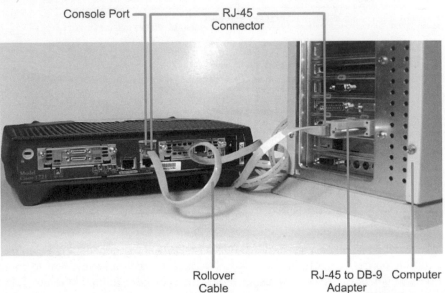

Besides connecting the console rollover cable as shown in Figure 1-15, a terminal emulator must be installed and configured to use the proper settings. These settings make the terminal emulator software act like one of the terminal models that used to be sold as standalone pieces of hardware. (The online curriculum states that the emulator must act like an old terminal type called a VT-100 terminal, but many terminal types actually work.) Most any terminal emulator can be used, with an emulator called HyperTerminal being relatively popular. HyperTerminal is included with some Microsoft OSs, and it can be downloaded for free from http://www.hilgraeve.com. Figure 1-16 shows the HyperTerminal configuration screen, reflecting the correct default terminal settings for using the console port of a router, as follows:

- 9600 bps

- 8 data bits

- No parity

- 1 stop bit

- No flow control

Figure 1-16   HyperTerminal Configuration Settings

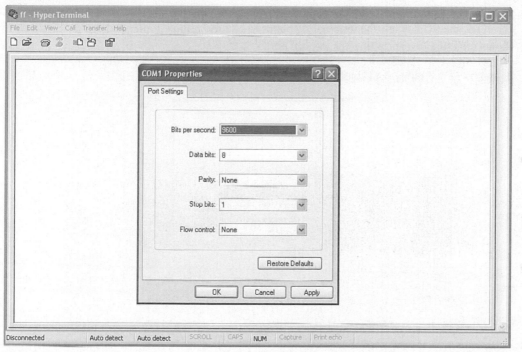

The speed setting of 9600 bps (default) brings up an interesting point about how the console and aux ports work. Both ports are considered to be asynchronous ports. *Asynchronous communications* means that both devices on each end of the cable (the PC and console port in this case) must use the same speed—in this case, 9600 bps. However, an asynchronous device does not attempt to adjust its clock based on what the other device is doing. In contrast, you may recall that the section titled "WAN Clocking on DTE and DCE Devices" earlier in this chapter explained a concept of clocking and synchronization by which the DTEs (routers) adjusted their clocks. In that case, the router's serial interfaces use synchronous communications, because they synchronize their clock speeds, whereas the console and aux ports use asynchronous communications, because they do not synchronize their clock speeds.

Note

The online curriculum also uses the term *RS-232* when referring to the console and aux ports. RS-232 is an old-style connector used on some early models of routers, but routers mainly use RJ-45 instead of RS-232 for the console connectors today.

Lab 1.2.5   Connecting Console Interfaces

In this lab, you connect a PC to a router using a console or rollover cable.

Cabling a Router Auxiliary Port

Cabling a router's aux port requires slightly more effort than cabling the console port. The router must have an external modem connected, with the modem typically using a different connector than the typical RJ-45 connector on the rollover cable. However, after the router aux port is cabled to a modem, the PC is cabled to a modem, and the terminal emulator is configured correctly, the PC can use the terminal emulator to call the remote router and log in. Figure 1-17 shows a picture of the cabling for the aux port.

Figure 1-17   Router Aux Cabling

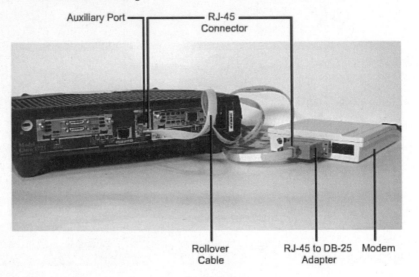

Comparing the Console and Auxiliary Ports

One of the main benefits of the console and aux ports is that both allow ***out-of-band management*** of routers. Most of the time, when a network engineer needs to execute commands on a router, the engineer telnets to the router. However, Telnet sends IP packets, with those IP packets going over the IP network. In some cases, the problem may be that packets cannot reach the remote router, so telnetting to that remote router will not work. The engineer then needs a way to log in to a router using a communications link that is outside the IP network, like a console cable or a phone call between two modems and the aux port. The term *out-of-band* simply refers to the fact that the communications link is "outside the bandwidth" used for sending IP packets.

Figure 1-18 shows the main benefit of the two out-of-band management ports of a router.

Figure 1-18   Out-of-Band Access to a Remote Router

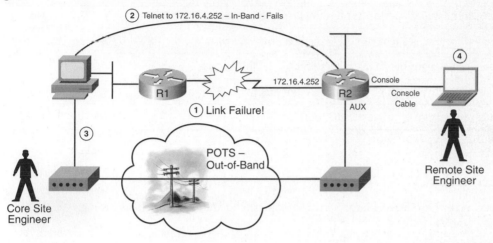

Figure 1-18 begins with the core site network engineer, on the left, logged in to remote router R2 using Telnet. The figure shows the following steps:

1. The link between R1 and R2 fails.

2. The telnet from the core engineer's PC fails.

3. The core site engineer can use a modem to call the remote router (R2) via the remote router's aux port.

4. Alternatively, if an engineer is at the remote site, the remote site engineer can access R2 via the console port.

Both the console and aux ports were designed to be used for out-of-band management of a router. The main difference is that the console is meant for local access when the engineer is next to the router, and the aux port is intended for remote access when the engineer is not even at the same site as the router. Beyond that basic difference, however, some functions are best performed at the console port and others can be performed only at the console port. For that reason, the console port is used more often than the aux port when the engineer is close to the router. Table 1-6 summarizes some of the key comparison points between these two management ports.

Note

The term POTS stands for plain old telephone system, which is just a reference to the worldwide network that allows a typical phone call to be made. It is also called the public switched telephone network (PSTN).

Table 1-6   Comparison of Router Console and Auxiliary Ports

Feature	Console	Auxiliary
Uses short cable, requiring the terminal to be close to the router	Yes	No
Intended for use as a remote-access method using modems and the PSTN	No	Yes
Router sends error messages to this port by default	Yes	No
Password recovery can be performed from this port	Yes	No
Sends router boot messages to this port	Yes	No

Summary

This chapter introduced a large variety of topics related to computer networking.

The major difference between a WAN and a LAN is the geographic area that is covered. A LAN connects workstations, printers, servers, and other devices within a building or other small area. A WAN is used to connect multiple LANs, typically over a large geographic area. The primary characteristics of a WAN include the ability to connect devices separated by wide geographic areas, the use of service providers to make these connections, and the serial connections used to access bandwidth.

WANs operate at the physical layer (OSI Layer 1) and the data link layer (OSI Layer 2). Several organizations define WAN Layer 1 and 2 standards, including ITU, ISO, IETF, and EIA. Routers understand the Layer 1 and 2 details of both LANs and WANs, plus they use Layer 3 routing logic. The Layer 3 logic allows the routers to send packets over any type of LAN or WAN link, making good use of the different types of physical networks.

Routers are specialized computers whose primary purpose is to forward packets. Routers include the following components that help the router forward packets:

- **Cisco IOS**—The OS that runs on Cisco routers

- **CPU**—Executes instructions in the OS

- **RAM or DRAM**—Stores items used for the router's work, such as the routing table

- **NVRAM**—Stores the initial (startup) configuration file

- **Flash memory**—Acts as permanent memory, typically holding the Cisco IOS software

- **ROM**—Holds the bootstrap program and POST diagnostic programs

- **LAN interfaces**—Can be used to receive and forward packets

- **WAN interfaces**—Can be used to receive and forward packets

- **Management ports**—Include the router's console and auxiliary ports and can be used to access the router's CLI

A router's LAN interfaces typically connect to a LAN switch via a straight-through cable. A router's serial interface may connect to a WAN link via a serial cable, connected to a router serial port on one end and an external CSU/DSU on the other end of the cable. The CSU/DSU connects to the leased-line cable from the telco. For WAN links, the router acts as DTE, accepting clocking and synchronization from the CSU/DSU, acting as the DCE.

Check Your Understanding

Complete all the review questions listed here to test your understanding of the topics and concepts in this chapter. Answers are listed in Appendix A, "Answers to Check Your Understanding and Challenge Questions."

1. Which of the following statements accurately describe differences between a LAN and a WAN? (Choose two)

   A. A LAN makes data connections across a broad geographic area, and a WAN makes a local connection in a building.

   B. Companies can use a WAN to connect remote locations, and a LAN can make a local connection in a building.

   C. WANs are usually faster than LANs.

   D. Only WANs require a CSU/DSU to be used on the ends of the cable.

2. Network professionals belong to organizations that plan and define standards used in networking. Which of the following are recognized industry organizations? (Choose two.)

   A. IETF

   B. UAS-K

   C. ISO

   D. EIA

   E. OSI-N

   F. ITU

3. Which of the following are true about a router? (Choose three.)

   A. Routers enable different IP networks or IP subnets to communicate with each other.

   B. Routers choose paths between networks using MAC address information.

   C. Path selection is one of the main functions of a router.

   D. Protocols are specialized chips on a router's motherboard to store routing tables.

   E. Routers have a central processing unit and memory.

   F. Only one network can be connected to a router at a time.

4. Which of the following are main components of a router? (Choose three.)

   A. ROM

   B. Flash memory

   C. CTG interfaces

   D. NV-ROM

   E. RAM

5. Which of the following statements describe the function of RAM in a router? (Choose two.)

   A. RAM stores the necessary Cisco IOS software for the router to begin booting.

   B. RAM is not necessary if extra NVRAM is available.

   C. RAM stores the current configuration information.

   D. RAM is maintained when the router is turned off.

   E. RAM stores routing tables for the router.

6. Which of the following statements are true about DTE? (Choose two.)

   A. DTE is an acronym for digital transfer enhancement.

   B. DTE provides clocking information to the provider.

   C. DTE usually resides on the customer's premises.

   D. DTE is an acronym for data terminal equipment.

   E. DTE is always connected to the first serial interface on a router.

7. Which of the following statements are true about DCE? (Choose two.)

   A. DCE is an acronym for digital clocking equipment.

   B. DCE provides clocking to the DTE.

   C. DCE is an acronym for data circuit-terminating equipment.

   D. DCE can be connected to the aux port on a router.

8. The term WAN refers to which layers of the OSI model? (Choose two.)

   A. Transport

   B. Data link

   C. Network

   D. Physical

   E. Session

   F. Presentation

9. Which of the following physical ports and/or cables on a router require clocking to be configured in a back-to-back connection? (Choose one.)

   A. Serial port with DTE cable

   B. Console

   C. Aux port

   D. Ethernet

   E. Serial port with DCE cable

10. Which of the following statements are true about router interfaces? (Choose two.)

    A. Interfaces must be connected to serial cables.

    B. LAN interfaces can work with straight-through or rollover cables.

    C. Ethernet interfaces usually use RJ-45 connectors.

    D. Interfaces can accept smart serial connectors.

11. What are possible functions of a console port? (Choose two.)

    A. Storing routing information

    B. Accessing the router to change configurations

    C. Telnet access to the router

    D. Password recovery

    E. Backup to the smart serial connections

12. In the following figure, which setting is different from the default for connecting to a Cisco router?

    A. Bits per second

    B. Data bits

    C. Parity

    D. Flow control

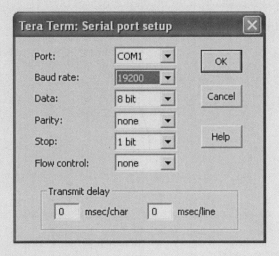

13. Which of the following are data-link encapsulations for WAN? (Choose three.)

   A. Frame Relay

   B. RIP

   C. IETF

   D. High-Level Data Link Control (HDLC)

14. Which of the following are used in WANs? (Choose two.)

   A. Hub

   B. Router

   C. Modem

   D. Multiport repeaters

   E. Bridges

15. Which of the following describe the function of flash memory in a router? (Choose three.)

   A. Holds the Cisco IOS software image

   B. Replaces the need for RAM chips

   C. Keeps its contents when a router is rebooted

   D. Can store multiple versions of Cisco IOS software

   E. Backs up configuration files

16. Which of the following are true about out-of-band router management? (Choose three.)

   A. Can be performed using the console port with a rollover cable

   B. Can be performed using Ethernet interfaces

   C. Provides access to Telnet services

   D. Can allow troubleshooting when a link is down

   E. Can be performed using a dialup connection

17. Which of the following are true about the items shown in the following figure? (Choose three.)

   A. Item B contains serial interfaces.

   B. Items C and D can be used for router management.

   C. Item C can use a crossover cable.

   D. Item B can accept either DTE or DCE cables.

   E. Item A can be used for a DCE.

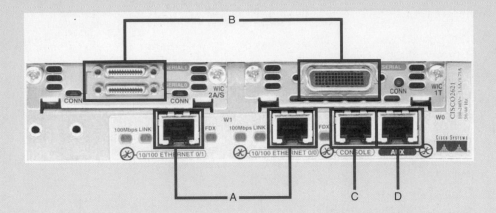

18. Which statement is true about a router? (Choose one.)

    A. The running configuration is stored in ROM, and flash memory holds the Cisco IOS software.

    B. NVRAM stores the startup configuration file, and RAM stores the running configuration.

    C. RAM stores the startup configuration file, and NVRAM stores the running configuration.

    D. Flash memory stores the running configuration, and ROM stores the Cisco IOS software.

Challenge Questions and Activities

These questions require a deeper application of the concepts covered in this chapter and are similar to the style of questions you might see on a CCNA certification exam. You can find the answers in Appendix A.

1. Which type of cable is used in the connections marked in the following figure?

   A. PC1 to R1: _____

   B. R1 to R2: _____

   C. R2 to SW2: _____

   D. R2 to PC2: _____

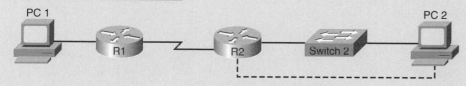

2. Router R1 has been used in a lab for the last several years. R1 connects to router R2 using a back-to-back serial connection, using its serial interface that does not have a built-in CSU/DSU. R1 also has a single Ethernet interface connected to a single PC without using a hub or switch. To save money, the IT manager has decided to use R1 for a new site being installed into the network, as shown in the bottom half of the following figure. Which of the following answers is true regarding other opportunities to save money with this new installation?

   A. R1 can use the serial cable that was formerly attached to R2, but not the serial cable that was formerly attached to R1.

   B. R1 can use the same Ethernet cable that it formerly used.

   C. If R1 changed its serial interface to use an integrated CSU/DSU, R1 could use the same serial cable as before.

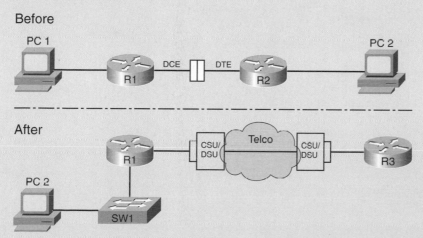

CHAPTER 2

Introduction to Routers

Objectives

Upon completion of this chapter, you should be able to answer the following questions:

- What is the purpose of Cisco IOS?

- How does Cisco IOS operate at a basic level?

- What are some of the features of Cisco IOS?

- What methods can be used to establish a command-line interface (CLI) session with the router?

- How does a user move between user executive (EXEC) mode and privileged EXEC mode?

- How does a user establish a HyperTerminal session on a router?

- How does a user log in to a router?

- How does the help feature in the CLI work?

- What messages indicate an error has occurred?

- What are the basic troubleshooting commands?

Key Terms

This chapter uses the following key terms. You can find the definitions in the Glossary:

command-line interface (CLI)   page 40

modes   page 43

executive mode (EXEC mode)   page 43

user EXEC mode   page 43

privileged EXEC mode   page 43

configuration mode   page 45

global configuration mode   page 46

interface configuration mode   page 46

routing protocol configuration mode   page 46

Cisco IOS images   page 47

platform   page 47

feature set   page 47

Cisco Software Advisor   page 50

ROM Monitor (ROMMON)   page 50

boot ROM   page 50

booting   page 52

power-on self test (POST)   page 54

bootstrap   page 55

Cisco Technical Assistance Center (TAC)   page 55

configuration register   page 57

boot field   page 57

setup mode   page 59

hostname   page 64

console password   page 65

enable password   page 65

command recall   page 70

terminal history   page 70

history buffer   page 70

Chapter 1, "WANs and Routers," reviewed some of the basic functions of routers. Before routers can route packets, they must be connected to one or more LANs and WANs. The router must also learn routes, either through static configuration or by using dynamic routing protocols. This chapter, along with Chapters 3, 4, and 5, focuses on different parts of what must happen for routers to be able to forward packets. This chapter focuses on Cisco IOS, which is the operating system (OS) that runs in a Cisco router. The IOS user interface allows network engineers to use, look at, configure, and otherwise change how IOS behaves on a particular router. Chapter 3, "Configuring a Router," then explains the router configuration process, which is the process by which a network engineer can tell a router the details of how the router should work.

This chapter has two main sections. The first section introduces the concept of Cisco IOS and its command-line interface (CLI). The second section covers the process by which a router initializes after it is powered on, plus additional details about how to get help from IOS from the CLI.

Operating the Cisco IOS CLI

As mentioned in Chapter 1, routers are computers that are designed for the purpose of routing packets. Just like any other computer, routers need an operating system—something that controls the hardware components of the computer and performs the core functions of the router. But unlike a PC, which has an OS plus lots of other software packages that enable word processing, web browsing, e-mail, and the like, Cisco puts all the important software features of a router into one large OS, called *Cisco IOS*. The IOS provides all the core features of a router, including the following:

- Controlling the sending and receiving of packets in the router's physical interfaces
- Storing packets in RAM until the outgoing interface is available to forward the packet
- Routing (forwarding) packets
- Dynamically learning routes using routing protocols

This section introduces the concept of the IOS CLI, along with a few details about IOS itself that can be viewed using the CLI.

The Cisco IOS CLI

Most PC OSs today provide a nice graphical screen to the end user. The user can either click with a mouse or use a keyboard to tell the PC what to do. These graphical user interfaces (GUIs) are generally intuitive, with OS vendors spending a lot of time trying to create a user interface that people like to use.

The router's user interface is called the ***command-line interface (CLI)***. The CLI is not graphical—instead, it is a text-based user interface. The CLI enables the user to enter commands on a keyboard with the router typically reacting by displaying a series of text messages on the user's screen. As compared with a modern PC OS, the user interface is rather basic. However, the CLI is powerful because it unlocks thousands of router commands and options, allowing the administrator to make choices not available on the GUI. After you complete the learning curve to get comfortable with the CLI, you can begin to experiment with the many features of Cisco routers and Cisco IOS.

The IOS CLI can be accessed using a terminal emulator. Many freeware and shareware terminal emulators exist, including HyperTerminal (as mentioned in Chapter 1, and found at http://www.hilgraeve.com). The user can use the PC with the terminal emulator installed, enter commands at the keyboard that the terminal-emulator window displays, and see response messages from the router displayed in the terminal-emulator window.

In addition to installing terminal-emulator software on a PC, the router user also needs to have some physical means with which to communicate with the router. The PC can physically access the router by using one of these three methods:

- **Router console port**—Uses cables between the PC and the router console port

- **Router auxiliary (aux) port**—Uses modems and a telephone circuit between the PC and the router aux port

- **Telnet**—Uses the IP network between the PC and the router

Figure 2-1 shows a graphical perspective of accessing a router CLI.

Figure 2-1   Three Methods to Access a Router CLI

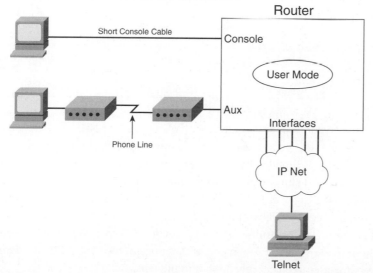

If you have a working router in the classroom, a good short exercise to do at this point is to use a terminal emulator and telnet into a router, doing some simple commands like **show version** and **show flash**. (The **show version** command displays information about the version of IOS

> **Note**
>
> Throughout this chapter, the term "user" refers to the user of a router's CLI, which is typically a network engineer. The end users of the network never need to access a router's CLI.

> **Note**
>
> The console and aux ports can be accessed without any specific configuration in the router. However, a router must be configured and operational on at least one interface, with a Telnet password configured, before Telnet users can access a router's CLI.

running in the router, and the **show flash** command shows information about the contents of the router's flash memory.) In case you do not have any routers handy, Figure 2-2 shows an image of a HyperTerminal window, with the terminal emulator using the console to log in to a router and issue a command.

Note

In this book, commands entered in the CLI appear in bold.

Figure 2-2   Terminal Emulator (HyperTerminal) Accessing a Router

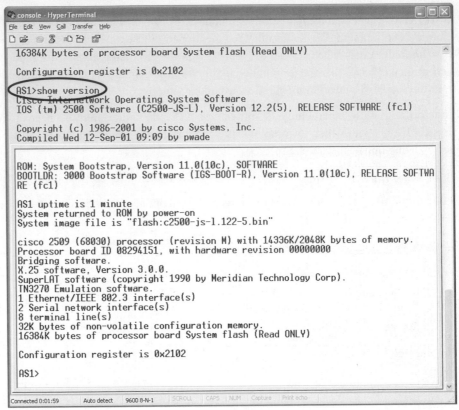

Figure 2-2 shows the HyperTerminal window with lots of text in it. The circle added to the figure focuses your attention on specific text. It shows a line of AS1>**show version**. The AS1> part is the command prompt supplied by the router, with the router waiting for the user to enter something. The user entered **show version**, which the terminal emulator put on the screen. Then, the user pressed the Enter or Return key. As a result, the router interpreted the entered text (**show version**) as a command, with the router generating some text messages in reply. The router then sent all the text in the following lines, eventually displaying the command prompt AS1> at the bottom of the window. At the end of the process, the router CLI is again waiting for the HyperTerminal user to enter something into the window.

Router EXEC Modes

The IOS CLI has many different areas or parts, called *modes*. The mode shown in Figure 2-2 is called *executive mode (EXEC mode)*. The term *EXEC mode* comes from *command executive*, which is the part of IOS that looks at the command entered by the user, executes the command, and provides a response to the user.

To provide a basic level of security, IOS creates two different levels of EXEC mode by default: *user EXEC mode* and *privileged EXEC mode*. The main difference between the two is that privileged EXEC mode allows commands that can disrupt router operations, whereas user EXEC mode does not allow the user to use these disruptive commands. For instance, privileged mode accepts the **reload** command, which tells the router to reboot itself, but user mode does not allow this command. Table 2-1 lists some of the key features of and differences between these two EXEC modes.

Table 2-1   Comparing User and Privileged EXEC Modes

Mode	How the Command Prompt Ends	How to Access the Mode	Accepts Commands That Do Not Disrupt the Operation of the Router	Accepts Commands That Might Disrupt the Operation of the Router
User	>	Telnet, console, or aux port	Yes	No
Privileged	#	By using the **enable** command from user mode	Yes	Yes

Interestingly, a user can reach user mode by logging in using Telnet, the console port, or the aux port. However, to get to privileged mode, the user must use the **enable** command from user mode. After the user supplies the correct enable password, IOS places the user in privileged mode, as shown in Figure 2-3. Also, a privileged mode user can choose to go back to user mode by using the **disable** command.

The text boxes in the top center and bottom center of Figure 2-3 show examples of what you might see displayed on the screen when moving between user mode and privileged mode. The circles show the two modes, user mode and privileged mode.

Note

Privileged mode is popularly called enable mode, mainly because the **enable** command is used to reach this more-powerful EXEC mode.

Figure 2-3   Navigating to and from User and Privileged (Enable) Modes in a Router

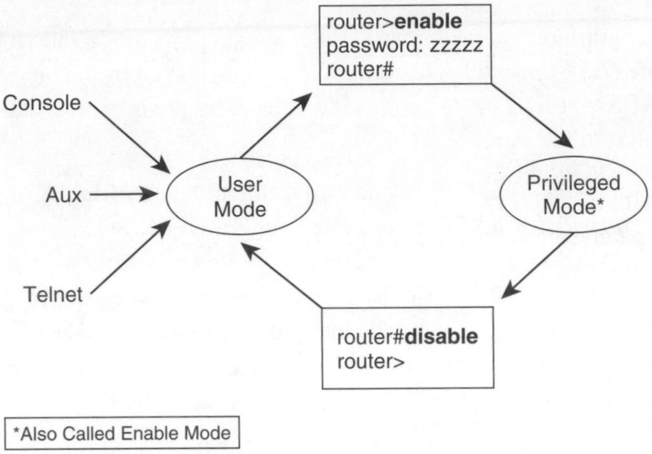

The next section provides an example that shows a complete process of how to move between the EXEC modes, as well as information about other CLI modes called configuration modes.

Router Configuration Modes

This section covers the configuration process on Cisco routers. First, you will learn about the concept of configuration, including what it is and what network engineers need to configure on routers. Following that, you will see an example of router configuration, including several configuration modes.

Perspectives on What Needs to Be Configured on a Router

When you buy a Cisco router, it comes with the Cisco IOS installed. You can take the router out of its cardboard shipping box and connect the power, console, and interface cables, completing the physical installation. However, even though the physical installation of a router might be 100 percent correct and complete, the router will not route any packets until the router has been configured. This section explains the concept of router configuration.

Configuring routes on a router is like setting up new bus routes in a city. For bus routes, after the buses and equipment are in place, the new drivers need to be told where to go on their new routes. For example, imagine that you run the bus service for a city. You order new buses and hire new drivers, knowing that you need to add new bus routes in certain parts of the city. But buying the buses and hiring the drivers is not enough. You still have to tell the drivers when and where to drive the buses so that people can get to all the new destinations on the new bus routes.

Similarly, network engineers plan and install internetworks using routers, but the routers need to know where to route the packets. The routers cannot actually route packets until they know more details about the internetwork in which they are installed. So, after a network engineer receives and installs new routers, the engineer still needs to configure the routers, which means that you must tell the routers some basic parameters about what to do.

Interestingly, routers do not need a lot of configuration to work correctly. Figure 2-4 shows a small internetwork with two routers, two LANs, and one point-to-point WAN link. The figure lists the small set of parameters that must be configured on the two routers, R1 and R2, for them to be able to route packets in this internetwork.

Figure 2-4   Minimum Requirements for Configuring Two Routers

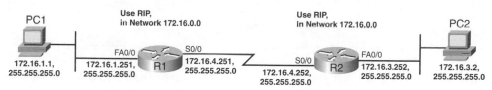

The routers simply need to be configured with the correct IP addresses and masks, along with a routing protocol. After the routers know their IP address and mask on each interface, the routers can do the same math covered in Chapter 10 of *Networking Basics CCNA 1 Companion Guide* (or module 10 of the CCNA 1 course) and learn about the subnets connected to the interfaces. To learn routes from each other, the two routers need to use the same routing protocol, so in this case both routers must be configured to use RIP. By configuring the details shown in Figure 2-4, routers R1 and R2 can be made to route packets to each other.

Packet Tracer configuration file NA02-0204 creates a network similar to the network in Figure 2-4. By clicking the routers from real-time mode, you can view a copy of each router's routing table and see the subnet numbers for each subnet.

Configuration Process and Configuration Modes

Cisco routers cannot be configured from either EXEC mode; instead, the user must use the CLI's *configuration mode*. Example 2-1 shows how to configure R1 from Figure 2-4. The process starts when the engineer connects to the console of R1 as the router is just completing the boot process.

Example 2-1   Configuration Process on R1

```
Press return to get started!
router>enable
router#configure terminal
router(config)#interface fastethernet0/0
router(config-if)#ip address 172.16.1.251 255.255.255.0
router(config-if)#no shutdown
router(config-if)#interface serial0/0
router(config-if)#ip address 172.16.4.251 255.255.255.0
router(config-if)#no shutdown
router(config-if)#router rip
router(config-router)#network 172.16.0.0
router(config-router)#end
router#
```

Example 2-1 shows the text that would be visible inside a terminal emulator of a PC connected to R1's console. For formatting purposes, books from Cisco Press show the text entered by the user a little differently from the text created by the router. The text entered by the user is shown in bold, and the text supplied by the router is shown in nonbold. (An actual terminal emulator does not change the bolding of the text.)

Example 2-1 shows three separate types of configuration modes, described as follows in the order in which they appear:

1. The **configure terminal** EXEC command moves the user from privileged EXEC mode into *global configuration mode*, as signified by a command prompt that ends in (config)#. This mode allows the user to enter configuration commands that apply to the whole router, or to enter configuration commands that move the user to a more specific configuration mode.

2. The **interface** command moves the CLI from global configuration mode into *interface configuration mode*, as signified by a prompt ending in (config-if)#. This mode allows the user to configure details about a specific interface. For example, R1's FA0/0 interface's IP address is configured with the next command, **ip address 172.16.1.251 255.255.255.0**, which was entered in configuration mode for interface FA0/0.

3. The **router rip** command moves the CLI into a *routing protocol configuration mode*, as signified by a prompt ending in (config-router)#. For RIP to work correctly in a Cisco router, IOS needs to know the IP networks about which RIP could advertise, or share information about, with other routers. The **network 172.16.0.0** command needs to be entered in router configuration mode to tell IOS to advertise about network 172.16.0.0.

Note

The commands entered in configuration mode are called *configuration commands*, whereas the commands entered in EXEC mode are called *EXEC commands*.

After being configured as shown in Example 2-1, the IOS in routers R1 and R2 routes packets between the subnets shown in Figure 2-4. However, the configuration details go beyond the scope of what is covered in Module 2 of the online curriculum. So, if the configuration process, and particularly the configuration commands, seem a little confusing at this point, do not worry—Chapter 3 covers the configuration process more thoroughly.

The next section takes a closer look at Cisco IOS.

Cisco IOS Fundamentals

Most every decision, protocol, and process implemented by a router is performed by IOS. In fact, the key to Cisco's dominance in the router marketplace is the quality, function, and features available in IOS. This section covers a few of the basics of IOS, including some details about the files that contain IOS and the memory a router uses to store the IOS.

Cisco IOS Features and Filenames

Cisco IOS is the operating system for the majority of Cisco routers. You can use a small, inexpensive Cisco router or a large, expensive one, old or new, and find the same CLI and the same IOS commands, doing the same things, due to the consistency of IOS. For example, the configuration shown in Example 2-1 could be used on the vast majority of Cisco router models with any of the different IOS versions in the last 10 years. This consistency makes life much easier for the average network engineer.

Although Cisco IOS appears to be the same on the majority of Cisco routers, there are many different *Cisco IOS images*. An IOS image is a file that contains the entire IOS. Cisco creates different IOS images for a large variety of reasons, including the following:

- Cisco manufactures many different models of router hardware, with each model being a member of a router *platform*, *series*, or *family*. The routers in a router platform are similar, typically using the same chips. Router platforms need to use different IOS images because each router platform typically uses different CPU chips. The number that represents a router platform or family is typically included in the name of the IOS. For example, the Cisco 1700 series of routers includes the 1760 models, as well as many others, with the names of the IOS images including the text 1700.

- Some IOS images have fewer features and some have more features, to provide flexible pricing. Thus, companies that want the extra features can order an IOS image that has the extra features, but that company has to pay more. For example, a company that wants to route only IP packets can use a basic (and less expensive) IOS image, and a company that also wants to route Novell IPX and AppleTalk packets can use a more expensive IOS. (Cisco calls the different sets of functions in an IOS image a *feature set*.)

- Cisco updates the software over time with new features and bug fixes. Cisco creates new IOS images for each new version of IOS software.

- Some IOS images are compressed to save storage space, and some are not.

When a network engineer needs to download a new IOS image for a router, the engineer must go through the types of items in this list to determine the right IOS image to download and use on a particular router. However, the part of IOS that a network engineer sees on a regular basis—the CLI and the many commands—works the same on different models of Cisco routers and on different versions of software.

As mentioned before, Cisco puts the entire IOS into a single file called an IOS image. Routers typically store the IOS image in flash memory in the router. To distinguish between IOS images, Cisco has a standard for naming the IOS image files, with the filename describing information about the IOS image such as the feature set, the model of router, and the version number. Figure 2-5 shows an example of an IOS filename.

Figure 2-5   Cisco IOS Filename Example

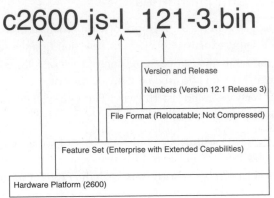

Knowing that the IOS image files have a naming standard is important at this point in the course, but the details of the naming standard are not important for now. Chapter 5, "Managing Cisco IOS Software," covers IOS filenames in more detail.

Storing Cisco IOS in Flash Memory and RAM

Routers, like computers, need a permanent place to keep their operating system. Computers use hard drives to store the OS, but routers, because they do not have disk drives, use flash memory to store the OS. When a router boots, the OS is copied from flash memory to RAM, where it is used by the router's CPU.

Routers use flash memory for several reasons. Originally, Cisco chose flash memory because it gave routers better availability. Flash memory has no moving parts, whereas disk drives spin the disks inside the disk drive. As a result, routers experience fewer failures. Today, flash memory has become more popular as a technology for consumers as well, which has driven down the cost of flash memory used by routers. For example, many companies sell a device called a USB flash drive, which is a flash memory device that connects to a USB port on a PC.

Before installing a new IOS into a router, you need to check to see if the flash memory in the router has enough space to hold the new IOS. The size of the IOS image depends on several factors. IOS images that have larger and more expensive feature sets generally require more space. Also, the later the version of IOS, the more memory that is required, mainly because each new IOS version has more features added to it. To check the amount of flash memory in a router, you can use the **show flash** command, as shown in Example 2-2.

Note

In its fourth-quarter 2005 issue, Cisco's *Packet Magazine* listed comments from readers that showed a couple of routers that had been working nonstop for over five years (http://www.cisco.com/packet).

Example 2-2   Output from the **show flash** Command

```
R1>show flash
System flash directory:
File Length Name/status
1 8022152 /c2500-i-l.121-16.bin
[8022216 bytes used, 366392 available, 8388608 total]
8192K bytes of processor board System flash (Read ONLY)
```

Example 2-2 shows that R1 has 8192 KB of flash memory. (This value is the same as 8,388,608 bytes and 8 MB. For example, 8192 KB times 1024 bytes/KB is 8,388,608 bytes.) The command output also shows that only about 366 KB (366,392 bytes) is currently unused. So, if the new IOS image were less than 366,392 bytes, it could be copied into flash memory. However, no current IOS images are that small. So, the engineer could delete the current contents of flash memory and then copy the new IOS image into flash memory, assuming the new image is less than 8192 KB in size. If the new image is larger than 8192 KB, the router would need to have a larger flash memory installed before the new IOS image could be copied into flash memory in the router.

Similar to other computers, routers copy all or part of IOS into RAM when the router is powered on. To determine if a router has enough RAM to hold the IOS, you need to know how much RAM is required for a particular IOS, and whether the router has that much RAM. Example 2-3 shows the output of a **show version** command, which lists the amount of RAM available in a router.

Example 2-3   Finding the Amount of Router RAM Using the **show version** Command

```
R1>show version
Cisco IOS Software, 1841 Software (C1841-ADVIPSERVICESK9-M), Version 12.3(11)T3,
  RELEASE SOFTWARE (fc4)
Technical Support: http://www.cisco.com/techsupport
Copyright  1986-2005 by Cisco Systems, Inc.
Compiled Tue 25-Jan-05 14:20 by pwade

ROM: System Bootstrap, Version 12.3(8r)T8, RELEASE SOFTWARE (fc1)

R1 uptime is 1 minute
System returned to ROM by power-on
System image file is "flash:c1841-advipservicesk9-mz.123-11.T3.bin"
Cisco 1841 (revision 4.1) with 117760K/13312K bytes of memory.
Processor board ID FTX0906Y03T
2 FastEthernet interfaces
4 Serial(sync/async) interfaces
1 Virtual Private Network (VPN) Module
DRAM configuration is 64 bits wide with parity disabled.
191K bytes of NVRAM.
31744K bytes of ATA CompactFlash (Read/Write)

Configuration register is 0x2102
```

The highlighted output from the **show version** command in Example 2-3 lists the RAM as two parts. By adding the two numbers together, you can determine the amount of available RAM in the router. The example shows that this router has 131,072 KB of RAM.

The **show version** command lists how much RAM a router has installed, but you also need to determine the amount of RAM required for a particular new IOS. With the appropriate login credentials, which can be obtained by anyone with a Cisco router that has a current maintenance contract with Cisco, you can log in to Cisco.com and use *Cisco Software Advisor*. This tool allows you to choose an IOS image that can be downloaded and installed into the flash memory of a router. Cisco Software Advisor lets you select details such as router model, feature set, and version, telling you how much flash memory and RAM are required to store and run that particular IOS image.

Two Alternative OSs

Before moving on to the second major section of this chapter, this section describes a few details about other OSs that Cisco routers can use. These two OSs, or operating environments, are called *ROM Monitor (ROMMON)* and *boot ROM*.

ROMMON is an operating environment used for very special purposes. The main uses of ROMMON mode are as follows:

- To provide a low-level debugging tool that is available even when flash memory has been erased or corrupted

- To provide a means of putting a normal IOS file into flash memory in case flash memory is erased or becomes corrupted

- To provide a means to recover or reset router passwords

ROMMON is a rudimentary OS that provides a basic, and sometimes cryptic, user interface. ROMMON is not IOS. It does not accept IOS commands, and it cannot route IP packets. The ROMMON software is stored in a ROM chip instead of flash memory, so it should always be available, even if some other network engineer made a mistake and erased all the contents of flash memory.

Password recovery is the most popular reason for the average network engineer to use ROMMON. If you do not remember a router's password, you can use ROMMON mode to at least bypass the router's passwords from the console. By bypassing the passwords, the user can then reset all the passwords. For more details on that process, simply go to Cisco.com and search on the word **password**. The first hit in the search typically points to a document that describes how to perform password recovery from the console.

Note

ROMMON mode is only accessible only from the console, meaning that password recovery can also be performed only from the console. For this reason, routers can be made much more secure by simply locking the door to the room where the routers are located.

The other alternative OS is called the boot ROM IOS, or sometimes RX-boot mode. Like ROMMON, the boot ROM software resides in the ROM chips, which means that this software can be loaded even if there is no working IOS in flash memory. However, unlike ROMMON, the *boot ROM* software is an IOS image, although a very basic one. The purpose of this basic IOS is to allow an engineer to load new IOS images into flash memory when the image cannot be loaded due to other issues.

Table 2-2 summarizes some of the key features and facts about these two alternatives to IOS.

Table 2-2   Key Features and Facts About Alternative OSs

Operating Environment	Alternative Name	Command Prompt	Typical Use
ROM Monitor	ROMMON	> or ROMMON>	Low-level debugging and password recovery
Boot ROM	RX boot	Router(boot)>	Copying a new IOS into flash memory (under certain conditions)
IOS	—	Router>	Normal router operations

Starting, Configuring, Accessing, and Using a Router

This section continues the introduction to routers by covering four main topics:

- The events that occur when the router first starts working after being powered on

- A process for creating a simple configuration for the router

- A review of how to access a router's CLI using a terminal emulator and the router's console port

- Descriptions and examples of how to use the router's CLI, particularly how to use the CLI's built-in help features

Initial Booting of a Router

Before a computer can do any useful work, it must be connected to an electrical outlet, and the power must be turned on. However, it usually takes several minutes before the computer is ready to do any useful work. During that time, the computer checks the hardware to make sure it is working and loads the OS into RAM, among other things. After all the overhead work is complete, the PC screen displays a logo or desktop that makes you know that it can be used. The process of doing the overhead work to make the computer ready to use is called *booting*, or the boot process, or rebooting the computer.

As mentioned in Chapter 1, routers are computers built for a specific set of purposes. Because routers are computers, routers use a boot process as well. When booting, the router generates messages about the boot process and sends them out the console port. If the engineer connects a PC to the console port before turning on the router, the PC's terminal emulator can display all the boot messages. Some of the messages can be pretty cryptic, but others identify useful information about the process. Of particular interest, the router output during the boot process includes the following:

- The version of IOS being loaded

- The number of interfaces

- The types of interfaces

- The amount of NVRAM

- The amount of flash memory

Example 2-4 shows boot messages sent to a router's console, with the highlighted sections showing the information mentioned in the preceding list. Some of the more cryptic and less useful parts of the output have been omitted to save space.

Example 2-4   Initial Boot Messages

```
System Bootstrap, Version X.X(XXXX) [XXXXX XX], RELEASE SOFTWARE
Copyright  1986-199X by Cisco Systems
1721 processor with 4096 Kbytes of main memory
Notice: NVRAM invalid, possibly due to write erase.
! output omitted
IOS (tm) 1721 Software (XXX-X-X), Version [XXXXX XXX]
Copyright  1986-199X by Cisco Systems, Inc.
Processor board ID 10226279
R4700 CPU at 100Mhz, Implementation 33, Rev 1.0
MICA-6DM Firmware: CP ver 2730 - 5/23/2001, SP ver 2730 - 5/23/2001.
Bridging software.
X.25 software, Version 3.0.0.
SuperLAT software (copyright 1990 by Meridian Technology Corp).
TN3270 Emulation software.
Primary Rate ISDN software, Version 1.1.
2 Ethernet/IEEE 802.3 interface(s)
24 Serial network interface(s)
4 Low-speed serial(sync/async) network interface(s)
6 terminal line(s)
1 Channelized T1/PRI port(s)
DRAM configuration is 64 bits wide with parity disabled.
125K bytes of non-volatile configuration memory.
32768K bytes of processor board System flash (Read/Write)
Configuration register is 0x2102
```

Besides the information in the boot messages sent to the console, the router also gives some indication about the boot process through the LEDs on the back of the router. Some routers come with an LED labeled OK, which lights up after the bootstrap program has been loaded. (More information about the bootstrap program is covered in the upcoming section titled "Loading the Bootstrap Program.") Also, each interface has an LED as well, with the router lighting the LED when the interface is busy. When interfaces are sending a lot of traffic, the LEDs might even appear to be on all the time. Figure 2-6 shows a picture of the back of a 2500 series router.

Figure 2-6   Back of a 2500 Series Router, Including LEDs

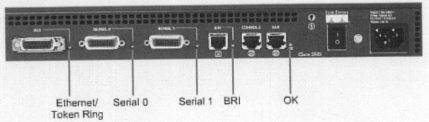

Ethernet/   Serial 0   Serial 1   BRI   OK
Token Ring

The messages sent to the console, and the OK LED, provide some outward evidence about a router's boot process. The next few pages take a closer look at some of the hidden internal details of a router's boot process. Specifically, routers take four steps when booting:

1. The router performs a power-on self test (POST) operation to verify that the hardware components are working.

2. The router loads a bootstrap program that results in some software executing on the router's CPU.

3. The router, using the bootstrap program, loads an IOS image into RAM and switches from using the bootstrap software to using the IOS software.

4. The router loads an initial configuration into RAM, called the startup configuration, which tells the router its operating parameters (such as IP addresses and routing protocol details).

The next four short sections explain more details about each of these four steps.

Performing a Power-On Self Test

The *power-on self test (POST)* process occurs on most every computer. The chips that make up the computer—the CPU, RAM, flash, and so on—must be tested to ensure they work before the router will attempt to use them. The POST process occurs immediately after power-on of the router, testing the individual components.

For comparison, if you turn off a PC, turn it back on, and immediately watch the screen, you typically see some messages about how the computer is testing its memory (RAM), which is another example of the POST process.

Loading the Bootstrap Program

When the POST process has completed, the router then needs to somehow get software loaded into RAM so that the CPU can use, or execute, the software. However, a chicken-and-egg problem exists: the CPU normally controls the process of moving data from permanent storage into RAM, but the CPU typically executes only software that sits in RAM, and RAM is empty at this point in the booting process. So, the CPU can't do anything useful if RAM is empty, including moving the OS into RAM.

Routers and other computers use a bootstrap process to overcome this problem. When the router completes the POST process, the electronics on the motherboard are wired so that a very basic program called the *bootstrap* program is loaded into RAM. After it is in RAM, the CPU can run the bootstrap program, whose main job is to then copy the full OS—the IOS image in this case—into RAM.

The term bootstrap is used throughout the computing world to describe the same process of getting a nonworking CPU up to a fully working state. However, the term bootstrap actually originated centuries ago, referring to the strap used to hold boots on your feet. Today, the computing world uses several variations on this old term, such as "boot" and "reboot," to refer to initializing a computer.

Routers automatically load the bootstrap program from the ROM chip, assuming the POST process successfully completes. Figure 2-7 shows a reminder of the fact that the bootstrap program resides in ROM, and it is loaded into RAM by the router.

Figure 2-7   Loading the Bootstrap Program from ROM

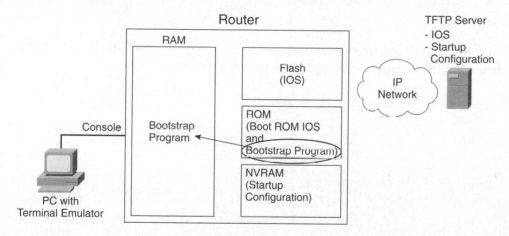

The bootstrap program for a given router resides in ROM. ROM by definition cannot be changed, meaning that the bootstrap program on a router cannot be easily replaced. The only way to upgrade the bootstrap program is to physically obtain a new ROM chip from Cisco, remove the old ROM chip, and install the new one.

Thankfully, the bootstrap program practically never needs to be replaced. However, some very rare problems might be related to the version of the bootstrap program. When working with the *Cisco Technical Assistance Center (TAC)*, which helps Cisco customers with problems with Cisco equipment, the TAC might be interested in knowing the version of bootstrap software on a router. To see the version of the bootstrap program, simply connect to the console port as covered in Chapter 1 (and as reviewed later in this chapter, in the section "Cabling and Accessing a Router Console Port") before turning on the router. One of the first messages generated by the router tells you the version of bootstrap software, as shown in Example 2-5.

Note

The output in Example 2-5 lists X as placeholder text for the digits of the version, but the actual digits would be numeric.

Example 2-5   Finding the Version of the Bootstrap Program

```
System Bootstrap, Version X.X(XXXX) [XXXXX XX], RELEASE SOFTWARE
Copyright  1986-199X by Cisco Systems
1721 processor with 4096 Kbytes of main memory
Notice: NVRAM invalid, possibly due to write erase.
!output omitted
```

Loading the Cisco IOS

One of the most important tasks for the bootstrap program is to load, or copy, the IOS image from permanent memory into a router's RAM. To do so, the bootstrap program must first determine from what permanent storage location it should get the IOS image. The bootstrap program has three main alternatives from which to get the IOS image:

A. Flash memory

B. An external TFTP server

C. ROM

Figure 2-8 shows the three options for the location of the IOS file. The arrowed lines show the idea that the IOS software is then copied into the router's RAM.

Note

Figure 2-8 shows three alternative locations to store the IOS image, but only one IOS image is loaded into RAM at any one time.

Figure 2-8   Loading the IOS—Three Options

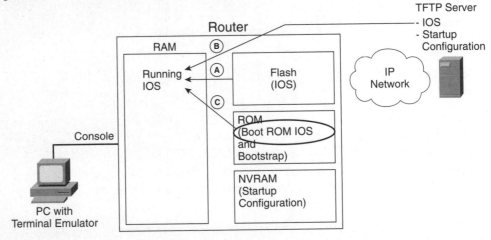

Of the four-step process described in the last few pages (POST, load the bootstrap, load an IOS image, and load a configuration file), the loading of an IOS image into RAM is the first step that requires a choice by the router. Routers automatically perform the POST when the router is powered on, and then the router automatically loads the bootstrap program from ROM. The network engineer who owns the router cannot change the first two steps. For the third part of the process, however, a network engineer can tell the router the location and name of the IOS image to load.

Routers load an IOS image from flash memory by default, although loading an IOS image from a TFTP server might be done when testing a new IOS image. Most routers use an IOS image that is stored in flash memory because flash sits inside the router. However, when testing a new version of IOS on a router, a network engineer might prefer to download the IOS image from Cisco and put that image (file) on a TFTP server. Then the router can load the new IOS from the TFTP server rather than copy that IOS image into flash memory. If the engineer finds that the new IOS image works well, the engineer can take the time and effort to copy the IOS image into flash memory on the router. (Note that in Figure 2-7 the IOS copied from the TFTP server indeed goes into RAM to be used by the router, and not into flash memory to be stored.)

Finally, the IOS image in ROM is the limited-function boot ROM IOS, mentioned earlier in the chapter in the section "Two Alternative OSs." This can be useful in some cases when copying a new IOS into flash memory.

Cisco provides two tools with which to tell the router which IOS image to load. Both tools are covered in more detail in Chapter 5, but this chapter covers the basics. The first tool is called the *configuration register*, or simply config register. The config register is a 16-bit value stored in the router, typically listed as a four-digit hexadecimal number, like 0x2102. (The 0x in front of 2102 means that the number that follows is a hexadecimal number.) The last hex digit of the config register is called the *boot field*, and the boot field tells the bootstrap program what software to load, as follows:

- **Boot field of hex 0**—Load ROMMON

- **Boot field of hex 1**—Load boot ROM IOS

- **Boot field of hex 2 through F**—Load an IOS from another location, typically from flash memory

If a router initializes when the boot field is 0 or 1, the router knows exactly what to do. However, if the boot field is any other value, the router must use another tool, called the **boot system** configuration command. The **boot system** command, found inside the configuration file used by the router when the router is first powered on, can tell the router the location and filename of the IOS image. For example, this command can list the name of a file in flash memory, or the IP address of a TFTP server along with the name of a file. So, when the boot field is anything besides 0 or 1, the router uses the **boot system** command and the following logic, which Chapter 5 covers in more depth:

1. Attempt to load the IOS image listed in the first **boot system** command found in the router's configuration file.

2. If the attempt to load that IOS image fails, attempt to load the IOS image listed in the next **boot system** command found in the configuration file

3. If an IOS image has not been successfully loaded after all **boot system** commands have been tried, or if no **boot system** commands exist, load the first IOS image found in flash memory.

Ironically, most routers default to use a configuration register of 0x2102, with no **boot system** commands, meaning that these routers simply load the first IOS image in the router's flash memory.

Loading the Startup Configuration into RAM

IOS knows how to route packets and how to learn routes, but each router needs at least some basic configuration to tell it what to do. For example, each router needs to know the IP address and mask to use for each interface, and they also typically need to have a routing protocol configured—the same routing protocol as other neighboring routers.

Under normal circumstances, a router keeps all its configuration commands in a single file, called the startup-config file. The purpose of the startup-config file is to tell the router what configuration settings to use when the router is initialized. The file is stored in a special type of permanent memory called nonvolatile RAM (NVRAM), so its contents are not lost when the router loses power. Figure 2-9 shows the basic process.

Figure 2-9   Loading IOS from Flash Memory and Startup-config from NVRAM

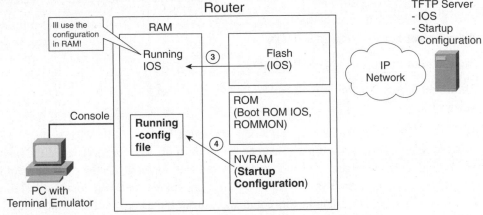

Figure 2-9 shows the typical actions taken at Steps 3 and 4 of the four-step list of actions a router takes when it is initialized (POST, load bootstrap, load IOS, and load a configuration file). Step 3 shows the most likely action for loading an IOS image, with the router taking the IOS image from flash memory. Step 4 shows the loading of the startup-config file from NVRAM into RAM so that it can be used by the IOS. Note that the configuration loaded into RAM is called the running-config file because it is the configuration actually used by the IOS that is executing, or running, at the current time.

Figure 2-9 shows the typical actions that happen on most every Cisco router in the world. However, just as a router has several locations from which it can find the IOS image to load into RAM, a router has several locations from which it can get the startup-config file. The options are as follows:

■ The router can choose to ignore the startup-config file in NVRAM, so the router starts with no configuration. This process is useful when performing password recovery, and it can be accomplished using the configuration register.

■ The router can be configured to load an initial configuration from a TFTP server, based on the existence of **boot config** commands in the NVRAM startup-config file.

■ The router can search for an available TFTP server by sending broadcasts and try to find an appropriate configuration file on the server.

■ The router can load the startup-config file in NVRAM as shown in Figure 2-9, which is the default.

The list outlines the options for loading the configuration, but IOS does follow a consistent sequence under normal circumstances. Assuming the configuration register is not configured to tell IOS to ignore the NVRAM configuration, IOS first looks in NVRAM. If no configuration is found, it then looks for a TFTP server, as described in the preceding list. If none is found, IOS does not load any configuration, assuming that the engineer will log in from the console and add configuration.

The next section looks at what happens when the router IOS completes all these steps but does not find a startup-config file to use.

Creating an Initial Configuration Using Setup Mode

Example 2-2 showed a configuration process using configuration mode. Chapter 3 covers much more detail about the configuration process, configuration mode, and commands used to manipulate the configuration files. However, IOS provides another tool for configuring routers, called *setup mode*, which is covered here. Setup mode is a method by which the router sends a series of questions to the console. If the user replies to the messages, the router builds an initial configuration for the router, copies it into NVRAM (startup-config file), and copies it into RAM (running-config file).

You can get into setup mode in two ways. First, you can simply enter the **setup** command from privileged mode. The second way is to boot the router when NVRAM is empty. When a router boots with an empty NVRAM, the router does not have any initial configuration to use, so the router sends a question to the console user, asking if the user wants to use setup mode to create an initial configuration. This section focuses on the process to reach setup mode when initializing a router that has an empty NVRAM.

NVRAM might be empty for the following reasons:

- The router was just unpacked from its shipping box and has not yet been configured.

- A user issued a privileged mode EXEC command such as **erase startup-config** or **write erase**, both of which erase the contents of the startup-config file in NVRAM.

If NVRAM is empty when the router initializes, the bootstrap program attempts to notify anyone sitting at the console by sending the messages shown in Example 2-6.

Note

The messages in Example 2-6 go to the console, but the boot process continues, and other messages show up at the console as well. Unless you are watching and reading the messages at the console during the boot process, you will miss the messages shown in the example.

Example 2-6   Initial Boot Messages Implying NVRAM Is Empty

```
System Bootstrap, Version X.X(XXXX) [XXXXX XX], RELEASE SOFTWARE
Copyright  1986-199X by Cisco Systems
1721 processor with 4096 Kbytes of main memory
Notice: NVRAM invalid, possibly due to write erase.
!output omitted
```

If a router completes the initialization process with no configuration loaded, the router cannot route any packets. So, the router gives the network engineer an opportunity to use setup mode to easily configure the router. To do so, the router poses a question to the engineer by sending a message to the console. The first few lines in Example 2-7 show the messages that the router sends to the console, asking the network engineer if he or she would like to use the *initial configuration dialog*, which is a fancy phrase to refer to setup mode. In the example, the user enters **yes** in response, beginning the setup process. Note that the example highlights the first question posed by the router, with the first text response in bold (**yes**).

Example 2-7   Setup Mode Questions and Answers

```
--- System Configuration Dialog ---

Would you like to enter the initial configuration dialog? [yes/no]: yes
At any point you may enter a question mark '?' for help.
Use ctrl-c to abort configuration dialog at any prompt.
Default settings are in square brackets '[]'.
Basic management setup configures only enough connectivity
for management of the system, extended setup will ask you
to configure each interface on the system

Would you like to enter basic management setup? [yes/no]: no
First, would you like to see the current interface summary? [yes]:
Any interface listed with OK? value "NO" does not have a valid configuration

Interface                 IP-Address      OK? Method Status       Protocol
Ethernet0                 unassigned      NO  unset  up           down
Serial0                   unassigned      NO  unset  down         down
Serial1                   unassigned      NO  unset  down         down
```

Setup involves a process by which the router sends messages, and eventually a question, to the console, and the user enters an answer to the question at the keyboard. The router asks questions about some of the basic things that can be configured on a router, and the engineer's answers to those questions tell the router what configuration commands to create. The router often suggests a default answer, shown in brackets. The user can always quit the process by pressing Ctrl-C at any point in the process.

Assuming the engineer completes the setup process, the router has gathered the basic information it needs to start performing some functions, including routing packets. However, the user needs to answer one last set of questions to determine whether the router uses the information it gathered during the setup process. Example 2-8 shows the three options given to the engineer.

Example 2-8   The Three Options at the End of the Setup Process

```
[0] Go to the IOS command prompt without saving this config.
[1] Return back to the setup without saving this config.
[2] Save this configuration to nvram and exit. Enter your selection [2]:
```

The text for each of these three options might be meaningful, but a paraphrase of each item might be a little more helpful:

- **Option 0**—Ignore all the answers that were given in setup mode, and give the user a user mode command prompt. As a result, the router will still not have any configuration.

- **Option 1**—The user answered some of the questions incorrectly, so ignore all the answers given in setup mode. Start setup again so that the user can answer correctly this time.

- **Option 2**—Use the answers given in setup mode, creating a startup config file in NVRAM and an identical running-config file in RAM. (The user also sees a new user mode command prompt.)

Lab 2.2.1   Router Configuration Using Setup

In this lab, you use the System Configuration dialog (setup) to establish some of the basic router configuration parameters.

Accessing a Router

As covered several other places in the online curriculum, a PC with a terminal emulator can be used to access the CLI of a router. This section reviews the cabling details between the PC and a router's console port along with the terminal-emulator settings. Additionally, this section covers information about the passwords required for access to each of the modes of the CLI.

Cabling and Accessing a Router Console Port

To successfully log in to a router via its console, you must install the correct cabling and then configure the terminal emulator correctly. The trickiest part of the cabling is that the PC uses a serial port to communicate with the router, and the PC's serial port typically is not an RJ-45 connector. You can use the following steps to correctly install the cabling, with the details related to the PC serial port at Step 2:

Step 1   Connect a rollover cable to the router console port. (The console port is typically an RJ-45 jack, and the rollover cable also typically has an RJ-45 connector.)

Step 2   Connect a converter to the other end of the rollover cable. For example, many PC serial ports use a DB-9 serial port connector, so an RJ-45-to-DB-9 converter would be used.

Step 3   Connect the DB-9 end of the converter to the serial port on the PC.

Figure 2-10 shows a picture of the cabling components.

Figure 2-10   Console Cabling

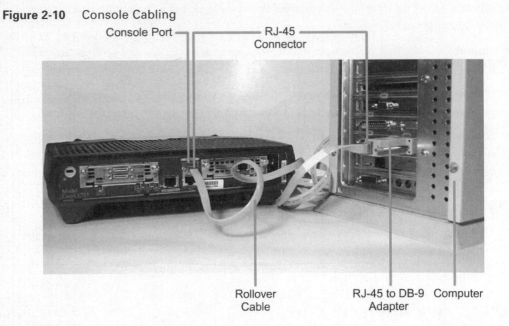

When physically connected to the console as shown in Figure 2-10, the PC must use a terminal emulator with the proper settings. A terminal emulator simply provides a window on the screen. The emulator displays any text sent by the router over the console cable. Also, any text entered on the PC is sent to the router over the console cable, with the text comprising commands to

Note

Although the term *bits per second (bps)* is commonly used today, you might occasionally see a reference to *baud* instead of bps when referring to the speed of a link.

tell the router what to do. The emulator's settings must be as follows to match the default settings on the router console port:

- 9600 bps
- 8 data bits
- No parity
- 1 stop bit
- No flow control

Note

The terminal emulators used to access a router are sometimes called ASCII terminal emulators because they use the ASCII character set.

As mentioned in Chapter 1, many people use the HyperTerminal terminal emulator from Hillgraeve (http://www.hillgraeve.com), because it was often included with Microsoft OSs. Table 2-3 lists some of the more popular terminal emulators for different OSs, as mentioned in the online curriculum.

Table 2-3   Common Terminal Emulators for Different OSs

PC Operating System	Software
Windows 9x, NT, 2000, and XP[1]	HyperTerminal (included with Windows software), ProComm Plus, and TeraTerm
Windows 3.1	Terminal (included with Windows software)
Macintosh	ProComm, VersaTerm, ZTerm (supplied separately)

[1] Some versions of Windows XP no longer include HyperTerminal.

Lab 2.2.4   Establishing a Console Connection with HyperTerminal

In this lab, you connect a workstation to the router by using a console cable and configure HyperTerminal to establish a console session with the router.

Review of Router EXEC and Configuration Modes

As covered earlier, in the section "The Cisco IOS CLI," the Cisco IOS CLI has several modes, with each mode meant for different purposes. Example 2-9 shows a progression in which a user logs in from the console and then moves through the various modes on the router. The example also lists notes mentioning which mode is seen at each point. To create this example, the user moved to each new mode and then pressed Enter once in that new mode, resulting in another command line. By doing so, the output shows a line in each mode with no command entered on the line, leaving just the command prompt on that line. Focusing on the command prompt for each mode is important, because the router command prompt actually tells the user in which mode the CLI sits at any given point in time.

Example 2-9   CLI Modes as Implied by Different Command Prompts

```
Press return to get started!
router>
!User Mode shown above
router>enable
router#
!Enable Mode shown above
router#configure terminal
router(config)#
!Global Config Mode shown above
router(config)#interface fastethernet0/0
router(config-if)#
!Interface Config Mode shown above
router(config-if)#ip address 172.16.1.251 255.255.255.0
router(config-if)#end
router#
!Enable Mode shown above
router#disable
router>
!User Mode shown above
```

Example 2-9 also shows several ways to navigate between the different modes of the CLI. The user begins in user mode, moving to privileged mode by using the **enable** command. From there, the **configure terminal** command moves the user into global configuration mode. Either pressing Ctrl-z or using the **end** command moves the user back to privileged mode, and the **disable** command moves the user back to user mode.

It is important to note that the command prompt differs depending on the CLI mode. A router's command prompt begins with its *hostname*, with the router in Example 2-9 using a router's default hostname of "router." The end of the command prompt identifies the CLI mode. Table 2-4 shows the prompts and their corresponding mode (assuming a hostname of "router").

Note

Many other configuration modes exist in addition to those shown in Table 2-4.

Table 2-4   Command Prompts Used by Different CLI Modes

Prompt	Configuration Mode
router>	User mode
router#	Privileged mode
router(config)#	Global config mode
router(config-if)#	Interface config mode

Router Password Basics

The router used to create Example 2-9 did not have any passwords configured. However, each router can (and should) be configured to require passwords. IOS can be configured to require a different password to reach user mode from the console (called the ***console password***), another password for reaching user mode from the aux port (called the aux password), and another for reaching user mode using Telnet (called the Telnet or vty password). Then, another password, called the ***enable password,*** can be required for anyone in user mode to reach enable or privileged mode. Figure 2-11 shows a diagram of the process and the names of the passwords.

Figure 2-11   Console, Aux, vty, and Enable Passwords

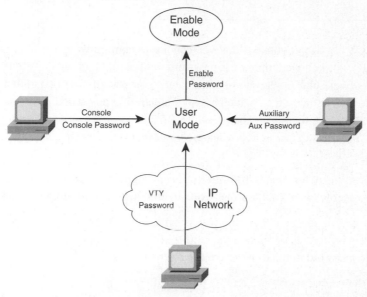

When configured to require passwords, the router prompts the user to supply the passwords. Example 2-10 shows the same process of getting into user mode and enable mode from the console as in Example 2-9, but this time with IOS being configured to require console and enable passwords. Note that the router does not display the password that is entered, so the example simply lists a string of the letter *z* to represent the password being entered.

Example 2-10   Example Password Prompting by a Router

```
Press return to get started!
password:zzzzz
!Console Password Required above
router>
!User Mode shown above
router>enable
password:zzzzz
!Enable Password Required above
router#
!Enable Mode shown above
```

Interestingly, IOS has two commands that you can use to configure the enable password. Module 3 of the online curriculum covers password configuration completely, but Module 2 only briefly mentions some key points about the enable password. The two global configuration commands that can configure the enable password are **enable password** *pw* and **enable secret** *pw*, where *pw* represents the text of the password. Together, these two configuration commands define what IOS expects to be entered when the user enters the **enable** command and the router prompts the user for a password. The following list explains the combinations:

Note

All passwords on Cisco routers are case-sensitive.

- If only one of the two commands (**enable secret** or **enable password**) is configured, IOS expects the user to enter the password as defined in that single configuration command.

- If both the **enable secret** and **enable password** commands are configured, the router expects the password as defined in the **enable secret** command. In this case, the router ignores the password defined in the **enable password** command.

- If neither the **enable secret** nor **enable password** command is configured, the behavior varies. If the user is at the console, the router automatically allows the user access to enable mode. If the user is not at the console, the router rejects the **enable** command.

The reason that IOS has two commands to configure the same type of password is that IOS first included the **enable password** command, but IOS used a weak encryption method for the password. (The IOS global configuration command **service password-encryption** performed the weak encryption of the password defined in the **enable password** command.) As a result, it was relatively easy for hackers to find the enable password defined with the **enable password** command. Cisco then added the **enable secret** command with much better encryption, but it never got rid of the old **enable password** command.

Using a Router CLI

The remainder of this chapter focuses on tools that make using the router CLI a little easier. It is important that you get comfortable with the process of using the CLI before you move on to the rest of the chapters.

This section focuses on five main topics:

- How to find commands available from the CLI

- How to find the available options on a known command

- How to retrieve an old command so you can repeat it

- How to edit the command line to change something about the command

- How to interpret the automatic help that occurs when you mistype a command

How to Find the Commands Available from the CLI

To find the names of the commands available from the IOS CLI, you simply need to enter **?** using the keyboard. As soon as you enter **?**, the router supplies a list of commands that you can enter from that mode of the CLI. Example 2-11 shows the results of entering **?** from enable mode in router R1.

```
Example 2-11    Finding IOS Commands Using ?
R1#?
Exec commands:
access-enable     Create a temporary Access-List entry
access-profile    Apply user-profile to interface
access-template   Create a temporary Access-List entry
archive            manage archive files
bfe                For manual emergency modes setting
cd                 Change current directory
clear             Reset functions
clock             Manage the system clock
configure         Enter configuration mode
connect           Open a terminal connection
copy              Copy from one file to another
debug             Debugging functions (see also 'undebug')
delete            Delete a file
dir               List files on a filesystem
disable           Turn off privileged commands
disconnect        Disconnect an existing network connection
elog              Event-logging control commands
enable            Turn on privileged commands
erase             Erase a filesystem
exit              Exit from the EXEC
--More--
```

In Example 2-11, the user entered **?** at the R1# command prompt. As soon as the user entered **?**, the router immediately sent the rest of the text to the screen. A printed book cannot really show the process well, so if you have routers available, log in and try to use **?**. If not, use Packet Tracer for a simulated router CLI, entering **?** to see the results.

When the router needs to send many lines of text to your screen, it only attempts to fill the screen. Then the router waits for you to ask for more lines of output. To inform you that it has more text to display, the router lists the last line of output as --More--, as shown at the bottom of Example 2-11. When you are ready to read more output from the router, use one of the following three options:

- Press the Spacebar to get another screen's worth of messages

- Press the Enter or Return key to get one more line of output

- Press any other key to stop command output altogether

Keep in mind that **?**, when entered from a command prompt, shows only the commands available from that CLI mode. For example, Example 2-11 shows help obtained by using **?** from enable mode, so the help includes all commands available in enable mode, including the highlighted **erase** and **clear** commands. The **erase** command can be harmful (specifically, erasing NVRAM and flash memory), so that command cannot be used in user mode. So, if the user requested help from user mode (by again entering **?**), the help output would not list the **erase** command.

How to Find the Available Options on a Command

When you know the command you want to use, you need to know what parameters or options you can enter on the command. So, you can enter **?** at any point on the command line, and the router will provide some help by telling you the options you have at each point. Example 2-12 shows how to get help, using the **show interfaces** command as an example.

Example 2-12   Getting Help for the Options on a Command

```
R1#show ?
  aaa                     Show AAA values
  aal2                    Show commands for AAL2
  access-expression       List access expression
  access-lists            List access lists
  accounting              Accounting data for active sessions
  adjacency               Adjacent nodes
  aliases                 Display alias commands
  alignment               Show alignment information
  archive                 Archive of the running configuration information
  arp                     ARP table
! lines omitted for brevity
R1#show i?
```

Note

The term *help* in this section refers to the helpful information learned when using **?**.

Example 2-12   Getting Help for the Options on a Command   *continued*

```
idb    interfaces   inventory   ip
ipv6   isis         iua

R1#show in?
interfaces   inventory

R1#show int?
interfaces

R1#show interfaces ?
  Async              Async interface
  BVI                Bridge-Group Virtual Interface
  CDMA-Ix            CDMA Ix interface
  CTunnel            CTunnel interface
  Dialer             Dialer interface
  FastEthernet       FastEthernet IEEE 802.3
  Loopback           Loopback interface
  MFR                Multilink Frame Relay bundle interface
  Multilink          Multilink-group interface
  Null               Null interface
  Serial             Serial
! lines omitted for brevity
  <cr>

R1#show interfaces serial ?
  <0-4>  Serial interface number

R1#show interfaces serial 0/0
Serial0/0 is administratively down, line protocol is down
  Hardware is GT96K Serial
  Description: frame link
  MTU 1500 bytes, BW 1544 Kbit, DLY 20000 usec,
     reliability 255/255, txload 1/255, rxload 1/255
  Encapsulation FRAME-RELAY, loopback not set
! lines omitted for brevity
```

Example 2-12 shows two main styles of when you can enter **?** in the middle of a command. The first is to enter **?** after a space, as shown with the command **show ?** at the beginning of the example. With this style, IOS supplies help about the possible options that follow the **show** command, such as **serial** and **fastethernet**.

The second style of using **?** inside a command is to use **?** without a space in front of it. This style of using **?** tells you about all the options that begin with the letters in front of **?**. For example, the command **show i?** lists all the options after the command **show** that begin with the letter "i." Following that, the command **show in?** shows all the options after the command **show** that begin with the letters "in."

Help, obtained by using **?**, also tells you when a command is considered to be complete. When the help lists <cr> as the last line of the help output, it means that you can enter a "carriage return," which is either the Enter or Return key. (The term *carriage return* came from the days of typewriters.) For example, the **show interfaces ?** command in Example 2-12 lists many options, with the last one being <cr>. That means that the user could just press Enter, issuing the **show interfaces** command, and it would be accepted by IOS.

On a related note, pressing the Tab key can help you learn command options as well. The Tab key spells out the rest of a word in a command, assuming the letters typed so far are unambiguous. As you can see in Example 2-12, two options on the **show** command start with "in"—the **interfaces** option and the **inventory** option. (Look at the line in the example that lists **show in?**.) So, if you enter **show in**<*tab*>, where <*tab*> represents pressing the Tab key, nothing happens. However, if you enter **show int**<*tab*>, the CLI would instantly change the command line to read **show interfaces**, because only one option on the **show** command starts with "int."

Although you can use the Tab key to spell out the rest of a command or command option if you have entered enough of the command or option, you can simply use the abbreviated version of the command or option as well. For example, the command **sh int** works just as well as **show interfaces** because the only IOS EXEC command that starts with "sh" is the **show** command, and the only option on the **show** command that starts with "int" is the **interfaces** option.

Recalling Old Commands to Save Typing Effort

The remaining topics in this chapter describe tools that help you save keystrokes or help you figure out when you have mistyped. This section describes the features in the CLI that you can use to avoid entering the same command over and over. For example, imagine that you are troubleshooting a problem with a router. As you troubleshoot the problem, you seem to be using the same three or four commands over and over to test whether something you did solved the problem. So, you keep repetitively entering the commands.

Instead of entering the commands over and over, you could use the *command recall* and *terminal history* features of the IOS CLI. IOS remembers the commands you have entered from the CLI and stores a copy of the commands in RAM in a place called the *history buffer*. By pressing the Up Arrow key, or the key combination Ctrl-p, you instruct IOS to look in the history buffer that holds the old commands and insert the old command on the command line. If you press the Up Arrow key once, you get the last command you issued. If you press it twice, IOS goes back two commands in the command history buffer. If you press the Up Arrow key three times, you get the command three back in the history buffer, and so on. So, in the case where you keep typing the same commands, you can just press the Up Arrow key a few times until the command you want to use again shows up on the command line, and then press Enter to use the command. Table 2-5 lists some commands related to using the terminal history and command recall features.

Table 2-5   Commands and Key Combinations Related to Command Recall

Command	Description
Ctrl-p or Up Arrow key	Recalls the previous command and places it on the command line. Repeated use continues the process, going further back in the command history buffer. (The *p* stands for "previous.")
Ctrl-n or Down Arrow key	After repeated use of Ctrl-p, these keys go forward in the history buffer. (The *n* stands for "next.")
show history	An EXEC mode command that displays the contents of the current history buffer.
terminal history size *number-of-lines*	An EXEC mode command that sets the number of commands that IOS saves in the history buffer for this user. (The default is 10.)

Note

If you can, try out the Up Arrow key when using a real router's CLI; this feature does work from a router CLI in Packet Tracer.

Note

The online curriculum has a helpful Interactive Media Activity related to the details shown in Table 2-5.

Changing the Command on the Command Line

Recalling old commands and pressing Enter allows you to reissue the same command you entered earlier, but in some cases, you might need to use a similar, but not exactly same, command. For example, you might have issued the command **show interfaces serial 0/0**, which shows status and statistical information about serial interface 0/0. You might later use the Up Arrow key to recall the command to the command line, but maybe now you need to look at serial interface 1/0. You could just enter **show interfaces serial 1/0**, but you can also recall the old command and use the CLI's enhanced editing mode to move around the command line, edit the command, and then press Enter to issue the new command.

The best way to check out and understand enhanced editing mode is to use the CLI of a real router. However, you can see the basics using the following simple explanation. Imagine that you used the Up Arrow key to retrieve a command. The following line might be the line displayed on the terminal emulator's screen:

```
R1#show interfaces serial 0/0_
```

Note that the underscore at the end of the line shows the current location of the cursor on the command line after the command is recalled. Now, you want to instead issue the **show interfaces serial 1/0** command, changing the first 0 to 1. To do so, you first would press the Left Arrow key twice, resulting in the following command line:

```
R1#show interfaces serial 0_0
```

Note that the Left Arrow key did not delete any text, but it did move the cursor backward in the command line. Note also that the cursor is below the slash (/), which is one character to the right of the first 0. Next, to delete the 0 to the left of the cursor, you would press the Backspace key, resulting in the following line:

```
R1#show interfaces serial /0
```

Note

The Delete and Insert keys do not have any useful effect on the CLI command-line text.

The Backspace key deletes the character that was to the left of the cursor, leaving the cursor under the same character (/) as before. Finally, to insert a 1, you simply enter **1**, resulting in the following command line:

```
R1#show interfaces serial 1/0
```

At this point, the command has been changed. You can press the Enter or Return key to issue the command. You do not have to move the cursor to the end of the line.

Although it took a page of text to describe the process, with a little practice, most people can work faster by recalling and editing commands instead of retyping all the commands.

This example of changing the command from **show interfaces serial 0/0** to **show interfaces serial 1/0** requires the use of just two special keys: Left Arrow and Backspace. However, CLI enhanced editing mode, which is on by default, enables you to use several other keys and key sequences that are useful for moving around the command line. For instance, if a recalled command has 70 characters and you want to change the first few characters, you can either press the Left Arrow key 70 times or you can press Ctrl-a, which moves the cursor to the beginning of the command line. Table 2-6 lists the keys and key sequences supported by the CLI enhanced command-line editing feature.

Table 2-6   CLI Enhanced Editing Feature

Key or Key Sequence	Description
Ctrl-b (or Left Arrow key)	Moves back one character
Ctrl-f (or Right Arrow key)	Moves forward one character
Esc-b	Moves back one word
Esc-f	Moves forward one word
Ctrl-a	Moves to the beginning of the command line
Ctrl-e	Moves to the end of the command line

Most people leave the CLI enhanced editing mode on, but you can disable it with the **terminal no editing** EXEC command. (You use the **terminal editing** command to turn enhanced editing back on.) For human end users, it makes sense to leave enhanced editing turned on. However, some people create scripts, which are programs that can act like a human user. These scripts can issue commands to a router and examine and process the output of the commands, all to automate some repetitive task with the router. When using scripts, it might be useful to disable enhanced editing mode.

 Lab 2.2.9   Command-Line Fundamentals

In this lab, you log in to a router in both user and privileged modes. You use several basic router commands to determine how the router is configured. You also become familiar with the router help facility and use the command history and editing features.

Automatic Help When a Command Is Mistyped

When you enter something on the command line in the IOS CLI and then press Enter or Return, IOS tries to interpret the command you entered. However, if the command has an error, IOS tells you what the problem is. This section describes three main ways that IOS tells you about such errors.

The three types of notifications are shown in Example 2-13 using three incorrect variations of the **show interfaces** command. The three types of error messages shown in the example are as follows:

- When a command is mistyped, with no options on the command, IOS supplies a message that begins with the words "unknown command," meaning that the command, as typed, is not a command as far as IOS is concerned. Example 2-13 shows this error message using the **shew** command, which is simply a misspelling of the **show** command.

- When any part of a command or option is mistyped, and the command has at least one option listed behind it, the router points to the first such error in the command line with a carat (^) character. Example 2-13 shows this error message using the **shew interfaces** command.

- When a command is typed correctly, but some required options are missing, the router issues a message that says "incomplete command."

Example 2-13   Error Messages When a Command Is Mistyped
```
R1#shew
Translating "shew"
% Unknown command or computer name, or unable to find computer address
R1#
R1#shew interfaces
     ^
% Invalid input detected at '^' marker.
R1#show interfaces serial
% Incomplete command.
R1#
```

Note that in the second case, the carat, or ^, points to the *e* in the word "shew." In the last error of Example 2-13, note that the **show interfaces** command is valid, and the **show interfaces serial 0/0** command is valid. However, **show interfaces serial**, with no additional parameters, is not a valid command as far as IOS is concerned. If **show interfaces** includes the type of interface in the command (**serial** in this case), the command must also include the number of the interface. To determine the missing next parameter, the user could have recalled the command with the Up Arrow key and entered **?** to find help for the next parameter.

show version Command

To close this chapter, this short section reviews some of the details shown in the output of the **show version** command. This command lists a lot of information related to the topics covered in this chapter. Now that the chapter is essentially complete, it is useful to consider some of the many small pieces of information shown by the **show version** command.

Example 2-14 lists the output of a **show version** command.

Example 2-14   The **show version** Command

```
R1#show version
Cisco IOS Software, 1841 Software (C1841-ADVIPSERVICESK9-M), Version 12.3(11)T3,
  RELEASE SOFTWARE (fc4)
Technical Support: http://www.cisco.com/techsupport
Copyright  1986-2005 by Cisco Systems, Inc.
Compiled Tue 25-Jan-05 14:20 by pwade

ROM: System Bootstrap, Version 12.3(8r)T8, RELEASE SOFTWARE (fc1)

R1 uptime is 20 minutes
System returned to ROM by power-on
System image file is "flash:c1841-advipservicesk9-mz.123-11.T3.bin"
Cisco 1841 (revision 4.1) with 117760K/13312K bytes of memory.
Processor board ID FTX0906Y03T
2 FastEthernet interfaces
4 Serial(sync/async) interfaces
1 Virtual Private Network (VPN) Module
DRAM configuration is 64 bits wide with parity disabled.
191K bytes of NVRAM.
31744K bytes of ATA CompactFlash (Read/Write)

Configuration register is 0x2102
```

The highlighted portions of the command output in Example 2-14 focus on the following items that were discussed throughout this chapter. This list also references the values shown in the example for cross-reference:

- **IOS version and descriptive information**—Version 12.3(11)T3

- **Bootstrap ROM version**—12.3(8r)T8

- **Router uptime**—20 minutes

- **Last restart method**—Returned to ROM by power-on

- **System image file and location**—flash:c1841-advipservicesk9-mz.123-11.T3.bin

- **Router platform/series/model**—Cisco 1841

- **Amount of RAM**—117760K/13312K bytes

- **Amount of NVRAM**—191K bytes

- **Amount of flash memory**—31744K bytes

- **Configuration register setting**—0x2102

Summary

Cisco IOS is the OS that runs inside Cisco routers. IOS provides the core logic of routers, including the routing (forwarding) of packets and the dynamic learning of routes using routing protocols. IOS also controls the router's network interfaces, which provide access to various physical networks.

Cisco IOS software provides a command-line interface (CLI) to allow users to access, use, and control IOS. A terminal emulator can be used to access the CLI, using one of three main methods of connecting to the router:

- Using cabling to the router's console port

- Using a modem to dial in to the router's aux port

- Using Telnet over an IP network

Access via any of these three methods can be password protected using the console, auxiliary, and Telnet passwords, respectively.

The CLI includes a wide variety of modes. Two of these modes, user EXEC mode and privileged (enable) EXEC mode, allow the user to enter commands. The IOS command executive (EXEC) interprets the commands, does what the command says to do, and sends messages back to the user. User EXEC mode allows commands that are not disruptive to the router's operations, whereas privileged mode (also called enable mode) allows more powerful and possibly more disruptive commands. Enable mode access can be password protected as well.

Configuration mode allows the user to enter configuration commands, which are commands that tell IOS what parameters to use when routing packets. Refer to Table 2-4 earlier in the chapter for a summary of the command prompts typically seen with the various IOS CLI modes mentioned so far in this book.

Users can navigate between modes using several commands. The user begins in user mode, moving to privileged mode by using the **enable** command. From there, the **configure terminal** command moves the user into global configuration mode. Either pressing Ctrl-z or using the **end** command moves the user back to privileged mode, and the **disable** command moves the user back to user mode.

IOS supports a large variety of features to help the user navigate the CLI. Most importantly, **?** can be used to view a list of available commands in a given mode and get help information about the options on each command. Also, if a command has been mistyped, IOS might display a carat symbol (^) to tell the user where the problem is in the command. In addition, the enhanced editing mode provides a set of editing-key functions that allows the user to edit a command line as it is being typed.

Check Your Understanding

Complete all the review questions listed here to test your understanding of the topics and concepts in this chapter. Answers are listed in Appendix A, "Answers to Check Your Understanding and Challenge Questions."

1. Which statement best describes CLI?

   A. It is a graphical user interface allowing easy "point-and-click" configuration.

   B. It is an access point for ROM Monitor configurations.

   C. It is a text-based interface using a keyboard.

   D. It is required for remote management of routers.

2. When scrolling through output from a terminal session, the --More-- prompt indicates which of the following? (Choose two.)

   A. Press the Enter or Return key for the next page.

   B. Press the Spacebar for the next page.

   C. Press the Spacebar for the next line.

   D. Press the Enter or Return key for the next line.

3. Which of the following statements are true about the different EXEC levels of access to a router? (Choose three.)

   A. User EXEC mode allows configuration changes to the router.

   B. Privileged EXEC mode permits commands that can change the router's operation.

   C. Central_Office# is an example of a privileged mode prompt.

   D. Central_Office(config)# is an example of a privileged mode prompt.

   E. Central_Office> is an example of a user mode prompt.

   F. User EXEC mode is also known as enable mode.

4. Which two commands ask the router to display a list of valid syntax to follow the word "show"?

   A. **show ?**

   B. **show help**

   C. **sh?**

   D. **sh ?**

5. What is the likely reason for the following output from a router?

```
Central_Office# config trem
                      ^__
```

A. The user is in the wrong mode for the **configure** command.

B. The prompt indicates that the user cannot configure the router.

C. The ^ indicates that the letter *r* is not valid.

D. The word **config** should be entered as **configure**.

6. Which of the following are true about the terminal history? (Choose three.)

A. Previous commands can be recalled using Ctrl-p.

B. The command history is stored in NVRAM.

C. The command history is stored in RAM.

D. Previous commands can be recalled using Ctrl-h.

E. **show history** lists the commands in the history buffer.

F. The command history can be recalled by entering the command **show commands**.

7. Which command moves a user from the Router(config-router)# prompt to EXEC mode?

A. Ctrl-a

B. Ctrl-z

C. **exit**

D. Ctrl-p

E. **end**

F. **exec**

8. Choose three true statements about setup mode.

A. It can be accessed using the **setup** command.

B. It is loaded by default instead of a saved configuration in NVRAM.

C. It loads by default when a router is new and booted for the first time.

D. It is an interactive dialog creating a configuration using a question-and-answer format.

E. After setup mode is entered, the configuration is applied unless the router is rebooted.

9. A user tries to access a router's enable mode by using the password configured in the **enable password** command. The router, however, denies access to the user. What are two possible explanations for this problem?

    A. The **enable** command was attempted from the Router> prompt.

    B. The **enable secret** command is configured.

    C. The password was set using the **enable password** command from the Router# prompt.

    D. The Caps Lock key was on when was entered the enable password.

10. The command **configure terminal** is used from enable mode. When **configure terminal** is entered, which of the following are true? (Choose two.)

    A. The router enters interface configuration mode.

    B. The router enters global configuration mode.

    C. The router will accept a **router rip** command at this point.

    D. IP addresses can be assigned from the resulting mode.

    E. Telnet access can be configured from the resulting mode.

11. Which command puts a router into routing protocol configuration mode?

    A. **router rip**

    B. Ctrl-z

    C. **interface s0/0**

    D. **network 201.203.50.0**

12. Which of the following best describes the sequence of the startup process of a router?

    A. Performing POST, loading the startup-config file, entering setup mode, loading the operating system

    B. Loading the bootstrap, loading the operating system, running POST, loading a configuration file

    C. Performing POST, loading bootstrap, loading IOS, loading the startup configuration

    D. Loading the bootstrap, performing POST, running the setup procedure, starting the operating system

13. Which of the following are operating environments for a router? (Choose three.)

    A. Boot ROM (RX BOOT)

    B. RIP

    C. ROM Monitor (ROMMON)

    D. IOS

    E. OSPF

    F. IGRP

14. Where can a router find an IOS image to load during startup? (Choose three.)

   A. Flash memory

   B. BIOS

   C. An external TFTP server

   D. POST

   E. ROM

   F. RAM

15. Which of the following are information displayed by the Cisco IOS software **show version** command? (Choose three.)

   A. The names and versions of flash files

   B. The startup configuration file

   C. Router uptime and last restart method

   D. System image file and location

   E. Configuration register

   F. Routing protocol database

16. What are the three methods to access the router's CLI?

   A. Terminal connection through the console port using a rollover cable

   B. Telnet via a console cable

   C. Terminal via a crossover cable

   D. Telnet via an Ethernet connection

   E. Modem connection via the aux port

   F. Aux port via a crossover cable

Challenge Questions and Activities

These questions require a deeper application of the concepts covered in this chapter.

1. Answer the following questions about the topology in the figure. PC3 and PC8 are on the same subnet.

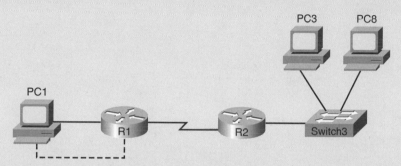

A. For PC3 to successfully ping PC8, is a routing protocol necessary on SW3?

B. If a user on PC8 wants to change a configuration on R1, what program can be used to access R1?

C. With the current cable configuration, can PC1 successfully use the console connection into R1? Why?

2. Using this router output, answer the following questions about the IOS:

```
System flash directory:
File        Length       Name/status
1           5427524      c2600-i-mz.122-12c.bin
2           845             startup1
[5428500 bytes used, 28125932 available, 33554432 total]
32768k bytes of processor board System flash (Read/Write)
```

A. What command produced this output?

B. What is an alternative command that can provide the currently used image name?

C. Will this IOS image run on a Cisco 2501 router?

D. If an engineer wants to upgrade the router IOS image to an image that is twice as large as the current one, will the router be able to handle it?

CHAPTER 3

Configuring a Router

Objectives

Upon completion of this chapter, you should be able to answer the following questions:

- What are the commands to name a router?

- How does an administrator set passwords on a router?

- What are the **show** commands used for?

- What steps and commands are necessary to configure a serial interface?

- What steps and commands are necessary to configure an Ethernet interface?

- How does a network engineer execute changes to a router?

- How does a network engineer save changes to a router?

- How does a network engineer configure an interface description?

- How does a network engineer configure a message-of-the-day banner?

- What steps and commands are necessary to configure host tables?

- What is the purpose of backup documentation?

- What steps and commands are necessary to recover a password on a router?

Key Terms

This chapter uses the following key terms. You can find the definitions in the Glossary:

Chapters 1 and 2 covered a wide variety of processes and terminology about how to configure a Cisco router. This chapter focuses on some of the most popular features to configure in a router. Specifically, this chapter explains how to configure IP addresses, serial and Ethernet interfaces, passwords, hostnames, login banners, and interface descriptions. Along the way, the chapter includes some related topics, such as how to look at how the router is working by using **show** commands, how to save the configuration after you have completed configuring the routers, and how to back up the configuration in case someone later inadvertently erases a router's configuration.

This chapter has two major sections. The first section shows how to take an internetwork with routers, Ethernet interfaces, and serial interfaces, from a totally unconfigured state to a working state, with the routers routing packets. The second section focuses on commands and processes related to documenting a router configuration.

Module 3 of the online curriculum includes several labs that reinforce the topics covered in this chapter. If at all possible, and at the direction of your instructor, please do the labs as you read the chapter. Doing the labs at the same time will help reinforce the concepts. You can also practice about half the commands shown in this chapter by using the Packet Tracer tool.

Configuring a Router for Basic Routing

This section explains basic router configuration under the assumption that the physical installation of some new routers has already been completed. (The Cisco Networking Academy Program curriculum covers many details about physical installation of cabling for both LANs and WANs, and those details are not repeated here.) Most of the discussions for the next several chapters assume that the physical installation has been correctly completed.

The examples in this chapter use the same simple internetwork used in Chapter 2, "Introduction to Routers," repeated here as Figure 3-1. Figure 3-1 shows two new routers. Neither router has any configuration at the start of the chapter. By the end of this section, you will see how to configure the routers to operate correctly, how to use **show** commands to verify the correct operation, and how to save the configuration so that the routers will still work after they are powered off and powered on again.

Figure 3-1   Internetwork with Two Routers Used in Basic Router Configuration Examples

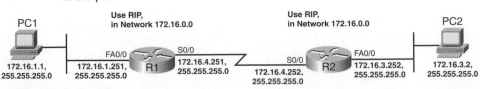

Reviewing the Configuration Modes

The Chapter 2 section "The Configuration Process and Configuration Modes" covered the basics of the configuration process. Before examining the specific configuration commands, it is helpful to review the process briefly.

By using the **configure terminal** command from privileged EXEC mode, the CLI moves into global configuration mode. From there, a user can use global configuration commands, but not other commands. Global configuration commands configure settings that apply to the entire router; for example, the **hostname** command assigns the router's hostname.

Some other configuration commands define settings that apply to one part of a router, so these commands are not global configuration commands. To use these other configuration commands, the CLI user must move to another configuration mode besides global configuration mode, or the command will be rejected. For example, the **ip address** command sets the IP address used by a single router interface. So, Cisco IOS requires that the CLI user first move from global configuration mode into interface configuration mode for that particular interface. Then the IOS will accept the **ip address** command, as shown in Example 3-1.

Note

Just as a reminder of the overall process, Example 3-1 begins with the user entering user EXEC mode, then enable mode, and then configuration mode.

Example 3-1   Global and Interface Configuration Modes

```
Press return to get started!
router>enable
router#configure terminal
router(config)#hostname fred
fred(config)#ip address 172.16.1.251 255.255.255.0
                        ^
% Invalid input detected at '^' marker.

fred(config)#interface fastethernet0/0
fred(config-if)#ip address 172.16.1.251 255.255.255.0
fred(config-if)#^Z
fred#
```

Example 3-1 shows the following steps:

Step 1   The user logs in from the console, moves to enable mode, and then enters configuration mode by using the **configure terminal** privileged mode EXEC command.

Step 2   The user changes the hostname using the **hostname fred** global configuration command.

Step 3   The user incorrectly tries to use the **ip address 172.16.1.251 255.255.255.0** command. This command is an interface mode subcommand that must be issued from interface mode.

Step 4   The user moves to interface configuration mode using the **interface fastethernet 0/0** command and then correctly uses the **ip address** interface subcommand.

Step 5   The user presses Ctrl-z to exit configuration mode, moving back to enable mode.

Cisco IOS includes a large number of subconfiguration modes, such as the interface configuration mode shown in Example 3-1. Each of these additional configuration modes can be reached using a global command. For example, interface configuration mode for interface fastethernet0/0 is reached using the **interface fastethernet0/0** global configuration command. From there, commands that define settings just for that interface—such as the IP address—can be used.

Table 3-1 lists the subconfiguration modes most likely to be used throughout the Networking Academy curriculum, plus a few others. The table lists the global command used to reach each config mode, as well as the resulting command *prompt*. (Each configuration mode can be recognized by a unique command prompt, all of which begin with "*hostname*(config," where *hostname* is the router's hostname.)

Table 3-1   Router Configuration Modes and Command Prompts

Mode	Global Command Used to Reach This Mode	Prompt
Interface	**interface**	Router(config-if)#
Controller	**controller**	Router(config-subif)#
Map-class	**map-class**	Router(config-map-list)#
Line	**line**	Router(config-map-class)#
Router	**router**	Router(config-line)#

Packet Tracer   You can use the Packet Tracer tool to gain experience with the CLI. Packet Tracer file NA02-0301 has a topology just like Figure 3-1. From topology mode, just click a router icon, and you can navigate as shown in Example 3-1.

Configuring Ethernet and Serial Interfaces

After an internetwork has been physically installed, configuring the routers to route IP packets takes only three configuration commands, as follows:

How To ⌕

Step 1   The engineer must configure each router with the correct IP address and subnet mask, using the **ip address** {*address mask*} interface subcommand, as previously shown in Example 3-1.

Step 2   The engineer must administratively enable the interface by configuring the **no shutdown** interface subcommand.

Step 3   If installed in a lab environment, the engineer must set the serial interface clock rate (on the router connected to the DCE cable) using the **clock rate** interface subcommand.

Example 3-2 shows the configuration process to configure R1 in Figure 3-1 for the first two steps in the list. Step 3 will be explained in Example 3-3.

Note

Cisco conventions use braces—{}—to enclose command parameters that are required, and brackets—[]—to list command parameters that are optional.

Example 3-2   Configuring IP Addresses on R1's Serial and Ethernet Interfaces

```
Router#configure terminal
Enter configuration commands, one per line.  End with CNTL/Z.
Router(config)#interface fastethernet 0/0
Router(config-if)#ip address 172.16.1.251 255.255.255.0
Router(config-if)#no shutdown
*Jan 13 17:34:59.529: %LINK-3-UPDOWN: Interface FastEthernet0/0, changed state to up
*Jan 13 17:35:00.530: %LINEPROTO-5-UPDOWN: Line protocol on Interface FastEthernet0/0,
  changed state to up
Router(config-if)#interface s0/0
Router(config-if)#ip address 172.16.4.251 255.255.255.0
Router(config-if)#no shutdown
Router(config-if)#
*Jan 13 17:34:48.002: %LINK-3-UPDOWN: Interface Serial0/0, changed state to down
Router(config-if)#end
Router#
```

Note

Most Cisco engineers habitually abbreviate the words used to refer to types of router interfaces. For example, most people abbreviate FastEthernet as "FA" or "Fa," serial as "S," and Ethernet as "E."

Example 3-2 shows the basic configuration and how to enable each interface. Note that the example begins with the user assigning IP address 172.16.1.251 to R1's FastEthernet0/0 interface, followed by a **no shutdown** command. IOS puts a router interface into a shutdown state, or administratively disabled state, if no cable is plugged into the interface when the router is first enabled. The user can switch between a **shutdown** (down on purpose) and **no shutdown** (up on purpose) state by using the **shutdown** and **no shutdown** interface subcommands, respectively.

Note that Example 3-2 shows the messages generated by the router after the **no shutdown** commands were issued. Cisco routers and switches send log messages to the console port whenever certain events (such as interfaces changing status) occur. For interface FastEthernet0/0, the log messages imply that the interface came up. However, the log message generated after the **no shutdown** command was used on the serial interface implies that the interface is still not working. In this case, router R2 (on the other end of the serial link) was not yet configured, and its interface was in a shutdown state. When R2 is configured, R1 would send log messages to the console to tell the engineer that the interface just came up.

After configuring the IP addresses on the other router (R2) and enabling its interfaces, the small internetwork of Figure 3-1 is mostly working. However, a few other items typically need to be configured to make the internetwork more useful: the serial interface clock rate and routes.

Lab 3.1.7   Configuring an Ethernet Interface

In this lab, you configure an Ethernet interface on the router with an IP address and a subnet mask.

Configuring Clock Rate on a Serial Link

If the internetwork of Figure 3-1 is created in a lab, the serial link is probably created by connecting a DTE serial cable and a DCE serial cable between two router serial ports. This practice is explained in the Chapter 1 section "Creating Inexpensive Leased Lines in a Lab." If you do not remember the details, it is worth a few minutes to review that section.

When creating a WAN link by connecting cables in a lab, the routers need an additional command: **clock rate**. This command tells the router that has the DCE cable plugged into it the speed at which it should clock the serial link. With a leased line installed by a telco, the CSU/DSU on the link supplies clocking to the router, and the **clock rate** command is not needed. In a lab, the CSU/DSUs are not needed to create the leased line, which saves money but requires the **clock rate** command.

The format of the **clock rate** command includes the speed in bits per second (bps), but a router supports only specific speeds. Many routers support only 1200, 2400, 9600, 19,200, 38,400, 56,000, 64,000, 72,000, 125,000, 148,000, 500,000, 800,000, 100,0000, 1,300,000, 2,000,000, or 4,000,000 bps. For example, the **clock rate 64000** command would be accepted, but the **clock rate 65000** command would be rejected. Other router platforms may support other speeds as well, but routers do not allow just any speed. To find the speeds supported on a particular type of router, use the **clock rate ?** command in serial interface configuration mode.

Packet Tracer configuration file NA02-0301-unconfigured has a topology that is similar to Figure 3-1 but does not include the majority of configurations shown in this chapter. Note that this Packet Tracer configuration file already has the **clock rate 64000** command configured, but you can practice the command by changing the speed to another valid setting.

Lab 3.1.5   Configuring a Serial Interface

In this lab, you configure a serial interface between two routers so that they can communicate.

Configuring Routes

At this point in the configuration process, both R1 and R2 may have successfully configured IP addresses on each interface, and the interfaces may all be up and working. However, the hosts on the two LANs may not be able to send packets to each other, because the two routers do not have all the required routes. In particular, each router is missing a route to the LAN subnet on the other side of the internetwork. Example 3-3 shows the routing tables in the two routers.

Example 3-3   Routing Tables on Routers R1 and R2—Connected Routes Only

```
! The following command is on router R1
R1#show ip route
Codes: C - connected, S - static, R - RIP, M - mobile, B - BGP
       D - EIGRP, EX - EIGRP external, O - OSPF, IA - OSPF inter area
       N1 - OSPF NSSA external type 1, N2 - OSPF NSSA external type 2
       E1 - OSPF external type 1, E2 - OSPF external type 2
       i - IS-IS, su - IS-IS summary, L1 - IS-IS level-1, L2 - IS-IS level-2
       ia - IS-IS inter area, * - candidate default, U - per-user static route
       o - ODR, P - periodic downloaded static route
Gateway of last resort is not set


     172.16.0.0/24 is subnetted, 2 subnets
C       172.16.4.0 is directly connected, Serial0/0
C       172.16.1.0 is directly connected, FastEthernet0/0
```

```
! The following command is on router R2
R2#show ip route
Codes: C - connected, S - static, R - RIP, M - mobile, B - BGP
       D - EIGRP, EX - EIGRP external, O - OSPF, IA - OSPF inter area
       N1 - OSPF NSSA external type 1, N2 - OSPF NSSA external type 2
       E1 - OSPF external type 1, E2 - OSPF external type 2
       i - IS-IS, su - IS-IS summary, L1 - IS-IS level-1, L2 - IS-IS level-2
       ia - IS-IS inter area, * - candidate default, U - per-user static route
       o - ODR, P - periodic downloaded static route
Gateway of last resort is not set


     172.16.0.0/24 is subnetted, 2 subnets
C       172.16.4.0 is directly connected, Serial0/0
C       172.16.2.0 is directly connected, FastEthernet0/0
R2#ping 172.16.4.251

Type escape sequence to abort.
Sending 5, 100-byte ICMP Echos to 172.16.4.251, timeout is 2 seconds:
!!!!!
Success rate is 100 percent (5/5), round-trip min/avg/max = 28/28/32 ms
```

Example 3-3   Routing Tables on Routers R1 and R2—Connected Routes Only   *continued*

```
R2#ping 172.16.1.251

Type escape sequence to abort.
Sending 5, 100-byte ICMP Echos to 172.16.1.251, timeout is 2 seconds:
.....
Success rate is 0 percent (0/5)
```

Routers add a ***directly connected route*** to their routing tables after the interface is both configured with an IP address and up and working. Directly connected routes, or simply *connected
routes*, are routes for subnets that are directly connected to a router. For example, R1 has two
directly connected routes: one for subnet 172.16.1.0/24 (off interface FA0/0) and one for
172.16.4.0/24 (off interface S0/0). However, R1 does not have a route to reach R2's LAN subnet—namely, 172.16.2.0/24. Conversely, R2 has two directly connected routes, because it has
two up and working interfaces, but it does not have a route to reach R1's LAN subnet of
172.16.1.0/24. So, as shown at the end of Example 3-3, R2 can ping R1's 172.16.4.251 IP
address, because R2 has a route to reach that (connected) subnet. However, R2 fails when pinging 172.16.1.251, R1's LAN IP address, because R2 does not have a route to reach subnet
172.16.1.0/24.

Chapters 6 and 7 cover the details of how to configure routes in Cisco routers, either through
static configuration commands (Chapter 6, "Routing and Routing Protocols") or through
dynamic routing protocols such as RIP (Chapter 7, "Distance Vector Routing Protocols"). For
this chapter, however, the examples configure RIP correctly, using the **router rip** and **network
172.16.0.0** commands on both R1 and R2. By doing so, both routers learn the missing routes.
Chapter 7 explains the meaning behind these commands and explains more about how RIP
works.

Summarizing the Working Configurations for R1 and R2

Before we move on to the next several commands, Example 3-4 summarizes the configuration
required to create working router configurations for the internetwork shown in Figure 3-1. Note
that the configuration assumes that RIP will be used to dynamically learn routes and that the
network exists in a lab, so the **clock rate** command is needed on one of the serial interfaces.
Also note that Example 3-4 shows the output of the **show running-config** command, but the
output has been edited to only show the commands covered in this chapter.

Example 3-4   R1 and R2 Configuration

```
! Configuration on R1
R1#show running-config
hostname R1
!
interface fastethernet0/0
 ip address 172.16.1.251 255.255.255.0
!
interface serial0/0
 ip address 172.16.4.251 255.255.255.0
 clock rate 64000
!
router rip
 network 172.16.0.0
```

```
! Configuration on R2
R2#show running-config
hostname R2

interface FastEthernet0/0
 ip address 172.16.2.252 255.255.255.0
!
interface Serial0/0
 ip address 172.16.4.252 255.255.255.0
!
router rip
 network 172.16.0.0
```

The **show running-config** and **show startup-config** commands show whether each interface
has been administratively enabled. If the output of the **show running-config** command lists a
shutdown command under an interface, the interface is administratively disabled, or "shut
down." However, when configured to be in a "no shutdown" (enabled) state, the output of the
show running-config command does not list either the **shutdown** or **no shutdown** command.
So the absence of both the **shutdown** and **no shutdown** commands means that the interfaces in
Example 3-4 are administratively enabled.

Configuring Hostnames and Passwords

The hosts on the two LANs in Figure 3-1 now should be able to send and receive packets to
and from each other. This section examines two other configuration settings—router hostnames
and router passwords—that, although not absolutely required, are added in most every router
configuration in the world.

Configuring a Router's Hostname

Giving each router a unique name is just plain common sense. With Cisco routers, the **hostname** *name* global configuration command assigns a text name to a router. Once configured, IOS uses the hostname as the beginning part of the command prompt.

Example 3-5 shows the configuration of R1's hostname. At the beginning of the example, no hostname has been configured, so the hostname is the default setting of "router."

Example 3-5   Assigning a Hostname to a Router

```
router#configure terminal
router(config)#hostname R1
R1(config)#end
R1#
```

Example 3-5 also shows an obvious reminder that when you enter a configuration command in configuration mode and press Enter at the end of the line, IOS immediately uses the command. In this case, once the **hostname R1** command was entered, IOS started using R1 as the beginning of the command prompt.

Lab 3.1.2   Command Modes and Router Identification

In this lab, you identify the basic router modes of user EXEC and privileged EXEC. You also use commands to enter specific modes. In addition, you name the router.

User and Enable Mode Passwords

As covered in the Chapter 2 section "Router Password Basics," routers have a separate password for each of the three methods to reach user mode: the console, the aux port, and Telnet. Additionally, after the user enters the **enable** command, the router expects the user to enter the enable password at the password prompt to reach privileged mode, which is also called enable mode. Figure 3-2 shows these passwords and the general idea of their use.

IOS uses the term *line* to refer to the console, aux port, and Telnet connections into a router. So, the console password, auxiliary password, and *Telnet password* are configured using *line configuration mode*. Once inside the respective line configuration modes, two commands define what IOS should do about a password on that line:

- The **password** *text* command defines the characters that must be entered when the router asks for a password.

- The **login** command tells IOS that a password is required, causing IOS to display a password prompt for the end user.

Figure 3-2 Console, Aux, VTY, and Enable Passwords

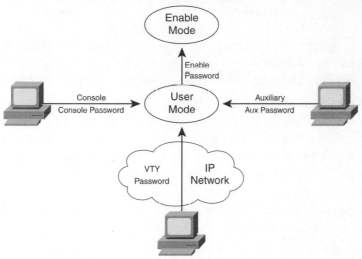

Example 3-6 shows the configuration for the console, aux, and vty passwords on router R1.

```
Example 3-6     Configuring Console, Aux, and VTY Passwords on Router R1
R1#conf t
Enter configuration commands, one per line.  End with CNTL/Z.
R1(config)#line con 0
R1(config-line)#login
% Login disabled on line 0, until 'password' is set
R1(config-line)#password height
R1(config-line)#line aux 0
R1(config-line)#password depth
R1(config-line)#login
R1(config-line)#line vty 0 4
R1(config-line)#password anything-else
R1(config-line)#login
R1(config-line)#^Z
R1#
```

The commands themselves are relatively basic, but Example 3-6 shows a couple of subtle points. Note that although the single console line is referred to as **line con 0**, and the single aux line is referred to as **line aux 0**, the **line vty 0 4** command refers to a range of Telnet connections into the router. The "0 4" means IOS has configured five concurrent Telnet connections into the router, numbered 0 through 4. Because the end user cannot choose which of the router's Telnet (vty) lines to use when telnetting to a router, all the vty lines are typically assigned the same password text, as shown at the end of Example 3-6.

Also note the error message after the **login** command under **line con 0**. Example 3-6 shows the **login** command preceding the **password** command. In that case, the **login** command tells IOS to display a password prompt on the screen and wait for the user to enter a password. However, at that point, a console password has not been configured. The message means that IOS will not prompt the user for the password until the engineer also configures a console password using the **password** subcommand.

Chapter 2 already covered the details of how to configure the enable password. The password required by the **enable** command is set by either the **enable password** *pw* or **enable secret** *pw* command, where *pw* represents the text of the password. The enable secret password is much more secure because it is stored in the configuration as a Message Digest 5 (MD5) hash. (The password configured with the **enable password** command can be encrypted using the **service password-encryption** global configuration command, as mentioned in Chapter 2, but the encryption is weak and can be easily broken.) The following list summarizes the behavior with the two commands that can define the enable password:

Note

There is no benefit to configuring both the **enable secret** and **enable password** commands at the same time. In most routers today, only the **enable secret** command is used.

- If only one of the two commands (**enable secret** or **enable password**) is configured, but not both, IOS expects the user to enter the password as defined in that single configuration command.

- If both the **enable secret** and **enable password** commands are configured, the router expects the password as defined in the **enable secret** command. The router will not accept the password defined in the **enable password** command.

- If neither the **enable secret** nor **enable password** command is configured, the behavior varies. If the user is at the console, the router automatically allows the user access to enable mode. If the user is not at the console, the router rejects the **enable** command.

Lab 3.1.3 Configuring Router Passwords

In this lab, you configure a password for console login to user mode and configure a password for virtual terminal (Telnet) sessions.

Examining Operational Status Using show Commands

After the routers are configured, you need to be able to examine them to see if they are working properly. Some of the best troubleshooting and testing commands on a router are the **ping**, **traceroute**, and **telnet** commands, all of which are covered at various points in the Networking Academy CCNA 1 course and the *Networking Basics CCNA 1 Companion Guide* book. These commands are also covered in this book in the second half of Chapter 4, "Learning About Other Devices."

Additionally, IOS supplies a large number of **show** command options that network engineers can use to examine a router's current operational status. In fact, the IOS **show** command may well be the single most important IOS command. It is an EXEC command that has countless options. Its basic function is to display, or show, information about what the router is doing or how the router is configured. For example, two of the more popular **show** command options used for basic troubleshooting are the **show interfaces** command and the **show ip interface brief** command. Example 3-7 shows these commands on R1, as soon as it is working as configured in the examples in the earlier parts of this chapter.

Example 3-7   The **show interfaces** and **show ip interface brief** Commands on R1

```
R1>show ip interface brief
Interface                  IP-Address      OK? Method Status
  Protocol
FastEthernet0/0            172.16.1.251    YES manual up                      up
Serial0/0                  172.16.4.251    YES manual up                      up
Serial0/1                  unassigned      YES unset  administratively down down
R1>show interfaces serial 0/0
Serial0/0 is up, line protocol is up
  Hardware is PowerQUICC Serial
  Internet address is 172.16.4.251/24
  MTU 1500 bytes, BW 1544 Kbit, DLY 20000 usec,
     reliability 255/255, txload 1/255, rxload 1/255
  Encapsulation HDLC, loopback not set
  Keepalive set (10 sec)
  Last input 00:00:06, output 00:00:04, output hang never
  Last clearing of "show interface" counters 03:52:36
  Input queue: 0/75/0/0 (size/max/drops/flushes); Total output drops: 0
  Queueing strategy: fifo
  Output queue: 0/40 (size/max)
  5 minute input rate 0 bits/sec, 0 packets/sec
  5 minute output rate 0 bits/sec, 0 packets/sec
     1636 packets input, 104854 bytes, 0 no buffer
     Received 1565 broadcasts, 0 runts, 0 giants, 0 throttles
     1 input errors, 0 CRC, 1 frame, 0 overrun, 0 ignored, 0 abort
     1634 packets output, 104709 bytes, 0 underruns
     0 output errors, 0 collisions, 70 interface resets
     0 output buffer failures, 0 output buffers swapped out
     11 carrier transitions
     DCD=up  DSR=up  DTR=up  RTS=up  CTS=up
```

First, look at the **show ip interface brief** command output. Many engineers use this command first when logging in to a router. The **show ip interface brief** command lists the interfaces, their IP addresses, and the interface status, with only one line of output per interface. Several IOS commands list two states for each router interface; interfaces that are working must be in an "up and up" state, as is the case with two of the interfaces shown in Example 3-7. Router interfaces that are not in the "up and up" state cannot send and receive packets. So, this example shows that R1's FA0/0 and S0/0 interfaces are configured with IP addresses that match

Figure 3-1, and the interfaces are both up and working. (Chapter 9, "Basic Router Troubleshooting," reviews the other combinations of interface state values, along with some reasons why an interface might not be in an "up and up" state.)

The **show interfaces s0/0** command shows more detail about a particular interface, interface S0/0 in this case. The first half of the command output lists basic configuration settings, and the last half of the output lists statistics for the interface. So, not only can you tell if the interface is "up and up" per the first line of output, and see the IP address and mask from the third line of output, you can also tell if packets are currently being sent and received on the interface.

Another important command on routers is the **show ip route** command. Routers route packets by comparing the destination IP address of each packet with the contents of the IP routing table, so basic troubleshooting ought to include an examination of the routing table. Example 3-8 shows the IP routing table on router R1, followed by a few explanatory comments.

Example 3-8   The show ip route Command on Router R1

```
R1>show ip route
Codes: C - connected, S - static, R - RIP, M - mobile, B - BGP
       D - EIGRP, EX - EIGRP external, O - OSPF, IA - OSPF inter area
       N1 - OSPF NSSA external type 1, N2 - OSPF NSSA external type 2
       E1 - OSPF external type 1, E2 - OSPF external type 2
       i - IS-IS, su - IS-IS summary, L1 - IS-IS level-1, L2 - IS-IS level-2
       ia - IS-IS inter area, * - candidate default, U - per-user static route
       o - ODR, P - periodic downloaded static route

Gateway of last resort is not set


     172.16.0.0/24 is subnetted, 3 subnets
C       172.16.4.0 is directly connected, Serial0/0
C       172.16.1.0 is directly connected, FastEthernet0/0
R       172.16.2.0 [120/1] via 172.16.4.252, 00:00:24, Serial0/0
```

The output in Example 3-8 begins with a legend that describes many codes and their meanings. For example, C represents connected routes, and R represents RIP-learned routes. The actual routing table entries are listed at the bottom of the example, showing the two connected routes with a C in the first column and the one RIP-learned route with an R in the first column. Focusing on the RIP-learned route, note that the destination subnet (172.16.2.0) is listed, with a next-hop router of 172.16.4.252, which is R2's IP address on the serial link. According to this last route in the routing table, R1 uses its interface S0/0 when forwarding packets to subnet 172.16.2.0.

Most **show** commands can be issued from user mode. However, the **show running-config** and **show startup-config** commands are notable exceptions. The **show running-config** command, which shows the running configuration file stored in RAM, and the **show startup-config** command, which shows the configuration file in NVRAM, are both allowed only in enable mode.

(Example 3-4 earlier in this chapter shows an example of the kinds of output shown from a **show running-config** command.)

Although looking at the configuration files is an easy way to troubleshoot basic configuration problems, in some companies, the security rules allow only a few engineers to know the enable password. The rest of the engineers are allowed access to only user mode. So, it is helpful to understand **show** commands so that you can examine the router's operations without being able to look at the router configuration. For reference, Table 3-2 lists the **show** commands mentioned in the corresponding module of the online curriculum, plus a few other popular **show** commands.

Table 3-2   Router Commands Mentioned in the Networking Academy CCNA 2 Online Curriculum

Command	Description
show interfaces [*type number*]	Displays all the statistics for all the interfaces on the router. To view statistics for one interface, the interface type and number can be included in the command—for example, Router#**show interfaces serial 1**.
show controllers [*type number*]	Displays information specific to the interface hardware, for all interfaces or for a specific interface—for example, Router#**show controllers serial 0/0**.
show clock	Displays the time set in the router.
show hosts	Displays a cached list of hostnames and addresses.
show users	Displays all users who are connected to the router.
show history	Displays a history of commands that have been entered.
show version	Displays information about the currently loaded software version along with hardware and device information.
show arp	Displays the router's Address Resolution Protocol (ARP) table.
show flash	Displays the contents of a router's flash memory.
show protocols	Displays the global and interface-specific status of any configured Layer 3 protocols.
show startup-config	Displays the saved configuration located in NVRAM.
show running-config	Displays the contents of the currently running configuration file, the configuration for a specific interface, or map class information.
show ip route	Displays IP routes known to the router.
show ip interface brief	Displays a single line of output per interface, including the IP address configured and the interface status.

Lab 3.1.4   Using Router show Commands

In this lab, you become familiar with the basic router **show** commands.

Changing the Configuration

When you configure a router from configuration mode, the new commands are added to the running configuration, in RAM, as soon as you press the Enter key at the end of each command. The commands may be 100 percent correct, or they may not. This section covers some of the basics of what to do if the commands added to the running configuration are incorrect, and what to do as soon as the running configuration is correct and you want to save it.

What to Do if the Configuration Is Incorrect

After configuration changes have been made, you should look at the running configuration using the **show running-config** command. After looking at the configuration, if some of the commands are incorrect, you have several options—some easy and some drastic—for fixing the problems.

For the simple changes, you can either reenter the command or use the **no** version of the command. For example, all the configuration commands covered in this chapter can simply be reentered in the correct configuration mode, with the corrected values, to replace the incorrect parameters. Alternatively, if a command was configured but was not needed, you can get into the same configuration mode and issue the same command prefaced by the word **no**.

Example 3-9 shows how to change the configuration of R1 as compared with its configuration shown in Example 3-4, under the following assumptions:

- The hostname shown in Example 3-4 was incorrectly configured as R1. It should have been Router1.

- The FA0/0 IP address should have been 172.16.1.1, not 172.16.1.251 as shown in Example 3-4.

- There should be no console password, meaning that it should be removed.

Example 3-9   Changing the Configuration

```
! The following shows the configuration before the changes
Router1#show running-config
Building configuration...
! lines that are not related to this example are omitted
hostname R1
!
interface FastEthernet0/0
 ip address 172.16.1.251 255.255.255.0
!
line con 0
 login
 password height
! Next, the settings are changed.
R1#configure terminal
Enter configuration commands, one per line.  End with CNTL/Z.
R1(config)#hostname Router1
Router1(config)#int fa0/0
Router1(config-if)#ip address 172.16.1.1 255.255.255.0
Router1(config-if)#line con 0
Router1(config-line)#no password height
Router1(config-line)#no login
Router1(config-line)#^Z
Router1#
*Jan 13 22:32:09.850: %SYS-5-CONFIG_I: Configured from console by console
Router1#show running-config
Building configuration...
! lines that are not related to this example are omitted
hostname Router1
!
interface FastEthernet0/0
 ip address 172.16.1.1 255.255.255.0
!
line con 0
!
```

The configuration process in Example 3-9 follows the same process for configuring the hostname and IP address, but with the new values shown. Because a router can have only one hostname, the **hostname Router1** command simply replaces the old **hostname** command setting. Similarly, a router interface can have only one primary IP address on an interface, so the **ip address 172.16.1.1 255.255.255.0** command replaces the old IP address.

To remove the **password** and **login** commands from the console line, the commands (as configured earlier, in Example 3-4) were issued again, but with the word **no** in front. This process is often referred to as "using the 'no' version of the command." By doing so, the command is removed, or, for cases in which the command sets some value to one of two values, the **no** command sets the value to the opposite. In this case, the **no password** and **no login** commands simply delete the commands from the configuration; note that at the end of the example, the console does not have anything configured.

A more drastic way to fix an incorrect configuration is to reload the router using the **reload** command. This process assumes that if you want to revert to the startup configuration file that was last saved, and that if the newly added and incorrect configuration has not yet been saved to the startup-config file using the **copy running-config startup-config** command, the router can be reloaded.

Similarly, you could simply start over completely by erasing the startup-config file using the **erase startup-config** command and then reloading the router. This might be practical in a lab environment, where it may be quicker to just start over, particularly if you already saved the incorrect configuration using the **copy running-config startup-config** command.

The final option for correcting configuration errors is to use either the **copy startup-config running-config** command or the **copy tftp running-config** command. These commands copy the startup configuration or a configuration file from a TFTP server, respectively, into the running-config file. These options can be useful when you know that the startup-config file or a file saved on a TFTP server has the complete and correct configuration you want to use.

The unfortunate part of using the **copy** command to copy another configuration file into the running configuration file is that the **copy** command does not actually replace the running configuration file in all cases. Unfortunately, the reasons are best understood after you have learned a large number of configuration commands. Effectively, any **copy** command that copies into the running configuration does the equivalent of what would happen if the same commands were entered from configuration mode. In many cases, the configuration commands replace the old configuration commands, as was shown in Example 3-9. In fact, if the configuration files use only the commands covered in this chapter, the process using these **copy** commands would work fine. However, in some cases, particularly when using configuration commands that create any kind of list, these **copy** commands may not fix all the errors.

Chapter 11, which covers a type of configuration list called Access Control Lists (ACLs), explains the problem with the **copy** command when trying to fix configuration errors in an ACL.

What to Do After the Configuration Is Correct

As soon as the new configuration in RAM is correct, the engineer should save a copy of the configuration. At a minimum, the **copy running-config startup-config** privileged EXEC command should be used to save a copy of the new configuration in the startup-config file in NVRAM. At that point, if the router were reloaded, the router would come up with the new configuration commands loaded.

Additionally, the configuration should be saved outside the router. The **copy running-config tftp** command is commonly used to copy the configuration into a file somewhere in the IP network. Alternatively, the engineer can simply copy and paste the output of a **show running-config** command from the terminal emulator, although doing so could be time-consuming for a large network.

Later in this chapter, the section "Using TFTP to Back Up a Configuration" shows examples of copying the configuration to a TFTP server. That section also includes a table summarizing the commands used for copying the configuration files.

 Lab 3.1.6   Making Configuration Changes

In this lab, you configure some basic router settings and bring interfaces up and down.

Next, the second major section of this chapter looks at the processes and basic commands that can be used to document the router configuration for others.

Documenting the Router Configuration

Imagine that you just took a new job working for a company with a network that has 100 routers and a few hundred LAN switches. On your first day on the job, the lead network engineer unfortunately calls in sick. And of course, the network breaks, and your boss says to you, "I know it's your first day, but could you take a crack at troubleshooting and fixing a problem?" After feeling the adrenaline start to flow, you realize that your chances of finding and fixing the problem are much better if the lead engineer did a good job of standardizing and documenting configurations. Otherwise, you're in for a pretty rough first day.

The network should be well documented by the network engineers. The documentation should include drawings, called engineering drawings, that show the physical installation, the logical IP topology with subnets, the circuits leased from the telco, and so on. The documentation should also include a copy of all the router and switch configuration files stored on a server. These files should be readily available to the engineering staff so that it can recover when the router and switch configurations have been changed.

Engineers should define a standard for their internetworks about how the routers (and switches) are configured. The creation of standards for network consistency helps reduce network complexity, unplanned downtime, and events that may affect network performance. For example, the engineer picks the subnet numbers and router IP addresses used in the network. A company's configuration standard should define whether the routers' IP addresses are always the first IP address in the subnet, the last, or some other convention. The router hostnames need to match the names used in any drawings of the internetwork.

Configuration standards make the network much easier to troubleshoot and change. With standards, anyone knowledgeable about networking could look at diagrams of the network and the written configuration standards and quickly understand the most important details about the network.

Along with following standards and documenting the network, the router configurations themselves can help provide some information about the routers and the network. Specifically, an engineer can add a text description to an interface, documenting details about that interface, and add a text banner that the user sees when logging in to the router. Both items help a user remember details about the router, without taking a lot of time. The router can also be configured with hostnames of other routers and switches, allowing the person using the router CLI to refer to names instead of IP addresses. The next three sections examine all three of these tools on a router, including how to configure each.

Configuring Interface Descriptions

An interface description is text that is added to an interface configuration on a router for the purpose of documentation. The information might include the name of the device on the other end of the cable, or the user group that the interface supports. For WAN interfaces, many engineers add the WAN circuit number, which is a number the telco needs to know when you call the telco to report a failure on a WAN link. Whatever the information, anything can be entered and later viewed.

The **description** *text* interface subcommand adds a description to an interface. To see the description, the **show interfaces** or **show running-config** commands can be used. Example 3-10 shows an example of interface descriptions.

Example 3-10   Configuring and Viewing Interface Descriptions

```
R1#conf t
Enter configuration commands, one per line.  End with CNTL/Z.
R1(config)#int fa0/0
R1(config-if)#description R1 Fa0/0 is connected to SW1's FA0/11 interface
R1(config-if)#int s0/0
R1(config-if)#description R1 S0/0 is connected to R2's S0/0. R2 is in Atlanta
R1(config-if)#^Z
R1#show running-config
Building configuration...
! lines that are not related to this example are omitted
interface FastEthernet0/0
 description R1 Fa0/0 is connected to SW1's FA0/11 interface
 ip address 172.16.1.251 255.255.255.0
!
interface Serial0/0
 description R1 S0/0 is connected to R2's S0/0. R2 is in Atlanta
 ip address 172.16.4.251 255.255.255.0
```

Example 3-10   Configuring and Viewing Interface Descriptions *continued*

```
! lines that are not related to this example are omitted
R1#show interfaces fa0/0
FastEthernet0/0 is up, line protocol is up
  Hardware is PQUICC_FEC, address is 0007.8580.7208 (bia 0007.8580.7208)
  Description: R1 Fa0/0 is connected to SW1's FA0/11 interface
  Internet address is 172.16.1.251/24
```

Lab 3.2.3   Configuring Interface Descriptions

In this lab, you practice choosing a description for an interface and use interface configuration mode to enter that description.

Configuring Login Banners

A login banner is a text message supplied to the user at some point when he or she logs in to a router. IOS supports many types of banners, with the most common being the ***message-of-the-day (MOTD) banner***. The MOTD banner is supplied to users who access the router from the console, aux port, or via Telnet, with the banner being displayed before the user logs in. Many routers show a banner that reads something like this:

```
Restricted Access—Authorized Users Only. Violators Will Be Prosecuted!
```

Example 3-11 shows an example of how to configure an MOTD banner on a router using the **banner motd** *delimiter banner-text delimiter* command. Note that the command uses a delimiter to define the beginning and end of the message. The delimiter is a single character that cannot be anywhere in the banner text. IOS sees the first (delimiter) character and then scans until it finds the next one, treating all the text in between as the banner text. This style of configuration allows the banner to be multiple lines long, as shown in Example 3-11.

Example 3-11   Configuring Message-of-the-Day Banners

```
R1#conf t
Enter configuration commands, one per line.  End with CNTL/Z.
R1(config)#banner motd $ This is line 1 of the banner
Enter TEXT message.  End with the character '$'.
This is line 2
Don't mess with my router, under penalty
The banner ends when I type the dollar sign, like this $
R1(config)#^Z
R1#exit

R1 con0 is now available
```

Example 3-11   Configuring Message-of-the-Day Banners   *continued*

```
Press RETURN to get started.


 This is line 1 of the banner
This is line 2
Don't mess with my router, under penalty
The banner ends when I type the dollar sign, like this


User Access Verification


Password:
R1>
```

The best way to get a sense of how the **banner** command works is to use it on a real router, but Example 3-11 does show most of the interesting points about the **banner** command's quirks. The first line of the banner is entered on a single line, and the user presses the Enter key. Assuming that the line has only a starting delimiter, and the same character is not repeated on that line as an ending delimiter, IOS supplies a message (highlighted in Example 3-11) that tells the user to keep typing and to end the banner with another delimiter, which in this example is a dollar sign ($). (The first non-blank character typed after the **motd** keyword will be the delimiter.) Then, each line is typed, and Enter is pressed, until a line has a "$" in it. At that point, IOS ends the banner.

The end of Example 3-11 shows the user exiting EXEC mode and the banner being displayed. Note that the MOTD banner is indeed displayed before the password prompt.

Lab 3.2.5   Configuring Message-of-the-Day (MOTD)

In this lab, you enter an MOTD on the router, which will allow all users to view the message upon entering the router.

Configuring Local Host Tables

Users of the IOS CLI often need to refer to other routers' and switches' IP addresses in commands. For example, to troubleshoot a problem, the **ping** command might be used. For a user at R1 in Figure 3-1 to ping router R2's serial IP address, the user at R1 might use the command **ping 172.16.4.252** or the command **ping R2**. To use the command that refers to R2 by name, R1 must somehow resolve that name into IP address 172.16.4.252.

IOS supports two methods for resolving a name into its corresponding IP address. The first method is to tell the router to use a DNS server using the **ip name-server** *address1* [*address2…address6*] command. This global configuration command identifies the IP address of a name server, with IOS allowing up to six DNS servers to be configured. Then, the DNS administrator must add names and IP addresses to the DNS—for example, an entry for name R2 with IP address 172.16.4.252. When the user enters the name **R2** at the CLI, the router asks the DNS for assistance, which resolves the name into IP address 172.16.4.252. Then the **ping** command can send the ICMP echo messages to 172.16.4.252.

The second method for IOS to resolve names into IP addresses is to statically configure the names and addresses on the router. To do so, the **ip host** *name address1* [*address2…address8*] global configuration command is used. This command defines local names that can be used only on the router at which the commands are configured. Example 3-12 shows how R1 might configure the hostname of R2, with some deeper explanations following the example.

Example 3-12   Configuring and Using Local Hostnames on R1

```
R1#configure terminal
R1(config)#ip host R2 172.16.2.252 172.16.4.252
R1(config)#ip host R2-fa 172.16.2.252
R1(config)#ip host R2-s 172.16.4.252
R1(config)#^Z
R1#pingR2-fa

Type escape sequence to abort.
Sending 5, 100-byte ICMP Echos to 172.16.2.252, timeout is 2 seconds:
!!!!!
Success rate is 100 percent (5/5), round-trip min/avg/max = 28/28/32 ms
R1#ping R2-s

Type escape sequence to abort.
Sending 5, 100-byte ICMP Echos to 172.16.4.252, timeout is 2 seconds:
!!!!!
Success rate is 100 percent (5/5), round-trip min/avg/max = 28/28/32 ms
R1#show hosts
Default domain is not set
Name/address lookup uses static mappings


Codes: UN - unknown, EX - expired, OK - OK, ?? - revalidate
       temp - temporary, perm - permanent
       NA - Not Applicable None - Not defined


Host                    Port  Flags      Age Type  Address(es)
R2                      None  (perm, OK)  0  IP    172.16.2.252
                                                   172.16.4.252
R2-fa                   None  (perm, OK)  0  IP    172.16.2.252
R2-s                    None  (perm, OK)  0  IP    172.16.4.252
```

The configuration in Example 3-12 shows three **ip host** commands. Two of the commands define a single IP address. When these names (R2-s and R2-fa) are referenced in the **ping** commands in the second half of the example, IOS uses the information in the **ip host** commands to find the single correct IP address to use, as highlighted in the example. For instance, the **ping R2-fa** command sends an ICMP echo to IP address 172.16.2.252, the IP address in the **ip host R2-fa 172.16.2.252** command.

The IOS **telnet** command can take advantage of the **ip host** command's ability to list several IP addresses associated with a single name. Routers normally use many interfaces, each with a different IP address. The **telnet** command, when referencing a hostname for which several IP addresses have been associated, attempts to telnet to the first IP address. If no response is received, the **telnet** command tries the next IP address associated with the name. For example, with the **ip host R2 172.16.2.252 172.16.4.252** command on R1, the user at R1 can enter the **telnet R2** command. R1 then attempts to telnet to 172.16.2.252, and if that fails, it attempts to telnet to 172.16.4.252. Essentially, it allows the user to telnet to the router, and as long as at least one of the IP addresses on the other router is reachable, the telnet works.

Configuring hostnames on a router improves documentation, as long as the hostnames are kept up-to-date and accurate. The end of Example 3-12 shows the output of the **show hosts** command, which summarizes all the information configured on the **ip host** commands. Someone unfamiliar with R2 could log in to R1, see the hostnames, and quickly be able to start testing the network to figure out what the network looks like.

The information listed in the output of the **show hosts** command is called a *hostname cache*. The text "perm" in a line means that the hostname and IP address were configured in an **ip host** global configuration command. When the router uses a name server, once the router associates a name with an IP address, it keeps or caches the information in the hostname cache. The entries learned from the DNS would be listed as "dynamic" instead of "perm."

 Lab 3.2.7   Configuring Host Tables

In this lab, you create IP host tables by associating router names with IP addresses.

Backing Up the Configuration

The configuration process from the CLI updates the running configuration file, which is stored in RAM. Because the contents of RAM are lost when a router loses power or is reloaded, it is important to keep copies of the configuration file. At a minimum, the running configuration file needs to be copied into the startup-config file, stored in NVRAM, so that it will be available to the router the next time it is reloaded. However, it is also a good practice to keep a backup copy of the configuration outside each router. This section covers some of the tools used to back up a router's configuration file and includes a few comments about good standards when backing up the configuration files.

Using TFTP to Back Up a Configuration

The IOS **copy** command can be used to copy files inside a router, including the running-config file (RAM) and the startup-config file (NVRAM). Additionally, the **copy** command can be used to copy files to and from TFTP (and FTP) servers outside a router.

The **copy** command has two main parameters: the source file and the destination file, in that order. For example, the **copy running-config startup-config** command copies the configuration file called running-config (the source) to the destination file startup-config. Figure 3-3 shows the movement of files using the **copy** command between three locations:

- The running configuration file in RAM

- The startup configuration file in NVRAM

- A TFTP server in the network

Figure 3-3   File-Copying Details on a Cisco Router

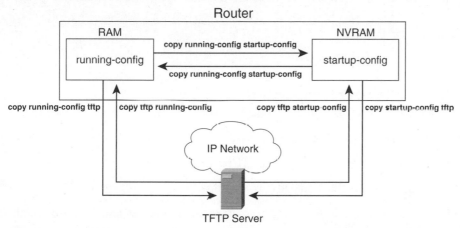

As with any server defined by TCP/IP, the server itself is simply software that runs on some computer. So, the TFTP server shown in Figure 3-3 can be any PC. In fact, the PC is often the laptop used by a network engineer. You can create a *TFTP server* by installing TFTP server software onto any computer. Many freeware and shareware TFTP servers exist; for example, the SolarWinds TFTP server (http://www.solarwinds.net) can be downloaded and used for free, and it works well in a lab environment.

When the **copy** command refers to a TFTP server, the command itself does not include all the details required to transfer the file. Instead, IOS then issues a series of prompt messages, asking the CLI user for input. Example 3-13 shows a running configuration copied to a TFTP server, and then later another configuration copied from the TFTP server to the running configuration.

Example 3-13   Copying to and from a TFTP Server

```
! First, the running-config is copied to the TFTP server
R1#copy running-config tftp
Address or name of remote host []? 172.16.2.1
Destination filename [R1-confg]?
Write file R1-confg to 172.16.2.1 ? [confirm]:
Writing R1-confg  !!!  [OK - 880 bytes]
880 bytes copied in 0.869 secs (1013 bytes/sec)
R1#
! Next, the file is copied from the TFTP server back to R1's running-config
R1#copy tftp running-config
Address or name of remote host []? 172.16.2.1
Source filename []? R1-confg
Destination filename [running-config]?
Accessing tftp://172.16.2.1/R1-confg...
Loading R1-confg from 172.16.2.1 (via Serial0/0): !
[OK - 880 bytes]
880 bytes copied in 0.869 secs (1013 bytes/sec)
R1#
```

In Example 3-13, the **copy running-config tftp** command prompts the user to enter the following information before actually performing the copy:

- The IP address or name of the TFTP server

- The name of the file to be written to the TFTP server

- Confirmation that the user wants to copy the file

Note that the default filename (R1-confg) was suggested in brackets in the second prompt line, and the user just pressed Enter to accept that filename, as shown by the absence of anything after the "?" on that line.

In some cases IOS makes up a default filename using the hostname, a dash, and the word "config." In other cases, the router makes up a shorter name. The shorter names are used when the TFTP server restricts the length of the name, typically eight characters, as is the case in Example 3-13. Another TFTP server may have allowed longer names, so IOS would have picked "R1-config" as the default filename.

Configurations can also be backed up using a terminal emulator. Most emulators support a feature that enables the emulator to capture all the text sent to the emulator window. So, you could use that feature, enter a **show running-config** command, and capture the configuration, without having to install and use a TFTP server. Alternatively, terminal emulators also allow you to select, copy, and paste text, so you could again enter a **show running-config** command and copy/paste the text into a file. Both of these methods are useful for occasional backup tasks, but in most medium to large networks, using a centralized TFTP server may be more practical.

Where to Keep the Backup Configuration Files

Backing up a router's configuration file to a TFTP server is a good idea, but it is important to go a step further. In fact, the online curriculum lists three places in which you might want to save the configuration files:

- A TFTP server
- A network (file) server
- A disk in a safe place

The preceding section mentioned good reasons to back up the configuration onto a TFTP server outside the router. To appreciate why you should put a copy on a disk and store it in a safe place, consider a scenario in which you work at a small company. You are the only person who will ever care about the router configurations. You could use a TFTP server on your own laptop computer, back up the router configurations, and be reasonably safe. However, if that TFTP server (and all copies of the configuration files) were on your laptop, you may lose the configuration files. For instance, the disk drive on the laptop could fail, or someone might steal your laptop while you are traveling. Regardless, it is a good idea to put a copy of the configurations on some removable disk, such as a CD or DVD, and put the disk somewhere safe—maybe even offsite.

Now imagine you work in a network with 20 network engineers. One day, a router crashes and needs to be replaced. The configuration file needs to be copied into that router. Any of those 20 engineers might be involved in solving the problem and copying the configuration. So, it makes sense to store the backup configuration files on a network file server and document the location and names of the configuration files. Then, every engineer knows where to look for the configuration file and can help in the process of recovering from the failure.

Table 3-3 summarizes the commands used for looking at and copying configuration files in a Cisco router.

Table 3-3   Command Summary for Copying and Looking at Configuration Files

Command	Description
configure terminal	Moves the user from privileged EXEC mode to configuration mode.
copy startup-config running-config	Copies startup-config file's commands into the running configuration in RAM. It does not necessarily replace the contents.
copy tftp running-config	Loads configuration information from a network TFTP server into RAM.
copy running-config startup-config	Stores the current configuration from RAM into NVRAM. The startup-config file exactly matches the running-config file as a result.
copy running-config tftp	Stores the current configuration from RAM on a network TFTP server. The file on the server exactly matches the running-config file as a result.
erase startup-config	Erases the contents of NVRAM.
show startup-config	Displays the saved configuration, which is the contents of NVRAM.
show running-config	Displays the current configuration in RAM.

Lab 3.2.9   Backing Up Configuration Files

In this lab, you capture the running configuration of a router to an ASCII text file with HyperTerminal.

Summary

The router CLI includes several different command modes that are used for different purposes. The two EXEC modes—user and privileged (enable)—allow the user to enter EXEC commands, and the router replies with some information or by taking some action. For example, the **show interfaces** EXEC command, available in both user and enable modes, lists status and statistical information about interfaces.

Routers support many different configuration modes as well. The **configure terminal** command, used from privileged EXEC mode, puts the CLI user into global configuration mode. Global configuration mode is used to apply configuration statements that affect a whole router. Additionally, other subconfiguration modes can be reached to configure details that do not apply to the whole router. For example, the **interface serial0/0** command moves the CLI user from global config mode to interface config mode, whereas the **ip address** command can be used to assign an IP address to that one interface. Table 3-1, shown earlier in the chapter, lists several popular configuration modes and the command prompt shown by a router for each mode.

This chapter explained several basic configuration commands on routers. Some of these commands configure the router so that it can route packets correctly, while in other cases, the commands help document what the router should be doing. Table 3-4 summarizes the configuration commands covered in this chapter.

Table 3-4   Configuration Command Summary for Chapter 3

Configuration Command	Config Mode	Description
hostname *name*	Global	Sets the router's hostname.
interface *type number*	Global	Moves the user to interface config mode for the stated interface.
ip address *address mask*	Interface	Defines the IP address and subnet mask used on the interface.
description *text*	Interface	Documents some detail about the use or purpose of an interface.
shutdown	Interface	Administratively disables an interface.
no shutdown	Interface	Administratively enables an interface.
clock rate *speed*	Interface	If creating a serial link in a lab, sets the speed of the serial link.
router rip	Global	Moves the user to RIP config mode.
network *net-number*	Routing protocol (for example, RIP)	Enables RIP for all interfaces in the listed network.
**line {con 0	aux 0	vty 0 4}**	Global	Moves the user to line configuration mode for the listed line (console, auxiliary, or Telnet [vty]).
password *text*	Line	Defines the password required for users of that type of line.
login	Line	Tells IOS to display a password prompt for users of that line.
enable secret *pw*	Global	Defines the password required by the **enable** command.
enable password *pw*	Global	Defines the password required by the **enable** command if the **enable secret** command is not configured.

Table 3-4   Configuration Command Summary for Chapter 3   *continued*

Configuration Command	Config Mode	Description
banner motd *delimiter banner-text delimiter*	Global	Defines the possibly multiline text banner that is displayed to all users before they log in to a router.
ip host *name* {*address1* [*address2...address8*]}	Global	Defines names of other hosts and up to eight IP addresses associated with the name.
ip name-server *address1* [*address2...address6*]	Global	Defines the IP address(es) of the name server(s) used when the user of the router CLI references a name.

Just like a host computer used by an end user, a router may need to resolve IP names into the corresponding IP addresses. IOS supports the ability to use a DNS server, as well as static configuration of a set of local hostnames and addresses using the **ip host** global configuration command.

Configuration standards are developed for consistency, to reduce network complexity and downtime, and to maximize network performance. Some standards for configuration files include the number of files to maintain, how they are stored, and where they are stored. Interface descriptions, login banners, and MOTDs can be standardized to inform users about events such as downtime and to warn unauthorized users.

The chapter ended with some comments about the importance of keeping a backup copy of all router configurations. The backup copies of the configurations can be made by using a TFTP server, or the engineer can simply use a PC's copy/paste function to make a copy as well.

Check Your Understanding

Complete all the review questions listed here to test your understanding of the topics and concepts in this chapter. Answers are listed in Appendix A, "Answers to Check Your Understanding and Challenge Questions."

1. Which of the following statements are true about router CLI modes? (Choose two.)

   A. The prompt indicates which mode a user is in.

   B. Entering **exit** moves the router from a specific mode to user mode.

   C. Global configuration mode allows configuration of settings that apply to the entire router.

   D. Pressing Ctrl-Z moves the router from a specific configuration mode to global configuration mode.

2. Which of the following statements are true concerning passwords on a router? (Choose two.)

   A. A password must be set for a router to be accessed by a user.

   B. The password defined by the **enable password** command is used only if the password defined by the **enable secret** password has not been configured.

   C. The **enable password remote_access** command allows users to access the router via Telnet.

   D. The **login** command is used whenever a user accesses the router.

   E. By default, the **enable secret** password is encrypted, and the **enable** password is not.

3. Which of the following answers imply the correct CLI mode and correct IOS command required to configure remote access to a router with a password of **cisco**? (Choose three.)

   A. Router(config)#**line console 0**

   B. Router(config-router)#**login**

   C. Router(config-line)#**login**

   D. Router(config line)**enable password cisco**

   E. Router(config-line)# **password cisco**

   F. Router(config-line)#**logout**

4. If an engineer wants to verify changes that she has been making on a router, which of the following commands will allow her to check the router's current configuration before saving?

   A. **show flash**

   B. **show version**

   C. **show controllers**

   D. **show running-config**

   E. **show startup-config**

5. Where should the **clock rate** command be configured?

    A. On the router using the S0/0 interface

    B. On the router using the DTE cable

    C. On the Ethernet interface running at 56000 bits per second

    D. On interfaces connected to the DCE cable

    E. In global configuration mode

6. When in global configuration mode, which steps are necessary to edit an IP address on an Ethernet interface? (Choose two.)

    A. Shut down the interface with the **shutdown** command.

    B. Enter interface configuration mode.

    C. Connect the cable to the Ethernet interface.

    D. Configure the IP address and subnet mask.

7. A company has specified a set of rules about how to configure various settings on the devices in its networks. What are the benefits of this? (Choose two.)

    A. It is required to comply with international law.

    B. It makes it easier to recognize problems that may arise on a network.

    C. Design standards are necessary for access to the Internet.

    D. Consistent design standards can be quickly understood by different engineers assigned to support the company network.

8. What is the purpose of the **description** command?

    A. It provides a welcome message to all users entering the router.

    B. It allows the interface to operate according to design standards.

    C. It explains an interface configuration.

    D. It provides a security warning to invalid users.

9. Which of the following best describes the purpose of a delimiter when configuring a login banner?

    A. The delimiter keeps unauthorized users out of the router.

    B. The delimiter indicates when the message will expire.

    C. The delimiter indicates the beginning and ending of the free text field.

    D. The delimiter allows user level access to the router.

10. What is the purpose of a host table? (Choose two.)

    A. It allows a user's security level to be remembered on the router.

    B. It maps an IP address to a device name.

    C. It allows engineers to ping remote devices using names instead of IP addresses.

    D. It allows routers to establish secure relationships with neighboring routers.

    E. It maps the IP and MAC addresses of computers and printers on the LAN.

11. Which of the following commands is the proper format for configuring a host table?

    A. **host boston 172.16.27.6 172.16.62.4**

    B. **ip host boston 172.16.27.6**

    C. **ip host 172.16.27.6 172.16.62.4 boston**

    D. **host 172.16.27.6 172.16.62.4 boston**

12. Which of the following are possible locations to back up a configuration file? (Choose three.)

    A. The router's RAM

    B. A TFTP server

    C. A network server

    D. The router's bootstrap file

    E. A disk stored offsite in a safe place

    F. In the IOS image

13. What is the next step after entering the **copy running-config tftp** command?

    A. Enter the name of the file to be saved.

    B. Enter the IP address of the destination remote host.

    C. Enter the name of the file server backing up images.

    D. Enter the IP address of the local router interface that will send the file.

Challenge Questions and Activities

These questions require a deeper application of the concepts covered in this chapter and are similar to the style of questions you might see on a CCNA certification exam. You can find the answers in Appendix A.

1. When a user is setting up a back-to-back serial connection between routers, a **clock rate** command must be entered. If the user is unable to see the serial cables, which command will most likely provide information that will allow her to issue the command on the proper interface?

   A. **show interfaces serial 0/0**

   B. **show interfaces fa 0/1**

   C. **show controllers serial 0/0**

   D. **show clock**

   E. **show flash**

   F. **show controllers interface serial 0/0**

2. Examine the output of the **show startup-config** and **show running-config** commands on router R1. Which of the following answers is accurate at the point in time that the command output was gathered?

```
R1#show startup-config
hostname Router1
!
interface Serial0/0
 clock rate 256000
 description T1 link to router R2
!
banner motd # this router is connected to R2 at 512Kbps #
R1#show running-config
hostname R1
!
interface Serial0/0
! the clock rate command is not listed in the output of the show running-config
! command
!
 description 64 Kbps link to router R2
!
banner motd # this router is connected to R2 at 128Kbps #
```

   A. The actual clock rate of S0/0 is 64 kbps.

   B. The actual clock rate of S0/0 is 128 kbps.

   C. The actual clock rate of S0/0 is 256 kbps.

   D. The actual clock rate of S0/0 is 512 kbps.

   E. The actual clock rate of S0/0 is 1.544 Mbps.

   F. The current speed cannot be determined from the output.

CHAPTER 4

Learning About Other Devices

Objectives

Upon completion of this chapter, you should be able to answer the following questions:

- How is Cisco Discovery Protocol (CDP) enabled and disabled on a router?

- What information does the **show cdp neighbors** command provide?

- How can a user determine which neighbor devices are connected to local interfaces?

- How can a user gather network address information about neighbors using CDP?

- How are Telnet connections established and verified?

- How are Telnet connections suspended and disconnected?

- What are some alternative connectivity tests, and how are they performed?

- What methods can be used to troubleshoot remote terminal connections?

Key Terms

This chapter uses the following key terms. You can find the definitions in the Glossary.

If you are logged in to one router, the best way to learn information about that router is to use **show** commands, as covered in Chapter 3, "Configuring a Router." This chapter focuses on four Cisco IOS tools that, after you are logged in to one router, help you learn information about other routers and switches in the network.

The first major section of this chapter explains Cisco Discovery Protocol (CDP). CDP allows a Cisco router to learn information about neighboring devices, including other Cisco routers and switches.

The second half of the chapter covers three popular features of routers: Telnet, ping, and traceroute. The **telnet** command allows a user of a router CLI to telnet to another router or switch so that the user can then enter commands on the other device, thereby learning more about that other device. The **ping** and **traceroute** commands also supply more information about other networking devices, but their focus is to help troubleshoot problems in an internetwork.

Discovering Neighbors Using CDP

Routers, switches, and other Cisco devices can use the *Cisco Discovery Protocol (CDP)* to dynamically discover information about neighboring devices. The letters in the CDP acronym provide a good definition of CDP:

- CDP is a *Cisco*-proprietary protocol.
- CDP *discovers* information about neighboring devices.
- CDP defines *protocol* messages that flow between neighboring devices to discover the information.

CDP discovers a wide variety of information about neighbors. Before reading about the details of CDP, it is helpful to see a brief example of the information discovered by CDP. Figure 4-1 shows an internetwork that is used in several examples in this chapter. The figure is slightly different from the examples of Chapter 3. As compared with Figure 3-1, in Figure 4-1 R2 uses a different serial interface (S0/1), the switches are now named, and another router (R4) has been added to the internetwork.

CDP discovers information about neighboring devices—devices attached to directly connected network segments—but only about neighboring devices. For example, in Figure 4-1, R1 can discover information about SW1 and R2, but not about SW2 and R4. Similarly, R2 can discover information about R1 and SW2, but not about SW1 or R4. Example 4-1 shows a sample of the information CDP discovers on R2.

Figure 4-1   Internetwork with Three Routers and Two Switches, Used in the Chapter 4
Examples

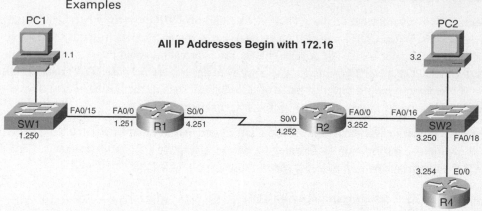

All IP Addresses Begin with 172.16

```
Example 4-1    Basic CDP Information on R2

R2#show cdp neighbors
Capability Codes: R - Router, T - Trans Bridge, B - Source Route Bridge
                  S - Switch, H - Host, I - IGMP, r - Repeater


Device ID       Local Intrfce   Holdtme     Capability    Platform      Port ID
SW2             Fas 0/0         163          S I          WS-C3550-2    Fas 0/16
R1              Ser 0/1         143          R            1760          Ser 0/0
```

The **show cdp neighbors** command lists a single line of output per neighboring device, but the
output has a lot of information. Each line lists the hostname of the other device. The Local
Interface column lists the local device's interface used to connect to the neighbor. For example,
R2's FA0/0 interface connects to the device called SW2. The last column, Port ID, lists the
neighboring device's interface. For example, comparing Example 4-1 to Figure 4-1, you can see
that SW2's FA0/16 interface is indeed connected to R2's FA0/0 interface. Finally, the Platform
column lists the device model of the neighboring device. In this case, SW2 is a Workgroup
Switch (WS) model 3550.

You can see the power of CDP in just this one simple example. Even if you do not have a diagram of the internetwork, just from this single command on one router, you can begin to form
an idea of the topology of the internetwork. Other CDP commands provide more information,
like Layer 3 addresses. You can literally do selected **show cdp** commands on various devices
and build a diagram of the entire internetwork.

This section examines the details of CDP, including what it is, how it works, and, most important, the kinds of information it provides at the router CLI.

CDP Protocol Operations

A router discovers information using CDP by listening for *CDP advertisements* sent by neighboring devices. When CDP is enabled on an interface, a router (or switch) sends CDP advertisements on a regular basis. The advertisements list information about the router sending the advertisement. The advertisements include a series of *Type Length Value (TLV)* data structures, each of which represents a different piece of information, such as the hostname, the device model number, or the interface out which the advertisement was sent.

Figure 4-2 shows a conceptual view of two CDP advertisements sent by R1 and SW2 toward R2. R2 learns the information by listening for and receiving the CDP advertisements. Each of the CDP advertisements in Figure 4-2 shows three sample TLVs.

Note

The physical connectors on routers are usually called interfaces. However, the physical connectors on switches are called both interfaces and ports. Generally speaking, both terms can be used as synonyms.

Figure 4-2   CDP Advertisements with TLVs

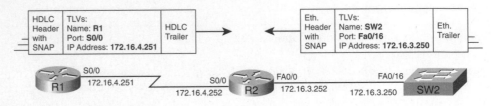

By default, all the routers and switches in Figure 4-2 would send periodic CDP advertisements, but the figure focuses just on the CDP advertisements sent by R1 and SW2. First, consider the CDP message from SW2. It lists interface FA0/16 in the message as the port on SW2 out which the message was sent. R2 happens to receive that CDP advertisement on R2's FA0/0 interface. These two facts give R2 enough information to list the information in the local interface and Port ID fields of the **show cdp neighbors** command listed earlier in Example 4-1. So, R2 can correlate the information it receives in the CDP message with the interface on which the information is received.

Figure 4-2 also implies the following details about how CDP messages are encapsulated:

- CDP encapsulates its messages inside data-link headers and trailers, without relying on any Layer 3 protocols.

- The data link layer protocol must support the use of a Subnetwork Access Protocol (SNAP) header.

Understanding the meaning and importance of both points requires a little more explanation. First, by not using IP or any other Layer 3 protocol, CDP can work even if IP does not work. For example, the information shown in Example 4-1 can be learned even if no IP addresses are configured on any of the devices in Figure 4-1. The requirement to use SNAP headers is a technical requirement from Cisco, but it limits the types of interfaces on which CDP can work. Fortunately, most data link protocols used today support SNAP. In particular, all the data link protocols covered in the Cisco CCNA Academy curriculum (Ethernet, HDLC, PPP, and Frame Relay) support SNAP.

CDP Versions 1 and 2

The CDP protocol has two versions, depending on the IOS version. On routers, CDP version 1 has been supported for a long time, beginning with IOS Version 10.3, which came out in the mid-1990s. CDP version 2 has been supported since the introduction of IOS 12.0T versions, which were released around 2000. As of the time of publication of this book, it is likely that most Cisco routers and switches already have been upgraded to an IOS that supports version 2. However, even if some devices support only version 1, CDP version 2 is backward-compatible.

The main difference between the two CDP versions relates to the TLVs (information) announced in a CDP advertisement. The following list details the types of information learned by CDP, with the last three items learned only when the devices support CDP version 2:

- Device ID (name of the device)
- Local Interface (the local device's interface or port)
- Holdtime (the time before the device will remove this CDP entry unless another CDP message refreshes the information)
- Capability (functions supported on the device)
- Platform (model series number of the device)
- Port ID (interface or port number information)
- VTP Management Domain Name (CDP version 2 only)
- Native VLAN (CDP version 2 only)
- Full/Half Duplex (CDP version 2 only)

CDP Timers

The CDP specifications define two important timers:

- *CDP update interval*
- *CDP holdtime*

CDP requires that a device send advertisements on a regular, periodic time cycle, called the CDP update interval, with a default update interval of 60 seconds. By repeatedly sending the CDP advertisements, the neighbor hearing the advertisements knows that the sending device is still alive and working.

The CDP holdtime defines how long the information in an advertisement should be considered valid. When a device receives another CDP advertisement, the holdtime timer is refreshed. When a device fails, the neighbor ceases to receive advertisements, and the holdtime defines how long the information is kept.

Figure 4-3 shows a graphical representation of the update interval and holdtime timers, using R1 and R2 as examples. To keep the figure less cluttered, it shows only the CDP advertisement sent by R1 to R2. This same advertisement process would work on each interface between each pair of neighbors.

Figure 4-3   CDP Update Interval and Holdtime

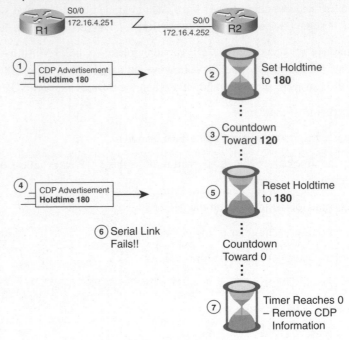

Figure 4-3 shows two periodic updates from R1, with the serial link failing after the second CDP message. The steps in the figure are explained as follows:

1. R1 sends the first CDP advertisement, which states a (default) holdtime of 180 seconds.

2. R2 receives the CDP advertisement, believes the information, and sets its holdtime for the information to 180 seconds.

3. R2 counts down from 180 seconds toward 120 seconds.

4. R1 sends its next periodic CDP advertisement 60 seconds after the first one.

5. R2 receives the CDP advertisement and resets its holdtime to 180.

6. The serial link fails.

7. R2's holdtime eventually counts down to 0, at which point R2 discards its CDP information about R1.

Cisco routers and switches default to send CDP updates on all interfaces, defaulting to use an update time of 60 seconds and a holdtime of 180 seconds. So, once you physically install an internetwork, and the interfaces reach an "up and up" state, CDP immediately uses the processes and messages described in this section to discover information about the internetwork. The next section takes a closer look at the information learned with CDP.

Information Learned by CDP

To view the information learned by CDP, a CLI user simply needs to use the correct parameters on the **show cdp** command. The **show cdp** command has many possible options, some of which display the information learned by CDP, and others that display information about how CDP is working. Table 4-1 shows the three styles of the **show cdp** command that list the information learned by CDP.

Table 4-1   **show cdp** Commands That List Information About Neighbors

Command	Description
show cdp neighbors [*type number*]	Lists one summary line of information about each neighbor, or just the neighbor found on a specific interface if an interface was listed
show cdp neighbors detail	Lists one large set (approximately 15 lines) of information, one set for every neighbor
show cdp entry *name*	Lists the same information as the **show cdp neighbors detail** command, but only for the named neighbor

Example 4-1 has already shown an example of the **show cdp neighbors** command. Next, Example 4-2 shows the **show cdp neighbors detail** and **show cdp entry R2** commands on router R1 of Figure 4-2. The paragraphs following the example explain the highlighted portions.

Example 4-2   The **show cdp neighbors detail** and **show cdp entry** Commands

```
R1>show cdp neighbors detail
-------------------------
Device ID: SW1
Entry address(es):
  IP address: 172.16.1.250
Platform: Cisco WS-C3550-24,   Capabilities: Switch IGMP
Interface: FastEthernet0/0,   Port ID (outgoing port): FastEthernet0/15
Holdtime : 169 sec

Version :
Cisco IOS Software, C3550 Software (C3550 I5Q3L2-M), Version 12.2(25)SE, RELEASE
  SOFTWARE (fc)
Copyright  1986-2004 by Cisco Systems, Inc.
```

Example 4-2   The **show cdp neighbors detail** and **show cdp entry**
Commands   *continued*

```
Compiled Wed 10-Nov-04 18:07 by yenanh


advertisement version: 2
Protocol Hello:  OUI=0x00000C, Protocol ID=0x0112; payload len=27,
  value=00000000FFFFFFFF010221FF000000000000000AB7DCB780FF0000
VTP Management Domain: ''
Native VLAN: 1
Duplex: full
! This line and the next line were added by the authors. This ends the first set of
! messages. The next set, which is for neighbor R2, follows.
-------------------------
Device ID: R2
Entry address(es):
   IP address: 172.16.4.252
Platform: cisco 1760,  Capabilities: Router
Interface: Serial0/0,  Port ID (outgoing port): Serial0/1
Holdtime : 151 sec


Version :
Cisco Internetwork Operating System Software
IOS (tm) C1700 Software (C1700-K8SV3Y7-M), Version 12.2(15)T5,  RELEASE SOFTWARE (fc1)
TAC Support: http://www.cisco.com/tac
Copyright  1986-2003 by cisco Systems, Inc.
Compiled Thu 12-Jun-03 10:32 by eaarmas


advertisement version: 2


R1>show cdp entry R2
-------------------------
Device ID: R2
Entry address(es):
   IP address: 172.16.4.252
Platform: cisco 1760,  Capabilities: Router
Interface: Serial0/0,  Port ID (outgoing port): Serial0/1
Holdtime : 131 sec


Version :
Cisco Internetwork Operating System Software
IOS (tm) C1700 Software (C1700-K8SV3Y7-M), Version 12.2(15)T5,  RELEASE SOFTWARE (fc1)
TAC Support: http://www.cisco.com/tac
Copyright  1986-2003 by cisco Systems, Inc.
Compiled Thu 12-Jun-03 10:32 by eaarmas


advertisement version: 2
```

Note

The output in Example 4-2 lists devices' hostnames. The names are not found by asking a DNS to perform name resolution; instead, the names are included in CDP advertisements.

Example 4-2 begins by listing several lines of information about SW1 and then several more lines about R2, all generated by the **show cdp neighbors detail** command. For SW1, the output lists the name (SW1), IP address, R1's interface connected to SW1 (FA0/0), SW1's interface on the other end of the cable (FA0/15), and the version of software. Example 4-2 also highlights a statement of the capabilities of SW1, listed as "Switch IGMP." This phrase means that SW1 is a switch, and that it understands a multicast protocol called Internet Group Management Protocol (IGMP).

The second half of the output of the **show cdp neighbors detail** command lists information about R2. In this case, the output identifies the neighbor as R2, as a 1760 router, with its capabilities listed as "router." As usual, CDP lists R1's local interface (S0/0) and the neighbor's (R2's) interface (S0/1). It also lists R2's IP address. Typically, a CDP advertisement lists the IP address out which the advertisement is sent. For example, R2 sent an advertisement to R1, out R2's S0/1 interface, whose IP address is 172.16.4.252, so R2 listed that IP address in the CDP advertisement.

Of particular importance, compare the output about R2 in the **show cdp neighbors detail** command with the output of the **show cdp entry R2** command at the end of the example: the lines of output are identical. So, to see detailed information about just one neighbor, use the **show cdp entry** command.

Note

CDP can also learn information about other Layer 3 protocols, such as Novell's IPX protocol and Apple Computer's AppleTalk protocol, provided the routers have enabled those protocols.

Configuring and Verifying CDP Operations

By default, Cisco routers and switches use CDP on every interface. However, engineers can disable CDP on a per-interface basis, or they can disable CDP globally, which means that CDP would be disabled on all interfaces. So, it is useful to know how to verify whether CDP is enabled globally and, if so, on which interfaces it is enabled. This section covers the details of how to verify where CDP is running and how to enable and disable CDP per interface and globally.

For reference, Table 4-2 lists the CDP commands that can be used to verify whether CDP is enabled and whether it is sending and receiving messages. These commands will be used in upcoming examples that verify where CDP has been enabled and disabled.

Table 4-2   Commands Used to Verify CDP Operations

Command	Description
show cdp	States whether CDP is enabled globally and lists the default update and holdtime timers
show cdp interface [*type number*]	States whether CDP is enabled on each interface, or a single interface if the interface is listed, and states update and holdtime timers on those interfaces
show cdp traffic	Lists global statistics for the number of CDP advertisements sent and received
clear cdp counters	Resets the counters shown in the **show cdp traffic** command to 0
debug cdp packets	Enables a debug that generates one message each time a CDP advertisement is sent or received

The following list states how to enable and disable CDP in a Cisco router:

- To globally enable CDP, use the **cdp run** global configuration command. To globally disable CDP, use the **no cdp run** global configuration command.

- To enable CDP on an interface, use the **cdp enable** interface subcommand. To disable CDP on an interface, use the **no cdp enable** interface subcommand.

To show both examples of these configuration commands and the verification commands in Table 4-2, Example 4-3 shows a process that alternates between configuration and verification commands. The output of the commands is straightforward, and the text following the example points out a few of the most important details. The example shows the following process:

1. Several **show** commands on R1 verify that, by default, CDP is enabled globally and on each interface.

2. CDP is then disabled on interface S0/0, which is connected to R2, using the **no cdp enable** interface subcommand.

3. The **show cdp interface** command shows that CDP is disabled.

4. CDP is disabled globally using the **no cdp run** global command.

5. The **show** commands confirm that CDP is disabled globally and that the traffic counters are not displayed.

6. CDP is then enabled globally and re-enabled on interface S0/0.

7. The **show cdp traffic** command shows statistics, but the counters were not reset to 0 when CDP was globally disabled.

8. The **clear cdp counters** command is used to reset the counters.

9. The **show cdp traffic** command's counters now show low numbers, but they show only global counters, not per-interface counters.

10. To verify that CDP messages are being sent and received on each interface, the **debug cdp packet** command is used.

Example 4-3   Verifying, Disabling, and Enabling CDP

```
! Step 1
R1#show cdp
Global CDP information:
        Sending CDP packets every 60 seconds
        Sending a holdtime value of 180 seconds
        Sending CDPv2 advertisements is  enabled
R1#show cdp interface
FastEthernet0/0 is up, line protocol is up
  Encapsulation ARPA
  Sending CDP packets every 60 seconds
```

Example 4-3   Verifying, Disabling, and Enabling CDP   *continued*

```
  Holdtime is 180 seconds
Serial0/0 is up, line protocol is up
  Encapsulation HDLC
  Sending CDP packets every 60 seconds
  Holdtime is 180 seconds
! Step 2 next
R1#configure terminal
Enter configuration commands, one per line.  End with CNTL/Z.
R1(config)#interface serial 0/0
R1(config-if)#no cdp enable
R1(config-if)#^Z
! Step 3 next: Notice that interface S0/0 is simply omitted.
R1#show cdp interface
FastEthernet0/0 is up, line protocol is up
  Encapsulation ARPA
  Sending CDP packets every 60 seconds
  Holdtime is 180 seconds
! Step 4 next: CDP is globally disabled
R1#configure terminal
Enter configuration commands, one per line.  End with CNTL/Z.
R1(config)#no cdp run
R1(config)#^Z
! Step 5 next
R1#show cdp
% CDP is not enabled
R1#sh cdp traffic
% CDP is not enabled
! Step 6 next: CDP is re-enabled globally and on interface S0/0
R1#configure terminal
Enter configuration commands, one per line.  End with CNTL/Z.
R1(config)#cdp run
R1(config)#interface serial 0/0
R1(config-if)#cdp enable
R1(config-if)#^Z
! Step 7 next
R1#show cdp traffic
CDP counters :
      Total packets output: 294, Input: 291
      Hdr syntax: 0, Chksum error: 0, Encaps failed: 0
      No memory: 0, Invalid packet: 0, Fragmented: 0
      CDP version 1 advertisements output: 0, Input: 0
      CDP version 2 advertisements output: 294, Input: 291
! Step 8 next
R1#clear cdp counters
```

continues

Example 4-3   Verifying, Disabling, and Enabling CDP   *continued*

```
R1#clear cdp counters
! Step 9 next
R1#show cdp traffic      _____
CDP counters :
      Total packets output: 1, Input: 0
      Hdr syntax: 0, Chksum error: 0, Encaps failed: 0
      No memory: 0, Invalid packet: 0, Fragmented: 0
      CDP version 1 advertisements output: 0, Input: 0
      CDP version 2 advertisements output: 1, Input: 0
! Finally, Step 10
R1#debug cdp packets
CDP packet info debugging is on
R1#
*Jan 13 19:39:26.713: CDP-PA: Packet received from R2 on interface Serial0/0
*Jan 13 19:39:26.713: **Entry  found in cache**
*Jan 13 19:39:28.532: CDP-PA: version 2 packet sent out on FastEthernet0/0
*Jan 13 19:39:43.449: CDP-PA: Packet received from SW1 on interface FastEthernet0/0
*Jan 13 19:39:43.449: **Entry  found in cache**
*Jan 13 19:40:13.410: CDP-PA: version 2 packet sent out on Serial0/0
```

Example 4-3 shows several steps that demonstrate how each command is used. The only piece of information lacking from the **show** commands is whether CDP is actually sending and receiving advertisements on a particular interface. (The **show cdp traffic** command lists only global statistics.) To tell if an interface is sending or receiving CDP advertisements, the **debug cdp packet** command is needed.

Creating a Network Map Using CDP Information

CDP has several practical purposes besides just answering a couple of curious questions for an engineer. For example, Cisco IP phones use CDP to communicate with LAN switches. Also, if CDP messages can pass over a link, you can be certain that the physical and data link layer protocols on the link are working. Besides these purposes, you can also use CDP information to construct a map of an internetwork. By comparing the output of the various **show cdp** commands from different devices in an internetwork, you can find the names, IP addresses, which interfaces connect which devices, and the types of devices.

Lab 4.1.4 in the online curriculum allows you to practice using the output of **show cdp** commands to construct a map of an internetwork. In that lab, you use **telnet** (as covered later, in the section "Telnet Basics") to move between routers, and then you use the **show cdp** command options to learn the information about neighboring routers. This type of exercise is very useful for helping you remember the detailed information available from CDP.

Packet Tracer

Example 4-4 gives you an opportunity to do an exercise similar to Lab 4.1.4. For this exercise, read the output from the CDP commands in the example, and try to draw a network diagram that includes network interfaces and IP addresses. To check your work, you can load Packet Tracer configuration NA02-0406. The output in Example 4-4 was actually taken from commands issued inside Packet Tracer.

Example 4-4   Using CDP to Construct a Network Map

```
R1#show cdp neighbors
Capability Codes: R - Router, T - Trans Bridge, B - Source Route Bridge
                  S - Switch, H - Host, I - IGMP, r - Repeater

Device ID    Local Intrfce   Holdtme   Capability   Platform      Port ID
SW1          Fa 0/0          180       S            WS-2950PT-10   Fa 2/0
R2           Ser 1/0         180       R            2621PT        Ser 1/0
R3           Ser 3/0         180       R            2621PT        Ser 2/0
R1#
```

```
! R2's output here
R2#show cdp neighbors detail
-------------------------
Device ID: SW4
Entry address(es):
Platform: cisco WS-2950PT-10, Capabilities: Switch
Interface: FastEthernet0/0, Port ID (outgoing port): FastEthernet0/0
Holdtime: 180

Version :
Cisco Internetwork Operating System Software
IOS (tm) C2950 Software (C2950-I6Q4L2-M), Version 12.1(20)
Copyright  1986-2004 by Cisco Systems, Inc.

advertisement version: 2
Duplex: full
-------------------------
Device ID: R1
Entry address(es):
  IP Address: 130.1.113.1
Platform: cisco 2621PT, Capabilities: Router
Interface: Serial2/0, Port ID (outgoing port): Serial3/0
Holdtime: 180

Version :
```

continues

Example 4-4   Using CDP to Construct a Network Map   *continued*

```
Version :
Cisco Internetwork Operating System Software
IOS (tm) C2600 Software (C2600-I-M), Version 12.2(13e)
Copyright  1986-2004 by Cisco Systems, Inc.

advertisement version: 2
Duplex: full
------------------------
Device ID: R2
Entry address(es):
  IP Address: 130.1.123.2
Platform: cisco 2621PT, Capabilities: Router
Interface: Serial3/0, Port ID (outgoing port): Serial2/0
Holdtime: 180

Version :
Cisco Internetwork Operating System Software
IOS (tm) C2600 Software (C2600-I-M), Version 12.2(13e)
Copyright  1986-2004 by Cisco Systems, Inc.

advertisement version: 2
Duplex: full
R2>show cdp neighbors
Capability Codes: R - Router, T - Trans Bridge, B - Source Route Bridge
                  S - Switch, H - Host, I - IGMP, r - Repeater
Device ID       Local Intrfce   Holdtme   Capability   Platform       Port ID
SW3             Fa 0/0          180            S        WS-2950PT-10   Fa 0/0
R1              Ser 1/0         180            R        2621PT         Ser 1/0
R3              Ser 2/0         180            R        2621PT         Ser 3/0
```

Lab 4.1.4   Creating a Network Map Using CDP

In this lab, you use CDP commands to get information about neighboring network devices.

Additional CDP Verification and Troubleshooting Commands

CDP includes several other commands not specifically covered throughout the other sections of this chapter. Table 4-3 lists the remaining commands and provides a description of each.

Table 4-3   Additional CDP Verification and Troubleshooting Commands

Command	Description
clear cdp table	Deletes the CDP table of information about neighbors
show debugging	Displays information about the types of debugging that are enabled for your router
debug cdp adjacency	Displays informational messages in real time when the status of a CDP neighbor changes
debug cdp events	Displays informational messages regarding any event that occurs with CDP
debug cdp ip	Displays informational messages each time a router learns IP information with CDP
cdp timers	A global configuration command that sets the CDP update timer
cdp holdtime	A global configuration command that specifies the CDP holdtime

Lab 4.1.6   Using CDP Commands

In this lab, you use CDP commands to obtain information about neighboring networks and devices.

Getting Information and Troubleshooting Remote Devices

Although CDP does provide some convenient and useful information about other devices, the **Telnet**, **ping**, and **traceroute** tools covered in this section also provide vital information about an internetwork. The **telnet** command allows the user to connect to other routers and switches and issue commands on the remote devices, learning about the devices' configuration and current operations. The **ping** and **traceroute** IOS EXEC commands enable an engineer to test Layer 3 by verifying whether IP packets can be delivered in an internetwork, and determine the route used by those packets.

Verifying Which Networking Layers Are Working

Each of the router features covered in this chapter tests a particular part of the TCP/IP networking model. For example, engineers use two of the tools, **ping** and **traceroute**, specifically for testing IP and IP routing, which are OSI Layer 3 functions. Engineers primarily use CDP and

Telnet for their core purpose of learning information about an internetwork, but both CDP and Telnet can be used to verify whether certain layers of the TCP/IP model are working.

As usual, when discussing networking models, most comparisons are made using the seven-layer OSI model. Figure 4-4 shows a diagram of the OSI model, including the layers of the model tested by CDP, **ping**, **traceroute**, and **Telnet**.

Figure 4-4   OSI Layers Tested by Various IOS Tools

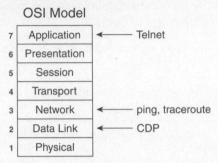

Although each tool focuses on one layer of the OSI model, each can be used to prove whether multiple layers are working. For example, the **ping** command tests whether the internetwork can forward a packet to some destination IP address, which is of course a Layer 3 function. However, **ping** really tests OSI Layers 1 through 3, because although IP and IP routing are Layer 3 functions, the IP packets cannot be forwarded if the underlying physical layer (Layer 1) and data link layer (Layer 2) functions are not working.

Telnet tests all seven layers of the OSI model because it focuses on the application layer, and the application layer cannot work unless the rest of the layers below it are working. For example, Telnet cannot work if the underlying Layer 3 IP addressing and routing are not working. Similarly, CDP encapsulates messages inside data-link frames, not relying on any Layer 3 protocols. So, when an engineer confirms that a router is receiving CDP advertisements on an interface, the engineer knows that the underlying Layer 1 and Layer 2 functions of that interface are working.

Telnet Basics

Telnet allows a user to gain access to the CLI of a remote device. To do so, Telnet defines a protocol that can be used between the devices and defines the functions performed by a *Telnet client* and a *Telnet server*. The user uses a Telnet client application, which is typically a software package that opens a single window on the user's computer. The Telnet client then connects to the remote device's Telnet server. At that point, anything entered in the Telnet client window on the user's PC is sent to the remote device, and the remote device tries to act on what was entered. For example, an engineer can sit at his desktop PC, open a Telnet client, and connect to a remote router's CLI. The engineer can then enter **show cdp neighbors**, executing the command at the router.

Figure 4-5 shows an example, with PC1 using a Telnet client to connect to router R1. The figure shows the output of a **show ip route** command, entered by the user at PC1 but executed on router R1.

Figure 4-5   Telnet Client/Server Operation

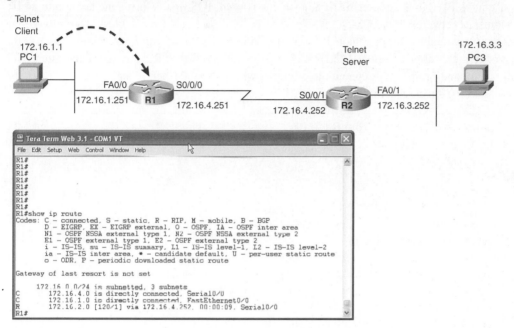

Cisco routers and switches include a built-in Telnet server so that engineers can remotely access the CLI. The only configuration required on the routers is that the *vty lines* must be configured to require a password, as shown in the section "User and Enable Mode Passwords" in Chapter 3. On the PC, all that is required is a Telnet client software package. Many freeware and shareware Telnet clients exist, including TeraTerm from Ayera Technologies (http://www.ayera.com) and HyperTerminal from Hilgraeve (http://www.hilgraeve.com).

Next, this section takes a closer look at the **telnet** command on Cisco routers, how to best use the **telnet** command to help troubleshoot a network problem, and some warnings about some quirky behavior with hostnames and the **telnet** command.

Cisco IOS **telnet** Command

Oftentimes, network engineers need to telnet to multiple different routers and switches when troubleshooting. If the engineer wants to connect to ten routers at the same time when troubleshooting a problem, she can open ten Telnet windows on her PC and switch between them to issue commands on the various routers. However, IOS includes a Telnet client as well, so once an engineer has access to one router's CLI, the engineer can use the IOS **telnet** command to telnet to other devices. The rest of the coverage of Telnet in this chapter specifically describes how to use the router **telnet** command. (The **telnet** command on Cisco switches works the same way.)

The **telnet** {*hostname* | *address*} command connects a CLI user to the host at the IP address or hostname listed in the command. If a hostname is used, IOS first resolves the name into an IP address, as covered in the Chapter 3 section "Configuring Local Host Tables." The **telnet** command then connects to the remote host, as shown in Example 4-5. In the example, a user at the console of R1 uses the **telnet 172.16.4.252** command to telnet to R2. Pay particular attention to the command prompts throughout the example, which show R1 before and after the Telnet session and R2 during the Telnet session.

```
Example 4-5     Telnet from R1 to R2
R1#telnet 172.16.4.252
Trying 172.16.4.252 ... Open


User Access Verification


Password:
R2>show ip interface brief
Interface          IP-Address      OK?    Method   Status                      Protocol
FastEthernet0/0    172.16.2.252    YES    NVRAM    up                          up
Serial0/0          unassigned      YES    NVRAM    administratively down       down
Serial0/1          172.16.4.252    YES    NVRAM    up                          up
R2>show users
    Line        User       Host(s)               Idle        Location
*   6 vty 0                idle                   00:00:00 172.16.4.251
R2>logout

[Connection to 172.16.4.252 closed by foreign host]
R1#
```

Example 4-5 shows the most typical method for telnetting to a remote host (the **telnet** command), but two other methods exist. The **connect** {*hostname* | *address*} command can be used as an alternative to **telnet**. Beyond that, just by entering an IP address or hostname on the command line in EXEC mode—without either the **telnet** or **connect** command in front of it—IOS assumes that the user wants to telnet to that name or address.

Two alternatives exist for terminating the Telnet connection:

- **exit** command

- **logout** command

When acting as a Telnet server, Cisco routers allocate a vty line for each incoming Telnet connection (as did R2 in Example 4-5). As shown in the output of the **show users** command on

R2, R2 has allocated vty line 0 for the single current Telnet connection into R2. Note that older IOS versions support vty lines 0 through 4, for a total of five allowed concurrent Telnet connections into a router. Later IOS versions support vty lines 0 through 15, allowing for 16 concurrent Telnet connections into a router.

 Lab 4.2.2   Establishing and Verifying a Telnet Connection

In this lab, you establish a Telnet connection to a remote router and verify that the application layer between source and destination is working properly.

Basic Telnet Troubleshooting

A failure of the **telnet** command means that any of the seven layers of the OSI model might be having a problem. Although a Telnet connection to a router or switch can fail for many reasons, three of the reasons are relatively common. The Networking Academy CCNA curriculum has covered the background behind all three reasons already. The three main reasons are as follows:

- IP routing is not working between the two devices.

- Name resolution is not working on the router at which the **telnet** command is used. (This condition occurs only when the **telnet** command refers to a hostname.)

- The router being telnetted to (the Telnet server) does not have its vty password configured.

An engineer can use the **ping** command to further isolate the problem based on the first two reasons. By pinging the IP address of the remote device, the engineer can verify whether routing works between the two devices. If that works, by pinging the hostname of the remote device, the **ping** command must first do name resolution, testing the name resolution process. If the **ping** of the hostname works, the engineer can look at the third common failure reason by connecting to the console of the remote device and looking at the vty configuration to see if the passwords are configured correctly.

Issues with the Default Name Resolution Method

Cisco IOS makes some interesting assumptions about when you want to use the telnet command. If you enter a command in EXEC mode, and the text is not recognized by IOS as a valid command, IOS assumes you want to telnet to a host of that name. This behavior, along with the default IOS behavior to use a DNS for name resolution, can cause the user to get a little frustrated. By default, here is what happens when a user simply mistypes a command, something as simple as typing **shw interfaces** instead of **show interfaces**:

1. IOS does not recognize the command (in this example, **shw**).

2. IOS tries to telnet to that name. The first step is to resolve the name (**shw**) into an IP address.

3. IOS broadcasts DNS resolution requests on all interfaces, looking for a DNS server to resolve the name.

4. Assuming no DNS servers hear the request, the user waits 30 to 40 seconds for IOS to finally time out its DNS request, *during which time the user cannot enter any other commands*!

In short, with all default configuration settings for name resolution, every time the user mistypes a command, he or she has to wait 30 to 40 seconds before getting a chance to enter the command again with the correct spelling. That can be frustrating for good typists and downright maddening for poor typists. To solve the problem in a lab, just add the **no ip domain-lookup** global configuration command to the routers' configurations, and IOS will no longer attempt to broadcast to find a DNS, and the mistyped commands will fail immediately.

The **no ip domain-lookup** command impacts only users of the routers; it does not impact end users at all. However, if the routers in an internetwork have been configured to use DNS, do not use this command, because it will disable DNS resolution.

Advanced Telnet: Suspending and Switching Between Telnet Connections

The "Telnet Basics" section earlier in this chapter showed how to simply telnet from one router to another, issue some commands, and then use the **exit** or **logout** commands to close or terminate the Telnet connection. However, the IOS **telnet** command also supports the ability to suspend a Telnet connection. *Suspending a Telnet connection* means that the user does not close or terminate the Telnet connection, but instead, the Telnet connection is temporarily set aside. By suspending a Telnet connection, the user can switch back and forth between router command prompts very quickly and easily. Example 4-6 shows an example. Again, pay close attention to the command prompts. Also, several comments have been added to clarify the steps in the example. The steps are as follows:

Note

The **show sessions** command lists information about the number of suspended Telnet connections.

Step 1   The user at R1 telnets into R2, logs in, and gets into enable mode.

Step 2   The user enters a command on R2, just to emphasize which router the user is using.

Step 3   The user suspends the Telnet connection, giving the user a command prompt back on R1.

Step 4   The user issues a command on R1, again to emphasize which router the user is using.

Step 5   The user resumes the suspended Telnet connection using the **resume 1** command.

Step 6   The user issues a command on R2 again, just to emphasize which router the user is using.

Example 4-6   Suspending and Resuming a Telnet Connection

```
! Step 1
R1#telnet 172.16.4.252
Trying 172.16.4.252 ... Open

User Access Verification

Password:
! The user is now telnetted into R2
R2>enable
Password:
! Step 2 next
R2#show ip interface brief
Interface            IP-Address      OK?   Method  Status                 Protocol
FastEthernet0/0      172.16.2.252    YES   NVRAM   up                     up
Serial0/0            unassigned      YES   NVRAM   administratively down   down
Serial0/1            172.16.4.252    YES   NVRAM   up                     up
R2#
! Step 3 next
! The user pressed "Ctrl-Shift-6", let go of all 3 keys, and then pressed "x" and let go.
! This key sequence suspends the telnet, putting the user back at R1.
! Step 4 next
! Next, the show sessions command lists the suspended telnet connection, connection
! number 1, which is used in the resume command that follows.
R1#show sessions
Conn Host            Address         Byte  Idle Conn Name
*  1 172.16.4.252      172.16.4.252          0     0 172.16.4.252
! step 5 next
R1#resume 1
[Resuming connection 1 to 172.16.4.252 ... ]
! step 6 next
R2#
R2#show ip interface brief
Interface            IP-Address      OK?   Method  Status                 Protocol
FastEthernet0/0      172.16.2.252    YES   NVRAM   up                     up
Serial0/0            unassigned      YES   NVRAM   administratively down   down
Serial0/1            172.16.4.252    YES   NVRAM   up                     up
```

Example 4-6 shows a couple of very important points. First, once telnetted to R2, the user had
to press Ctrl-Shift-6, then *x* to suspend the Telnet connection. Just to be clear, that means that
the user pressed the Ctrl key, the Shift key, and the number 6 key all at the same time, and then
let go of all three keys, and then pressed and released the *x* key. Doing so suspended the Telnet
connection.

After the Telnet connection is suspended, the user is back at the original router's command prompt, in this case R1. R1 can go back to the suspended Telnet connection by using the **resume** command. The **resume** command uses a connection number, listed in the output of the **show sessions** command. The **show sessions** command lists all suspended Telnet connections.

Finally, note that when the **resume 1** command connected the user back to the suspended Telnet connection to R2, the user did not have to enter any passwords. In fact, the user was right back where she was when she suspended the Telnet connection.

Lab 4.2.3   Suspending and Disconnecting Telnet Sessions

In this lab, you establish a Telnet session with a remote router and then suspend and re-establish a Telnet session.

Switching Between Multiple Telnet Connections

By creating, suspending, and resuming multiple Telnet connections, a user can easily switch between the CLIs of multiple routers. For example, the internetwork of Figure 4-1 shows three routers. If an engineer connected to the console port of R1 and used the CLI of R1, she could then telnet to both R2 and R4, use commands on each, and easily switch between R1, R2, and R4 while troubleshooting a problem.

This example also provides a good backdrop to discuss how IOS resumes a suspended Telnet connection. IOS uses the following logic when there is at least one suspended Telnet connection:

- If the **resume** *session-number* command is used, IOS resumes the suspended Telnet connection identified by the session number.

- If the **resume** command is used, without a session number, IOS resumes the most recently suspended Telnet connection.

- If a single number is entered on the command line, and there is a suspended Telnet connection using that same number, IOS resumes that Telnet connection.

- If the user presses the Enter key when the command line has no text on it, IOS assumes that the user wants to resume the most recently suspended Telnet connection, and IOS resumes that Telnet connection.

Example 4-7 shows the last three versions of the resume process in the preceding list. The example follows these overall steps:

Step 1   The user telnets from R1 to R2.

Step 2   The user suspends the Telnet connection, moving back to R1.

Step 3   The user telnets from R1 to R4.

Step 4   The user suspends the Telnet connection, moving back to R1 again.

Step 5   At R1, the user issues the **show sessions** command, which lists both suspended Telnet connections.

Step 6   The user resumes the Telnet connection to R4 by using the **resume** command, without a session number.

Step 7   The user suspends the Telnet connection, moving back to R1 again.

Step 8   The user resumes the Telnet connection to R2 by using the **1** command, which simply identifies the session number for the Telnet connection to R2.

Step 9   The user suspends the Telnet connection, moving back to R1 again.

Step 10   At the R1 command prompt, the user simply presses Enter, resuming the last-suspended Telnet connection (R2).

Example 4-7   Suspending and Resuming a Telnet Connection

```
! Step 1
R1#telnet 172.16.4.252
Trying 172.16.4.252 ... Open


User Access Verification


Password:
R2>
! Step 2 not shown. The user typed Ctrl-Shift-6 and then x to suspend
! Step 3 next
R1#172.16.2.254
Trying 172.16.2.254 ... Open


User Access Verification


Password:
R4>
! Step 4 not shown. The user typed Ctrl-Shift-6 and then x to suspend
! Step 5 next
R1#show sessions
Conn Host               Address             Byte  Idle Conn Name
   1 172.16.4.252       172.16.4.252           0     0 172.16.4.252
*  2 172.16.2.254       172.16.2.254           0     0 172.16.2.254
! Step 6 next - resumes the last-suspended telnet, namely the one to R4
R1#resume
[Resuming connection 2 to 172.16.2.254 ... ]
! The user had to press enter before seeing the next command prompt
R4>
! Step 7 not shown. The user typed Ctrl-Shift-6 and then x to suspend
! Step 8 next. Just a 1 on the command line resumes connection 1, to R2
```

continues

Example 4-7   Suspending and Resuming a Telnet Connection   *continued*

```
R1#1
[Resuming connection 1 to 172.16.4.252 ... ]
! The user had to press enter before seeing the next command prompt
R2>
! Step 9 not shown. The user typed Ctrl-Shift-6 and then x to suspend
! Step 10 next, but it is difficult to show. The user presses enter with
! no text on the command line, which connects the user back to the last-suspended
! telnet (R2)
R1#

[Resuming connection 1 to 172.16.4.252 ... ]
R2>
```

The last part of Example 4-7 points out what can be a risky feature. Many people press the Enter key out of habit, with nothing on the command line, just to clear the clutter from the screen. When there are no suspended Telnet connections, and the user presses the Enter key, IOS simply repeats the text of the command prompt, scrolling text off the top of the Telnet window. So, many people press the Enter key a few times to unclutter the screen. However, with at least one suspended Telnet connection, pressing Enter on an empty command line resumes a Telnet connection. With suspended Telnet connections, before doing any destructive commands, make sure that you know on which router you are entering the commands.

Lab 4.2.4   Advanced Telnet Operations

In this lab, you use the **telnet** command to remotely access other routers.

Number of Concurrent Telnets

To complete the coverage of Telnet for this chapter, this section mentions three methods to restrict the number of Telnet connections into a router and describes whether a router allows users to telnet into the router.

The first method prevents all Telnets into a router by simply not configuring a Telnet password. If a router's vty lines have not been configured with a password (as covered in the Chapter 3 section "User and Enable Mode Passwords"), the router rejects all incoming Telnet requests. So, to disable Telnet access to a router, simply do not configure vty passwords.

The second restriction relates to the maximum number of vty lines supported by IOS. IOS dynamically assigns a vty line for each user telnetted into a router. Older IOS releases support five vty lines (0 through 4), and more recent IOS releases support 16 lines (0 through 15).

Finally, the third way to limit Telnet connections is to configure a limit. The engineer can configure the maximum number of concurrent Telnet connections into a router by configuring the **session limit** *number* command in vty line configuration mode.

Cisco IOS ping and traceroute Commands

Two of the most useful TCP/IP troubleshooting tools are the *ping* and *traceroute* commands. Both commands test whether Layer 3 addressing and routing are working properly. This section covers the basics of each command, specifically as implemented on Cisco routers, and shows an example of each.

Cisco IOS **ping** Command

The IOS **ping** command sends a series of ICMP echo request messages (default five messages) to another host. According to the TCP/IP standards, any TCP/IP host that receives an ICMP echo request should reply with an aptly named ICMP echo reply message. If the **ping** command sends some number of echo requests and gets a reply to each request, a network engineer can have confidence that the route to reach the remote host and back is working well.

The IOS **ping** command tests whether packets can be routed to the remote host, as well as the time for the echo packet to go to the remote host, and the reply to come back. The **ping** command can also give the engineer some sense of the amount of packet loss happening over a route, because the command states how many of the echo reply messages were received correctly. To see all three types of information provided by the **ping** command, look at Example 4-8, which shows a **ping 172.16.2.254** command. The command output comes from router R1 in Figure 4-1, with 172.16.2.254 being router R4's LAN interface IP address.

Example 4-8   The **ping** Command on Router R1
```
R1#ping 172.16.2.254

Type escape sequence to abort.
Sending 5, 100-byte ICMP Echos to 172.16.2.254, timeout is 2 seconds:
!!!!!
Success rate is 100 percent (5/5), round-trip min/avg/max = 28/28/32 ms
```

The output of the **ping** command in Example 4-8 says that it is sending five 100-byte-long ICMP echo messages. Then, the output shows five exclamation points, each of which means that the **ping** command received an echo reply from 172.16.2.254. So, because five echo requests were sent, and five reply messages were received, the last line of output states that the command was 100 percent successful, going five for five. (If an echo reply is not received within 2 seconds, the **ping** command displays a period, which means no response was received.)

Also, the **ping** command notices the round-trip time, which is the time between when the echo request is sent and the corresponding echo reply is received. The **ping** command then lists the smallest, average, and largest round-trip time.

Cisco IOS **traceroute** Command

The **traceroute** command also tests whether the IP route to another host works, but it also identifies the routers in the route. Example 4-9 shows an example, using the same network as in Figure 4-1.

Example 4-9   The **traceroute** Command on Router R1

```
R1#traceroute 172.16.2.254

Type escape sequence to abort.
Tracing the route to 172.16.2.254

  1 R2 (172.16.4.252) 12 msec 16 msec 12 msec
  2 172.16.2.254 12 msec 12 msec *
```

Note

The **traceroute** command may not complete in some cases. To stop the command, press Ctrl-Shift-6.

The output of the **traceroute** command in Example 4-9 lists R2 (172.16.4.252) as the first router in the route between R1 and the destination. It also lists the minimum, average, and maximum round-trip time to reach that router. The second line lists the next device, which happens to be the destination in this case. If the route includes many routers, the command output keeps listing a line for each new router.

Chapter 9, "Basic Router Troubleshooting," and the corresponding Module 9 of the online curriculum go into slightly more detail about how **traceroute** works. Briefly, the **traceroute** command begins by sending a few packets (typically three) to the destination address listed in the command, but these packets have a *Time to Live (TTL) field* in the IP header set to 1. As covered in Chapter 10 of the *Networking Basics CCNA 1 Companion Guide*, routers decrement the TTL field by 1 when forwarding a packet, but if the router decrements a packet's TTL to 0, the router discards the packet. So, the first router that gets these three packets, R2 in this case, discards the packets. However, the router that discards the packets when decrementing TTL to 0 also sends an ICMP TTL Exceeded message to the IP address that sent the packet. So, in Example 4-9, the following process occurs due to the **traceroute** command:

1. R1 sends three packets, source 172.16.4.251, destination 172.16.2.254, with TTL=1.

2. R2 receives the packets, decrements the TTL to 0, and discards the packets.

3. R2 also sends an ICMP TTL Exceeded message back to 172.16.4.251 (R1) for each discarded packet.

4. The **traceroute** command on R1, upon seeing that all the ICMP TTL Exceeded messages came from the same IP address (172.16.4.252), now knows with confidence that 271.16.4.252 is the first router in the route to reach the destination. So, the **traceroute** command lists 172.16.4.252 as the first router in the route.

Summarizing the **ping** and **traceroute** Commands

Both **ping** and **traceroute** can be used from either user mode or privileged EXEC mode in IOS. They can also be used on most other OSs, although **traceroute** may be spelled a little differently on some OSs. For example, most Microsoft OSs have a **tracert** command instead of a **traceroute** command.

Note

The *Networking Basics CCNA 1 Companion Guide*, Chapter 1, Figure 1-30, shows a sample **tracert** command on Windows XP.

Packet Tracer   You can test the **ping** and **traceroute** commands, on both routers and PCs, by using Packet Tracer. By loading Packet Tracer configuration file NA02-0401-traceroute, you will see a working internetwork similar to Figure 4-1, but with an additional subnet. For example, you could use the **traceroute 172.16.5.1** command from R1 to see a three-router-long route in the **traceroute** command output. Also, you can use PC1 to do a **tracert** command as well.

 Lab 4.2.5a   Connectivity Tests—Ping

In this lab, you use the **ping** command to send ICMP datagrams to a target host.

 Lab 4.2.5b   Connectivity Tests—Traceroute

In this lab, you use the **traceroute** command to determine the path from a source to a destination.

Lab 4.2.6   Troubleshooting IP Address Issues

In this lab, you configure two routers and two workstations in a small WAN.

Summary

Cisco routers, switches, and other Cisco devices use CDP to obtain information about directly connected Cisco devices. The information includes the router interfaces on the local and neighboring devices, the model number and software version of the neighboring device, and the Layer 3 addresses if configured. CDP supports any physical medium and data link layer protocol as long as the data link supports the use of a SNAP header. CDP runs inside a data-link frame, so it is independent of any Layer 3 protocol. As a result, even if the Cisco devices do not have IP configured, or if IP is misconfigured, CDP can still learn information about neighboring devices.

By default, Cisco devices enable CDP on every interface. When a Cisco device boots up, CDP starts automatically and allows the device to detect directly connected Cisco devices that also use CDP. The **show cdp neighbors**, **show cdp neighbors detail**, and **show cdp entry** *name* commands display information about the devices that are directly connected to a router. Other commands, such as **show cdp timers**, list information about the operation of CDP.

CDP can be enabled or disabled on a router, both globally and per interface. IOS enables and disables CDP using the **cdp run** and **no cdp run** global configuration commands, respectively. If enabled globally, IOS enables or disables CDP per interface using the **cdp enable** and **no cdp enable** interface configuration subcommands, respectively, on a particular interface.

The IOS **telnet** command may be run from user or privileged EXEC mode. It allows a CLI user to remotely access another device. Alternatively, the **connect** command can be used, or the hostname or IP address can be entered on the command line without the **telnet** or **connect** command. As long as the name entered on the command line is not the same as a valid IOS command, IOS assumes that the user wants to telnet to a host by that name. To end a Telnet session, use the **exit** or **logout** commands, or simply do not enter anything in that Telnet connection until the inactivity timer expires (the default is 10 minutes).

The **ping** and **traceroute** commands are two excellent tools for testing IP routes. The **ping** command sends a packet to the destination host and then waits for a reply packet from that host. Using the ICMP echo protocol, the **ping** command determines whether a working route exists, determines the round-trip time for packets to go to the remote host and back, and, to some degree, tests the route's reliability based on packet loss. The **traceroute** command tests the same general features as **ping**, with the added benefit that it lists the routers at each hop of the route to the destination. The IOS **ping** and **traceroute** commands can both be performed at either the user or privileged EXEC levels.

Check Your Understanding

Complete all the review questions listed here to test your understanding of the topics and concepts in this chapter. Answers are listed in Appendix A, "Answers to Check Your Understanding and Challenge Questions."

1. What is the primary use for CDP?

A. Remote terminal access to devices on the network

B. To learn about all Cisco devices directly connected to an interface

C. To gather basic information about network devices from non-Cisco vendors

D. To provide responses to **ping** commands from the network administrator

2. What information does the **show cdp neighbors** command provide for each CDP neighbor? (Choose three.)

A. Device identifier

B. Runtime

C. Address list

D. Port identifier

E. Clock rate information

3. The **show cdp interface** command is used to display which one of the following?

A. The values of the CDP timers and the interface status

B. The interface configuration of the neighboring routers

C. The IP address of the neighbor device

D. The CDP holdtime

4. When used to test a network, which of the following does the **show cdp interfaces** command display?

A. Line and data link layer protocol status

B. How the router directs traffic across the network

C. The path that packets follow across the network

D. The names of routers on the network

5. What information is displayed by the **show cdp neighbors** command? (Choose four.)

A. Decremented holdtime value, in seconds

B. Local ports/interface types and numbers

C. Routing protocols running on the link

D. Neighbor device type, device ID, and port ID

E. CDP debug summary

F. Platform type of neighboring devices

6. Which of the following is true for the output of the command **show cdp entry** [*device-name*]?

   A. It displays the Layer 3 addresses configured on the interface that the neighbor uses to send CDP updates to the local router.

   B. It displays an interface list of the connected neighbor with IP addresses of that device's neighbors.

   C. It displays the list of the device numbers of all the neighboring routers.

   D. It displays all the Layer 2 addresses on the interfaces of the neighbor router.

7. What is a definition for Telnet?

   A. A command to determine whether a specific IP address is accessible. It works by sending a packet to the specified address and waiting for a reply.

   B. A command that uses Time to Live (TTL) values to generate messages from each router used along the path.

   C. A protocol that allows a user to gain access to the CLI of a remote device.

   D. An application that resides on devices in the network. The devices use the application to report errors to the network manager.

8. Which of the following are true about Telnet? (Choose two.)

   A. It is the basic test of only Layers 1 to 3 of the OSI model.

   B. The IOS telnet client allows for multiple concurrent suspended telnet connections.

   C. A user can suspend an IOS Telnet connection by pressing Ctrl-Shift-6 and then *x*.

   D. A Telnet response displays the path that packets take through the network.

9. What four important pieces of information do you receive after issuing a **ping** command? (Choose one.)

   A. The size and quantity of ICMP packets, the timeout duration, the success rate, and the round-trip time

   B. The size and quantity of the SNMP packets, the timeout duration, the success rate, and the round-trip time

   C. The size and quantity of ICMP packets, the MAC address, the success rate, and the round-trip time

   D. The size and quantity of SNMP packets, the timeout duration, the TCP status, and the round-trip time

10. In reply to the **ping** command, what do exclamation points (!) indicate?

   A. The number of successful echo requests

   B. The number of unsuccessful echo requests

   C. The number of hops before reaching the destination

   D. Layer 7 of the target device is working successfully

11. What information does testing a network by using the **traceroute** command provide?

   A. It determines if the line protocol is operational.

   B. It determines if a routing table entry exists for the target network.

   C. It maps every router that a packet goes through to reach its destination.

   D. It determines if upper-layer applications are functioning properly.

Challenge Questions and Activities

These questions require a deeper application of the concepts covered in this chapter and are similar to the style of questions you might see on a CCNA certification exam. Answers are listed in Appendix A.

1. A network engineer wants to verify information about R1's neighboring devices (including their IP address) for devices connected to R1's interface FA0/0. CDP is configured to work on all R1 interfaces except the FA0/0 interface. Choose the answers that show the correct CLI modes and commands with which the engineer can enable CDP in this case and then view the IP addresses of the devices connected to interface FA0/0. (Choose two.)

   A. Router#(config)**cdp enable fa0/0**

   B. Router#(config-int)**cdp enable**

   C. Router#(config-int)**cdp run**

   D. Router#**show cdp neighbors**

   E. Router#**show cdp neighbors detail**

   F. Router#**show cdp controllers**

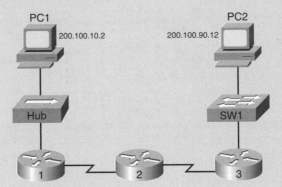

Device	Hostname	Interface	IP Address	Platform
Router1	Accounting	FA0/1 S0/1	200.100.10.1 200.100.20.1	2600
Router2		S0/0 S0/1	200.100.20.2	
Router3		S0/0 FA0/1		
SW1	N/A	FA0/8	N/A	

2. The preceding figure shows a sample network. A network engineer has only console access to the devices because vty passwords are not set. The engineer has been asked to complete a map of hostnames, network interfaces, IP addresses, and device platforms in the LAN. The completed portion of the map is shown in the accompanying table. Which steps should the network engineer take to gather the remaining information she needs to complete the table? (Choose one.)

   A. Console into Router1 and enter **show cdp neighbors**; telnet to Router2 and Router3 and repeat **show cdp neighbors** on each.

   B. Console into Router2 and enter **show cdp neighbors**.

   C. Console into Router3 and enter **show cdp neighbors detail**.

   D. Console into SW1 and enter **show cdp neighbors entry Router 3**.

   E. Console into Router2 and enter **show cdp neighbors**, and then telnet to Router3 and enter **show cdp neighbors**.

   F. Console into Router3 and enter **show cdp neighbors detail**.

CHAPTER 5

Managing Cisco IOS Software

Objectives

Upon completion of this chapter, you should be able to answer the following questions:

- What are the stages of the router boot sequence?

- How do Cisco devices locate and load Cisco IOS Software?

- What is the boot system command used for?

- What files are used by the Cisco IOS, and what are their functions?

- What are the configuration register values?

- What are the locations of different file types on a router?

- What are the Cisco IOS Software naming conventions?

- What are the steps and processes to save and restore configuration files using TFTP and copy-and-paste?

- What are the steps and commands to load an IOS image using TFTP?

- What are the steps and commands to load an IOS image using Xmodem?

- How can the **show** commands be used to verify the file system?

Key Terms

This chapter uses the following key terms. You can find the definitions in the Glossary.

As covered in Chapter 2, "Introduction to Routers," routers perform several functions at initialization, including picking which Cisco IOS image to load into RAM and use. Following that, the final initialization step relates to how the router finds and picks a configuration file to use, typically the startup-config file stored in NVRAM. To do both steps, the router must find, copy, move, and manipulate files—files that hold IOS images and files that contain configuration commands. This chapter closely examines the options and processes that routers use to manage these types of files.

The first half of this chapter reviews the boot process as covered in Chapter 2, adding more detail and explanations about how a router can pick which IOS image to load. The extra details include more information about troubleshooting problems when the IOS fails to load correctly, or when the router loads the wrong IOS image.

The second half of the chapter then examines several topics relating to how to move files into and out of a router. This part of the chapter again reviews some information from Chapter 2, but it goes deeper, covering information about the Cisco IOS File System (IFS), additional commands for moving files, and options for recovery when a router fails to load an IOS image. This section also reviews some of the basics about moving configuration files into and out of a router.

Router Boot Sequence and Loading Cisco IOS Images

When an engineer first powers on or reboots a router, the router goes through a four-step process, covered in Chapter 2. This section explains more details about the last two steps in the four-step initialization process:

1. Perform a power-on self test (POST).

2. Load a bootstrap program.

3. Load an IOS.

4. Load a startup configuration file.

The completion of these four steps ends with a working router. The POST process happens automatically, performing basic hardware tests. The bootstrap program completes the hardware testing and initializes software in the router. The router then loads an IOS image, enabling the router to route IP packets. Finally, the router loads an initial configuration file, which tells IOS the parameters it needs to know—things like IP addresses and routing protocols to use—so that the router can successfully route packets.

The last three steps require the router to copy the files into RAM, as shown in Figure 5-1. The figure shows a single place from which a router can load the bootstrap program (ROM), but three options each for getting the IOS file and the running configuration file. Normally, most routers load an IOS image that is stored in flash memory and an initial configuration stored in

NVRAM. However, the router can load these files from the other locations shown in Figure 5-1. This first section of the chapter examines the options for loading the IOS image, or IOS file. (Note that the "console" option for the configuration is not really a file, but a reference that means the user can connect to the console and enter the configuration from the keyboard.)

Figure 5-1   Moving the Bootstrap, IOS, and Configuration Files into RAM

In most networks, all the routers simply load the startup-config file in NVRAM into RAM as the

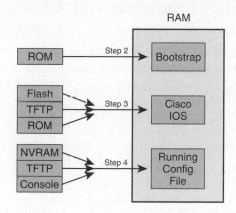

running-config file during the initialization process. However, in those same networks, each router may have different settings that affect how each router picks which IOS file to load. So, this section focuses on the process of how a router chooses which IOS to load. You also learn how a network engineer can troubleshoot and verify the choice of which Cisco IOS a router uses.

Choosing the Cisco IOS Image During the Router Boot Sequence

Cisco supplies a large number of options for how to change what IOS image a router loads. Routers use the following logic to attempt to load an IOS:

1. Load a limited-function IOS based on whether the configuration register's last hex digit is set to 0 or 1.

2. Load an IOS based on the configuration of **boot system** commands in the startup-config file.

3. Load the first file in flash memory as the IOS.

4. Use TFTP broadcasts to find a TFTP server, and download an IOS from that server.

5. Load a limited-function IOS from ROM.

Routers almost always pick their IOS based on either Step 2 or Step 3 of this list. Steps 2 and 3

Note

The online course has an interactive media activity that lets you exercise your memory of the last four steps in this list.

give engineers plenty of choices of how they can make the router load the correct IOS for normal operation of the router. Engineers can use Step 1 when performing some sort of maintenance; the OSs loaded at this step cannot route packets, but they can be used for some useful functions, such as password recovery. Finally, Steps 4 and 5 exist mainly as fail-safe mechanisms when the first three steps do not work.

The next several sections explain each of the steps in the list, in order.

Choosing the Cisco IOS Image Based on the Configuration Register

Under normal conditions, when routers reboot, they need to load a fully functioning IOS image. However, in some cases, engineers need to make a router load one of the two alternative OSs mentioned in Chapter 2: ROM Monitor (ROMMON) and a limited-function IOS called boot ROM (RXBoot). This first step in a router's decision process allows the engineer to tell the router to not load the IOS it would normally load, but instead to load one of the two alternative OSs.

To understand this first step in how a router chooses its IOS, you must first understand something about the *configuration register*. The configuration register is a 16-bit number that Cisco routers store in a hidden area of NVRAM that is not part of the startup-config file. The configuration register's value tells the router facts about several small operating parameters. For example, the configuration register has several bits that, when changed, change the speed of the router console port. Parts of the configuration register can also be used to tell the router which IOS to load.

The configuration register can be set in a couple of ways, and viewed using the **show version** command. The most commonly used way to set its value is to use the **config-register** global configuration command. However, when you set the configuration register's value, the value is used only after the router is reloaded. Example 5-1 shows the (default) value of the configuration register, the user changing the value, and the **show version** command stating that the new value will not be used until the next reload.

Example 5-1   Changing and Viewing the Configuration Register's Value

```
R1#show version
Cisco IOS Software, C1700 Software (C1700-ADVIPSERVICESK9-M), Version 12.3(11)T3,
  RELEASE SOFTWARE (fc4)
Technical Support: http://www.cisco.com/techsupport
Copyright  1986-2005 by Cisco Systems, Inc.
Compiled Wed 26-Jan-05 09:19 by pwade

ROM: System Bootstrap, Version 12.2(4r)XL, RELEASE SOFTWARE (fc1)

R1 uptime is 1 minute
System returned to ROM by power-on
System image file is "flash:c1700-advipservicesk9-mz.123-11.T3.bin"
```

```
Example 5-1    Changing and Viewing the Configuration Register's Value    continued
Cisco 1760 (MPC860P) processor (revision 0x200) with 91117K/7187K bytes of memory.
Processor board ID VMS06200J38 (2996972870), with hardware revision BB67
MPC860P processor: part number 5, mask 2
1 FastEthernet interface
2 Serial(sync/async) interfaces
2 Voice FXS interfaces
32K bytes of NVRAM.
32768K bytes of processor board System flash (Read/Write)

Configuration register is 0x2102
R1#configure terminal
Enter configuration commands, one per line.  End with CNTL/Z.
R1(config)#config-register 0x2101
R1(config)#^Z
R1#show version
! lines omitted for brevity

Configuration register is 0x2102 (will be 0x2101 at next reload)
```

The end of the output of both **show version** commands lists the value of the configuration register. The value is displayed with a 0x prefix, which the **show version** output uses to imply that the number following 0x is a hexadecimal number. The four-hex-digit (16-bit) value follows 0x. Of particular interest, note that the current value at the end of the example shows the current setting (hex 2102) and the setting that will be used at the next reload of the router (hex 2101).

Routers use the 4 low-order bits of the configuration register as the *boot field*. The boot field tells the router what to do in its first of the five decision steps listed in the preceding section. To appreciate this first decision step, you need to remember the basics about the two alternative OSs that may be loaded into a router: ROMMON and RXBoot. These two alternative OSs were covered in the Chapter 2 section "Two Alternative OSs." The key points about each are listed in Table 5-1.

Note

The low-order bits of the configuration register are the far-right bits when writing down the number.

Table 5-1   Comparing ROMMON and RXBoot OSs

Operating Environment	Alternative Name	OS Stored In	Typical Use
ROM Monitor	ROMMON	ROM	Low-level debugging and password recovery
Boot ROM	RxBoot	ROM	Copying a new IOS into flash memory (under certain conditions)

Depending on the value of the boot field and the age of the router, a router can choose to load ROMMON, load RXBoot, or move on to a later step in the five-step list for choosing an IOS to load. Only older routers, such as the Cisco 1600 and 2500 series routers, have an RXBoot IOS in ROM. Later, Cisco added all the features of the RXBoot IOS to ROMMON, so newer routers do not need (and do not have) an RXBoot IOS.

Table 5-2 shows the logic used by both older and newer routers for choosing an IOS. Note that the logic differs between the older and newer routers only when the boot field is hex 1.

Table 5-2   How Routers Use the Boot Field to Choose an IOS

Boot Field Value (Hex)	Boot Field Value (Binary)	Older Routers	Newer Routers
0	0000	Load ROMMON	Load ROMMON
1	0001	Load RXBoot	Skip to Step 3[1]
2–F	0010–1111	Skip to Step 2	Skip to Step 2

[1] The router ignores any boot system commands and immediately tries to load the first file found in flash memory.

If the router loads either ROMMON or RXBoot software, the process is complete, waiting for the network engineer to do whatever low-level maintenance function needs to be done. However, depending on the configuration register settings, the router may simply move on to Step 2 or even Step 3 of the process of finding an IOS to load. In fact, most production routers default to use a boot field of 2, because the configuration register defaults to 0x2102. As such, at Step 1 of the decision process, these same routers simply choose to move on to Step 2.

Choosing the Cisco IOS Based on **boot system** Commands

The IOS **boot system** *file-url* global configuration command gives an engineer a direct means of telling a router exactly what IOS to load. These commands can be added in configuration mode and saved in the startup-config file in NVRAM. Assuming the router reaches this step (step 2) of the process, the router looks in the startup-config file for any **boot system** commands and loads the IOS file listed in the commands. For example, imagine that the startup-config file holds a **boot system flash:c1700-advipservicesk9-mz.123-11.T3.bin** command. When the router reboots, the router then attempts to load the IOS file listed in the command. If the file is found—in this case in flash memory—all is well, and the router loads and uses the IOS.

In some cases, however, the **boot system** command may fail for one of several reasons. For example, it is easy to mistype such a long filename. As a result, the router will not find the file in flash memory and therefore will fail to load the IOS. Also, another engineer may have made a mistake and erased the IOS file from flash memory, so again the router will not find a file by that name in flash memory. Also, the file may be corrupted, and it is possible for the router to have a hardware error trying to access flash memory.

Cisco routers provide a couple of ways to prepare for cases in which the router fails when try ing to load the IOS listed in a **boot system** command. First, the engineer can configure multiple **boot system** commands, and the router will try each of them sequentially until one of them works. Alternatively, after the router has tried all the **boot system** commands, it moves on to Step 3, in which the router attempts to load the first file it finds in flash memory, no matter what its name is.

Example 5-2 shows a typical case of how to use multiple boot system commands in a single configuration.

Example 5-2   Configuring Multiple **boot system** Commands

```
Router#configure terminal
Router(config)#boot system flash:c1700-advipservicesk9-mz.123-11.T3.bin
Router(config)#boot system tftp c1700-advipservicesk9-mz.123-11.T3.bin 10.1.1.1
Router(config)#boot system flash:
Router(config)#boot system rom
Router(config)#end
Router#copy running-config startup-config
```

The configuration shows the following four **boot system** commands, with the three extra com-mands giving the engineer extra protection against potential problems:

1. The first **boot system** command simply references the specific IOS image in flash memory.

2. To be ready for the possibility that the file may be accidentally erased, the **boot system tftp** command points to a TFTP server at IP address 10.1.1.1, but with the same filename. In that case, the router attempts to contact the listed TFTP server, transfer a copy of the same IOS file, and load that into RAM.

3. The **boot system flash**: command next tells the router to look in flash memory, find the first file in flash (more on what "first file" means in the next section), and load that file as the IOS.

4. If all these commands fail, the router attempts to use the last boot system command, **boot system rom**, which simply tells the router to load ROMMON. This last step would then allow the engineer to begin the process of recovering and copying the IOS back into flash after someone else had erased the file.

Note

The router must have IP connectivity to the TFTP server before the router can successfully retrieve an IOS image from a TFTP server.

Beyond the meaning and the sequence of the **boot system** commands, you also should note the following points:

- The **copy running-config startup-config** command in the example is needed so that the **boot system** commands will not be lost when the router is rebooted.

- If the router loads the IOS from the TFTP server based on the second **boot system tftp** command, the IOS is copied from the server, into RAM, and used; the file is not stored in flash.

■ If you later add another **boot system** command, it is added to the end of the list of **boot system** commands. If you want to add a new command to the middle of the list instead of the end of the list, you must delete some of the commands by using the **no boot system** command, add the new **boot system** command, and then add the previously deleted commands back into the configuration.

 Lab 5.1.3   Using the boot system Command

In this lab, you display information about the Cisco IOS image that runs on the router.

Loading the First File in Flash Memory

At this point in the process, the router has considered the logic at the first two steps for choosing which OS to load. When a router fails to find and successfully load an IOS at Step 1 or 2, it then tries one last time to find an IOS in flash memory. The router looks in flash, finds the first file in flash, and attempts to use that file as the IOS. For instance, Example 5-3 shows the output of a **show flash** command on router R1, with the first file in flash (shown with a number 1 on the left) being the IOS image for this Cisco 1841 series router.

Example 5-3   Listing an IOS as the First File in Flash Memory

```
R1#show flash
-#- --length-- -----date/time------ path
1     22314120 Feb 16 2005 18:55:44 +00:00 c1841-advipservicesk9-mz.123-11.T3.bin
2         1536 Jan 31 2005 21:33:20 +00:00 sdmconfig-18xx.cfg
3      3885056 Jan 31 2005 21:33:50 +00:00 sdm.tar
```

Interestingly, a large number of Cisco routers, including Cisco routers purchased and shipped directly from Cisco, rely on Step 3 for choosing which IOS to load. These routers ship with a default configuration register of 0x2102, with no configuration file at all (so no **boot system** commands), and with the first file in flash memory being an IOS image. So, these new routers skip Step 1 based on a boot field of 2, find no **boot system** commands, and move on to Step 3 to look for the first file in flash memory.

You should be cautious, however, when relying on this step. A router's flash memory can hold many files, each of which is numbered as shown on the left side of Example 5-3. When new files are copied into flash, IOS typically assigns the new file a larger file number. At this step, the problem is that a router searches to find the first file—and only the first file—in flash. So, if the desired IOS image is not the first file in flash, practically speaking, you may be better off simply configuring a **boot system** command to specifically refer to the correct file in flash.

Broadcasting to Find a Cisco IOS on a TFTP Server

As mentioned earlier, most production routers have been configured so that they choose their IOS images at Step 2 or Step 3. Step 4 provides the router with one final effort to find and load an IOS, but frankly it is seldom used outside a Cisco lab environment. At this step, the router broadcasts on all interfaces to which a cable has been attached, looking for a TFTP server. If found, the router asks the TFTP server to send the router a specific file, with the file using a standard name based in part on the router's hostname, and in part on the configuration register value.

Loading a Limited-Function OS from ROM

The final step in this process allows the router to load one of the two limited-function OSs so that the engineer can begin the process of recovering from whatever caused the router to fail to load an IOS. This step is truly the last resort when a router boots. The router has given up trying to load a fully functional IOS, but the router knows that the next step for the network engineer will be to solve the problem and get an IOS loaded into the router. So, the router goes ahead and loads one of the limited-function OSs, as follows:

- If the router has an RXBoot OS (only on older routers), the router loads the RXBoot image.

- If the router does not have an RXBoot OS, the router loads ROMMON.

Note that in both cases, the OS loaded by the router can copy an IOS from a TFTP server or copy an IOS image from a PC attached to the console, both of which are covered in the upcoming section "Managing Cisco Router IOS and Configuration Files." Either process allows the router to recover so that it can be reloaded with a fully functional IOS.

Troubleshooting and Verifying the Choice of Cisco IOS

Routers fail to load an IOS, or load the wrong IOS, for a variety of reasons. First, the **config-register** and **boot system** commands may simply have been configured to incorrect values. Even if the **boot system** commands are configured correctly, the files may simply be missing from flash memory, or the file may not be on the TFTP server. When referencing a TFTP server, other problems could occur. For instance, the router may not have a working IP route to reach the TFTP server, or the TFTP server software may not be running at the time. It is also possible that the router has hardware problems that prevent flash memory from working.

Regardless of why the router loaded an incorrect IOS, or failed to load an IOS, the network engineer needs to take a structured approach to troubleshooting this type of problem. First, the engineer should determine how the router will apply the five-step IOS decision process, and then look to see why each step could have failed.

Determining How a Router Should Apply the Five-Step Decision Process

To determine how a router will load an IOS (or OS) the next time it reboots, the engineer needs to get an IOS up and working on the router. To do that, if ROMMON or RXBoot was loaded, the engineer must first copy a new IOS into the router from some external source. (The second half of this chapter includes coverage of how to copy a new IOS into a router.)

When the engineer has a router with the possibly wrong IOS loaded, the engineer should first look at the two configurable items that impact the five-step IOS decision process: the configuration register and the **boot system** commands. The engineer can see the configuration register only by looking at the output of the **show version** command; the **show running-config** and **show startup-config** commands do not list the value of the configuration register. After examining the configuration register, the engineer must examine the **boot system** commands in the startup-config file by using the **show startup-config** command. It is important to look at the startup-config file, because the **boot system** commands will not be used until the router reboots, and the running-config file will be lost when the router reboots.

Armed with the knowledge of the configuration register (as of the next reboot) and the parameters of any **boot system** commands, plus the details about the five-step IOS decision process covered earlier in this chapter, the engineer should be able to figure out which IOS images the router would try to load. For example, if the configuration register is set to 0x2101 as of the next reboot, and the router is a newer router such as a Cisco 1800 series router, the engineer should know the following:

1. The router sees the boot field of 1 and skips to Step 3 of the decision process (because Cisco 1841 routers are a newer series, they do not include an RxBoot OS).

2. The router skips Step 2 of the decision process due to the boot field of hex 1.

3. At Step 3, the router tries to load the first file in flash memory.

4. If loading the first file fails, the router broadcasts, looking for a TFTP server.

5. If the router fails to find a TFTP server, the router loads ROMMON.

Determining Which Steps Failed

After you determine which specific IOS images the router will attempt to load, you simply need to verify that the files are there and accessible. Consider the following examples:

- For any **boot system flash:filename** commands, you should verify that the file with that name is in flash, with the same spelling and capitalization. The names are case-sensitive.

- For **boot system tftp** *filename ip-address* commands, you should verify that the correctly spelled filename is on the TFTP server, that TFTP server software is installed and running on that computer, and that the router can **ping** the server's IP address.

- For a **boot system flash** command, with no filename listed, make sure the lowest-numbered file in flash is the IOS file that you want to load.

In some rare cases, the router hardware may have a problem and be unable to read the contents of flash memory. In these cases, it may be best to simply call the Cisco Technical Assistance Center (TAC) and get advice on how to attack the problem.

This concludes this chapter's detailed coverage of how a router chooses the IOS, or possibly ROMMON or RXBoot software, to load when the router initializes. The second major section of this chapter changes the focus to topics related to storing and moving files inside a router.

Lab 5.1.5   Troubleshooting Configuration Register Boot Problems

In this lab, you check and document the configuration register settings related to the boot method.

Managing Cisco Router IOS and Configuration Files

The first major section of this chapter covered many options for using an IOS image—an IOS file—that is already stored in flash memory in the router. This section changes the focus to look more closely at how IOS stores and references files, and how IOS can copy files to and from a router. First, this section looks at the Cisco IOS File System (IFS), and then it covers the file-naming standards for IOS files. Following that, this section concludes with coverage of how to copy both IOS files and configuration files.

Cisco IOS File System

The term *file system* refers to the general concept of how any OS organizes and stores its files. For example, most PCs have a disk drive called the C: drive, and directories (sometimes called file folders) can be added to separate files into different groups. For instance, Microsoft OSs typically come with a directory called C:\My Documents, and a file stored there might be called C:\My Documents\chapter5.doc. These details—naming the disk drive C:, the ability to have other directories, and the rules for naming the files stored in those directories—are all part of the file system on that OS.

IOS, like every other OS, has a file system, aptly named the ***Cisco IOS File System (IFS)***. Although the name may sound formal, assuming you have done all the earlier labs in class, you have seen and used the IFS many times without knowing or caring about its name or existence. So far in this book, you have used three general types of files defined and stored by IOS using the IFS, as listed and described in Table 5-3.

Table 5-3   Startup and Running Config Files, and IOS Flash Files

Common Name of File	Where File Is Stored	Formal IFS Name
startup-config	NVRAM	nvram:startup-config
running-config	RAM	system:running-config
IOS (various names)[1]	Flash (permanent), typically moved to RAM at boot time	flash:filename

[1] The format of the actual filenames for IOS files is covered in the next section.

The file system created by Cisco IOS has gone through three major design steps over the years. The original early IOS releases (up through Version 10.2, which was released around 1994) used a variety of sometimes-confusing keywords to refer to what we know of today as the startup-config and running-config files. Next, at IOS Version 10.3 (early-mid 1990s), Cisco formalized the standard use of the names *startup-config* and *running-config* for all commands referring to the initial and currently used configuration files, respectively. The third step was the formal introduction of the IFS with IOS Version 12.0, when Cisco officially named the startup-config file *nvram:startup-config* and named the running-config file *system:running-config*. As a result, today's most current IOS releases support three variations of commands that reference the configuration files:

- The pre-Version-10.3 style

- The new style as of Version 10.3 (which is the most commonly used style)

- The style of commands that use the full IFS names for the configuration files

Table 5-4 lists the two newest styles of these commands.

Table 5-4   Two Most Recently Added Styles of Configuration File Commands

Function	New Command as of Cisco IOS 10.3	New Command with IFS (Version 12.0)
Copy a config file from a server to the running config[1]	copy rcp running-config copy tftp running-config	copy rcp: system: running-config copy tftp: system:running-config copy ftp: system:running-config
Copy the running config to a server[1]	copy running-config rcp copy running-config tftp	copy system: running-config rcp: copy system:running-config tftp copy system:running-config ftp
Display the contents of the running config[1]	show running-config	more system: running-config

Table 5-4   Two Most Recently Added Styles of Configuration File Commands   *continued*

Function	New Command as of Cisco IOS 10.3	New Command with IFS (Version 12.0)
Erase the contents of running config	**erase running-config**	**erase system: running-config**
Erase the contents of startup config	**erase startup-config**	**erase nvram:**

[1] For each of the commands in these rows, the keyword **startup-config** could be substituted, and the commands would do the same function for the startup-config file instead of the running-config file.

Table 5-4 lists a couple of particularly important points. The first three rows all **show** commands related to the running-config file, but the commands can all be changed to use **startup-config** instead of **running-config** to copy or display the startup-config file. Also, with the IFS, to erase the startup-config file, the **erase nvram:** command or the **erase nvram:startup-config** command can be used.

Also, it is important to note the order of the parameters in the **copy** command. The syntax is **copy** *source destination.* For example, **copy running-config startup-config** (or the abbreviated **copy run start**) copies a configuration from the running configuration to the startup configuration so that it will load on reboot. The **copy run tftp** command copies the running configuration to a TFTP server.

The last column of Table 5-4 lists prefixes added to IOS as part of the IFS. These prefixes have the same sort of meaning as a drive letter with a PC's OS. For example, a PC's hard disk drive may be drive letter C:, and the CD or DVD drive may be D:. With IFS, nvram: of course refers to NVRAM, and system: refers to system files held in RAM, including the running-config file. Table 5-5 lists the prefixes defined by IFS, along with a brief description.

Table 5-5   Cisco IFS File System Prefixes

Prefix	Description
bootflash:	Boot flash memory
flash:	Flash memory
flh:	Flash load helper log files
ftp:	FTP server
nvram:	NVRAM
rcp:	Remote copy protocol (RCP) network server
slot0:	On routers with Personal Computer Memory Card Industry Association (PCMCIA) flash memory cards, the first PCMCIA flash card

Table 5-5   Cisco IFS File System Prefixes   *continued*

Prefix	Description
slot1:	Second PCMCIA flash memory card
system:	Contains the system memory, including the running configuration
tftp:	TFTP network server

Table 5-5 mentions a couple of prefixes relating to flash memory that may not be obvious at first glance. Many routers have flash memory that is attached to the motherboard, so IFS references that type of flash simply as flash:. However, some models of routers have removable PCMCIA flash cards, and in some cases, routers have two PCMCIA card slots. On these routers, commands can refer to the first slot (slot 0) as both **flash:** and **slot0:**. If a second PCMCIA card slot exists, commands must specifically use the prefix **slot1:** to display and copy files.

Although the details in this section may seem a bit overwhelming, thankfully, you can still use commands that use keywords such as running-config, startup-config, and flash. The remainder of this chapter uses the simplest and most concise commands that can be used to look at and copy the files.

Cisco IOS Filenames

Before starting the coverage of moving IOS and configuration files in a router, it is important to understand a bit about IOS filenames. To appreciate IOS filenames, you need to know a bit more about IOS and how Cisco supports a very large set of customer requirements. As a result of these requirements, Cisco offers a large number of different IOS files to its customers. The four main points you need to understand about IOS follow:

- The differences in *Cisco IOS versions* and releases

- The differences between router model series/Cisco IOS platforms

- The differences in *Cisco IOS feature sets*

- Other minor differences, including whether the IOS is compressed or relocatable

First, Cisco needs to offer its customers different IOS files when upgrading or fixing the IOS. Just like any other software, Cisco adds features to IOS over time and fixes problems with the software. So, when Cisco plans for new major versions of IOS, each major version includes a large number of new features. (When learning the basics of IOS, it may not be obvious, but the number of features in IOS is huge, and Cisco adds features frequently.) After Cisco creates a new major version, it does not add new features to that specific version of IOS, but Cisco does change that IOS version over time to fix various problems or bugs that are uncovered.

To support the various versions and releases, Cisco must create different files for each IOS version number and, inside that version, for each maintenance release. For example, Cisco has four versions of IOS that begin with 12: 12.1, 12.2, 12.3, and 12.4. Inside each version, Cisco has several maintenance releases. So, someone might say something like, "We're running 12.1(3)," which means major Version 12.1, with maintenance release 3. The IOS filename, as supplied by Cisco, has some text such as "121-3," with the version number (12.1, but without the period) before the dash, and the release number (3) after the dash.

Next, Cisco must offer a different IOS file for each model series of Cisco router. Each model series, sometimes called a router platform, has hardware differences, including possibly using a different set of microprocessors. So, the IOS that runs on a Cisco 1700 series router will not run on a Cisco 2600 series router or an 1841 model router. So, Cisco must supply different IOS files for customers who use different platforms. For example, two routers, a Cisco 1760 and a Cisco 2620, might both run IOS 12.1(3) software, but the IOS files for each router would be different files, with different names, to support the different platforms. So, Cisco puts the model series number into the IOS filename as well.

The next difference in IOS files relates to the IOS feature set. One way to get the general idea of an IOS feature set is to use the analogy of buying a car. You go to the car dealer and walk around the lot. All the cars on the lot will meet your need for basic transportation, but you may have other requirements as well. An inexpensive basic commuter car may just have cloth seats, with a basic radio, an engine without much horsepower, and not many extras. A big SUV may have seating for seven adults, roomy cargo space, lots of nice extras, and tons of horsepower, but it costs more money. However, if you have a family of seven or you need to drive your group of friends around town, you might really need the large but more expensive SUV.

Similarly, all Cisco IOS images route packets, but IOS can do so much more. A recent IOS command reference (Version 12.3T) has over *7000* different commands and a large number of features, but many Cisco customers want to use only a small set of the features. So, Cisco creates different IOS images, some with a small number of common features (the equivalent of a small commuter car), some with a medium number of features, and some with all the features (like a large SUV). However, the more features and functions in the IOS feature set, the more money you have to pay.

To get a more specific idea about common IOS feature sets, examine the following list:

- **IP Base**—Provides basic IP routing functions, including all the features covered in this book.

- **IP Voice**—Supports the same features as IP Base, plus support for voice sent inside IP packets (voice over IP, or VoIP).

- **IP/FW 3DES**—Includes the features of IP Base, plus a firewall feature and Triple Digital Encryption Standard (3DES) encryption. This feature set provides many security features.

- **IP/ADSL/IPX/AT/IBM Plus**—Includes IP, IPX, and AppleTalk (AT) routing, support for many proprietary protocols from IBM, and support for asymmetric DSL (ADSL), which is the type of DSL most typically found installed in the United States today.

- **Enterprise Services**—Includes most every feature used in the largest enterprises.

Note

This list is a sampling of common IOS feature sets. Many other feature sets are available.

Note

Cisco IOS filenames include a two- or three-letter code that implies the feature set.

Additionally, Cisco may offer multiple *file formats* of IOS files. The file format differs mainly on two features:

- Whether the file is compressed
- Whether the file is relocatable

Compressed IOS files require less space in flash memory, but they require more time when the router reboots, because the router has to uncompress the file before loading it. With a relocatable IOS file, the router does not have to copy the whole IOS into RAM, instead leaving most of it in flash memory, which saves some space in RAM. IOS files that cannot be relocated must be fully copied into RAM when the IOS is loaded.

Because of all these differences, Cisco supplies a different IOS file for each combination of unique router platform, each version and release, each feature set, and each file format. So, when you need to download a new IOS from Cisco, you go through the process of picking the platform, version and release, feature set, and finally the file format. At that point, you can download a new IOS image from Cisco. (You can go to http://tools.cisco.com/ITDIT/IST-MAIN/servlet/index and use the Cisco IOS Software Selector tool to get a little more insight into this whole process.)

Cisco names the IOS files so that all four different items are implied by the name. Although it is not important for the course (or for real life) to memorize all the possible options in the file-names, it is useful to know the general format of the filenames, and at least be able to find the router platform, plus the version and release number. Figure 5-2 shows a sample IOS filename, including the four components of the filename.

Figure 5-2   Format of IOS Filenames

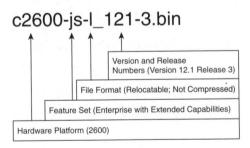

The following section explains a few details about managing IOS files by copying them into and out of the router.

Copying and Managing Cisco IOS Images

When you order a new Cisco router, Cisco ships the router with the requested IOS already installed into flash memory. However, you may want to make a backup copy of the IOS file in case someone accidentally erases the IOS in flash memory. You may also want to upgrade to a different IOS version or feature set later, so you will need to be able to copy the IOS into a router. All of these cases require that you be able to either copy IOS images into flash memory or copy them from flash memory.

This section covers the three main ways to copy IOS files into and out of a router. First, you can use the **copy** command while IOS is running, which is the most typical way to copy the IOS. The other two topics in this section—how to copy an IOS using a protocol called Xmodem, and how to copy an IOS using a ROMMON command called **tftpdnld**—are mainly used when you have a bad problem and cannot get any IOS to load in a router.

Copying Using the Cisco IOS **copy** Command

The IOS **copy** command provides a way to copy files to and from flash memory in the router and a server in the network. It supports three main protocols:

- Trivial File Transfer Protocol (TFTP)

- Remote Copy (RCP)

- File Transfer Protocol (FTP)

TFTP tends to be the most commonly used option, and it has been supported in IOS longer than RCP and FTP, so the examples here use TFTP.

The process of copying an IOS image into flash memory is relatively simple, as shown in Example 5-4, but visualizing the process on a printed page takes a little imagination. The **copy tftp flash** command tells the router to interact with the user, with the router asking several questions, waiting for user input. Example 5-4 shows the text entered by the CLI user in bold and uses highlights to show places where the router output stopped, waiting for user input.

Example 5-4   Copying an IOS File from a TFTP Server into Flash Memory

```
R1# copy tftp flash
Address or name of remote host []? 192.168.119.20
Source file name []?C2600-js-l_121-3.bin
Destination file name [C2600-js-l_121-3.bin]?
Accessing tftp://192.168.119.20/C2600-js-l_121-3.bin
Erase flash: before copying? [confirm]
Erasing the flash file system will remove all files Continue? [confirm]
Erasing device eeeeee...eeeeeeeeeeeee...erased
Loading C2600-js-l_121-3.bin from 192.168.119.20 (via FastEthernet 0/0):
    !!!!!!!!!!!!!!!!!!!!!!!!!!!!!!!!!!!!
Verifying Check sum.........................OK
[OK-8906589 bytes]
8906589 bytes copied in 277.45 secs
R1#
```

Note

The router displays a series of the letter *e* as the erasure of flash memory proceeds and then displays a series of ! as the actual file copying occurs.

The steps in Example 5-4 run as follows:

1. The user enters the **copy tftp flash** command.

2. The router asks for the hostname or IP address of the TFTP server and waits for a response.

3. The user enters 192.168.119.20 and presses Enter.

4. The router asks for the name of the source file to be taken from the TFTP server and waits for a response.

5. The user enters C2600-js-l_121-3.bin and presses Enter.

6. The router asks for the name it should use when storing the file in flash memory, which defaults to the same name as the source file, as shown in brackets. The router then waits for a response.

7. The user presses Enter to accept the default of using the same filename.

8. The router displays several lines and then asks if the user wants to erase flash memory before copying the file. The router then waits for a response.

9. The user presses Enter, taking the default action of erasing all the flash files.

10. The router asks if the user is sure about erasing flash memory, again asking the user to confirm.

11. The user presses Enter, taking the default action of erasing flash memory.

12. The router erases flash memory and then copies the file. Progress on the erasure of flash memory is shown by the router's displaying another *e* every few seconds, and progress on the copy is shown by displaying another ! every few seconds.

The best way to learn the process is to practice it using a real router, as suggested in the upcoming lab exercise. However, Example 5-4 does have one step that needs particular attention. The **copy tftp flash** command asks the user if the router should erase flash memory, with a default answer of "confirm," as shown in the example. In some cases, you need to erase flash before copying the file, particularly if there is not enough available space in flash for the new IOS file. However, if there is enough space in flash, you may not want to erase flash first. If that is the case, simply respond with **no** when answering this question.

You can also copy the IOS from flash memory to an external server. For instance, you may want to keep a copy of the IOS on a server just in case someone mistakenly erases flash. To make a copy of the IOS on a server, you can use the **copy flash tftp** command. As with the **copy tftp flash** command, IOS then prompts the user for the name or IP address of the server, the name of the (source) file in flash memory, and the name to use when storing the file on the TFTP server.

In a perfect world, network engineers would always be able to use the **copy** command as shown in this section to copy IOS files. However, when a router cannot load an IOS—for instance, flash memory has been erased—the engineer needs some way to copy a new IOS into flash memory. The next two sections describe how to copy IOS files into flash memory using two other tools, both of which use ROMMON mode.

 Lab 5.2.5   Managing IOS Images with TFTP

In this lab, you back up a copy of a router IOS from flash memory to a TFTP server.

Copying Using the ROMMON **tftpdnld** Command

When a router cannot load an IOS, it typically boots into ROMMON mode so that the engineer can recover from the problem. If the engineer decides to copy an IOS into flash memory as part of the solution to the problem, two options exist: the *tftpdnld* command (meaning "TFTP download"), or a feature called Xmodem, which is covered in the next section.

The ROMMON **tftpdnld** command can work only if the following conditions are met:

- The IP network is working well enough that the broken router can send IP packets to and from a TFTP server.

- The TFTP server has the appropriate IOS file available for download.

Because ROMMON is a very basic OS, you have to work a little harder to download an IOS using TFTP, as compared with the IOS **copy** command. The **tftpdnld** command does not prompt you for input as does the IOS **copy** command. Instead, you must define all the same information by setting environment variables. These variables supply the required information to the **tftpdnld** command. For example, if the TFTP server's IP address is 192.168.1.1, you first need to set the TFTP_SERVER environment variable by using the **TFTP_SERVER=192.168.1.1** command. Then, when you use the **tftpdnld** command, it uses 192.168.1.1 as the IP address of the TFTP server.

Besides setting the obvious parameters that are also used in the IOS **copy** command—settings such as the server IP address and filenames—you also need to set basic IP parameters in the router using environment variables. ROMMON does not understand any of the configuration in the startup-config file. ROMMON allows the router to act like an IP host, with an IP address, subnet mask, and default gateway. (ROMMON does not support the routing of IP packets or the use of any routing protocol, but it lets the router send and receive packets and use a default gateway.) Table 5-6 lists all the environment variables that need to be set to support a **tftpdnld** command from ROMMON.

Note

Although the IOS **copy** command supports FTP and RCP, the ROMMON **tftpdnld** command supports only TFTP.

Table 5-6   Environment Variables Needed for the **tftpdnld** Command

Environment Variable	Description
IP_ADDRESS	The IP address of the router's first LAN interface[1].
IP_SUBNET_MASK	The subnet mask used on the router's first LAN interface.
DEFAULT_GATEWAY	The IP address of the default gateway on the same LAN.
TFTP_SERVER	The IP address of the TFTP server.
TFTP_FILE	The full name of the file to download from the TFTP server. The name may include the directory structure.

[1] A router's first LAN interface is the LAN interface with the lowest interface number.

Setting and viewing the variables is relatively simple. To set a variable, just enter the variable name, an equals sign, and the value to which it should be set. The ROMMON **set** command displays the value of all ROMMON environment variables. When the environment variables have been set correctly, downloading a new IOS is relatively simple. Example 5-5 shows how to set the environment variables and then download a new IOS using **tftpdnld**.

The second half of the example shows the **tftpdnld** command. The command confirms that the

Example 5-5   Copying an IOS File from a TFTP Server Using ROMMON and **tftpdnld**

```
rommon 8>IP_ADDRESS=10.0.0.1
rommon 9>IP_SUBNET_MASK=255.255.255.0
rommon 10>DEFAULT_GATEWAY=10.0.0.254
rommon 11>TFTP_SERVER=192.168.1.1
rommon 12>TFTP_FILE=GAD/c2600-i-mz.121-5
rommon 13> set
IP_ADDRESS=10.0.0.1
IP_SUBNET_MASK=255.255.255.0
DEFAULT_GATEWAY=10.0.0.254
TFTP_SERVER=192.168.1.1
TFTP_FILE=GAD/c2600-i-mz.121-5

rommon 14 > tftpdnld
IP_ADDRESS: 10.0.0.1
IP_SUBNET_MASK: 255.255.255.0
DEFAULT_GATEWAY: 10.0.0.254
TFTP_SERVER: 192.168.1.1
TFTP_FILE: GAD/c2600-i-mz.121-5
Invoke this command for disaster recovery only.
WARNING: all existing data in all partitions on flash will be lost!
Do you wish to continue? y/n: [n]: y
```

Example 5-5   Copying an IOS File from a TFTP Server Using ROMMON
and **tftpdnld**   *continued*

```
Receiving GAD/original_2003_Jan_22/c2600-i-mz.121-5 from
192.168.1.1!!!!.!!!!!!!!!!!!!!!!!!!!.!!
File reception completed.
Copying file GAD/original_2003_Jan_22/c2600-i-mz.121-5 to flash.
Erasing flash at 0x607c0000
program flash location 0x60440000
rommon 15>
```

user wants to erase flash memory before proceeding. Assuming the user answers yes, the router erases flash memory and then copies the file into flash memory. The ROMMON **reset** command can then be used to reload the router, and, assuming the boot field is set to anything besides a hex 0, the router should boot the new IOS from flash memory. (If the boot field is set to 0, you can reset its value using the **confreg** ROMMON command.)

Copying Using ROMMON and Xmodem

Using *Xmodem* to copy a new IOS into a router's flash memory should be your last resort when trying to get an IOS to load into a Cisco router. The first option is to use the IOS **copy** command to copy the correct IOS into flash, assuming you can get some copy of IOS up and working. If the router cannot load an IOS directly, using ROMMON and the **tftpdnld** command is the next best option, but this option requires a working IP network and working TFTP server. The Xmodem option described here works when no IOS will load in the router and when there is no IP connectivity between the router and a TFTP server.

The Xmodem protocol defines a method to transfer files over an asynchronous serial line. Xmodem was first created to support transferring files over dialed links that used modems. Because the word "transfer" was frequently abbreviated as "xfer," Xmodem seemed like a good short name for a protocol for transferring files using modems and dialed serial links.

To transfer an IOS file into a router using the Xmodem protocol, you need three basic components:

- A router running ROMMON software so that the ROMMON **xmodem** command can be used

- A PC with the IOS file and a terminal emulator that supports Xmodem—for example, HyperTerminal

- A connection between a PC and the router that connects to the router's console or the aux ports

Figure 5-3 shows the basic setup for using Xmodem to transfer an IOS file from a PC into a router.

Figure 5-3   Components Required for Xmodem Transfer over the Console

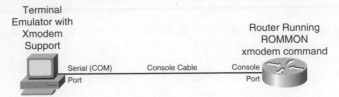

After you have all three components in place, transferring the file requires a few simple steps. Before actually transferring the file, though, consider the speed of the file transfer from the console. The default console speed is 9600 bps, which, when converted to bytes per second, is 1200 Bps. Most IOS files today—even those with a limited feature set—may be over 10 MB. So, imagine you need to transfer a 12-MB IOS file. To transfer 12,000,000 bytes at 1200 Bps, the theoretical best time would be 10,000 seconds, which is a little under 3 hours. So, transferring an IOS using Xmodem, with the default console speed, is a very slow process.

To speed up the process, you can change the speed of the console port up to its maximum speed of 115.2 kbps. To change the speed, you must change the value of the configuration register; to change the register from ROMMON, you need to use the ROMMON **confreg** command. The **confreg** command prompts the user with a series of questions. The answers to the questions tell ROMMON to what value the configuration register should be changed. As it turns out, the console speed can be changed by changing some of the bits in the configuration register, as shown in Example 5-6.

Example 5-6   Setting the Configuration Register from ROMMON

```
rommon 1 >confreg
Configuration Summary
!output omitted
console baud: 9600
boot: the ROM Monitor
do you wish to change the configuration? y/n [n]: y
enable "diagnostic mode"? y/n [n]:
!output omitted
enable "ignore system config info"? y/n [n]:
change console baud rate? y/n [n]: y
enter rate: 0 = 9600, 1 = 4800, 2 = 1200, 3 = 2400
4 = 19200, 5 = 38400, 6 = 57600, 7 = 115200 [0]: 7
change the boot characteristics? y/n [n]:
Configuration Summary
enabled are:
break/abort has effect
console baud: 115200
boot: the ROM Monitor
do you wish to change the configuration? y/n [n]:
rommon 2>
```

Example 5-6 focuses on how to set the console bit rate to a different value, but the command allows the user to change any of the bits in the configuration register. Note that the configuration register does not immediately change. It requires a reset or power off/on to take effect, just like when setting the configuration register using the IOS **config-register** command. Of particular importance, when you do reload the router, the console bit rate changes, so the terminal emulator settings also need to be changed to match the same speed—in this case, 115.2 kbps.

Regardless of the console speed, the transfer of the IOS file from the PC to the router's flash memory requires two basic steps:

Step 1   The engineer issues the ROMMON **xmodem** command to prepare the router to receive the file.

Step 2   The engineer tells the terminal emulator to send the file using Xmodem.

Example 5-7 shows the steps used by the **xmodem** command.

Example 5-7   A Router Preparing to Receive a File Using ROMMON's **xmodem** Command

```
rommon 2 > xmodem -c c2600-is-mz.122-10a.bin
Do not start the sending program yet...
Warning: All existing data in bootflash will be lost!
Invoke this application only for disaster recovery.
Do you wish to continue? y/n [n]: y
Ready to receive file c2600-is-mz.122-10a.bin ...
```

The **xmodem** command does not transfer the file; it just prepares ROMMON to receive the file. Note also that, as with **tftpdnld**, ROMMON erases the contents of flash, so the **xmodem** command prompts the user to make sure the user wants to erase flash.

Next, the engineer must tell the terminal emulator to send the file using Xmodem. These details of how to tell the emulator to send a file using Xmodem protocol differ depending on the terminal-emulator program. Figure 5-4 shows a sample image of a typical user interface. After you click the Send button, the Xmodem file transfer should take place, but the process of updating the IOS is not finished. Assuming the filenames were entered correctly, the PC should send the file, and the router should erase flash memory, store the file in flash, and display some messages to that effect. However, to get the router working again, you need to follow these steps:

Step 1   Use the **confreg** command to reset the configuration register to its original setting.

Step 2   Use the **reset** command to reload the router (or turn it off and then on).

Step 3   Change back the terminal-emulator configuration to use a speed of 9600 bps.

Figure 5-4   Starting an Xmodem File Transfer Using a Terminal Emulator

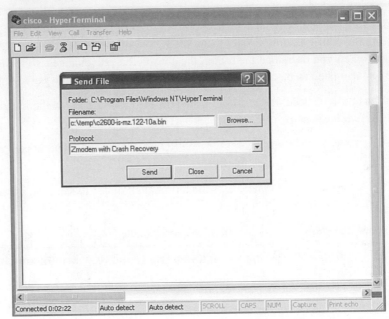

 Lab 5.2.6b   Managing IOS Images with ROMMON and Xmodem

In this lab, you recover a Cisco 1700 series router using ROM Monitor (ROMMON) (rommon >) due to a missing or corrupt IOS boot flash image.

Verifying Cisco IOS Images

This short section concludes this chapter's coverage of how routers move and manipulate IOS files by examining a few details on some important **show** commands and the information they give you about IOS files. The two main types of information you might want to find include the following:

- Information about the IOS that the router is currently using

- Information that determines what IOS images the router will attempt to load the next time it reboots

All the information can be found with the three commands listed in Table 5-7, which also lists the information shown by each.

Table 5-7   Important **show** Commands When Working with IOS Files

Command	Information Supplied
show version	IOS filename currently in use IOS version currently in use Location from which current IOS file was loaded Configuration register value—current and at next reload
show startup-config	Any **boot system** commands
show flash	The filenames, and file numbers, of the files in flash memory

The **show version** command lists most of the information relevant to examining IOS files. Example 5-8 shows an example of the output, with the items listed in Table 5-7 highlighted in the output.

Example 5-8   Key Items in the Output of the **show version** Command

```
R1#show version
Cisco IOS Software, C1700 Software (C1700-ADVIPSERVICESK9-M), Version 12.3(11)T3,
  RELEASE SOFTWARE (fc4)
Technical Support: http://www.cisco.com/techsupport
Copyright  1986-2005 by Cisco Systems, Inc.
Compiled Wed 26-Jan-05 09:19 by pwade


ROM: System Bootstrap, Version 12.2(4r)XL, RELEASE SOFTWARE (fc1)


R1 uptime is 1 minute
System returned to ROM by power-on
System image file is "flash:c1700-advipservicesk9-mz.123-11.T3.bin"


Cisco 1760 (MPC860P) processor (revision 0x200) with 91117K/7187K bytes of memory.
Processor board ID VMS06200J38 (2996972870), with hardware revision BB67
MPC860P processor: part number 5, mask 2
1 FastEthernet interface
2 Serial(sync/async) interfaces
2 Voice FXS interfaces
32K bytes of NVRAM.
32768K bytes of processor board System flash (Read/Write)

Configuration register is 0x2102
```

The remainder of this chapter covers a few details about router configuration files and router password recovery.

Copying and Managing Cisco IOS Configuration Files

Whereas most of this chapter focuses on IOS images, or IOS files, this section examines configuration files one last time. IOS includes two main configuration files:

- **startup-config**—Stored in NVRAM and holds the configuration that will be used the next time the router is reloaded

- **running-config**—Sits in RAM and holds the configuration commands currently being used in the router

The two files do not have to contain the same commands. In fact, when you configure new commands in configuration mode, IOS updates only the running-config file. So, after commands are configured in configuration mode, the two configuration files are different. Then, after the engineer uses the **copy running-config startup-config** command, the two files are again identical.

Figure 5-1 at the beginning of the chapter showed the three main methods of adding configuration commands to the running-config file: by a user from the CLI, from the startup-config file in NVRAM when the router initializes, and from a TFTP server. This section takes a close look at two of these methods:

- Using the **copy tftp** command
- Using a PC's copy-and-paste function

Copying the configuration to a computer allows the engineer to keep backup copies of the configuration. Copying the configuration into the running-config file may give the engineer a more convenient method for typing and adding configuration commands to routers.

Copying Configuration Files Using the IOS **copy** Command

The process of copying configuration files between a router and a TFTP server is covered in both Chapter 3 (in the section "Using TFTP to Back Up a Configuration") and in this chapter. The process requires that you use either the **copy tftp running-config** command, which copies the file from the server into the running-config file, or the **copy running-config tftp** command, which copies the file from the router's running-config file to the TFTP server. With both commands, you follow the same basic processs:

Step 1   Enter either the **copy tftp running-config** or **copy running-config tftp** command, and press Enter.

Step 2   Respond to the prompt with the IP address or hostname of the TFTP server, and press Enter.

Step 3   Respond to the next prompt with the filename to be used on the TFTP server, and press Enter.

Step 4   Respond to the third prompt by simply pressing Enter to confirm that you want to transfer the file.

Example 5-9 shows two examples of this four-step process, one copying a file out of the router, and one copying a file into the router.

Example 5-9   Copying to and from a TFTP Server

```
! First, the running-config is copied to the TFTP server
R1#copy running-config tftp
Address or name of remote host []? 172.16.2.1
Destination filename [R1-confg]?
Write file R1-confg to 172.16.2.1 ? [confirm]:
Writing R1-confg  !!!  [OK - 880 bytes]
880 bytes copied in 0.869 secs (1013 bytes/sec)
R1#
! Next, the file is copied from the TFTP server back to R1's running-config
R1#copy tftp running-config
Address or name of remote host []? 172.16.2.1
Source filename []? R1-confg
Destination filename [running-config]?
Accessing tftp://172.16.2.1/R1-confg...
Loading R1-confg from 172.16.2.1 (via Serial0/0): !
[OK - 880 bytes]
880 bytes copied in 0.869 secs (1013 bytes/sec)
R1#
```

Lab 5.2.3   Managing Configuration Files with TFTP

In this lab, you back up a copy of a router configuration file and reload the backup configuration file from a TFTP server into RAM on a router.

Copying Configuration Files Using Copy and Paste

Most Windows-based applications have a copy-and-paste feature that makes it easy to duplicate text between applications. Because configuration files are all text-based, they can be copied and pasted as well. This section covers a couple of variations on how a network engineer may take advantage of the copy-and-paste feature of a PC to copy configuration commands to and from the running-config file in a router. The first method simply uses a text-editor window and a terminal-emulator window, copying the text between the two. The second method uses some text-capture and text-sending features typically included in most terminal emulators.

Copy and Paste Between the Emulator and a Text Editor

Every PC OS supports a variety of applications called text editors. All of these applications allow the user to enter text into the editor, change the text, and save the file in an aptly named text file. Some of these text editors, such as Notepad on Microsoft OSs, are relatively simple, and others, such as Microsoft Word, are very sophisticated. For the purpose of copying the configuration to and from a router, a simple text editor such as Notepad will work just fine.

An engineer can use Notepad (or any other editor) to enter configuration commands. Then, she can select and copy the text, as shown in Figure 5-5. After that, the PC is ready to paste the text into another window. Figure 5-5 shows a window from a PC, with the Notepad editor. The user has entered four configuration commands, selected the text, and is ready to select the Copy function on the Edit menu.

Note

More sophisticated word processor applications, such as Microsoft Word, add hidden formatting characters to the files. Using a simple text editor such as Notepad can avoid some of the problems associated with the additional formatting characters.

Figure 5-5   Entering Commands into a Text Editor and Copying the Command Text

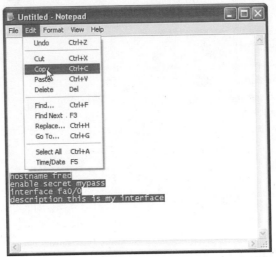

When the PC has a copy of the text that was shown in the text-editor screen, the user can paste the text into another window. Assuming that the engineer wants to add the configuration commands to a router's configuration, she must log in to the router using a terminal emulator, *from that same PC*, and get into configuration mode. When in configuration mode, the engineer can use the Paste feature of the OS, which sends the text to the chosen window—in this case, the terminal emulator. Pasting the text into the window works just like someone typing the exact same text into the window. In this case, the commands are added straight into configuration mode. Figure 5-6 shows the results, with the four commands being pasted into the terminal-emulator window as if the user just typed them.

Figure 5-6   Pasting Text into a Terminal-Emulator Window

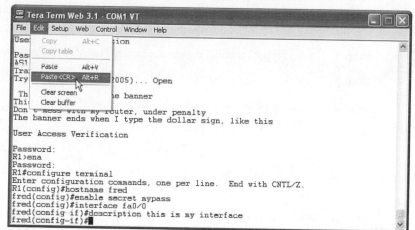

Note

Figure 5-6 shows that the text has already been pasted, but it also shows the menu item that the user chose to paste the text.

Using copy and paste as shown in Figure 5-5 and Figure 5-6 may not seem to be worth the effort, and it may not be for such a small number of configuration commands. However, when configuring the same commands on many routers, the engineer can enter the commands into an editor on the PC and then copy and paste the commands into several routers' configurations, saving time and effort. Engineers can also copy from the terminal-emulator window and paste the text into the text editor to make backup copies of the configuration. In fact, when performing labs during class, you can easily copy and paste from the terminal emulator into an editor such as Notepad and then save the file on your PC for later reference.

Note

The copy-and-paste function can be helpful when copying IOS files by copying and pasting the long IOS filenames into the terminal-emulator window, which helps avoid typos.

Using a Terminal Emulator's Text Capture Feature

Additionally, the online course describes a variation of the copy-and-paste process that uses a feature of most terminal emulators. Most terminal emulators have a feature by which you can tell the emulator to capture all text displayed by the emulator and then put the text into a text file. Emulators also typically have a feature by which you can tell the emulator to take the content of a text file and send it into the window as if you had entered all the text in the file into that window.

These two features together allow network engineers to use a simple three-step process to back up the configurations of routers:

Step 1   Use the emulator's text-capture feature to capture the output of a **show running-config** or **show startup-config** command.

Step 2   Because the capture process may capture extraneous characters or other unneeded text, edit the file to prepare it to be used as a backup configuration file.

Step 3   Should the router ever lose its configuration, use the emulator's "send text file" feature to send the contents of the backup configuration file back to the router and into configuration mode.

For Step 1, you need to use the emulator's text-capture feature to capture the output of a **show running-config** command. The following list describes how to use the text-capture feature of the popular HyperTerminal emulator to make a backup copy of the running-config file:

Step 1   In the HyperTerminal window, choose **Transfer > Capture Text**.

Step 2   Specify the name for the text file to the capture configuration.

Step 3   Click the **Start** button to start capturing text.

Step 4   Display the configuration to the screen by entering **show running-config**.

Step 5   Press the **Spacebar** when each --More-- prompt appears, which continues with the configuration until the end is reached.

Step 6   When the complete configuration has been displayed, stop the capture by choosing **Transfer > Capture Text > Stop**, as shown in Figure 5-7.

Note that in Figure 5-7, the user has already started the text capture, so the menu shows only an option to stop the current capture. If no text capture were currently in progress, the menu would list a Start option instead.

Figure 5-7   Stopping the HyperTerminal Text-Capture Feature

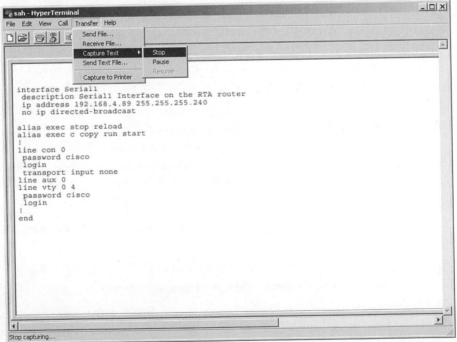

One of the main reasons for making a copy of the configuration file is to be able to paste the configuration back into the router if its configuration is erased. However, the text captured in Step 1 typically needs to be edited to make it ready to be pasted back into the router on the fateful day that the configuration is lost. The captured text file may have items that are not needed when pasting the configuration back into the router. For example, the **show running-config** command itself is not needed. To remove the extra text, you can edit the file with a tool such as Notepad.

To edit the file from Notepad, complete the following steps:

Step 1   Open the Notepad application. (On Microsoft OSs, go to **Start > Run**, enter **notepad**, and click **OK**).

Step 2 Select **File > Open**.

Step 3   Find the captured file and select it.

Step 4   Click **Open**.

The following types of lines typically need to be deleted to be ready to paste the configuration back into the router:

```
show running-config
Building configuration...
Current configuration:
- More -
Any lines that appear after the word End
```

You can also add commands to the backup configuration file. For example, many people add comment lines to document the configuration. When they are pasted back into the router, the router ignores and discards the comment lines, but they are useful when reviewing the file on your PC. To add a comment line, simply add a new line to the file, with the first character being an exclamation mark (!). Additionally, you may also want to add the **no shutdown** command under each interface so that when the configuration is pasted back into the router, the router attempts to bring up each interface. Finally, don't forget to save the file. With Notepad, choose **File > Save**.

That last step occurs when you want to add the configuration back into the router. You can then restore the backup configuration from a HyperTerminal session by using the text-transfer feature. The following steps detail the process:

Step 1   Log in to the router using HyperTerminal.

Step 2   Go into router global configuration mode.

Step 3   From the HyperTerminal window, choose **Transfer > Send Text File**.

Step 4   Select the name of the file for the saved backup configuration.

Step 5   The lines of the file are entered into the router as if they are being typed. Look for any errors.

Step 6   After the configuration is entered, press Ctrl-Z to exit global configuration mode.

Step 7   Restore the startup configuration with **copy running-config startup-config**.

This process can also be very useful in the classroom labs. For example, when starting a new lab, you might first use the command **erase startup-config** at the enable router prompt and then restart the router by entering **reload**. Then, the router comes up with no configuration, after which you could use this process to reconfigure the router based on a configuration file you have saved on your PC.

You should be aware of one last important point about pasting configurations back into a router, regardless of which method you use. If the configurations were originally copied when the router was working, the configuration does not include any **no shutdown** commands on the interfaces, because IOS considers **no shutdown** to be the default. So, if an interface currently happens to have a **shutdown** command configured, pasting the configuration back into the router will not bring the interface out of the shutdown (administratively disabled) state. So, after pasting the configuration back into a router, be sure to look at the interface status of each interface, and use the **no shutdown** command as needed to bring the interfaces back up.

Recovering from Lost Passwords

This final section of the chapter covers an important topic in real life. If you forget the **console**, **telnet**, and **enable** passwords on a router, you need to find a way to get back into the router and reset or recover the passwords. Lab 5.2.6A in the online curriculum describes how to reset lost passwords. This section briefly introduces the concept of password reset, or password recovery, but it is very useful to perform the lab in class and practice the password recovery process.

The password recovery process requires the engineer to reboot the router and tell it to ignore the configuration in NVRAM. If the router manages to boot without using the configuration in NVRAM, the router will not have any passwords configured. In fact, the router will have nothing configured. From that point, the engineer can log in from the console and get into enable mode, and the router will not request a password. Then the engineer can reconfigure new passwords or display any unencrypted passwords using the **show startup-config** command. The overall password recovery process runs like this:

Step 1   Connect to the console of the router.

Step 2   Reload the router (or turn it off and back on).

Step 3   Press the **Break** key on the keyboard in the first 30 seconds of the reload.

Step 4   When the router responds by entering ROMMON mode, change the configuration register (with the **confreg** ROMMON command) to tell the router to ignore the startup-config file. (Typically, that means setting the configuration register's third octet to 4—for example, 0x2142.)

Step 5   Reload the router (typically using the **reset** ROMMON command)

Step 6   When the router has completed booting, log in to the router from the console, and enter enable mode.

Step 7   Use the **copy startup-config running-config** command to load the configuration into the router.

Step 8   Enter configuration mode, and reconfigure new passwords.

This list does not include every detail, but it does give the overall flow of the process used on most every model of Cisco router. The details of the password recovery process differ slightly from router model to router model. If you go to Cisco.com and use the search tool to search for "password," the first reference listed is typically a web page that includes password recovery procedures for most every model of Cisco product, including routers and switches. This is a helpful web page to bookmark if you will be working with Cisco products on a regular basis.

Caution

The password recovery process requires the user to connect to the console; for this reason alone, routers and switches should be kept in a locked room to prevent unauthorized access.

Lab 5.2.6A   Password Recovery Procedures

In this lab, you gain access to a router with an unknown privileged mode (enable) password.

Summary

A Cisco router chooses the location from which it should load a stored copy of an IOS image based on several rules. In most cases, engineers set up a hierarchy of choices, first making a router attempt to load an IOS from flash memory; if that fails, the router attempts to load an IOS from a TFTP server; and if that fails, the router may have to load a limited-function OS such as ROMMON or RXBoot. The engineer can control this process by changing the boot field of the configuration register (the last 4 bits, or last hex digit) using the **config-register** command, and by configuring **boot system** commands.

Under normal conditions, a router engineer configures the router so that the router firsts looks for **boot system** commands in the startup-config file. If multiple **boot system** commands exist, the router attempts each command, in order, until it manages to successfully load an IOS. If all the **boot system** commands fail, the router then attempts to load the first file found in flash memory.

To troubleshoot the boot process, you should look at the **boot system** commands in the startup-config file by using the **show startup-config** command. Additionally, you should look at the configuration register's value as listed at the end of the **show version** command output. Note that the configuration register value changes only when the router is reloaded.

Cisco creates the filenames of IOS files with four parts:

- The hardware platform
- A code that represents the feature set
- A code that represents the file format
- The version and release number

Note that the version and release numbers increase as Cisco modifies and changes the IOS over time.

Cisco routers use two internal configuration files: the startup-config file and the running-config file. The startup-config file is stored in NVRAM and is copied into RAM to be used as the running-config file when the router is reloaded. The running-config file resides in RAM and is the configuration file currently used by the router. The files may be different at times, because configuration changes made in configuration mode modify only the running-config file. However, in practice, most people then save the running-config file using the **copy running-config startup-config** command, so the files end up being identical.

It is useful and important to keep a backup copy of the configuration files on an external device. The **copy running-config tftp** command can be used to copy the configuration to an external TFTP server. Additionally, you can use a text editor's simple copy-and-paste mechanisms when logged in to a router to copy the output of a **show running-config** command into a file. Additionally, most terminal emulators support the ability to perform a text-capture function, which causes the emulator to copy everything sent to the screen into a text file. So, the engineer could enable the text-capture feature and then issue a **show running-config** command to make a backup copy of the configuration.

Check Your Understanding

Complete all the review questions listed here to test your understanding of the topics and concepts in this chapter. Answers are listed in Appendix A, "Answers to Check Your Understanding and Challenge Questions."

1. Which of the following is *not* a boot option that can be set with the **boot system** command?

   A. Cisco IOS Software will boot in ROM monitor mode.

   B. Cisco IOS Software will automatically boot from flash memory.

   C. Cisco IOS Software will automatically boot from a TFTP server.

   D. Cisco IOS Software will automatically boot from a previous IOS image.

2. Which of the following are information displayed by the **show version** command? (Choose two.)

   A. Detailed statistics about each page of the router's memory

   B. The name of the system image and its location

   C. The names and sizes of all files in flash memory

   D. The status of configured network protocols

   E. The router platform and router uptime

3. Which command is used to discover the configuration register setting?

   A. **show register**

   B. **show running-config**

   C. **show version**

   D. **show startup-config**

4. What information is not implied by the Cisco image filename system?

   A. The capabilities of the image

   B. The platform on which the image runs

   C. Where the image runs

   D. The size of the image

5. Which of the following is the first step of the recommended procedure for loading a new Cisco IOS Software image to flash memory from a TFTP server?

   A. Enter the **copy start run** command to start downloading the new image from the server.

   B. Erase flash memory.

   C. Back up a copy of the current software image to the TFTP server.

   D. Enter the **copy tftp flash** command to start downloading the new image from the server.

6. What is the first location in which a newer 2600 series router looks for an IOS if the router configuration register is set to 0x2101?

   A. Setup mode

   B. TFTP server

   C. ROM

   D. Flash memory

7. Which of the following has a limited version of router Cisco IOS Software?

   A. ROM

   B. Flash memory

   C. TFTP server

   D. Bootstrap

8. Which answer best characterizes how a router looks for an IOS if the router configuration register is set to 0x2102?

   A. The first file in Flash memory

   B. TFTP server

   C. ROM

   D. The startup-config file, to check for **boot system** commands

9. Which of the following is the default sequence used by the router to locate the Cisco IOS?

   A. Flash memory, NVRAM, TFTP server

   B. NVRAM, TFTP server, flash memory

   C. NVRAM, flash memory, TFTP server

   D. Flash memory, TFTP server, ROM

10. Which of the following is not displayed by the Cisco IOS **show version** command?

   A. Statistics for configured interfaces

   B. The type of platform running the Cisco IOS Software

   C. The configuration register setting

   D. The Cisco IOS Software version

11. Which of the following statements are true regarding Xmodem? (Choose two.)

   A. Xmodem is the fastest way to load an IOS.

   B. Xmodem is run through Fast Ethernet interfaces using crossover cables.

   C. Xmodem is an option when there is no IP connectivity.

   D. An IOS can be loaded via the console or aux ports using Xmodem.

12. Why is it important to create a Cisco IOS Software image backup?

   A. To verify that the copy in flash memory is the same as the copy in ROM

   B. To provide a backup copy of the current image before copying the image to a new
       router

   C. To create a backup copy of the current image so that the RXBoot program runs easily if
       there is a problem

   D. To create a backup copy of the current image before updating with a new version

13. Which command is issued to upgrade an old version of the Cisco IOS Software by down-
       loading a new image from the TFTP server?

   A. **boot system tftp 131.21.11.3**

   B. **copy tftp flash**

   C. **show flash**

   D. **tftp ios.exe**

Challenge Questions and Activities

These questions require a deeper application of the concepts covered in this chapter or are similar to the style of questions you might see on a CCNA certification exam. Appendix A lists the answers.

1. An engineer has completed the required information in support of the **tftpdnld** command and then enters the **set** command. Which of the following is an example of the output of the **set** command?

    A.
    ```
    IP_ADDRESS=10.0.0.1
    IP_SUBNET_MASK=255.255.255.0
    DEFAULT_GATEWAY=10.0.0.254
    TFTP_SERVER=192.168.1.1
    TFTP_FILE=c1700-bnsy-1.122-11.p
    ```

    B.
    ```
    IP_ADDRESS-10.0.0.1
    HOST_ADDRESS-255.255.255.0
    DEFAULT_GATEWAY-10.0.0.254
    GATEWAY_MASK-255.0.0.
    TFTP_FILE-c1700-bnsy-1.122-11.p
    ```

    C.
    ```
    IP_ADDRESS=10.0.0.1
    USER_HOST_ADDRESS=255.255.255.0
    DEFAULT_GATEWAY=10.0.0.254
    DNS_SERVER=192.168.1.1
    TFTP_FILE=c1700-bnsy-1.122-11.p
    ```

    D.
    ```
    IP ADDRESS= 10.0.0.1
    IP SUBNET MASK= 255.255.255.0
    DEFAULT GATEWAY= 10.0.0.254
    TFTP SERVER= 192.168.1.1
    TFTP FILE= c1700-bnsy-1.122-11.p
    ```

2. When upgrading the IOS image on a router, an engineer enters the **show flash** command. The output follows:

    ```
    Router# show flash
    903848 bytes of flash memory on embedded flash (in XX).
    file  offset  length  name
    0     0x40    1204637 xk09140z
    [903848/2097152 bytes free]
    ```

If the new image is 7.2 MB in size, what will happen if the upgrade is attempted?

A. The upgrade will fail because there is not enough room in flash memory for the new image.

B. The upgrade will succeed without the current image having to be erased.

C. The upgrade is possible, but the current image must be erased.

D. There is not enough information to answer this question without also entering the **show version** command.

CHAPTER 6

Routing and Routing Protocols

Objectives

Upon completion of this chapter, you should be able to answer the following questions:

- What is the purpose of static routing?

- How are static and default routes configured?

- What methods can be used to troubleshoot static and default route configurations?

- What is the difference between static and dynamic routing?

- What are the main classes of routing protocols?

- What are distance vector routing protocols?

- What are link-state routing protocols?

- What are Interior Gateway Protocols (IGPs)?

- What are Exterior Gateway Protocols (EGPs)?

- How is the Routing Information Protocol (RIP) enabled?

Key Terms

This chapter uses the following key terms. You can find the definitions in the Glossary.

This chapter covers some of the most important topics in networking today. As introduced in Module 10 of the Networking Basics CCNA 1 course, routers forward (route) IP packets so that the packets reach the correct destination host. To route packets, routers must have routes in their IP routing tables. Each entry in a router's IP *routing table* has important information, including the following vital information:

- The destination subnet (subnet number and subnet mask)

- Directions that tell the router to what other router or host to send the packet next (outgoing interface and next-hop router)

In effect, *routing* works a little like someone driving a car. For example, imagine someone needs to drive to Smallville, and she approaches an intersection that has a road sign that says "Smallville." Next to "Smallville," the sign has a right-pointing arrow, and maybe a road number, such as "Highway 3," telling her to turn right at Highway 3. Similarly, you can think of a packet arriving at a router as a car approaching an intersection. The router's routing table is analogous to the road sign, listing the possible destinations, and which road to take at the intersection to reach that destination. The router actually decides where to forward the packet based on the routing table, so the analogy breaks down a bit at that point, but at the end of the process, the router has forwarded the packet out the next link, getting the packet one step closer to the final destination.

Routers must have routes in their routing tables for routers to forward, or route, packets. This chapter focuses on two of the three general methods by which a router can add these IP routes to its IP routing table. The three methods, as introduced in Module 10 of the CCNA 1 course, are as follows:

- **Connected routes**—Adding a route to locally connected subnets when a router's interface reaches an "up and up" state

- *Static routes*—Adding a route due to the engineer adding an **ip route** command to the router's configuration

- *Dynamic routing protocols*—Adding routes using routing protocols, which cause routers to dynamically exchange routing information with other routers

The first section of this chapter provides a thorough explanation of static routes. The second section of this chapter explains some of the theory regarding routing protocols. The third section covers the basic features of the most popular IP routing protocols, including basic configuration details for the Routing Information Protocol (RIP).

Introduction to Static and Connected IP Routes

Each router learns about the subnets directly connected to it for each interface that is both configured with an IP address and is up and working. Additionally, most routers learn the vast majority of IP routes using a dynamic routing protocol. However, many engineers find it useful to statically configure some IP routes. This section covers the details of how to configure these static routes and gives a couple of examples of cases in which engineers typically want to use static routes.

Before getting into static routes, the following section reviews the concept of connected routes, as first introduced in Module 10 of the CCNA 1 course (and Chapter 10 of *Networking Basics CCNA 1 Companion Guide*).

Learning Connected Routes

Subnets to which a router's interfaces are connected are called *connected subnets*. Routers automatically add routes to their IP routing tables for directly connected subnets, called ***directly connected routes***. A router adds a directly connected route for each interface that has been configured with an IP address, and is up and working.

For example, Figure 6-1 shows a sample internetwork, with the IP routing tables of R1 and R2. The *routing tables* contain connected IP routes only at this point.

Figure 6-1   Connected Routes Only, on R1 and R2

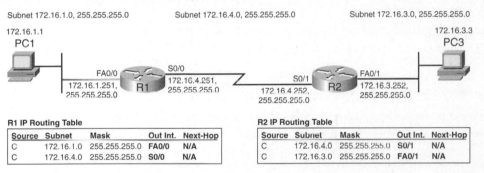

> **Note**
>
> A router's routing table lists all IP networks and subnets known by the router, and directions about the interface out which the router should forward packets destined for those networks and subnets.

Figure 6-1 shows a conceptual view of the IP routing tables in R1 and R2. The fields in the routing table need some explanation, mainly because the focus of this section is how to add entries to this table. Keep in mind that the routers were able to learn the entries in each table only because the routers are connected to these IP subnets. The following fields make up the table:

- **Source**—This column refers to how the router learned the route—in other words, the source of the routing information. *C* is shorthand for "connected."

- **Subnet/Mask**—These two fields together define a set of IP addresses, either an IP network or IP subnet. When routing packets, routers compare the destination IP address of packets to this field in each route in the routing table, looking to find the matching route.

- **Out Int.**—The abbreviation for "output interface" or "outgoing interface," this field tells the router out of which interface to send packets that match this route.

- **Next-Hop**—Short for ***next-hop router***, this field is meaningless for routes to connected subnets. For routes in which the packet is forwarded to another router, this field lists the IP address of the router to which this router should forward the packet.

Although every working router learns some connected routes, they do not always use static routes. The next section describes the mechanics of how to create static routes, and reasons why network engineers sometimes use static routes.

Static Routes

A static route is simply a route that is added using a configuration command in a router. After it is configured, IOS adds the route, including details such as the subnet number, mask, output interface, and next-hop router, into a new entry in that router's IP routing table. After it is added, the router can then route packets whose destination IP address matches the static route.

Engineers use static routes for several reasons. They could configure static routes for all routes in any internetwork, but typically it is not worth the effort. However, static routes can be very useful in several cases, including the following:

- The internetwork is small, may seldom change, or has no redundant links.

- The routers need to use dial backup to dynamically call another router when a leased line fails.

- An enterprise internetwork has many small branch offices, each with only one possible path to reach the rest of the internetwork.

- An enterprise wants to forward packets to hosts in the Internet, not to hosts in the enterprise network.

This section shows how to configure static routes, including static default routes, and provides samples of each of these four typical reasons for using static routes. Along the way, you learn about the basic mechanics of configuring and verifying static routes.

Configuring Static Routes in a Small, Nonredundant Network

In a small internetwork that has no redundancy and seldom changes, the network engineer may simply choose to configure static routes and not bother with an IP routing protocol. Frankly, most engineers would still choose to use a dynamic routing protocol even in a small internetwork, but such an internetwork provides a good example for showing the mechanics of configuring static routes with the **ip route** global configuration command.

This section shows how to configure two static routes in the internetwork shown earlier in Figure 6-1 and repeated here as Figure 6-2. Figure 6-2 shows the two missing routes that need to be added, one on each router, so that both R1 and R2 know how to reach each of the three subnets in the internetwork.

Figure 6-2   Each Router Needs One More Route to Know All Routes

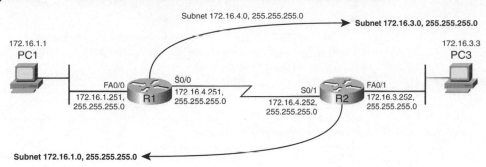

The internetwork has three subnets: 172.16.1.0, 172.16.4.0, and 172.16.3.0, all with masks of 255.255.255.0. Both routers know how to reach two of the subnets, as shown in Figure 6-1. So, each router needs a route to reach the remaining subnet, respectively, as shown in Figure 6-2.

Cisco IOS supports two main styles of configuring static routes using the **ip route** global configuration command. First, when point-to-point topologies such as leased lines are used, the command can simply refer to the outgoing interface. Example 6-1 shows how R1 can add a static route to reach subnet 172.16.3.0/24.

Example 6-1   R1: Configuring a Static Route Using the Outgoing Interface

```
R1#show ip route
Codes: C - connected, S - static, R - RIP, M - mobile, B - BGP
       D - EIGRP, EX - EIGRP external, O - OSPF, IA - OSPF inter area
       N1 - OSPF NSSA external type 1, N2 - OSPF NSSA external type 2
       E1 - OSPF external type 1, E2 - OSPF external type 2
       i - IS-IS, su - IS-IS summary, L1 - IS-IS level-1, L2 - IS-IS level-2
       ia - IS-IS inter area, * - candidate default, U - per-user static route
       o - ODR, P - periodic downloaded static route
Gateway of last resort is not set


     172.16.0.0/24 is subnetted, 2 subnets
C       172.16.4.0 is directly connected, Serial0/0
C       172.16.1.0 is directly connected, FastEthernet0/0

R1#configure terminal
Enter configuration commands, one per line.  End with CNTL/Z.
R1(config)#ip route 172.16.3.0 255.255.255.0 serial 0/0
R1(config)#^Z
R1#show ip route
Codes: C - connected, S - static, R - RIP, M - mobile, B - BGP
       D - EIGRP, EX - EIGRP external, O - OSPF, IA - OSPF inter area
       N1 - OSPF NSSA external type 1, N2 - OSPF NSSA external type 2
```

continues

Example 6-1   R1: Configuring a Static Route Using Outgoing Interface   *continued*

```
        E1 - OSPF external type 1, E2 - OSPF external type 2
        i - IS-IS, su - IS-IS summary, L1 - IS-IS level-1, L2 - IS-IS level-2
        ia - IS-IS inter area, * - candidate default, U - per-user static route
        o - ODR, P - periodic downloaded static route
Gateway of last resort is not set


     172.16.0.0/24 is subnetted, 3 subnets
C       172.16.4.0 is directly connected, Serial0/0
C       172.16.1.0 is directly connected, FastEthernet0/0
S       172.16.3.0 is directly connected, Serial0/0
```

The details in the **ip route** command are relatively straightforward, but the output of the **show ip route** command has a few surprises. The top of Example 6-1 shows R1's routing table before the static route is added, so R1 has its two connected routes only, as discussed with Figure 6-1. Next, the engineer adds the static route using the **ip route** command. This command simply lists the destination subnet, including the mask, because both numbers must be known to truly know which IP addresses are in a subnet. Then, the command lists the interface that R1 should use to forward packets to subnet 172.16.3.0—namely, R1's S0/0 interface.

Note

When a single classful IP network uses only one subnet mask, the **show ip route** command lists that single mask, in prefix notation, as shown in Example 6-1.

The **show ip route** command now lists the new static route (on the last line in Example 6-1). The subnet number and outgoing interface are both listed, but the mask is hidden three lines above, as /24. The /24 is *prefix notation*, which lists the number of network and subnet bits used in the structure of the IP subnet. For example, /24 means the listed subnet has 24 network and subnet bits; in other words, it is using a mask of 255.255.255.0. Finally, note the code on the left side of the last line—S. According to the legend at the top of the output of the **show ip route** command, it means that this route is a statically configured route.

Example 6-2 shows the other style of configuring the **ip route** command. This style can be used in all topologies, whereas the style shown in Example 6-1—with the **ip route** command referencing the outgoing interface—can be used only when point-to-point topologies are used. With this style, the next-hop router's IP address is configured, and the router figures out the outgoing interface. Example 6-2 shows the static route for subnet 172.16.1.0/24 as configured on router R2.

The configuration and IP routing table entry in Example 6-2 are relatively straightforward, but the mechanics of how R2 will use this route may not be obvious at first glance. R2 should forward packets destined for subnet 172.16.1.0/24—for instance, a packet sent to 172.16.1.1—out R2's S0/1 interface toward R1. When such a packet arrives at R2, the packet matches R2's static route. R2 wants to send the packet to 172.16.4.251 next, so it figures out which of its interfaces is on the same subnet as 172.16.4.251. In this case, R2's S0/1 interface, with IP address 172.16.4.252, is on the same subnet as next-hop router 172.16.4.251, so R2 sends the packet out its S0/1 interface.

Example 6-2   R2: Configuring a Static Route Using the Next-Hop IP Address

```
R2#conf t
Enter configuration commands, one per line.  End with CNTL/Z.
R2(config)#ip route 172.16.1.0 255.255.255.0 172.16.4.251
R2(config)#^Z
R2#show ip route
Codes: C - connected, S - static, R - RIP, M - mobile, B - BGP
       D - EIGRP, EX - EIGRP external, O - OSPF, IA - OSPF inter area
       N1 - OSPF NSSA external type 1, N2 - OSPF NSSA external type 2
       E1   OSPF external type 1, E2 - OSPF external type 2
       i - IS-IS, su - IS-IS summary, L1 - IS-IS level-1, L2 - IS-IS level-2
       ia - IS-IS inter area, * - candidate default, U - per-user static route
       o - ODR, P - periodic downloaded static route
Gateway of last resort is not set


     172.16.0.0/24 is subnetted, 3 subnets
C       172.16.4.0 is directly connected, Serial0/1
S       172.16.1.0 [1/0] via 172.16.4.251
C       172.16.3.0 is directly connected, FastEthernet0/0
```

Using Static Routes for Dial Backup Using Administrative Distance

One of the most popular reasons for configuring static routes occurs when a router is configured to use dial backup. As it turns out, dial backup configuration also requires you to consider a concept called *administrative distance*. This section covers the basics of dial backup to give you some insights into one of the most popular reasons to use static routes and to provide a good backdrop from which to think about administrative distance.

This section explains details of dial backup not covered in the online curriculum. The curriculum focuses on the concept of administrative distance and how a static route can be assigned an administrative distance to make the router use the route only when the same subnet is not learned by a routing protocol. Depending on the goals of your particular class, this section may be considered optional.

Dial Backup Basics

Dial backup provides a way for a router to use some permanent WAN services, such as a leased line, but when that leased line fails, the router can use the telephone network and replace the failed WAN link. Most often today, the link would use *Integrated Services Digital Network (ISDN)* services, oftentimes an ISDN *Basic Rate Interface (BRI)* line. Figure 6-3 shows the basic idea.

Figure 6-3   Conceptual View of Using ISDN Dial Backup

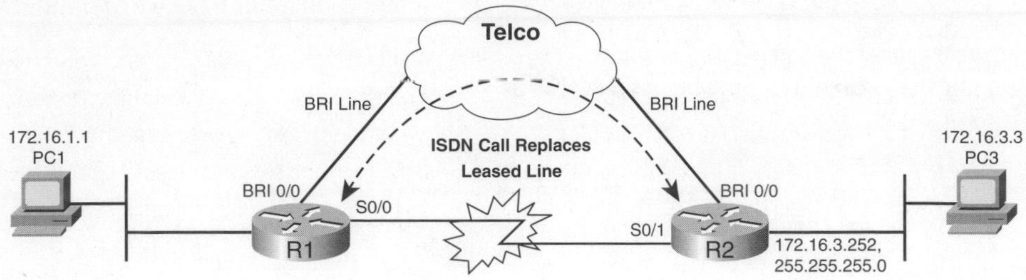

Figure 6-3 shows each router with an ISDN BRI interface, connected to an ISDN line. You can think of an ISDN line as being similar to a local telephone line, except that it supports digital data at speeds up to 128 kbps. Just as you can pick up your home phone and call someone, the routers can now do the equivalent with a BRI line: one router calls the other router, and the two routers can forward packets to each other.

Note

The complete coverage of dial backup and ISDN BRI configuration is in Chapter 4, "ISDN and DDR," in *WAN Technologies CNAP 4 Companion Guide*.

The routers in Figure 6-3 use the leased line normally, with the ISDN BRI lines sitting idle. While the leased line is up, the routers can learn routes using a routing protocol such as RIP. However, when the leased line fails (as shown in Figure 6-3), the routers lose all their RIP-learned routes. For example, R1 learns a route to 172.16.3.0/24 using RIP, but when the leased line fails, R1 also loses its RIP-learned route for 172.16.3.0/24. At that point, the routers use dial backup to react and make an ISDN call so that they can still send packets to one another.

Administrative Distance on Static Routes

You may find this explanation of dial backup to be fascinating, but you may also wonder what all this has to do with static routes. As it turns out, dial backup configuration uses static routes. Although this book does not cover all the details of dial backup configuration, the need for static routes becomes obvious if you consider the following facts, especially the third point in this list:

- When the leased line is up, the routers learn routes using a dynamic routing protocol.

- When the leased line fails, the routers also lose the routes learned by the dynamic routing protocol.

- Before dial backup dials an ISDN call, at least one router must try to route a packet out its BRI interface.

- A router needs a static route to be configured, referencing the BRI interface as the outgoing interface, to try to route a packet out its BRI interface.

In short, some styles of dial backup configuration require a static route, and these static routes tell a router to try to route the packets out a BRI interface. For example, R1's configuration might include a command like this:

```
ip route 172.16.3.0 255.255.255.0 bri0/0
```

This command solves one problem for dial backup configuration, because now packets destined for the LAN subnet on the right—subnet 172.16.3.0/24—are routed out R1's BRI0/0 interface.

However, this command creates yet another problem: which route does R1 use when the leased line is up? R1 will have a static route that references interface BRI0/0, and a RIP-learned route that references R1's S0/0 interface, so which is better? By design, the engineer wants to route packets over the leased line when it is working and use the (probably slower) ISDN lines only when the leased line fails. As it turns out, with the **ip route** command shown previously, R1 would use the static route instead of the RIP-learned route, therefore always using the dialed call over the BRI interface, all due to the concept of administrative distance.

The administrative distance of a route tells a router which route to use when the router learns the same route via multiple methods. For example, when the leased line is working, R1 learns a RIP route for 172.16.3.0/24, and it has the static route that references interface BRI0/0. In such cases, the router uses the route with the *lowest* administrative distance. RIP-learned routes have an administrative distance of 120 by default, and static routes have an administrative distance of either 0 or 1 by default. For instance, if the **ip route 172.16.3.0 255.255.255.0 bri0/0** command is configured, it has a lower administrative distance than the RIP-learned route, and R1 uses the static route.

An engineer can set a static route's administrative distance on the **ip route** command. For instance, to make dial backup work as designed—with the static route used only when the RIP route has been lost—the following configuration command could be used:

```
ip route 172.16.3.0 255.255.255.0 bri0/0 130
```

This command sets the route's administrative distance to 130. In this case, when R1 has learned a RIP route to 172.16.3.0/24, R1 uses the lower-administrative-distance (default 120) RIP route. If R1 loses the route—say, when the leased line fails—R1 then uses the next-best route, which coincidentally is needed to make dial backup work. (Static routes that the router puts in the routing table, and removes, in these cases are called *floating static routes* because they float into and out of the routing table.)

The administrative distance can be used to compare routes learned by multiple different routing protocols as well. For example, RIP uses a metric called *hop count*, which is the number of routers (hops) between a router and the destination subnet. OSPF uses a totally different metric, called *cost*. As a result, if a router uses both RIP and OSPF (which makes sense in some cases), the router might learn (with RIP) a hop-count-3 route to a subnet, and (with OSPF) a cost-54 route to the same subnet. It is impossible to look at the metrics and tell which route is best, so the router uses the administrative distance, choosing the OSPF route because, by default, OSPF has a lower administrative distance (110) than RIP (120).

Note

Some people like to think of routing protocol metrics as allowing an apples-to-apples comparison of routes when using a single routing protocol, and administrative distance as allowing an apples-to-oranges comparison of routes learned via multiple methods.

Statically Defined Default Routes

Engineers sometimes use static routes to define a special route called a *default route*. The name pretty much defines its function: a default route tells a router where to send packets that do not match any of that router's other IP routes. When a router does not have a default route, and the router receives a packet whose destination address is not found in the router's IP routing table, the router discards the packet. With a default route, the router forwards the packet based on the instructions in the default route.

Default routes can be most useful in two major cases:

- In enterprise routers that have only one possible physical path to forward packets to the rest of the internetwork

- To route packets from one company into the Internet, when the company has a single connection to the Internet

Figure 6-4 shows a sample enterprise network in which both types of static default routes may be useful. The enterprise uses subnets of registered Class B network 130.1.0.0. Each branch office has one router, with the only link back to the headquarters site. The enterprise network also has one link to an ISP for its Internet connection.

Figure 6-4   Two Typical Cases for Static Default Routes

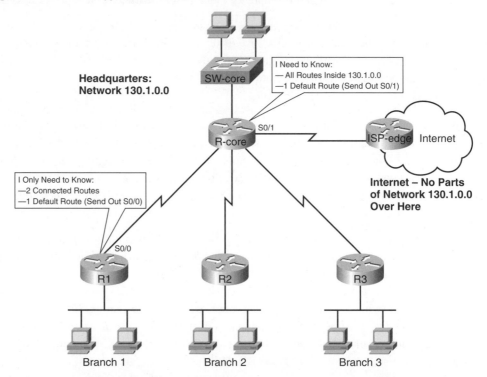

The branch-office routers can work quite well with only a static default route, plus the two connected routes it would learn anyway. For example, R1 will have two connected routes: one for the LAN subnet, and one for the connected WAN subnet. Then, R1 simply needs a default route

that sends traffic to all other destinations out R1's S0/0 interface toward router R-core. In fact, R1 does not need to know about any other subnets in network 130.1.0.0. Even if R1 had learned the specific routes for those subnets, all those routes would direct traffic out R1's S0/0 interface toward router R-core.

In this same enterprise, router R-core can either use a default route for forwarding packets to destinations in the Internet, or learn routes from the ISP's router. R-core could learn routes, using a dynamic routing protocol between itself and router ISP-edge, for all routes known inside the entire Internet. As of publication of this book, this means that R-core would learn about 250,000 routes from the ISP, chewing up a large amount of memory unnecessarily. Even if router R-core knew all those routes, each one would tell router R-core to send the packets out its S0/1 interface toward the Internet.

The typical option used on routers such as R-core—those that have a single possible path to reach the Internet—is to use a static default route pointing toward the Internet. In this case, R-core would use a default route pointing out its S0/1 interface toward the ISP's router. For any packets destined for hosts outside the enterprise, R-core forwards the packets into the Internet, which the routers at the ISP know how to forward.

> **Note**
>
> R-core still needs to know all the specific routes for network 130.1.0.0, typically learned via some routing protocol.

Although Figure 6-4 shows the two typical cases for configuring a static default route, the simple configuration is the same in both cases. For example, on branch router R1, the command would be as follows:

```
ip route 0.0.0.0 0.0.0.0 S0/0
```

To imply the concept of a "default" route that matches all packets, the subnet and mask fields in this command are both 0.0.0.0 by convention. The reasoning behind the subnet and mask of 0.0.0.0 relates to how you use a Boolean AND to find a subnet number. Normally, you AND an address and mask together to find the subnet. If any packet were to arrive at R1, and R1 did an AND of the destination address and the 0.0.0.0 mask, the result would be subnet number 0.0.0.0. So, the router could do this same Boolean AND math, and every packet would match the default route. (For a refresher on how a Boolean AND works, refer to Chapter 10 of *Networking Basics CCNA 1 Companion Guide* or Module 10 of the CCNA 1 online curriculum.)

In short, to configure a static default route, just use the same **ip route** command as before, but use a subnet number and mask of 0.0.0.0.

Verifying Static Routes

Verifying whether static routes work correctly requires a few steps. The following list points out the highlights:

- Because the routes are added in configuration mode, once the network engineer is convinced that the routes are configured correctly, she saves the configuration (**copy running-config startup-config**) to ensure that the routes still exist after the next reload of the router.

- When configured, the routes should be visible in the output of the **show ip route** command, with an *S* in the left column, unless one of the following is also true:

    — If the outgoing interface is down, the route is not in the routing table.

    — If the network engineer sets the administrative distance on the **ip route** command, and the static route has a higher administrative distance than the administrative distance of another route to the same subnet, the static route is not listed in the routing table.

- As with testing any routes, regardless of how they were learned, the **ping** and **traceroute** commands can help verify if all required routes between a source and destination are working.

In particular, the **traceroute** command works very well for testing routes. The **ping** command tells you whether the complete end-to-end route works, but the **traceroute** command tells you the first router that has a problem. Example 6-3 shows sample **traceroute** command output, with the **traceroute** command never completing, which requires the user to stop the command by using a break sequence.

Example 6-3   R2: Results from a Failed traceroute Command

```
R1#traceroute 172.16.55.1
Type escape sequence to abort.
Tracing the route to 172.16.55.1
  1 172.16.33.1 20 msec 22 msec 21 msec
  2 172.16.44.2 31 msec 32 msec 31 msec
  3  *   *   *   *
  4  *   *   *   *
  5  *   *   *   *
! User typed "CTL-Shift-6" to stop the command
R1#
```

The command output in Example 6-3 confirms that the **traceroute** command's packets successfully got to a router whose IP address is 172.16.33.1, and to a router whose address is 172.16.44.2, but no further. Now, the engineer can **telnet** to the last router in the **traceroute** command's output (172.16.44.2) and continue troubleshooting, getting closer to the root cause of the problem.

Chapter 9, "Basic Router Troubleshooting," covers more details about the troubleshooting process and methods.

Lab 6.1.6   Configuring Static Routes

In this lab, you configure static routes between routers to allow data transfer between routers without the use of dynamic routing protocols.

Dynamic Routing Overview

As mentioned at the beginning of this chapter, routers add IP routes to their routing tables using three methods: connected routes, static routes, and routes learned by using dynamic routing protocols. This section focuses on the concepts behind routing protocols in general and covers basic terms and concepts related to routing protocols. This section also explains some of the core features of two major types of routing protocols: distance vector routing protocols and link-state routing protocols.

Terminology Related to Routing Protocols

Before diving into the functions and concepts of routing protocols, you need to review and understand a few terms. These terms were covered in the *Networking Basics CCNA 1 Companion Guide* and online curriculum. However, it is important to distinguish some terms and their meanings before getting into the details of how they work.

The terms *routing protocol*, *routed protocol*, and *routable protocol* are used in networking, and all relate to routing in some way. These terms are generally described as follows:

- **Routing protocol**—A set of messages, rules, and algorithms used by routers for the overall purpose of learning routes. This process includes the exchange and analysis of routing information. Each router chooses the best route to each subnet (path selection) and finally places those best routes into its IP routing table. Examples include RIP, EIGRP, OSPF, and BGP.

- **Routed protocol and routable protocol**—Both terms refer to a protocol that defines a packet structure and logical addressing, allowing routers to forward or route the packets defined by that protocol. Routers forward, or route, packets defined by routed and routable protocols. Examples include IP and IPX (a part of the Novell NetWare protocol model).

> **Note**
>
> The term *path selection* sometimes refers to a part of the job of a routing protocol, in which the routing protocol chooses the best route.

Although routing protocols (such as RIP) are different from routed protocols (such as IP), they do work very closely together. The routing process forwards IP packets, but if a router does not have any routes in its IP routing table that match a packet's destination address, the router discards the packet. Routers need routing protocols so that the routers can learn all the possible routes and add them to the routing table so that the routing process can forward (route) routable protocols such as IP.

This section focuses on routing protocols. For a relatively detailed discussion of how routers forward, or route, routed protocols such as IP, refer to Chapter 10 of *Networking Basics CCNA 1 Companion Guide*.

Routing Protocol Functions

Cisco IOS software supports several IP routing protocols. IP routing protocols exchange routing information about IP routes; other routable protocols have their own associated routing protocols; for example, Novell's Network Link State Protocol (NLSP) is a routing protocol that learns IPX routes. All IP routing protocols perform the same general functions:

- Learn routing information about IP subnets from other neighboring routers.

- Advertise routing information about IP subnets to other neighboring routers.

- If more than one possible route exists to reach one subnet, pick the best route based on a metric.

- If the network topology changes—for example, a link fails—react by advertising that some routes have failed, and pick a new currently best route. (This process is called *convergence*.)

Figure 6-5 shows a simple example that uses the *Routing Information Protocol (RIP)* as the routing protocol. R2 advertises a route for subnet 172.16.3.0/24 to both R1 and R3, which is listed as the first function in the preceeding list. R3 learns the route to 172.16.3.0/24 and then ad vertises that route to R1, which is the second function in the preceding list. Then, R1 hears of two routes to reach 172.16.3.0/24: one with metric 1 from R2, and one with metric 2 from R3. R1 chooses the lower-metric route through R2, which is the third function from the preceding list.

Figure 6-5   Three of the Four Basic Functions of Routing Protocols

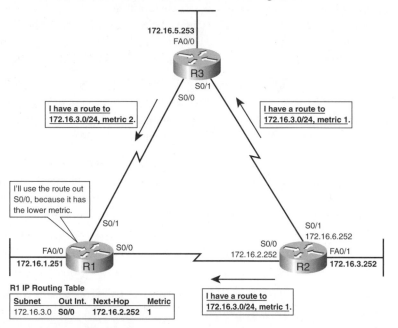

The last function of a routing protocol listed here is to converge when the network changes. The term *convergence* refers to a process that occurs when the topology changes—that is, when either a router or link fails or comes back up again. When something changes, the best routes available in the network may change. Convergence simply refers to the process by which all the routers collectively realize something has changed, advertise the information about the change to all the other routers, and then choose the currently best routes for each subnet. The ability to converge quickly, without causing loops, is one of the most important features of every routing protocol.

The online curriculum uses a different but equally true view of the meaning of the term convergence:

> When all routers in an internetwork operate with the same knowledge, the internetwork is said to have converged.

The routing protocols must recognize changes in the network topology and ensure that all routers know about the changes for the internetwork to converge.

In Figure 6-5, convergence might occur if the link between R1 and R2 fails. In that case, R1 should stop using its old route for subnet 172.16.3.0/24 (directly through R2) and instead send packets to R3.

Interior and Exterior Routing Protocols

IP routing protocols fall into one of two major categories: *Interior Gateway Protocols (IGPs)* and *Exterior Gateway Protocols (EGPs)*. The definitions for each are as follows:

- **IGP**—A routing protocol that was designed and intended for use inside a single *autonomous system (AS)*

- **EGP**—A routing protocol that was designed and intended for use between different autonomous systems

Note

The terms IGP and EGP include the word *gateway* because routers used to be called gateways.

These definitions use another new term: autonomous system (AS). An AS is an internetwork under the administrative control of a single organization. For instance, an internetwork created and paid for by a single company is probably a single AS, and an internetwork created by a single school system is probably a single AS. Other examples include large divisions of a state or national government, where different government agencies may be able to build their own internetworks. Each ISP is also typically a single different AS.

Some routing protocols work best inside a single AS, by design, so these routing protocols are called IGPs. Conversely, one current routing protocol, *Border Gateway Protocol (BGP)*, works best to exchange routes between routers in different autonomous systems, so it is called an EGP.

Note

In some cases, a single company, or more likely a single ISP, may act as if it is more than one AS for technical reasons beyond the scope of the CCNA or CCNP curriculum.

Each AS can be assigned a number, called (unsurprisingly) an *autonomous system number (ASN)*. Like public IP addresses, the Internet Assigned Numbers Authority (IANA, http://www.iana.org) controls the worldwide rights to assign ASNs, delegating that authority to other organizations around the planet, typically to the same organizations that assign public IP addresses. For example, in North America, the American Registry for Internet Numbers (ARIN, http://www.arin.net/) assigns public IP address ranges and ASNs.

Figure 6-6 shows a small view into the worldwide Internet. Two companies and three ISPs use IGPs (OSPF and EIGRP) inside their own networks, with BGP being used between the ASNs.

Figure 6-6   Comparing Locations for Using IGPs and EGPs

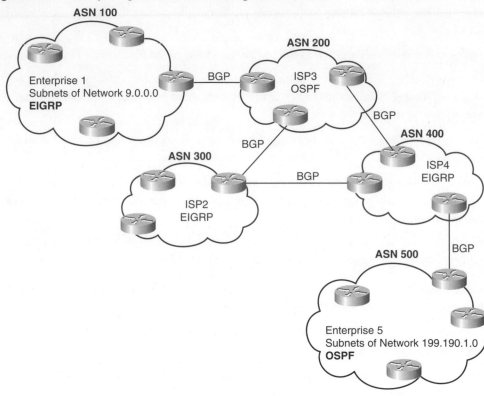

So far, this section has essentially answered the questions of what routing protocols do and where to use them (IGP versus EGP). The next section explores how various types of routing protocols work.

How Routing Protocols Work: Routing Protocol Algorithms

This section explains how routing protocols accomplish the goal of learning routes, choosing the best route among competing routes, and converging to use new routes when the network topology changes. A routing protocol's underlying algorithm determines how a routing protocol does its job. In the computing world, the term *algorithm* generically refers to a process that a computer can use to solve a problem. The term ***routing protocol algorithm*** simply refers to the algorithm used by different routing protocols to solve the problem of learning all routes, choosing the best route to each subnet, and converging in reaction to changes in the internetwork. Three main branches of routing protocol algorithms exists for IGP routing protocols:

- Distance vector (sometimes called Bellman-Ford after its creators)

- Link state

- Balanced hybrid (sometimes called enhanced distance vector)

This section examines the first two of these algorithms, and the CCNA 3 course and book cover balanced hybrid.

Distance Vector Routing Protocol Features

Distance vector routing protocols advertise a small amount of simple information about each subnet to their neighbors. Their neighbors in turn advertise the information to their neighbors, and so on, until all routers have learned the information. In fact, it works a lot like how rumors spread in a neighborhood, school, or company. You might be out in the yard, stop to talk to your next-door neighbor, and tell your neighbor the latest gossip. Then, that neighbor sees his other next-door neighbor, and tells him the same bit of gossip—and so on, until everyone in the neighborhood knows the latest gossip. Distance vector protocols work the same way, but hopefully, unlike rumors in a real neighborhood, the rumor has not changed by the time everyone has heard about it.

For example, consider what occurs in Figure 6-7, which is a duplicate of the network in Figure 6-5. Figure 6-7 shows a distance vector protocol—specifically, RIP—sending just a subnet number and metric to its neighbors.

Figure 6-7   How RIP Advertises Routes

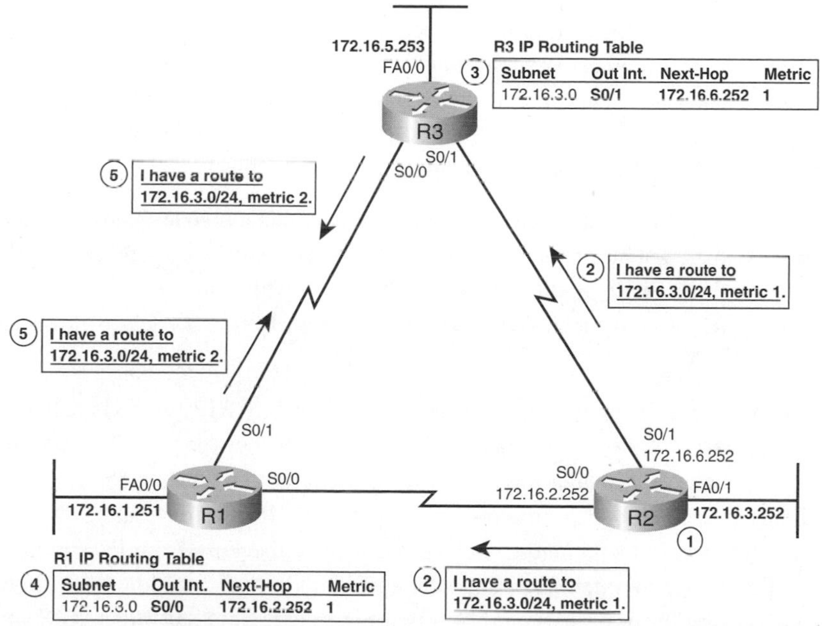

In that case, Figure 6-7 shows how the routers advertise and learn routes for subnet 172.16.3.0:

1. Router R2 learns a connected route for subnet 172.16.3.0.

2. R2 sends a ***routing update*** to its neighbors, listing a subnet (172.16.3.0) and a distance, or metric (1 in this case).

3. R3 hears the routing update and adds a route to its routing table for subnet 172.16.3.0, referring to R2 as the next-hop router.

4. Around the same time, R1 also hears the routing update sent directly to R1 from R2. R1 then adds a route to its routing table for subnet 172.16.3.0, referring to R2 as the next-hop router.

5. R1 and R3 send a routing update to each other, for subnet 172.16.3.0, metric 2.

By the end of this process, both R1 and R3 have heard of two possible routes to reach subnet 172.16.3.0—one with metric 1, and one with metric 2. Each router uses its respective lower-metric (metric 1) routes to reach 172.16.3.0.

Interestingly, distance vector protocols repeat this process continually on a periodic basis. For example, RIP sends periodic routing updates every 30 seconds by default. As long as the routers continue to hear the same routes, with the same metrics, the routers' routing table does not need to change. However, when something changes, the routers react and converge to use the then-best working routes.

Distance vector protocols also send full updates each time they send a regular periodic routing update. Essentially, distance vector routing protocols include all their known routes in the routing update, with some restrictions explained in Chapter 7, "Distance Vector Routing Protocols." So, these routing updates are called *periodic full routing updates*. (The more-advanced routing protocols, which were invented after distance vector protocols, use partial updates, reducing the amount of overhead created by routing protocols.)

Like all routing protocols, distance vector protocols must define a ***metric*** that determines how good each route is. With distance vector protocols, the metric essentially represents a distance from a router to a subnet. For example, consider Figure 6-8, which shows an internetwork with eight routers, using RIP as a distance vector routing protocol. Router R1 learns three separate routes to reach subnet X.

Figure 6-8 provides a good example of the simple metric used by RIP, which is called ***hop count***. The hop count is simply the number of routers, or hops, between a router and the destination subnet. For example, consider the number of routers (hops) between router R1 and subnet X, over the route at the top of Figure 6-8 (through routers R2, R3, R4, and R8). From R1's perspective, that route would be a metric (hop count) 4 route, because from R1's perspective, there are four other routes between itself and subnet X. Similarly, the middle route would be a three-hop route, and the lower route would be a two-hop route. Note that Figure 6-8 shows the routing updates received by R1, each advertising the number of hops associated with each route. As a result, R1 has three routes to subnet X to consider:

- The four-hop route through R2

- The three-hop route through R5

- The two-hop route through R7

Figure 6-8   Using a Hop Count Metric to Choose a Route

Note

All routers in Figure 6-8 would send full periodic updates, but to reduce the clutter, the figure shows only the parts of the routing updates related to the upcoming explanations.

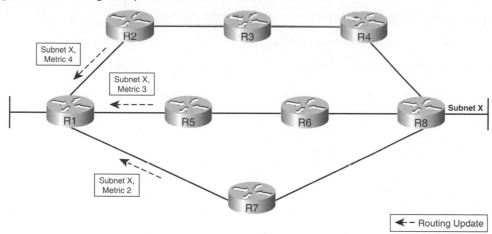

R1 picks the best route to reach subnet X, and in this case, it picks the two-hop route through R7 because that route has the lowest metric.

This example not only shows the idea behind using a metric to pick the best route to reach a subnet, but also provides a good example to show why distance vector logic is called "distance vector" in the first place. Although you can look at Figure 6-8 and know what the network topology looks like, consider for a moment what R1 has learned through this whole process: just three messages from its neighboring routers (R2, R5, and R7), a subnet (X), and a metric for each competing route. In fact, the information learned by R1 can be represented as in Figure 6-9.

Figure 6-9   A Graphical Representation of the Distance Vector Concept

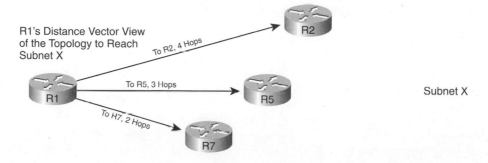

Effectively, all R1 knows about subnet X is three vectors. The length of the vectors represents how far away the subnet is over a particular route, and the direction of the vector represents the

next-hop router. So, with distance vector logic, routing protocols do not learn a lot about the network when they receive routing updates. All the routing protocols know is some concept of a vector: a vector's length is the distance (metric) to reach a subnet, and a vector's direction is through the neighbor that advertised the route.

To summarize, distance vector protocols use the following concepts:

- They send full periodic routing updates.

- The updates include a list of subnets and their respective distances (metrics), but nothing else.

- Routers do not know the details about the network's topology beyond a neighboring router.

- Like all routing protocols, if multiple routes to the same subnet exist, the router chooses the route with the lowest metric.

One of the reasons why distance vector logic keeps things simple, and uses little bandwidth, is that distance vector logic was created in the 1980s, when routers were lucky to have 32 KB of RAM. (That is not a typo—32 KB, not MB.) Also, router CPUs were much less powerful than the processor in an average MP3 player today. Networks did not have a lot of bandwidth back then either, so distance vector protocols were designed to send only a little information about the internetwork.

The next section examines the link-state routing protocol algorithm.

Link-State Routing Protocol Features

Link-state routing protocols send much more information in their routing updates than distance vector routing protocols. As a result, link-state routing protocols require much more CPU processing on the routers, but with the positive result of having much faster convergence of routes when something changes in the network. Link-state protocols were first created in the early 1990s, roughly ten years after the original distance vector protocols. By that time, routers had much faster CPUs and much more RAM, and networks used much faster links. As a result, the designers of the link-state routing protocols created algorithms that solved many of the problems with the earlier distance vector protocols, such as slow convergence, by taking advantage of the availability of more bandwidth, RAM, and CPU.

Like distance vector protocols, link-state protocols send routing updates to neighboring routers, which in turn send updates to their neighboring routers, and so on. At the end of the process, like distance vector protocols, routers that use link-state protocols add the best routes to their routing tables, based on metrics. Other than that, these two types of routing protocol algorithm have little in common.

This section covers the most basic mechanics of how link-state protocols work, with the examples using Open Shortest Path First (OSPF), the first link-state IP routing protocol, in the examples. The section begins by showing how link-state routing protocols flood routing information throughout the internetwork, and then it goes on to describe how link-state protocols process the routing information to choose the best routes.

Building the Same LSDB on Every Router

Routers using link-state routing protocols need to collectively advertise practically every detail about the internetwork to all the other routers. At the end of the process, called *flooding*, every router in the internetwork has the exact same information about the internetwork as all the other routers. This information, stored in RAM in a data structure called the *link-state database (LSDB)*, is then used in the other major step to find the currently best routes to each subnet. Flooding a lot of detailed information to every router sounds like a lot of work, and relative to distance vector routing protocols, it is.

Open Shortest Path First (OSPF), the most popular link-state routing protocol, advertises information in routing update messages, with the updates containing information called *link-state advertisements (LSAs)*. LSAs come in many forms, including the following two main types:

- **Router LSA**—Includes a number to identify the router (router ID), the router's interface IP addresses, the state (up or down) of each interface, and the cost (metric) associated with the interface.

- **Link LSA**—Identifies each link (subnet) and the routers that are attached to that link. It also identifies the state (up or down) of the link.

Using link-state protocols, each router creates a router LSA for itself and floods that LSA to other routers in routing update messages. To flood an LSA, a router sends the LSA to its neighbors; those neighbors in turn forward the LSA to their neighbors, and so on, until all the routers have learned about the LSA. Additionally, one router attached to a subnet also creates and floods a link LSA for each subnet (as needed). At the end of the process, every router has every other router's router LSA and a copy of all the link LSAs as well.

Figure 6-10 shows a general idea of the flooding process, with R8 creating and flooding its router LSA. Every router would create and flood a router LSA for itself, using the same general process used by R8, but the figure only shows the flooding of R8's router LSA to make the figure less cluttered. Also, some routers would also create and flood link LSAs, which describe a link or subnet to which multiple routers connect. Note that Figure 6-10 actually shows only a subset of the information in R8's router LSA.

Figure 6-10 shows the rather basic flooding process, with R8 sending the original LSA for itself, and the other routers flooding the LSA by forwarding it until every router has a copy. (There is a process to prevent routers from looping the LSAs around the network.)

The origins of the term *link state* can be explained by considering the (partial) contents of the router LSA shown in Figure 6-10. The bottom right part of the figure shows one of the four interface IP addresses that would be listed in R8's router LSA, along with the interface's state. Link-state protocols get their name from the fact that the LSAs advertise each interface (link) and whether the interface is up or down. So, the LSDB contains information about routers, interfaces, and subnets that are currently down, as well as information about routers, interfaces, and subnets that are currently up and working.

Note

Link-state protocols do not need to create link LSAs for all links. The Networking Academy CCNP curriculum covers this and many other details of link-state protocols.

Figure 6-10   Flooding LSAs Using a Link-State Routing Protocol

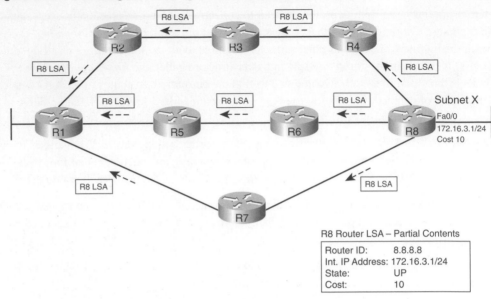

After the LSA has been flooded, even if the LSAs do not change, link-state protocols require periodic reflooding of the LSAs, similar to the periodic updates sent by distance vector protocols. However, distance vector protocols typically use a short timer; for example, RIP sends periodic updates every 30 seconds. With OSPF, the LSAs must be re-sent every 30 minutes. As a result, in a stable internetwork, link-state protocols actually use less network bandwidth for sending routing information than do distance vector protocols. If an LSA changes, the router immediately floods the changed LSA. For example, if a router interface changes from up to down, the LSA needs to be reflooded, because some routes may change as a result.

Applying Dijkstra SPF Math to Find the Best Routes

The link-state flooding process results in every router's having an identical copy of the LSDB in memory, but the flooding process alone does not cause a router to learn what routes to add to the IP routing table. Although incredibly detailed and useful, the information in the LSDB does not explicitly state each router's best route to reach a destination. Link-state protocols must use another major part of the link-state algorithm to find and add routes to the IP routing table—routes that list a subnet number and mask, an outgoing interface, and a next-hop router IP address. This process uses something called the *Dijkstra Shortest Path First (SPF) algorithm*.

The SPF algorithm can be compared to how humans think when taking a trip using a road map. Anyone can go to the store and buy the same road map, so anyone can know all the information about the roads. However, when you look at the map, you first find your starting and ending locations, and then you analyze the map to find the possible routes. If some of the routes look similar in length, you may decide to go over a longer route if the roads happen to be highways rather than little country roads.

In the analogy, the LSDB works like the map, and the SPF algorithm works like the human reading the map. The LSDB holds all the information about all the possible routers and links. The SPF algorithm defines how a router's CPU processes the LSDB, with each router considering itself to be the starting point for the route. The SPF algorithm calculates all the possible routes, and the cumulative metric for the entire route, for each possible destination subnet. In short, each router must view itself as the starting point, and each subnet as the destination, and use the SPF algorithm to look at the LSDB roadmap to find and pick the best route to each subnet.

Figure 6-11 shows a graphical view of the results of the SPF algorithm, run by router R1, when trying to find the best route to reach subnet 172.16.3.0/24 (based on Figure 6-10). Figure 6-11 shows R1 at the top of the figure rather than on the left. SPF creates a mathematical tree, and these trees are typically drawn with the base or root of the tree at the top of the figure and the subnet(s) at the bottom.

Note

Mathematical trees are used throughout the world of computing. The single node at the top is called the root, and the bottom parts are called leaves, as if it were a real tree—just turned upside-down.

Figure 6-11   SPF Tree to Find R1's Route to 172.16.3.0/24

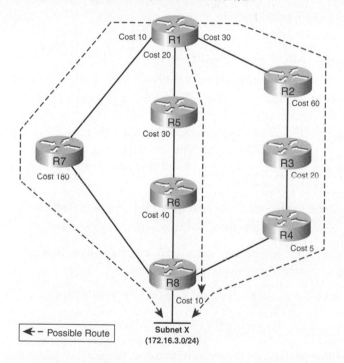

Figure 6-11 does not show the SPF algorithm's math (frankly, almost no one bothers looking at the math), but it does show a drawing of the kind of analysis done by the SPF algorithm on R1. Generally, each router runs the SPF process to find all routes to each subnet, and then the SPF algorithm can pick the best route. To pick the best route, a router's SPF algorithm adds the cost associated with each link between itself and the destination subnet, over each possible route.

Figure 6-11 shows the costs associated with each route beside the links, with the dashed lines showing the three routes R1 finds between itself and subnet X (172.16.3.0/24).

Table 6-1 references the three routes shown in Figure 6-11, with their cumulative costs, showing that R1's best route to 172.16.3.0/24 goes through R5 next.

Table 6-1   Comparing R1's Three Alternatives for the Route to 172.16.3.0/24

Route	Location in Figure 6-11	Cumulative Cost
R1-R7-R8	Left	10+180+10 = 200
R1-R5-R6-R8	Middle	20+30+40+10 = 100
R1-R2-R3-R4-R8	Right	30+60+20+5+10 = 125

As a result of the SPF algorithm's analysis of the LSDB, R1 adds a route to subnet 172.16.3.0/24 to its routing table, with the next-hop router of R5.

Reacting to Changes with Link-State Protocols

As soon as the internetwork is stable, link-state protocols reflood the LSAs on a regular basis, although the time period is rather long. (OSPF defaults to 30 minutes.) However, when an LSA changes, link-state protocols react swiftly, converging the network and using the currently best routes as quickly as possible. For example, imagine that the link between R5 and R6 fails in the internetwork of Figure 6-10 and Figure 6-11. The following list explains the process R1 uses to switch to use a different route. (Similar steps would occur for changes to other routers and routes.)

1. R5 and R6 flood LSAs that state that their interfaces are now in a "down" state. (In a network of this size, the flooding typically takes maybe a second or two.)

2. All routers run the SPF algorithm again to see if any routes have changed. (This process may take another second in a network this size.)

3. All routers replace routes, as needed, based on the results of SPF. (This takes practically no additional time after SPF has completed.) For example, R1 changes its route for subnet X (172.16.3.0/24) to use R2 as the next-hop router.

These steps allow the link-state routing protocol to converge quickly—much more quickly than distance vector routing protocols. Some of the reasons for distance vector routing protocols' slow convergence time are covered in Chapter 7.

Summarizing Features of the Link-State Routing Protocols

Link-state routing protocols, particularly OSPF, perform a valuable and important service in IP networks today. The Networking Academy Switching Basics and Intermediate Routing CCNA 3 course and *Companion Guide* cover OSPF and its configuration in more detail. However, for the CCNA 2 course, you should be aware of the main features of link-state routing protocols:

- All routers learn the same detailed information about all routers and subnets in the internetwork.

- The individual pieces of topology information are called LSAs, with all LSAs stored in RAM in the LSDB.

- Routers flood LSAs when they are created, on a regular but long time interval if the LSAs do not change over time, and immediately when an LSA changes.

- The LSDB does not contain routes, but it does contain information that can be processed by the Dijkstra SPF algorithm to find a router's best routes.

- Each router runs the SPF algorithm, with the LSDB as input, resulting in the best (lowest-cost/lowest-metric) routes being added to the IP routing table.

- Link-state protocols converge quickly by immediately reflooding LSAs and rerunning the SPF algorithm.

- Link-state protocols consume much more RAM and CPU than do distance vector routing protocols. If the internetwork changes a lot, link-state protocols can also consume much more bandwidth due to the (relative to distance vector protocols) large number of bytes of information in each LSA.

The next and final major section of this chapter discusses the specifics of the most popular IP routing protocols and some information about routing protocol configuration.

Routing Protocols Overview

This section explains and summarizes some of the main features of four IP routing protocols: RIP, OSPF, EIGRP, and BGP. It also explains how to configure RIP, leaving the details of OSPF and EIGRP configuration for the Networking Academy CCNA 3 course. First, this section provides a brief review of the IP routing process.

A Brief Review of IP Routing

Routers can be configured to perform many different functions, but most important, routers perform the following primary functions:

- The routing (also called forwarding or switching) of packets by comparing the destination IP address in the packet to the routes in the router's IP routing table

- Learning all possible routes to reach each subnet, and choosing the best of those routes to put in the router's IP routing table, by using a routing protocol (also called path determination)

This chapter has already explained quite a bit about the role of routing protocols. To briefly review the routing or forwarding process, consider Figure 6-12, which shows how the IP routing process forwards a packet from PC1 to PC3.

Figure 6-12   The IP Routing Process

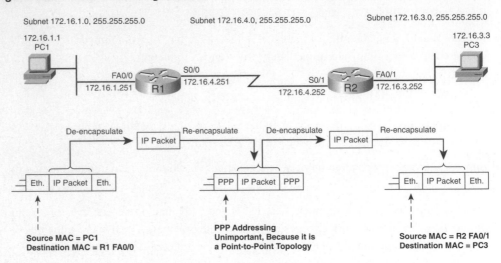

Figure 6-12 does not show every detail of the forwarding process, but it does point out two important facts about the routing process:

- The routing process forwards packets—which include the Layer 3 header but not the Layer 2 header and trailer—from one host to the other.

- Routing uses only data-link frames to deliver the packet from one device to the next.

For example, PC1 sends an IP packet in an Ethernet frame to router R1. When R1 routes the packet, R1 discards the old data link (Ethernet) header and trailer, and adds a new data link header and trailer (PPP in this case), before forwarding the packet. As a result, many people use the somewhat-redundant phrase "routers route packets" to refer to the fact that IP routing delivers packets from end to end through the network, but routing does not send data link layer frames from end to end.

Routing Protocol Features: RIP, OSPF, EIGRP, and BGP

The Cisco Networking Academy Program CCNA curriculum mentions several IP routing protocols. However, the courses focus on RIP (CCNA 2), OSPF (CCNA 3), and EIGRP (CCNA 3). The CCNA 2 curriculum formerly covered more detail about the Interior Gateway Routing Protocol (IGRP), an old proprietary routing protocol from Cisco, but due to its waning importance, this book includes the detailed IGRP coverage in the "Additional Topics of Interest" section for Chapter 7, which you can find on the CD-ROM accompanying this book.

This section summarizes some of the key features of the IP routing protocols. Some of the features have already been introduced—for example, this chapter has already explained the concepts behind routing protocol algorithms. This section explains some of the remaining features and compares the three most important IP IGPs (at least most important in the CCNA curriculum): RIP, OSPF, and EIGRP.

Each routing protocol uses a metric to make choices about path determination. As discussed in the section "Distance Vector Routing Protocol Features" earlier in this chapter, RIP uses the concept of *hop count*, which is the number of routers between a router and some subnet. OSPF uses the concept of *link cost*, with the SPF algorithm adding the cost of each link to determine the cost from a router, to a subnet, over each possible path. EIGRP uses a metric that is based on link bandwidth and link delay, applying a mathematical function to both to come up with an integer value for a metric.

Cisco has developed a couple of proprietary IP routing protocols in the past: *Interior Gateway Routing Protocol (IGRP)*, and its successor, *Enhanced Interior Gateway Routing Protocol (EIGRP)*. To run either routing protocol, you must use Cisco routers. However, when IGRP was announced, it worked better than the only other alternative at the time (RIP). Today, EIGRP works very well, competing with OSPF to be considered the best IGP IP routing protocol.

Some routing protocols, such as RIP, send *periodic full routing updates*. RIP sends updates every 30 seconds by default, regardless of whether anything has changed. The updates include all routes known by that router, with some restrictions, which means the updates are "full." Alternatively, other routing protocols (such as OSPF and EIGRP) send *partial updates*, which include only changes to routing information.

The actual routing update messages need to be sent to all other neighboring routers that care about that routing protocol. On a LAN, the routing protocol can choose to send the routing update messages as a LAN broadcast, meaning that all hosts receive and look at the packets, or as multicasts. Updates sent as multicasts can be optimized by LAN switches so that only the routers that care about that routing protocol receive those routing updates.

When a route fails, routing protocols typically still advertise the route, at least for a short time, but with a metric that implies the route has failed. Each routing protocol uses a special metric value, called an *infinite metric*, or simply *infinity*, to mean that a route has failed. For example, RIP uses hop count as the metric. A metric of 15 hops is a valid usable metric, but a metric of 16 means "infinity," and that the route has failed.

Finally, one last distinction between routing protocols is that they can all put multiple equal-metric (equal-cost) routes, for the same subnet, in the routing table at the same time. For instance, RIP may learn two different routes to subnet 172.16.3.0/24, both with metric 2, so RIP puts both into the routing table. The router then load-balances packets, sending some packets over one route and some packets over the other.

This section introduces many small points about routing protocols. To help keep track of the details, Table 6-2 summarizes the key points about the features of this section and how they are supported by the three main IP IGPs.

Table 6-2   Comparing Features of IGPs: RIP, EIGRP, and OSPF

Features	RIP1	OSPF	EIGRP
Algorithm	Distance vector	Link state	Advanced distance vector
Metric	Hop count	Link cost	Function of bandwidth, delay
Open standard or proprietary	Open (RFC 1058)	Open (RFC 2238)	Proprietary
Sends periodic updates?	Yes (30 seconds)	No	No
Full or partial routing updates	Full	Partial	Partial
Sends updates as broadcast or multicast	Broadcast	Multicast	Multicast
Metric considered to be "infinite"	16	16,777,215 ($2^{24} - 1$)	4,294,967,295 ($2^{32} - 1$)
Supports unequal cost load balancing?	No	No	Yes

[1] This table specifically refers to features of RIP Version 1 and not RIP Version 2.

Finally, before moving on to the last topic of this chapter, you should know about a few of the features of Border Gateway Protocol (BGP). BGP is the only real choice today for an Exterior Gateway Protocol (EGP), one that is specifically designed to exchange routing information between different autonomous systems. BGP is mainly used between ISPs, and sometimes between an ISP and its customers.

RIP Configuration

Understanding how RIP works, including its underlying distance vector logic, is much more difficult than configuring RIP. This section introduces RIP configuration, and Chapter 7 covers more about RIP concepts, configuration, troubleshooting, and the differences between RIP Versions 1 and 2. The Networking Academy CCNA 3 curriculum covers OSPF and EIGRP configuration.

RIP configuration requires two configuration commands:

- **router rip**
- **network** *classful-network-number*

The **router rip** command moves the user from global configuration mode to RIP configuration mode, and the **network** command tells the router on which interfaces to start using RIP. However, the **network** command does not list interfaces, but rather a Class A, B, or C network number. The router then uses the following logic to tell it on which interfaces to start using RIP:

> Find each interface whose interface IP address is in the listed classful network number, and use RIP on those interfaces.

For example, consider Figure 6-13, which shows the same simple internetwork as shown in Figure 2-4 in Chapter 2. To make RIP work in this sample internetwork, both R1 and R2 need the same two configuration commands, as shown in the figure.

Figure 6-13 Sample Network for Basic RIP Configuration—Single Network

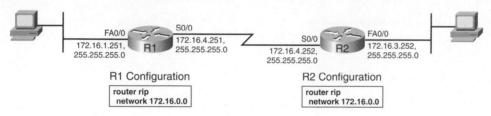

In this case, each router's **network** command tells the router to start using RIP on both interfaces. In this example, the logic on R1 works like this:

1. R1 looks for any interfaces whose IP address is in Class B network 172.16.0.0.

2. R1 sees that both its FA0/0 and S0/0 interfaces have IP addresses in network 172.16.0.0, so R1 starts sending RIP updates on both interfaces.

3. Similarly, R2 finds that both of its interfaces match the **network 172.16.0.0** command as well, because both interfaces are in network 172.16.0.0. So, R2 also begins sending RIP updates on both interfaces.

4. As a result, R1 and R2 begin to learn routes from each other using RIP.

Note that the RIP **network** command uses a classful network number as the parameter. A classful network number is a Class A, B, or C network number, as opposed to a subnet number or interface IP address. IOS does not have a way to enable RIP on an interface by referring directly to an interface. Instead, the **network** command lists a classful network number, and the router then looks at the IP addresses on all its interfaces and enables RIP on an interface in that classful network.

When a RIP **network** command matches an interface IP address, IOS enables RIP on that interface. When IOS enables RIP on an interface, RIP performs three actions related to that interface:

1. It starts sending RIP updates out the interface.

2. It starts listening for RIP updates coming in that interface from some other router.

3. It starts advertising a route to reach the subnet attached to the interface.

The first two actions seem pretty obvious, but the last action—advertising the subnet on that interface—can be better shown with a slightly different example. Figure 6-14 shows the same network topology, but with three different IP networks in use.

Figure 6-14   Sample Network for Basic RIP Configuration—Multiple Networks

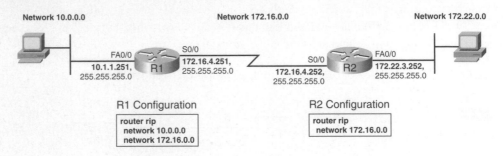

Figure 6-14 shows the different IP addresses and networks in use, and the routers' RIP configurations, but with R2 missing a **network** command. As shown, the following occur in this internetwork:

- R1 sends RIP updates out Fa0/0, listens for RIP updates in Fa0/0, and advertises subnet 10.1.1.0/24, all based on R1's **network 10.0.0.0** command.

- R1 sends RIP updates out S0/0, listens for RIP updates in S0/0, and advertises subnet 172.16.4.0/24, all based on R1's **network 172.16.0.0** command.

- R2 sends RIP updates out S0/0, listens for RIP updates in S0/0, and advertises subnet 172.16.4.0/24, all based on R2's **network 172.16.0.0** command.

The problem in this example is that R2 does not have a **network 172.22.0.0** command. So, R2 does not match its Fa0/0 interface with any **network** commands. R2 does not send and receive RIP updates on its Fa0/0 interface, which is no big deal in this case because no other routers are on the LAN off R2. However, R2 does not advertise network 172.22.0.0 either. So, as configured, even though R1 and R2 are sending routing updates to each other, R2 does not advertise network 172.22.0.0, and R1 does not learn routes to reach network 172.22.0.0. To solve the problem, R2 simply needs to add a **network 172.22.0.0** command under the **router rip** command.

Summary

Routers perform many functions, with the two most important being to route (forward) packets and to learn routes. The routing process requires the router to receive packets, match their destination address to the IP routing table, decide where to forward the packet next, and forward the packet. To make routing work well, routers add routes to the IP routing table via three main methods:

- Learning the routes for subnets connected to a router's interfaces

- Configuring static routes

- Using a dynamic routing protocol

Static route operations can be divided into these three parts. First, a network administrator uses the **ip route** command to configure a static route. Then the router installs the route in the routing table. Finally, the route is used to route packets.

Engineers use static routes for many purposes, although routers typically use dynamic routing protocols to learn the majority of routes. Static routes work well in dial backup scenarios, often requiring the static routes to use a higher administrative distance than the routing protocol. Remote routers that have only one possible path to reach the rest of an internetwork can easily use a static default route, because even if such a router learned all the specific routes in the internetwork, they would all use the same next-hop router and outgoing interface. Finally, the router connected to an enterprise's only connection to the Internet might use a static default route for forwarding packets into the Internet.

After static routes are configured using the **ip route** command, their existence can be verified using the **show running-config**, **show startup-config**, and **show ip route** commands. By default, a static route is added to the IP routing table only if the outgoing interface defined by the route is up and working.

An AS is a collection of networks under the same administration that share a common routing strategy; for instance, the internetwork created by one company, one school, or one organization is likely to be a single AS. The global Internet consists of most every AS in the world, with each AS having a registered (with IANA) unique AS number (ASN). Each AS connects to at least one ISP, and the world's ISPs have at least one path to reach all other ISPs. Inside each AS, the engineers responsible for the AS can choose the AS's set of rules and policies, including choosing which Interior Gateway Protocol (IGP) to use. BGP is typically used between ASNs.

The distance vector routing algorithm, also known as Bellman-Ford, determines the direction and distance to reach any subnet in an internetwork. Distance vector routing protocols send routing updates at a regular interval, with these updates including all known routes (except routes restricted by some mechanisms, as covered in Chapter 7). Routers can look at the received updates and add routes to their IP routing tables. Routers can also notice changes to the received updates, converging to a new set of routes.

The other major routing protocol algorithm covered in this chapter is the link-state algorithm, also knows as the Dijkstra algorithm or the SPF algorithm. Link-state routing algorithms advertise detailed topology information by sending routing updates, with the updates containing information called link-state advertisements (LSAs). The LSAs describe many details about the network topology, including each router, each router's interfaces and IP addresses, the state (up/down) of the interfaces, and information about each link (subnet) and its state. Each router collects the same set of LSAs for the internetwork into a data structure called the link-state database (LSDB). Then, each router applies the SPF algorithm to the LSDB, resulting in the router's finding the least-cost route to reach each subnet. The link-state protocol then adds that route to the IP routing table.

The three most commonly used IP IGPs are RIP, OSPF, and EIGRP. RIP uses distance vector logic, sending full updates every 30 seconds, and uses hop count for the metric. OSPF uses link-state logic, does not send full updates on a periodic basis, and uses cost as the metric. Refer to Table 6-2 for a summary that compares the three IGPs.

RIP configuration requires one **router rip** configuration command and one or more **network** *net-number* subcommands under **router rip**. The **network** command has a classful network number as its only parameter. The router then finds all its interfaces in that classful network and starts applying RIP to those interfaces, meaning that the router sends RIP updates on the interface, listens for RIP updates coming in the interface, and starts advertising the subnet connected to that interface.

Check Your Understanding

Complete all the review questions listed here to test your understanding of the topics and concepts in this chapter. Answers are listed in Appendix A, "Answers to Check Your Understanding and Challenge Questions."

1. Which of the following best describes one function of a router?

   A. It is responsible for reliable communication between LAN hosts.

   B. It is concerned with physical addressing of hosts on remote LANs.

   C. It determines the best path for traffic to take through a network.

   D. It uses routing protocols to put MAC addresses into the routing table.

2. Which of the following best describes the core function of path determination?

   A. Assigning administrative distances to routes

   B. Choosing the best of all the learned routes for each subnet

   C. Forwarding or switching packets in a LAN environment

   D. Keeping EGPs from leaving the autonomous system

3. What is the primary type of information used by the network layer when forwarding packets?

   A. An IP routing table

   b. ARP responses

   c. Data from a name server

   d. The bridging table

4. Which of the following statements describing the routing protocol exchange process are true? (Choose three.)

   A. Routers using OPSF can exchange information using LSAs.

   B. Routers using link-state protocols exchange routing tables every 90 seconds.

   C. Routers using RIP exchange routing tables at least every 30 seconds by default.

   D. Link-state protocols use hop counts to determine a route's value.

5. Which of the following best describes a routed protocol?

A. Its address provides enough information to allow a packet to be forwarded from host to host.

B. Its address provides the information necessary to pass data packets to the next-highest network layer.

C. It allows routers to communicate with other routers to maintain and update routing tables.

D. It allows routers to bind MAC and IP addresses.

6. Which of the following best describes a routing protocol?

A. A protocol through which routers learn about the possible IP routes

B. A protocol that specifies how and when MAC and IP addresses are bound

C. A protocol that assigns IP addresses to hosts as they boot on to the network

D. A protocol that allows a packet to be forwarded from host to host in a LAN

7. What is one characteristic of distance vector routing protocols?

A. They are not likely to count to infinity.

B. They work well on very large networks.

C. They are not prone to routing loops.

D. They are computationally simple.

8. Which of the following best describes the difference between an EGP and an IGP?

A. EGPs are used within autonomous systems, and IGPs are used between autonomous systems.

B. IGPs are routed protocols, and EGPs are routing protocols.

C. IGPs are used within autonomous systems, and EGPs are used between autonomous systems.

D. IGPs are used between ISPs, and EGPs are used in LANs.

E. An example of an EGP is OSPF, and an example of an IGP is BGP.

9. How do link-state routing protocols build routing tables?

A. By sending copies of link-state algorithms to neighbors after convergence occurs

B. By sending LSAs out each split horizon

C. By exchanging LSAs and running the SPF algorithm

D. By sending routing tables to the neighbor router and letting the table spread in a cascade effect

10. A corporate office has one large router connecting six subnets on six different Fast Ethernet interfaces, but it has no other interfaces, and no other routers exist. Which routing protocols could be configured for this router to learn routes to the six LAN subnets?

   A. RIP, because all networks are fewer than 16 hops away.

   B. OSPF, because the shortest path is easy to determine.

   C. The router could be configured with static routes to each subnet, removing the need for any routing protocol.

   D. No routing protocols are necessary.

11. Which of the following is predetermined by an administrator and does not require a routing algorithm?

   A. Static route

   B. Dynamic route

   C. Distance vector route

   D. OSPF

12. Which of the following best describes a default route?

   A. Urgent-data route manually entered by a network administrator

   B. Route used when part of the network fails

   C. Route used when the destination network is not listed explicitly in the routing table

   D. Preset shortest path

Challenge Questions and Activities

These questions require a deeper application of the concepts covered in this chapter and are similar to the style of questions you might see on a CCNA certification exam. Appendix A lists the answers.

1. Which of the following can be concluded from the following output? (Choose three.)

    ```
    KTN#show ip route
    Codes: C - connected, S - static, I - IGRP, R - RIP, M - mobile, B - BGP
           D - EIGRP, EX - EIGRP external, O - OSPF, IA - OSPF inter area
           N1 - OSPF NSSA external type 1, N2 - OSPF NSSA external type 2
           E1 - OSPF external type 1, E2 - OSPF external type 2, E - EGP
           i - IS-IS, L1 - IS-IS level-1, L2 -IS-IS level-2, ia - IS-IS inter area
           * - candidate default, U - per-user static route, o - ODR
           P - periodic downloaded static route


    Gateway of last resort is not set


    C    172.17.0.0/16 is directly connected, Serial0/0
    R    172.16.0.0/16 [120/1] via 172.17.1.1, 00:00:07, Serial0/0
    C    172.18.0.0/16 is directly connected, FastEthernet0/0
    S    172.16.3.0/16 is directly connected, Serial0/1
    ```

    A. 172.16.0.0/16 is two hops away.

    B. RIP is using the default administrative distance.

    C. The subnet mask for the routes shown is 255.255.255.0.

    D. A distance vector protocol is being used.

    E. A static route has been configured.

2. In the following figure, routers R1 and R2 have been configured to use RIP, and all router interfaces are in an "up and up" state. When host A issues the **ping 172.16.3.2** command, the command lists messages that say that the request timed out. Which of the following statements could be true about the reasons why PC A's ping fails?

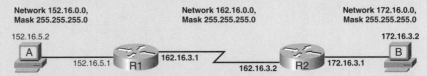

    A. PC A has connected to router R1 using a crossover cable.

    B. R1's RIP configuration does not include a **network 152.16.0.0** command.

    C. R1's RIP configuration does not include a **network 172.16.0.0** command.

    D. R2's RIP configuration does not include a **network 152.16.0.0** command.

    E. R2's RIP configuration does not include a **network 172.16.0.0** command.

CHAPTER 7

Distance Vector Routing Protocols

Objectives

Upon completion of this chapter, you should be able to answer the following questions:

- How do routing loops occur in distance vector routing?

- What are the methods used by distance vector routing protocols to ensure that routing information is accurate?

- What are the steps and commands to configure RIP?

- What is the purpose of the **ip classless** command?

- What are some methods and techniques used to troubleshoot RIP?

- How is load balancing configured in RIP?

- How are static routes configured in RIP?

- How can RIP operations be verified?

Additional Topics of Interest

Several chapters contain additional coverage of previous topics or related topics that are secondary to the main goals of this chapter. You can find the additional coverage on the CD-ROM. For this chapter, the following additional topics are covered:

- Interior Gateway Routing Protocol (IGRP) features

- IGRP metrics

- IGRP routes

- IGRP loop-avoidance features

- IGRP configurations

- Migrating from RIP to IGRP

- Verification of IGRP configurations

- Troubleshooting IGRP

Key Terms

This chapter uses the following key terms. You can find the definitions in the Glossary.

routing loops   page 228

routing tables   page 228

metric   page 229

route poisoning   page 230

infinity   page 230

counting to infinity   page 231

split horizon   page 234

triggered update   page 235

poison reverse   page 235

holddown   page 240

holddown timer   page 240

discontiguous network   page 247

flush timer   page 248

administrative distance   page 258

floating static route   page 259

classless routing protocol   page 261

classful routing protocol   page 261

classful routing   page 262

classless routing   page 262

This chapter focuses on two major topics related to Routing Information Protocol (RIP). The first section completes the explanation of the theory and concepts behind distance vector routing protocols—specifically, the features that prevent routing loops while a distance vector protocol converges. The second section covers the implementation of RIP, including how to configure versions 1 and 2 of RIP, a wide variety of brief configuration topics, and some basic tools to verify and troubleshoot RIP operation.

Note that this chapter focuses on RIP. Interior Gateway Routing Protocol (IGRP), the other distance vector protocol mentioned in this book, is covered in more depth in the "Additional Topics of Interest" section found on the CD-ROM.

Avoiding Loops When Converging Using Distance Vector Routing Protocols

The developers of the TCP/IP protocol first added distance vector routing protocols to the TCP/IP standards in the 1980s. Relative to today, the computer hardware at that time had slow CPUs and small amounts of memory, and the networks used relatively slow links. For example, a typical WAN link to a remote site might have been only 56 kbps, or about the speed of a single Internet dialup connection today. As a result, the designers of the first distance vector protocols had to keep them simple.

Unfortunately, the simplicity of distance vector protocols introduced the possibility of routing loops. *Routing loops* occur when the routers forward packets such that the same single packet ends up back at the same routers over and over again, wasting bandwidth and never delivering the packet. In production networks, the number of looping packets could congest the network to the point that the network becomes unusable, so routing loops must be avoided as much as possible. This section begins by reviewing the basics of distance vector protocols. It then shows how routing loops could occur and describes a variety of distance vector features that help prevent loops.

Review of Distance Vector Operation in a Stable Network

In a stable working network, distance vector protocols send periodic full routing updates on each interface. Figure 7-1 shows a simple internetwork with two routers, three LAN subnets, and one WAN subnet. The figure shows both routers' full *routing tables*, listing all four routes, and the periodic updates sent by each router.

Figure 7-1 Normal Steady-State RIP Operations

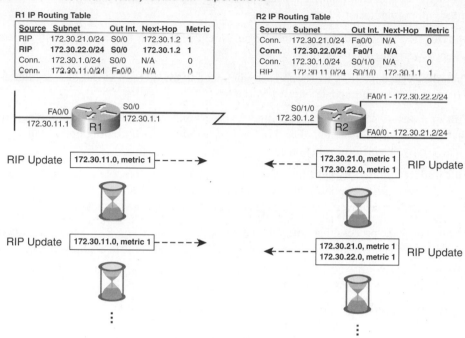

To begin, focus on some of the more important facts of how router R1 learns about subnet 172.30.22.0/24. (Subnet 172.30.22.0/24 is the subnet connected to R2's FA0/1 interface.)

- R2 considers itself to have a 0-hop route for subnet 172.30.22.0/24, so in the routing update sent by R2 (shown below the R2 router icon), R2 advertises a *metric* 1 (hop count 1) route.

- R1 receives the update, and because R1 has learned of no other possible routes to 172.30.22.0, this route must be R1's best route to the subnet.

- R1 adds the subnet to its routing table, listing it as a RIP-learned route.

- For the learned route, R1 uses an outgoing interface of S0/0, because R1 received R2's routing update on R1's S0/0 interface.

- For the learned route, R1 uses a next-hop router of 172.30.1.2, because R1 learned the route from a RIP update whose source IP address was 172.30.1.2.

At the end of this process, R1 has learned a new route. The rest of the RIP-learned routes in this example follow the same process.

Besides the process of advertising and learning routes, Figure 7-1 also highlights a few other particularly important facts:

- **Metric**—RIP uses hop count for the metric. Note that the RIP routers add 1 to the metric before advertising the route.

- **Periodic**—The hourglass icons represent the fact that the updates repeat on a regular cycle. RIP uses a 30-second update interval by default.

- **Full updates**—The routers send full updates, every time, instead of just sending new or changed routing information. (The term *partial update* refers to routing updates that include only changed information.)

- **Full updates limited by split horizon rules**—The routing protocol omits some routes from the periodic full updates due to split horizon rules. Split horizon is a loop-avoidance feature that will be covered in the next few pages.

Figure 7-1 shows the process that normally happens, by default, using RIP. The updates occur every 30 seconds, and as long as nothing changes, each periodic update contains the same full set of routes.

Route Poisoning

When a route fails, distance vector routing protocols risk causing routing loops until every router in the internetwork knows and believes that the original route has failed. As a result, distance vector protocols need to have a way to specifically identify which routes have failed.

Distance vector protocols spread the bad news about a route failure by poisoning the route. *Route poisoning* refers to the practice of advertising a route, but with a special metric value called *infinity*. Simply put, routers consider routes advertised with an infinite metric to have failed. Note that each distance vector routing protocol uses the concept of an actual metric value that represents infinity. RIP defines infinity as 16.

Figure 7-2 shows an example of route poisoning with RIP, with R2's FA0/1 interface failing, meaning that R2's route for 172.30.22.0/24 has failed.

Note

Even though routes poisoned by RIP have a metric of 16, the **show ip route** command does not list the metric's value—instead, it lists the phrase "possibly down."

Figure 7-2   Route Poisoning

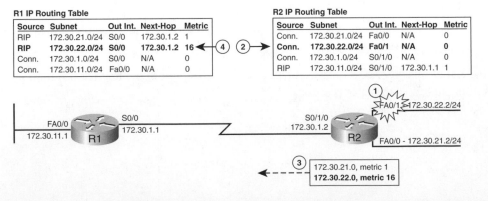

Figure 7-2 shows the following process:

1. R2's FA0/1 interface fails.

2. R2 removes its connected route for 172.30.22.0/24 from its routing table.

3. R2 advertises 172.30.22.0 with an infinite metric, which for RIP is metric 16.

4. R1 keeps the route in its routing table, with an infinite metric, as part of the loop-avoidance process.

Any metric value below infinity can be used as a valid metric for a valid route. With RIP, that means that a 15-hop route would be a valid route. Some of the largest enterprise networks in the world have at most four to five routers in the longest route between any two subnets, so a valid maximum valid metric of 15 hops is enough.

Problem: Counting to Infinity

Distance vector routing protocols risk causing routing loops between the time at which the first router realizes a route has failed until all the routers know that the route has failed. Without the loop-prevention mechanisms explained in this chapter, distance vector protocols can experience a problem called *counting to infinity*. Certainly, routers could never literally count to infinity, but they can count to their version of infinity—for example, to 16 with RIP.

Counting to infinity causes two related problems. Several of the distance vector loop-prevention features focus on preventing these problems:

- Packets may loop around the internetwork while the routers count to infinity, with the bandwidth consumed by the looping packets crippling an internetwork.

- The counting-to-infinity process may take several minutes, meaning that the looping could cause users to believe that the network has failed.

When routers count to infinity, they collectively keep changing their minds about the metric of a failed route. The metric grows slowly until the metric reaches infinity, at which point the routers finally believe that the route has failed. The best way to understand this concept is to see an example; Figure 7-3 shows the beginnings of the counting-to-infinity problem.

Figure 7-3 R2 Incorrectly Believes R1 Has a Route to 172.16.22.0/24

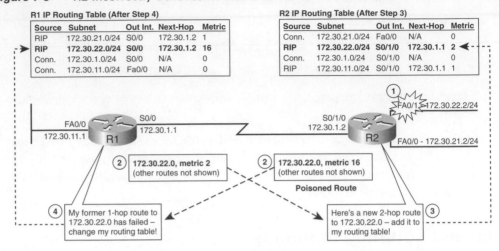

The key to this example is to know that R1's periodic update to R2 (left to right in Figure 7-3) occurs at almost the same instant as R2's poison route advertisement. Figure 7-4 shows the following process:

1. R2's FA0/1 interface fails, so R2 removes its connected route for 172.30.22.0/24 from its routing table.

2. R2 sends a poisoned route advertisement (metric 16 for RIP) to R1, but *at about the same time*, R1's periodic update timer expires, so R1 sends its regular update, including an advertisement of 172.30.22.0, metric 2.

3. R2 hears about the metric 2 route to reach 172.30.22.0 from R1. Because R2 no longer has a route for subnet 172.30.22.0, R2 adds the two-hop route to its routing table, next-hop router R1.

4. At about the same time as Step 3, R1 receives the update from R2, telling R1 that its former route to 172.30.22.0, through R1, has failed. As a result, R1 changes its routing table to list a metric of 16 for the route to 172.30.22.0.

At this point, R1 and R2 forward packets destined for 172.30.22.0/24 back and forth to each other. R2 has a route for 172.30.22.0/24, pointing to R1, and R1 has the reverse.

The looping occurs until R1 and R2 both count to infinity. Figure 7-4 shows the next step in their cooperative march toward infinity.

Figure 7-4   R1 and R2 Count to Infinity

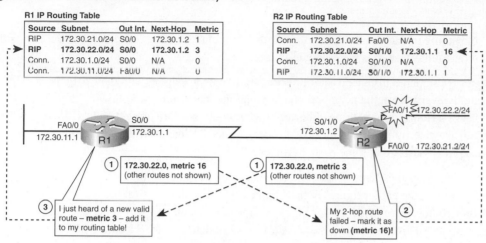

Figure 7-4 shows both routers' next periodic updates, as follows:

1. Both R1's and R2's update timers expire at about the same time. R1 advertises a poison (metric 16) route, and R2 advertises a metric 3 route. (Remember, RIP routers add 1 to the metric before advertising the route.)

2. R2 receives R1's update, so R2 changes its route for 172.30.22.0 to use a metric of 16.

3. At about the same time as Step 2, R1 receives R2's update, so R1 changes its route for 172.30.22.0 to use a metric of 3.

The process would continue through each periodic update cycle, with both routers eventually reaching metric 16. At that point, the routers could time out the routes and remove them from their routing tables.

Loop-Prevention Features

Thankfully, the distance vector protocols include features that prevent such problems as counting to infinity. This section covers several distance vector features that together eliminate the possibility of counting to infinity and solve other problems with distance vector protocols. The features are split horizon, poison reverse, triggered updates, and the holddown timer.

Split Horizon

In the simple internetwork used in Figure 7-3 and Figure 7-4, R2 has a connected route to 172.30.22.0, and R1 learns the route due to a routing update sent by R2. Both figures show R1 advertising subnet 172.30.22.0 in updates sent back to R2. However, there is little need for R1 to advertise that route to R2, because R1 learned that route from R2 in the first place. So, one way to prevent the counting-to-infinity problem shown in these figures is to have R1 simply not advertise subnet 172.30.22.0, using a feature called *split horizon*. Split horizon is defined as follows:

> In routing updates sent out interface *X*, do not include routing information about routes that refer to interface *X* as the outgoing interface.

Chapter 6 compared distance vector protocols to people gossiping with their neighbors, with eventually everyone in the neighborhood learning the latest rumors. Following that analogy, if you heard a rumor from your neighbor Fred, you would not turn around and tell Fred the same rumor. Likewise, split horizon means that when router R1 learns a route from router R2, R1 has no need to advertise that same route to router R2.

Figure 7-5 shows the effect of split horizon on routers R1 and R2 in the same familiar internetwork shown in the earlier figures in this chapter. R1's routing table (at the top of the figure) lists four routes, three of which have R1's 0/0 interface as the outgoing interface. So, split horizon prevents R1 from including those routes in the update sent by R1 out its S0/0 interface.

Figure 7-5   The Effects of Split Horizon Without Poison Reverse

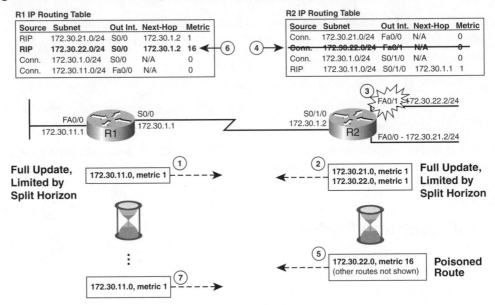

Figure 7-5 shows the following process:

1. R1 sends its normal periodic full update, which, due to split horizon rules, includes only one route.

2. R2 sends its normal periodic full update, which, due to split horizon rules, includes only two routes.

3. R2's FA0/1 interface fails.

4. R2 removes its connected route for 172.30.22.0/24 from its routing table.

5. R2 advertises 172.30.22.0 with an infinite metric, which for RIP is metric 16.

6. R1 temporarily keeps the route for 172.30.22.0 in its routing table, later removing the route from the routing table.

7. In its next regular update, R1, due to split horizon, still does not advertise the route for 172.30.22.0.

Split horizon prevents the counting-to-infinity problem shown in Figure 7-3 and Figure 7-4 because R1 does not advertise 172.30.22.0 at all. As a result, R2 never hears about an (incorrect) alternate route to 172.30.22.0.

Cisco IOS defaults to use split horizon on most interfaces, including all the interface types configured in this book.

Poison Reverse and Triggered Updates

Distance vector protocols can attack the counting-to-infinity problem when reacting to failed routes by ensuring that every router learns that the route has failed, through every means possible, as quickly as possible. The next two loop-prevention features do just that, and are defined as follows:

- *Triggered update*—When a route fails, do not wait for the next periodic update. Instead, send an immediate triggered update listing the poisoned route.

- *Poison reverse*—When learning of a failed route, suspend split horizon rules for that route, and advertise a poisoned route.

Figure 7-6 shows an example of each of these features, with R2's interface FA0/1 failing yet again. Note that the figure begins with all interfaces working and all routes known.

Figure 7-6   R2 Sending a Triggered Update, with R1 Advertising a Poison Reverse Route

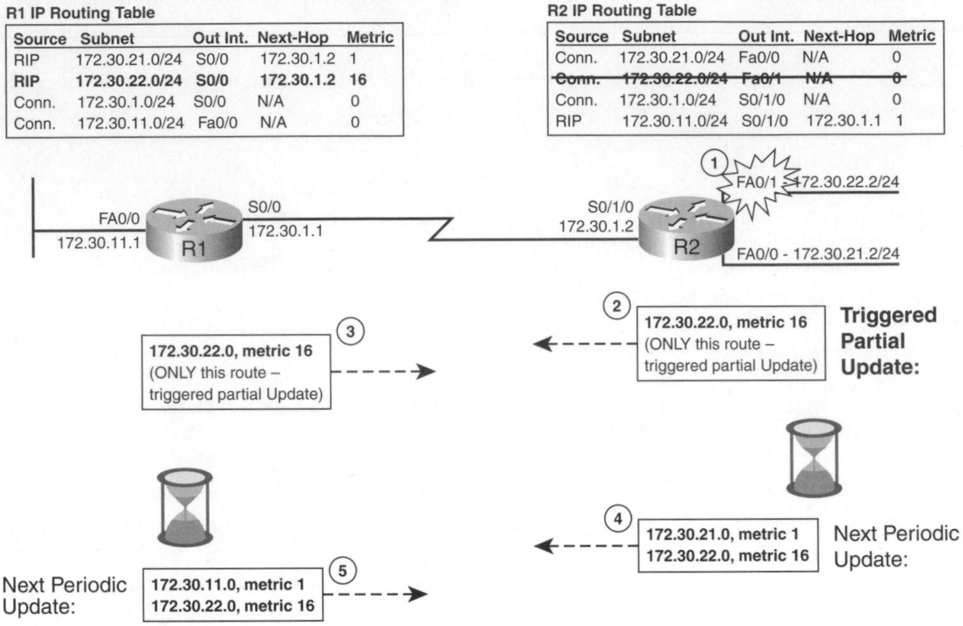

The process shown in Figure 7-6 runs as follows:

1. R2's FA0/1 interface fails.

2. R2 immediately sends a triggered partial update with only the changed information—in this case, a poison route for 172.30.22.0.

3. R1 responds by changing its routing table and sending back an immediate (triggered) partial update, listing only 172.30.22.0 with an infinite metric (metric 16). This is a poison reverse route.

4. On R2's next regular periodic update, R2 advertises all the typical routes, including the poison route for 172.30.22.0, for a time.

5. On R1's next regular periodic update, R1 advertises all the typical routes, including the poison reverse route for 172.30.22.0, for a time.

In this example, R2 reacts immediately by sending the triggered update. R1 also reacts immediately, suspending split horizon rules for the failed route, to send a poison reverse route. In fact, R2's poison route is not considered a poison reverse route, because R2 had already been advertising a route for 172.30.22.0. However, R1's poison route is a poison reverse route because it was advertised back to the router from which R1 learned about the failed route. In fact, some books also refer to poison reverse as *split horizon with poison reverse*, because the router ignores the split horizon rule for the failed route.

Using Holddown Timers to Prevent Loops in Redundant Networks

Split horizon prevents the counting-to-infinity problem from occurring between two routers. However, with redundant paths in an internetwork, which is true of most internetworks today, split horizon alone does not always prevent counting to infinity.

Figures 7-7, 7-8, and 7-9 show an example of how counting to infinity can occur when redundancy exists. To begin, Figure 7-7 shows a new internetwork with three routers. This figure shows the routes advertised in this internetwork when all links are up and working.

Figure 7-7   Periodic Updates in a Stable Triangle Internetwork

Note

Figure 7-7 omits the RIP updates that would be sent out the LAN interfaces.

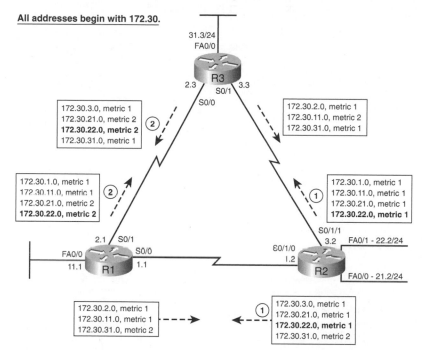

Besides providing the background needed to show how counting to infinity can occur in this internetwork, Figure 7-7 also provides a good example of how split horizon works. Again using subnet 172.30.22.0 as an example, the following process occurs in this internetwork (Step 3 is not shown in Figure 7-7):

1. R2 advertises a metric 1 route for 172.30.22.0 in its updates to both R1 and R3.

2. R1 advertises a metric 2 route for 172.30.22.0 to R3, while R3 advertises a metric 2 route for 172.30.22.0 to R2.

3. Both R1 and R3 add the metric 1 route, learned directly from R2, to their routing tables, and ignore the two-hop routes they learn from each other. For example, R1 places a route 172.30.22.0, using outgoing interface S0/0, next-hop router 172.30.1.2 (R2), in its routing table.

Split horizon prevents R1 and R3 from advertising subnet 172.30.22.0 back to R2. Note that Figure 7-7 shows all the route advertisements for 172.30.22.0 in bold text. R1 and R3 do not list 172.30.22.0 in their updates sent back to R2. In fact, all the routing updates shown in Figure 7-7 show the effects of split horizon.

Now that you have a good understanding of the internetwork shown in Figure 7-7, Figure 7-8 shows the same internetwork, but with the beginning of the counting-to-infinity problem. Yet again, R2's interface FA0/1 begins the example by failing.

Figure 7-8   Counting to Infinity in a Redundant Internetwork, Part 1

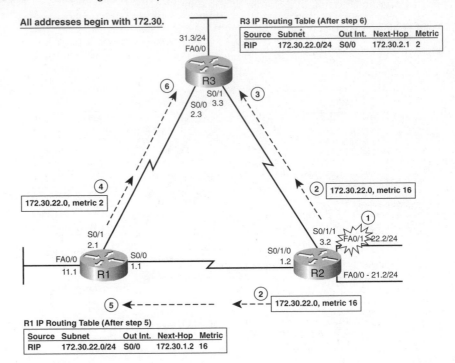

The process shown in Figure 7-8 is as follows:

1. R2's FA0/1 interface fails.

2. R2 immediately sends triggered partial updates poisoning the route for 172.30.22.0. R2 sends the updates out all still-working interfaces.

3. R3 receives R2's triggered update that poisons the route for 172.30.22.0, so R3 updates its routing table to list metric 16 for this route.

4. Before the update described in Step 2 arrives at R1, R1 sends its normal periodic update to R3, listing 172.30.22.0, metric 2, as normal. (Note that Figure 7-8 omits some of what would be in R1's periodic update to reduce clutter.)

5. R1 receives R2's triggered update (described at Step 2) that poisons the route for 172.30.22.0, so R1 updates it routing table to list metric 16 for this route.

6. R3 receives the periodic update sent by R1 (described at Step 4), listing a metric 2 route for 172.30.22.0. As a result, R3 updates its routing table to list a metric 2 route, through R1 as the next-hop router, with outgoing interface S0/0.

At this point, R3 has an incorrect metric 2 route for 172.30.22.0, pointing back to R1. Figure 7-9 shows how these three routers together count to infinity.

Figure 7-9   Counting to Infinity in a Redundant Internetwork, Part 2

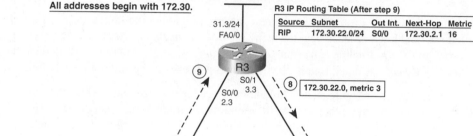

The following list describes the steps shown in Figure 7-9; these steps follow the steps shown in Figure 7-8:

7. R1 sends its next periodic update to R3, with poisoned route 172.30.22.0, metric 16.

8. Before the update described in Step 7 arrives at R3, R3 sends its next periodic update to R2, listing a metric 3 route for 172.30.22.0.

9. R3 receives R1's periodic update from R1 (as described in Step 7), and R3 changes its route for 172.30.22.0 to list an infinite metric.

10. R2 receives R3's periodic update (as described in Step 8), so R2 adds a metric 3 route for 172.30.22.0 to its routing table, listing R3 as the next-hop router, with outgoing interface S0/1/1.

The Holddown Process and Holddown Timer

The last loop-prevention feature covered in this chapter, a process called *holddown*, prevents the looping and counting-to-infinity problem shown in Figures 7-8 and 7-9. The routers in those figures used split horizon and could have easily been using triggered updates and poison reverse. Distance vector protocols use holddown to specifically attack the loops created by the counting-to-infinity problems that occur in redundant internetworks, similar to the example of Figures 7-8 and 7-9.

The term *holddown* gives a hint as to its meaning:

> After the route is considered to be down, *hold the route in a down state for a while* to give the routers time to make sure every router knows that the route has failed.

The holddown process tells a router to ignore new information about the failed route, for a time period called the holddown time, as counted using the *holddown timer*. The Cisco Networking Academy Program CCNA 3 online curriculum defines a more general definition of holddown, but when specifically looking at failed routes, the holddown process can be summarized as follows:

> After hearing a poisoned route, start a holddown timer for that one route. Until the timer expires, do not believe any other routing information about the failed route, unless the information is learned from the neighbor that originally advertised the working route.

The holddown concept may be better understood with an example. Figure 7-10 repeats the example of Figure 7-8, but with R3's holddown process preventing the counting-to-infinity problem. Figure 7-10 shows how R3 ignores any new information about subnet 172.30.22.0 due to holddown. As usual, the figure begins with all interfaces up and working, and all routes known, and with Step 1 being the failure of the same interface off router R2.

Figure 7-10 Using Holddown to Prevent Counting to Infinity

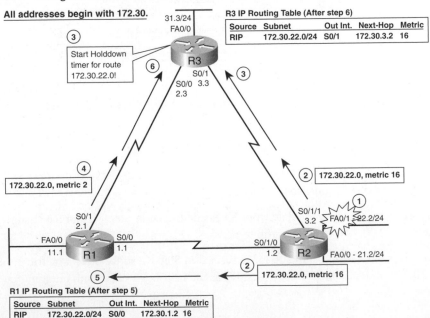

The process shown in Figure 7-10 is as follows, with Steps 3 and 6 differing from the corresponding steps for Figure 7-8:

1. R2's FA0/1 interface fails.

2. R2 immediately sends triggered partial updates, poisoning the route for 172.30.22.0. R2 sends the updates out all still-working interfaces.

3. R3 receives R2's triggered update that poisons the route for 172.30.22.0, so R3 updates its routing table to list metric 16 for this route. R3 also puts the route for 172.30.22.0 in holddown and starts the holddown timer (180 seconds by default with RIP) for the route.

4. Before the update described in Step 2 arrives at R1, R1 sends its normal periodic update to R3, listing 172.30.22.0, metric 2, as normal. (Note that Figure 7-10 omits some details in R1's periodic update to reduce clutter.)

5. R1 receives R2's triggered update (described in Step 2) that poisons the route for 172.30.22.0, so R1 updates its routing table to list metric 16 for this route.

6. R3 receives the update from R1 (described in Step 4), listing a metric 2 route for 172.30.22.0. Because R3 has placed this route in a holddown state, and this new metric 2 route was learned from a different router (R1) than the original router (R2), R3 ignores the new routing information.

As a result of R3's holddown logic described in Step 6, all three routers have a metric 16 route for 172.30.22.0. At this point, any future routing updates will list only metric 16 routes for this subnet—at least until a real route to the subnet becomes available again.

The definition of holddown allows the routers to believe the same router that originally advertised the route, even before the holddown timer expires. For example, the entire process of Figure 7-10 may occur within just a few seconds due to all the triggered updates. If R2's FA0/1 interface comes up again, R2 then advertises a metric 1 route for 172.30.22.0 again. If R1 and R3 would believe R2's advertisement, they could avoid waiting almost 3 more minutes for their holddown timers to expire for subnet 172.30.22.0. As it turns out, believing the routing update from the same router that originally advertised the route does not risk causing a loop, so holddown allows the routers (in this case, R1 and R3) to believe R2's advertisement.

Summarizing Loop Avoidance

Before closing this first major section of the chapter, it is useful to review the concepts it has covered. Although this section covered a lot of theory, some of which can be a little tricky, the main features can be summarized easily:

- During periods of stability, routers send periodic full updates. The updates list all known routes except the routes omitted due to split horizon rules.

- When changes occur that cause a route to fail, routers react by sending triggered partial updates with poisoned routes. Routers also suspend split horizon rules for that route, advertising a poison reverse route back toward the router from which the poisoned route was learned.

- All routers place a route in holddown state and start a holddown timer for that route after learning that the route has failed. The router ignores all new information about that route until the holddown timer expires, unless that information comes from the same router that originally advertised the good route to that subnet.

For reference, Table 7-1 defines many of the terms used so far in this chapter.

Table 7-1   Distance Vector Loop Avoidance Terminology

Term	Definition
Poison route	A route that was formerly advertised with a valid metric but is now advertised with an infinite metric. This advertisement means that the route has failed.
Poison reverse	A route that was formerly not advertised due to split horizon rules but is now advertised with an infinite metric. This advertisement means that the route has failed.
Split horizon	A per-interface feature, generally on by default, that limits the routes included in distance vector routing updates sent out each interface. For a given interface, any route whose outgoing interface is that same interface is not included in routing updates sent out that interface.
Infinity	With routing protocols, an actual number that is assigned to routes that have failed. For example, RIP, which has a maximum hop count of 15, uses 16 to mean "infinity."
Holddown	A process that a router applies to a route when the route fails, causing the router to ignore newly-learned alternate routes to reach that subnet. The router uses a timer, called the holddown timer, to determine how long to ignore newly-learned alternate routes. After the holddown timer expires, the router can believe newly-learned alternate routes without the risk of introducing routing loops.
Triggered update	A routing update that is not sent at a regular periodic interval but instead is caused, or triggered, based on some change in routing information.

The next section covers RIP configuration and troubleshooting.

Routing Information Protocol

Now that you understand many features that apply to any distance vector routing protocol and have seen many examples that use RIP, this section describes RIP in detail, covering its features, its configuration, and how to verify and troubleshoot a RIP installation. The section concludes with miscellaneous topics related to RIP, including how RIP chooses among equal-metric routes and what the **ip classless** command really does on a router.

Configuring RIP Versions 1 and 2

The first IP networks used RIP Version 1 (V1) because it was the first and only IP routing protocol early in the history of TCP/IP. As time went on, routers became more affordable, with faster CPUs, more memory, and faster links, all of which allowed the development of more advanced routing algorithms and routing protocols, such as OSPF and EIGRP. Around the same time, other developers enhanced the RIP protocol standard, calling the new standard RIP Version 2 (V2).

RIP V2 does not completely change RIP V1, but rather adds some advanced features. To add the features, RIP V2 puts more information in the routing update. These additions include authentication information so that a router has confidence that the routes it hears from a neighbor are from a legitimate router. Additionally, the V2 updates include the subnet mask with each route. By including the mask, RIP V2 supports variable-length subnet masking (VLSM), whereas RIP V1 could not support VLSM. In fact, the networking world uses the term *classless routing protocol* to refer to routing protocols that include the mask in routing updates, therefore supporting VLSM, which makes RIP V2 a classless routing protocol. RIP V1 would then be called a *classful routing protocol* by comparison. Classless and classful routing protocols are described in more detail in the section "Classful and Classless Routing Protocols, Routing, and Addressing" later in this chapter.

Table 7-2 summarizes many of the RIP features already covered in Chapter 6, with the key differences between RIP V1 and V2 highlighted at the bottom of the table.

Table 7-2   Comparing RIP Version 1 and 2 Features

Feature	V1	V2
RFC	1058	2453
Hop-count metric	Yes	Yes
15 is largest valid metric; 16 is infinity	Yes	Yes
Default 30-second update interval	Yes	Yes
Full periodic updates	Yes	Yes
Partial triggered updates when routes change	Yes	Yes
Uses route poisoning, poison reverse, split horizon, and holddown	Yes	Yes
Supports multiple equal-cost routes to same subnet (default 4, up to 6)	Yes	Yes
Sends updates as multicasts[1]	No	Yes
Sends mask in updates, thereby supporting VLSM[1]	No	Yes
Supports route tags	No	Yes
Supports authentication	No	Yes

[1] These features are enabled automatically after RIP V2 has been configured.

The next several sections examine the configuration for RIP V1 and V2 and how to configure a network to use both.

Configuring RIP V1

Chapter 6 introduced RIP V1 configuration in the appropriately titled section "RIP Configuration." Simply put, RIP V1 configuration requires two configuration commands:

- **router rip**

- **network** *classful-network-number*

The **router rip** command moves the user from global configuration mode to RIP configuration mode, and the **network** command tells the router on which interfaces to start using RIP. For example, in all the figures shown so far in this chapter, all router interfaces use an IP address in network 172.30.0.0. So, to configure RIP V1 to be used on every router, on every interface shown, in every figure so far in this chapter, you would simply need to add the commands shown in Example 7-1.

Example 7-1   Configuring RIP on All Interfaces on R1

```
R1#conf t
Enter configuration commands, one per line.  End with CNTL/Z.
R1(config)#router rip
R1(config-router)#network 172.30.0.0
R1(config-router)#^Z
R1#
```

Example 7-1 shows the configuration process and the actual configuration commands. By looking at the command prompts, you can see that the **router rip** global configuration command moves the user into RIP configuration mode, as shown with the R1(config-router)# command prompt. The **network** command requires a classful network, meaning a Class A, B, or C network number. (That is true of both V1 and V2 configuration.) The router then looks for all of its interfaces in that network and starts using RIP on those interfaces.

As a reminder from Chapter 6, when a router's RIP configuration matches an interface, Cisco IOS starts the following process:

1. Sends RIP updates out the interface.

2. Listens for RIP updates coming in that interface from some other router.

3. Advertises the subnet attached to the interface.

For an additional RIP configuration example, refer to Chapter 6, Figure 6-13, and the configuration process that is explained with it. The Chapter 6 example shows a router with multiple **network** commands.

> **Note**
>
> If you enter a **network** command and use a subnet number or IP address, the router accepts the command but changes the **network** command to list the Class A, B, or C network number.

 Packet Tracer configuration file NA02-0710-V1 includes a configuration that matches the topology of Figure 7-10, with the RIP configuration shown in Example 7-1.

 Lab 7.2.2   Configuring RIP

In this lab, you set up an IP addressing scheme using Class B networks and configure the RIP dynamic routing protocol on routers.

Configuring RIP V2

This section examines the simple configuration required when a network uses RIP V2, and RIP V2 only. To configure RIP V2 in internetworks that use RIP V2 only, simply add the **version 2** command under **router rip**. After they are configured, the routers send only V2 updates and process only received V2 updates. At that point, the core features of RIP V2, such as sending masks in routing updates, occur. Optional RIP V2 features, such as authentication, would then require additional configuration.

Packet Tracer Packet Tracer configuration file NA02-0710-V2 includes a configuration that matches the topology of Figure 7-10, with RIP V2 configured.

Using Both RIP V1 and V2

In some cases, an internetwork may need to use both RIP versions. For example, when migrating from RIP V1 to RIP V2, the engineers may decide to migrate to RIP V2 on some routers one weekend, more routers the next weekend, and so on. In other cases, there may be some business or company organizational reason to use both versions. Regardless of the reasons, to support both versions in the same internetwork, one or more routers need to use both versions at the same time.

Figure 7-11 shows an example network in which both RIP versions are used. The routers on the left can use the standard RIP V1 configuration, which omits the **version** command, defaulting to use version 1. The routers on the right can use the RIP V2 configuration, which includes the **version 2** command. Router R1 must use both RIP V1 and V2 and translate between the two versions, using RIP V1 on the left (S0/1) and RIP V2 on the right (S0/0).

Figure 7-11   RIP Version Migration: Speaking Both Versions

Note

A router using the default RIP configuration will not be fully compatible with a router configured to use only RIP V2.

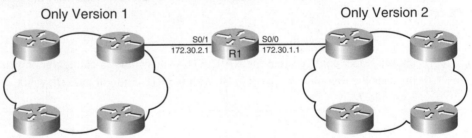

Cisco IOS provides commands that you can use to configure the RIP version for the whole router and provides other commands that you can use to override the RIP version on each interface. Essentially, you can tell a Cisco router to send RIP V1 updates, V2 updates, or both, for each interface. Likewise, you can tell the router to "receive"—meaning process—incoming updates that are V1, V2, or both. Because of all of these options, you can configure a Cisco router to support both RIP versions in several ways. For example, for R1 in Figure 7-11, you can use the following options:

- Configure R1 for RIP V1 (by omitting the **version** command) and then configure interface S0/0 to send and receive RIP V2 updates

- Configure R1 for RIP V2 (by including the **version 2** command) and then configure interface S0/1 to send and receive RIP V1 updates

Example 7-2 shows the configuration for the first of these two options.

Example 7-2   Configuring RIP Version 2 on an Interface

```
R1#configure terminal
Enter configuration commands, one per line.  End with CNTL/Z.
R1(config)#router rip
R1(config-router)#network 172.30.0.0
R1(config-router)#interface serial 0/0
R1(config-if)#ip rip send version 2
R1(config-if)#ip rip receive version 2
R1(config-if)#^Z
```

The configuration in Example 7-2 shows how R1 enables RIP V2 on interface S0/0 by using the **ip rip send version 2** and **ip rip receive version 2** interface subcommands. So, R1 sends and receives only RIP V2 updates on the right of Figure 7-11 and defaults to sending and receiving RIP V1 updates on the left.

Design Options Impacted by the RIP Version

The use of RIP V2 instead of RIP V1 allows the use of two powerful network design options. RIP V2 allows for the use of VLSM, whereas RIP V1 does not. VLSM gives the engineer much more flexibility when choosing which subnets to use and how many hosts to put into each subnet.

RIP V2 also allows a design choice called a *discontiguous network*. A discontiguous network occurs when at least one pair of subnets of the same classful network are separated by subnets of a different classful network. In Figure 7-12, 172.30.0.0 is the discontiguous network, because parts of it are separated by subnets of network 10.0.0.0.

Note

As a reminder, the term *classful network* refers to a single Class A, B, or C network.

Figure 7-12   Discontiguous Network 172.30.0.0

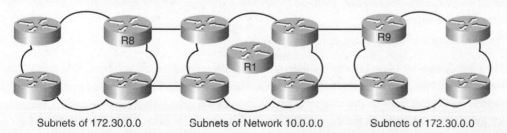

Subnets of 172.30.0.0   Subnets of Network 10.0.0.0   Subnets of 172.30.0.0

RIP V1 simply does not support discontiguous networks; RIP V2 supports them if all the routers have been configured with the RIP **no auto-summary** subcommand.

Other RIP Configuration Options

Although the RIP configuration can be a little tricky when supporting more than one RIP version on one router, for routers that use only one RIP version or the other, the configuration is straightforward. For V1, simply configure the **router rip** command and one or more **network** commands to match all the interfaces. For V2, add the **version 2** command under **router rip**.

RIP has several optional configuration settings as well:

- Adjust timers, such as the holddown and update timers

- Enable or disable split horizon per interface

- Explicitly configure RIP neighbors to support certain types of WAN connections

- Disable the sending of RIP updates on an interface (using the **passive-interface** command), while still receiving RIP updates

- Filter the contents of RIP updates

This section covers the basics of each of these items.

Adjusting RIP Timers

RIP uses several timers, including two that are covered in the Networking Academy CCNA 2 curriculum:

- Update timer

- Holddown timer

Note

Most installations do not change the RIP timers. If they are changed, the timers should be changed on all routers in the internetwork.

Additionally, RIP uses the concept of an invalid timer and a *flush timer*. (The flush timer determines when a router removes a route from the routing table after the route has been poisoned.) All of these timers can be reset with the following command, which is configured as a subcommand under **router rip**:

```
timers basic update invalid holddown flush
```

You might consider lowering the holddown timer to speed convergence. The online curriculum suggests that you can lower the holddown timer based on the following estimate: find the longest number of hops in the longest possible loop in the internetwork, and multiply that number by the update timer. In the case of Figure 7-10, with three routers in a triangle, the longest loop would be three hops, so the holddown timer could be changed to a value of 3×30, or 90 seconds. (The online curriculum shows four routers in a diamond shape, with a four-hop possible loop, suggesting a holddown timer of $4 \times 30 = 120$ seconds.) For instance, to change only the holddown timer, you could then use the command **timers basic 30 180 90 240**, which sets the holddown timer to 90 seconds and leaves the other timers at their default settings.

You should take care when adjusting any of the timers, because these all relate to loop-prevention in some way, and a poor choice could introduce temporary loops into an internetwork. Rather than tuning RIP so that RIP converges in 2 minutes instead of 3 minutes, the better option today is to use EIGRP or OSPF, which converge in less than 10 to 15 seconds in most cases.

Disabling Split Horizon

Split horizon helps prevent loops by avoiding the counting-to-infinity problem, as described earlier in the chapter in the section "Problem: Counting to Infinity." Cisco IOS enables split horizon on almost all interfaces, with the one exception being serial interfaces that are configured with some not-very-popular Frame Relay options. However, you can disable split horizon, per interface, by using the following interface subcommand:

```
no ip split-horizon
```

For example, to disable split horizon on interface S0/0, the engineer would enter configuration mode, type the **interface S0/0** command, and then use the **no ip split-horizon** command. Today, there are few if any good reasons to disable split horizon, other than for learning purposes.

Note

To re-enable split horizon on an interface, use the **ip split-horizon** interface subcommand.

Configuring Neighbors

RIP V1 sends its update messages to IP broadcast address 255.255.255.255. RIP V2 improves the update process by sending its update messages to the 224.0.0.9 multicast IP address. By using multicasts, only RIP-speaking routers should process RIP updates, reducing the overhead on the other hosts on a LAN.

Of course, these update packets must be inside a data-link frame before being sent out the physical interface. So, RIP V1 sends its updates as data-link broadcasts, and RIP V2 sends its updates as data-link multicasts. However, some WAN data links may not support the sending of data-link broadcasts or multicasts. In those cases, RIP must send its updates using IP and data-link unicast addresses. To do so, a RIP router must define the neighboring router's unicast IP address using the **neighbor** command. For example, in Figure 7-10, R1 might use the command **neighbor 172.30.1.2**, under **router rip**, to explicitly configure R2 as a neighbor.

Enabling the **passive-interface** Command

As mentioned earlier in the chapter in the section "Configuring RIP V1," RIP does three things on an interface that is matched using the RIP **network** command: advertises the subnet on that interface, sends updates out the interface, and listens for updates coming in that interface. After RIP is configured, it may be useful to then stop sending RIP updates on the interface. To do so, the configuration must still match the interface with a **network** command, and then the router must be told to stop sending updates with the **passive-interface** *interface* subcommand under **router rip**. The **passive-interface** command tells RIP to stop sending RIP updates out the listed interface.

Figure 7-13 shows an example in which it may be useful to make R1 stop sending RIP updates on its S0/0 interface. In this internetwork, the company has two separate divisions whose networks connect to each other. One division uses RIP, and the other uses OSPF. So, one (or more) router must learn routes with OSPF, and advertise them into RIP, and vice versa, so all the routes will be known. This process is known as *route redistribution*. In Figure 7-13, router R1 performs the route redistribution.

Figure 7-13 R1 Redistributing Between RIP and OSPF

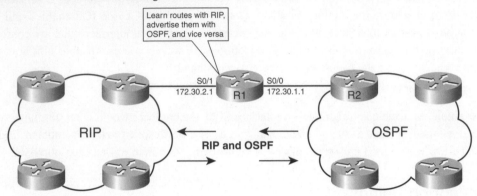

Example 7-3 shows R1's RIP configuration. Note that because both of R1's interfaces are part of network 172.30.0.0, the **network 172.30.0.0** command enables RIP on both interfaces. However, R2, which uses only OSPF, has no need to receive R1's RIP updates. So, R1 has used the **passive-interface** command, meaning that R1 no longer sends RIP updates out its S0/0 interface into the OSPF part of the internetwork.

Example 7-3 Configuring the **passive-interface** Command

```
R1#configure terminal
Enter configuration commands, one per line.  End with CNTL/Z.
R1(config)#router rip
R1(config-router)#network 172.30.0.0
R1(config-router)#passive-interface S0/0
R1(config-router)#^Z
R1#
```

Lab 7.2.7 Preventing Routing Updates Through an Interface

In this lab, you prevent a router from sending routing updates on an interface by using the **passive-interface** router subcommand.

Filtering Routes

Routers can use route filtering to filter the routes sent and received in RIP updates. Route filtering allows an engineer to limit which routers learn which routes. For example, if a particular subnet should be protected for security reasons, and only certain groups of people should be able to communicate with the hosts in that subnet, the engineer could filter routes.

Distance vector routing protocols support route filtering on any router for updates sent or received on any interface. However, link-state routing protocols work under the assumption that all routers need to learn about all routers and all links (subnets). As a result, link-state protocols can support route filtering, but only in certain locations in the internetwork.

The next section explains the main tools and commands to verify whether RIP is working properly.

RIP Verification and Troubleshooting

Cisco IOS includes several commands that show a direct correlation between the concepts used by RIP and the actual behavior of RIP on a particular router. This section covers the most commonly used commands for verifying and troubleshooting RIP.

Verifying RIP Operations Using **show** Commands

The following four **show** commands provide the most useful information for examining how RIP is working in a router:

- **show ip protocols**
- **show ip route**
- **show ip interface brief**
- **show ip rip database**

Example 7-4 shows the output of the **show ip protocols** command. This command supplies a large amount of specific information related to all IP routing protocols that are currently running in the router. In fact, if a router is running multiple routing protocols at one time, like R1 in Figure 7-13, this command would list detailed information about each of the routing protocols. This example shows command output from R1 in Figures 7-7 through 7-10 (the three-router internetwork using network 172.30.0.0). All three routers use default configuration as much as possible, with each router using the **router rip** and **network 172.30.0.0** commands, which enables RIP V1 on all interfaces on each router.

Note

Example 7-4 includes many comment lines— lines that begin with an exclamation point (!)— instead of listing the descriptions after the example.

Example 7-4   R1: Sample RIP **show ip protocols** Command

```
R1#show ip protocols
!!!!!!!!!!!!!!!!!!!!!!!!!!!!!!!!!!!!!!!!!!!!!!!!!!!!!!!!!!!!!!!!!!!!!!!!!!!!!!!!!!!!!
! The following line implies that RIP has indeed been configured on this router,
! with the update and holddown settings shown on the following lines.
Routing Protocol is "rip"
  Sending updates every 30 seconds, next due in 17 seconds
  Invalid after 180 seconds, hold down 180, flushed after 240
  Outgoing update filter list for all interfaces is not set
  Incoming update filter list for all interfaces is not set
  Redistributing: rip
!!!!!!!!!!!!!!!!!!!!!!!!!!!!!!!!!!!!!!!!!!!!!!!!!!!!!!!!!!!!!!!!!!!!!!!!!!!!!!!!!!!!!
! This next section lists the interfaces on which RIP has been enabled as a result
! of being matched by a network command.
  Default version control: send version 1, receive any version
    Interface            Send  Recv  Triggered RIP  Key-chain
    FastEthernet0/0      1     1 2
    Serial0/0            1     1 2
    Serial0/1            1     1 2
  Automatic network summarization is in effect
  Maximum path: 4
!!!!!!!!!!!!!!!!!!!!!!!!!!!!!!!!!!!!!!!!!!!!!!!!!!!!!!!!!!!!!!!!!!!!!!!!!!!!!!!!!!!!!
! The following lines essentially repeat the networks that are configured on
! the RIP network commands.
  Routing for Networks:
    172.30.0.0
!!!!!!!!!!!!!!!!!!!!!!!!!!!!!!!!!!!!!!!!!!!!!!!!!!!!!!!!!!!!!!!!!!!!!!!!!!!!!!!!!!!!!
! The following lines list the IP addresses of routers from which this router has
! received RIP updates. In this case, R1 has heard from R2 (172.30.1.2) and R3
! (172.30.2.3). It also shows how long ago R1 last received an update.
  Routing Information Sources:
    Gateway         Distance      Last Update
    172.30.1.2           120      00:00:17
    172.30.2.3           120      00:00:24
  Distance: (default is 120)
```

Verifying RIP should typically start with the **show ip protocols** command due to all the detailed information it lists. In particular, seeing the interface on which RIP is enabled, and the IP addresses of the neighboring routers from which the router has received recent updates, can be very helpful.

Example 7-5 shows examples of the other three **show** commands listed at the beginning of this section, again taken from router R1. In particular, the **show ip route** command lists all IP routes in the routing table while showing the RIP-learned routes with an "R" at the beginning of the line. The **show ip interface brief** command quickly lists the state of each interface, which is helpful because the **show ip protocols** command lists the interfaces on which RIP has been enabled, but it does not state whether those interfaces are up. Finally, the **show ip rip database** command lists all the best routes known by RIP.

Example 7-5   Sample RIP **show** Commands on R1

```
R1#show ip route
Codes: C - connected, S - static, R - RIP, M - mobile, B - BGP
       D - EIGRP, EX - EIGRP external, O - OSPF, IA - OSPF inter area
       N1 - OSPF NSSA external type 1, N2 - OSPF NSSA external type 2
       E1 - OSPF external type 1, E2 - OSPF external type 2
       i - IS-IS, su - IS-IS summary, L1 - IS-IS level-1, L2 - IS-IS level-2
       ia - IS-IS inter area, * - candidate default, U - per-user static route
       o - ODR, P - periodic downloaded static route
Gateway of last resort is not set

     172.30.0.0/24 is subnetted, 7 subnets
R       172.30.22.0 [120/1] via 172.30.1.2, 00:00:20, Serial0/0
R       172.30.21.0 [120/1] via 172.30.1.2, 00:00:20, Serial0/0
R       172.30.31.0 [120/1] via 172.30.2.3, 00:00:00, Serial0/1
C       172.30.2.0 is directly connected, Serial0/1
R       172.30.3.0 [120/1] via 172.30.2.3, 00:00:00, Serial0/1
                   [120/1] via 172.30.1.2, 00:00:20, Serial0/0
C       172.30.1.0 is directly connected, Serial0/0
C       172.30.11.0 is directly connected, FastEthernet0/0
R1#show ip interface brief
Interface              IP-Address      OK? Method Status                Protocol
FastEthernet0/0        172.30.11.1     YES manual up                    up
Serial0/0              172.30.1.1      YES manual up                    up
Serial0/1              172.30.2.1      YES manual up                    up
R1#show ip rip database
172.30.0.0/16     auto-summary
172.30.1.0/24     directly connected, Serial0/0
172.30.2.0/24     directly connected, Serial0/1
172.30.3.0/24
    [1] via 172.30.1.2, 00:00:00, Serial0/0
    [1] via 172.30.2.3, 00:00:08, Serial0/1
172.30.11.0/24    directly connected, FastEthernet0/0
172.30.21.0/24
    [1] via 172.30.1.2, 00:00:00, Serial0/0
172.30.22.0/24
    [1] via 172.30.1.2, 00:00:00, Serial0/0
172.30.31.0/24
    [1] via 172.30.2.3, 00:00:08, Serial0/1
```

Of particular importance, note the two numbers in brackets for each route listed in the **show ip route** command output. The first bracketed number highlighted in Example 7-5, 120, identifies the route's administrative distance. Chapter 6 introduced the concept of administrative distance, and it will be explained again later in this chapter in the section "Choosing Routes Based on Administrative Distance." The second number is the metric for the route.

Troubleshooting RIP Operations Using the **debug** Command

Note

Cisco IOS sends log messages to the console by default. Users telnetted into a router can also see log messages by using the **terminal monitor** command.

Cisco IOS supports a very important troubleshooting command called the **debug** command. The **debug** command has many options, including options related to RIP. Regardless of what options are added to the **debug** command, this command tells the router to do the following:

- Monitor some internal process (for example, RIP updates that are sent and received)

- When something happens related to that process, generate log messages

- Keep generating log messages until someone disables the debug using the **no debug** command

The best way to appreciate how the **debug** command works is to see an example. Example 7-6 shows the following process:

1. The console user uses the **debug ip rip** command.

2. The user gets a command prompt, at which she can type other commands.

3. Whenever the router receives or sends a RIP update, IOS generates messages that describe the contents of each sent and received RIP update.

Example 7-6   R1: Messages Generated by the **debug ip rip** Command

```
R1#debug ip rip
RIP protocol debugging is on
R1#
! Note that the debug command is finished, and the user can type more commands,
! as is shown next.
R1#show ip interface brief
Interface               IP-Address      OK?    Method  Status      Protocol
FastEthernet0/0         172.30.11.1     YES    manual  up          up
Serial0/0               172.30.1.1      YES    manual  up          up
Serial0/1               172.30.2.1      YES    manual  up          up
R1#
! The debug is still enabled. IOS generates the following messages over the next 15
! seconds or so.
! The first set of messages shows the contents of the update received from R2.
Feb  1 12:26:28.715: RIP: received v1 update from 172.30.1.2 on Serial0/0
Feb  1 12:26:28.715:      172.30.3.0 in 1 hops
Feb  1 12:26:28.715:      172.30.21.0 in 1 hops
Feb  1 12:26:28.719:      172.30.22.0 in 1 hops
```

Example 7-6   R1: Messages Generated by the **debug ip rip** Command   *continued*

```
Feb  1 12:26:28.719:       172.30.31.0 in metric 3
! The next set of messages shows the contents of the update sent to R2.
Feb  1 12:26:33.158: RIP: sending v1 update to 255.255.255.255 via Serial0/0
  (172.30.1.1)
Feb  1 12:26:33.158: RIP: build update entries
Feb  1 12:26:33.158:   subnet 172.30.2.0 metric 1
Feb  1 12:26:33.158:   subnet 172.30.11.0 metric 1
Feb  1 12:26:33.158:   subnet 172.30.31.0 metric 2
! The next set of messages shows the contents of the update sent to R3.
Feb  1 12:26:36.920: RIP: sending v1 update to 255.255.255.255 via Serial0/1
  (172.30.2.1)
Feb  1 12:26:36.920: RIP: build update entries
Feb  1 12:26:36.920:   subnet 172.30.1.0 metric 1
Feb  1 12:26:36.920:   subnet 172.30.11.0 metric 1
Feb  1 12:26:36.920:   subnet 172.30.21.0 metric 2
Feb  1 12:26:36.920:   subnet 172.30.22.0 metric 2
! The next set of messages shows the contents of the update received from R3.
Feb  1 12:26:38.623: RIP: received v1 update from 172.30.2.3 on Serial0/1
Feb  1 12:26:38.623:       172.30.3.0 in 1 hops
Feb  1 12:26:38.627:       172.30.21.0 in 2 hops
Feb  1 12:26:38.627:       172.30.22.0 in 2 hops
Feb  1 12:26:38.627:       172.30.31.0 in 1 hops
R1#no debug all
All possible debugging has been turned off
R1#
```

Example 7-6 shows several debug messages, including messages related to two RIP updates sent by R1 and two updates received by R1. These messages match the information shown in the updates of Figure 7-7. Because Figure 7-7 highlights the advertisement of subnet 172.30.22.0, Example 7-6 also highlights that particular route for easier comparison.

When finished, the user should disable the debug. To disable any debug, use the same **debug** command, with the same options, prefaced by **no**; for example, **no debug ip rip** would disable the debug in Example 7-6. Alternatively, the **no debug all** command can be used to disable all active debugs.

Lab 7.2.6   Troubleshooting RIP

In this lab, you set up an IP addressing scheme using Class B networks, configure RIP, and then verify and troubleshoot RIP to confirm that it is working correctly.

Choosing the Best Route Among the Possible Routes

Routers need to learn all the possible routes to reach each subnet and then choose which route to add to the routing table. However, in some cases, the router's choice may not be obvious. For example, when a router discovers multiple routes to reach the same subnet, and the metrics for those routes tie, the router may be able to add multiple routes to the routing table. Also, in some cases, a router may be running multiple routing protocols at the same time and learns about the same subnets with different routing protocols. In that case, the router needs a method to choose the best route other than using the metric. This section examines both topics.

Load Balancing over Multiple Equal-Cost Routes

When a router discovers multiple equal-cost routes to the same subnet, using a single routing protocol, the routing protocol can add multiple of those routes to the routing table. All the IGPs on Cisco routers use the following (default) rules when considering multiple equal-cost routes:

Note

Border Gateway Protocol (BGP), the only real option today for an Exterior Gateway Protocol (EGP), will support multiple equal-cost routes for the same subnet, but such cases are rare.

- By default, add up to four equal-cost (equal-metric) routes for the same subnet to the routing table at the same time.

- The number of concurrent equal-cost routes can be changed by using the **maximum-paths** *number* subcommand, to a value between 1 and 6.

When the IP routing table lists multiple routes to the same destination, the IP routing process then needs to choose how to load-balance the traffic over the multiple routes. The online curriculum mentions the following two options based on the internal routing process used by the router:

- **Process switching**—The slowest and highest-overhead option for how IOS forwards packets. However, with process switching, load balancing occurs per packet, with each successive packet going to the destination subnet using a different route.

- **Fast switching**—The next fastest option, with less overhead, for how IOS forwards packets. However, when using fast switching, the router balances traffic per destination IP address.

Cisco IOS load-balances the traffic over the multiple equal-cost routes, with different details of how the balancing occurs based on whether process switching or fast switching is used. For example, Figure 7-14 shows how R1 would use per-destination load balancing to balance packets if fast switching were used. The figure shows R1 with two routes to reach 172.16.2.0/24. R1 sends all packets destined for host 172.16.2.1 over the high route and all packets destined for host 172.16.2.2 over the low route.

Figure 7-14   Equal-Cost Load Balancing

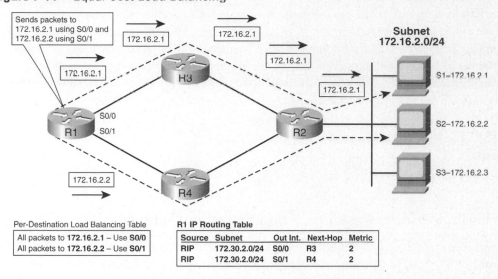

Figure 7-14 shows five packets (destined for host S1) going over the high route, and only one packet going over the low route, which is a common effect with per-destination load balancing. The routers cannot predict how many packets will be sent to each destination address. So, although load balancing takes place, per-destination load balancing risks the effect by which more packets go over one route versus the other, as shown in Figure 7-14.

Also note that when R1 starts sending packets to other hosts in subnet 172.16.2.0/24, R1 assigns either S0/0 or S0/1 as the outgoing interface for packets to each destination, alternating between the two routes. For example, R1 may assign packets sent to 172.16.2.3 to be sent over the high route, and packets sent to 172.16.2.4 to be sent over the low route.

Example 7-7 shows the output of the **show ip route 172.16.2.0** command, used on router R1 in Figure 7-14. Note that the asterisk shows which route will be used for the next packet (if balancing per packet) or for the next new destination IP address (if balancing per destination).

Note

Fast switching can be disabled by using the **no ip route-cache** interface subcommand.

Example 7-7   R1: Messages Generated by the **show ip route** Command

```
R1#show ip route 172.16.2.0
Routing entry for 172.16.2.0/24
  Known via "rip", distance 120, metric 2
  Redistributing via rip
  Last update from 172.16.3.3 on Serial0/0, 00:00:00 ago
  Routing Descriptor Blocks:
    172.16.3.3, from 172.16.3.3, 00:00:00 ago, via Serial0/0
      Route metric is 2, traffic share count is 1
  * 172.16.4.4, from 172.16.4.4, 00:00:00 ago, via Serial0/1
      Route metric is 2, traffic share count is 1
```

Although not mentioned in the online curriculum, a better option for process switching and load balancing exists, called *Cisco Express Forwarding (CEF)*. Historically, Cisco first created process switching logic, then improved router performance by creating fast switching logic, and then further improved the forwarding logic by creating CEF. CEF allows for load balancing either per packet (as with process switching, for example) or per destination (as with fast switching, for example), but with much faster forwarding and much less overhead than either process switching or fast switching incurs.

Lab 7.2.9   Load Balancing Across Multiple Paths

In this lab, you configure load balancing across multiple paths.

Choosing Routes Based on Administrative Distance

In some cases, one router may need to use multiple routing protocols. For example, router R1 in Figure 7-13, earlier in this chapter, exchanged routes between two divisions of one company, with one division using RIP and the other using OSPF. If multiple routers connect to both divisions, it is possible for routers such as R1—the routers running more than one routing protocol—to learn about a subnet using both routing protocols.

Because each routing protocol uses a different metric, a router cannot use the metric to determine which route is the best route. For example, a router may learn a metric 3 RIP route and a cost 54 OSPF route, both to subnet 172.16.2.0/24.

Routers determine the best route in these cases by choosing the route with the lowest *administrative distance*. The administrative distance is a number assigned to all the possible sources of routing information—routing protocols and static routes included. Table 7-3 lists the administrative distance for each routing information source, but the defaults can be changed.

Table 7-3   Default Administrative Distances in Cisco IOS

Protocol or Source of Routing Information	Default Administrative Distance
Connected interface	0
Static route	1
EIGRP summary route	5
External BGP	20
Internal EIGRP	90
IGRP	100
OSPF	110

Table 7-3   Default Administrative Distances in Cisco IOS   *continued*

Protocol or Source of Routing Information	Default Administrative Distance
IS-IS	115
RIP	120
External EIGRP	170
Internal BGP	200
Unknown	255

In the example in which router R1 learned the same route with both RIP and OSPF, assuming all defaults, R1 would choose the OSPF route as best based on the lowest administrative distance and would add only the OSPF-learned route to R1's routing table.

Integrating Static Routes with RIP

This section discusses two RIP configuration issues related to static routes: the use of floating static routes, and how to make RIP advertise a static default route.

Floating Static Routes

This section briefly describes one use of the administrative distance concept with static routes. Chapter 6 covered static routes, including how to change a static route's administrative distance when using dial backup.

A *floating static route* is a static route that the engineer wants to be used some of the time. The term *floating* comes from the idea that the static route leaves the routing table under some conditions and comes back into the routing table under other conditions. Floating static routes can be very useful for dial backup, using the following logic:

- When a permanent WAN connection is up, the router should ignore the static route and instead use the routes learned by the routing protocol. These routes will forward packets out the permanent WAN connection.

- When the permanent WAN connection is down, use the statically defined route that sends traffic over the dial backup link.

The Chapter 6 section "Using Static Routes for Dial Backup Using Administrative Distance" describes the details of how a floating static route works. Refer to that section in Chapter 6 if the concepts are not fresh in your mind.

Advertising Default Routes with RIP

In some cases, it makes sense to distribute a default route throughout an internetwork. Figure 7-15 shows a classic example in which all routers in an enterprise internetwork should forward Internet traffic to the router with the Internet connection, with that router forwarding the traffic to the Internet. The engineer wants all routers to use a default route to forward packets such that the packets get to router R-core, which will then use a default route to forward packets to the Internet.

Figure 7-15   Advertising a Default Route Using RIP

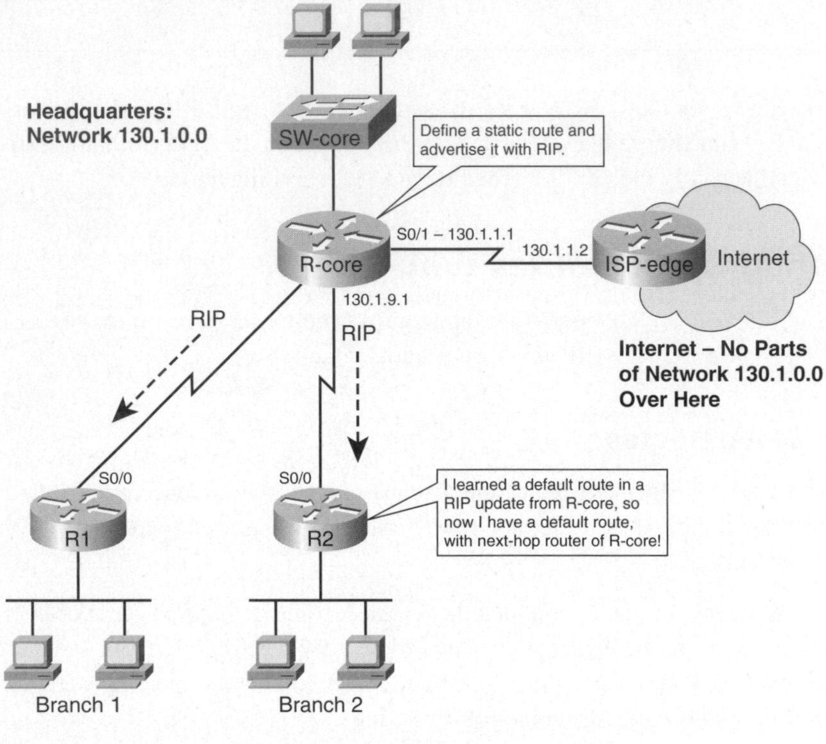

With the design shown in Figure 7-15, the following steps occur:

1. All routers in the enterprise internetwork learn about all subnets of Class B network 130.1.0.0 via RIP.

2. Router R-core defines a static default route pointing to the Internet.

3. Router R-core advertises a default route to the rest of the routers in the enterprise.

When R-core advertises the default route with RIP, the branch routers add a default route to their routing tables, pointing to R-core as the next-hop router. As a result, all packets destined for subnets outside network 130.1.0.0—in other words, packets destined for the Internet—are forwarded to R-core, which in turn forwards the packets to the Internet.

RIP can be configured to advertise a default route in several ways. Example 7-8 shows one option, in which R-core configures a static route that references the ISP's router at 130.1.1.2. Then, R-core's RIP configuration must include the **redistribute static** command, which tells R-core to advertise all static routes using RIP.

Example 7-8   Configuring Router R-core to Advertise a Default Route

```
ip route 0.0.0.0 0.0.0.0 130.1.1.2
!
router rip
 network 130.1.0.0
 redistribute static
```

Classful and Classless Routing Protocols, Routing, and Addressing

The terms classless and classful can be applied to three different topics related to TCP/IP:

- Classless and classful routing protocols
- Classless and classful routing
- Classless and classful addressing

Module 7 of the online curriculum covers classless and classful routing protocols and routing. This section describes all three concepts in this list to ensure that you have a basic understanding of each.

Classless and Classful Routing Protocols

The term *classless routing protocol* refers to a set of routing protocols that provide a particular set of functions. These functions do not change depending on the router configuration or internetwork. They are simply features of a particular routing protocol, or they are not. Classless routing protocols perform the following functions:

- Send subnet mask information in routing updates
- Support variable-length subnet mask (VLSM) because of the inclusion of the mask in routing updates
- Support designs that include discontiguous networks

A *classful routing protocol*, by definition, does not send mask information. As a result, it does not support VLSM, nor does it support discontiguous networks. Table 7-4 lists the different IP routing protocols and whether they are classless or classful.

Table 7-4   Classless and Classful Routing Protocols

Type	Routing Protocols
Classless	RIP V2, EIGRP, OSPF, IS-IS, BGP
Classful	RIP V1, IGRP

Classless and Classful Routing

The terms *classful routing* and *classless routing* refer to how each router uses its default route, assuming the router has a default route. These terms do not imply anything about the routing protocol(s) used on the router; instead, they refer to the routing, or forwarding, process. The terms are defined as follows:

- **Classless routing**—If a packet's destination IP address does not match a more specific route in the IP routing table, forward the packet based on the default route.

- **Classful routing**—If a packet's destination IP address does not match a more specific route in the IP routing table, forward the packet based on the default route, *but only if the routing table does not contain any subnets of that packet's classful IP network.*

Classless routing seems intuitive to most people: if the packet does not match any other routes, use the default. Classful routing, however, seems a bit complex, so an example can help. Consider router R2 in Figure 7-15 from earlier in the chapter. R2 learns routes to subnets of Class B network 130.1.0.0 and a default route. So, R2's routing table might look something like the output shown in Example 7-9.

Example 7-9   Routing Table for Router R2

```
R2#show ip route
! lines omitted for brevity


   130.1.0.0/24 is subnetted, 5 subnets
R      130.1.22.0 [120/1] via 130.1.9,1, 00:00:20, Serial0/0
R      130.1.21.0 [120/1] via 130.1.9.1, 00:00:20, Serial0/0
R      130.1.31.0 [120/1] via 130.1.9.1, 00:00:00, Serial0/1
C      130.1.9.0 is directly connected, Serial0/0
C      130.1.11.0 is directly connected, FastEthernet0/0
R*  0.0.0.0/0 [120/1] via 130.1.9.1, 00:00:10, Serial0/0
```

Example 7-9 shows that R2 knows about five subnets of Class B network 130.1.0.0 and a default route. Now imagine that a packet enters R2's LAN interface, with a destination address of 130.1.99.99. The packet's destination address does not match any of the more specific routes. If configured for classful routing, R2 would use the following logic:

1. 130.1.99.99 does not match any of the routes other than the default route.

2. 130.1.99.99 is in Class B network 130.1.0.0, and I know at least one route in network 130.1.0.0. So, using classful routing logic, I choose to not use the default route.

3. Because the packet did not match any of the routes inside network 130.1.0.0, and I have chosen to not use the default route in this case, discard the packet.

Each router uses either classless routing or classful routing, depending on the configuration of the **ip classless** global configuration command. With **ip classless** configured, the router uses classless routing, and with the **no ip classless** command configured, the router uses classful routing. Classless routing has been the IOS default since Cisco IOS Software Release 11.3.

Classless and Classful Addressing

The terms *classless addressing* and *classful addressing* refer to two methods of analyzing the structure of IP addresses. Although not covered in the Networking Academy CCNA 2 curriculum, it seems appropriate to provide a short description here to complete the classless and classful discussion in this chapter.

Classful addressing means that, when analyzing IP addresses, the addresses are considered to have a one-, two-, or three-octet network part, with the remainder of the addresses being the host part. In other words, the "class rules" apply. If subnetted, these addresses have a network part, a subnet part, and a host part. Table 7-5 summarizes the class rules that apply to classful addressing.

Table 7-5   Classful Addressing Rules

Class	Number of Network Octets	Number of Host Octets
A	1	3
B	2	2
C	3	1

Classless addressing ignores Class A, B, and C rules, treating each IP address as having only two parts: a subnet part and a host part. In a classless address, the subnet part (also called the prefix) contains what would have been the combined network and subnet parts with classful addressing. Figure 7-16 shows an example, with the structure of a Class B address and a mask of 255.255.255.0.

Note

With classless routing enabled, the packet would have been forwarded according to the default route in this example.

Figure 7-16   Classless and Classful Addressing Compared

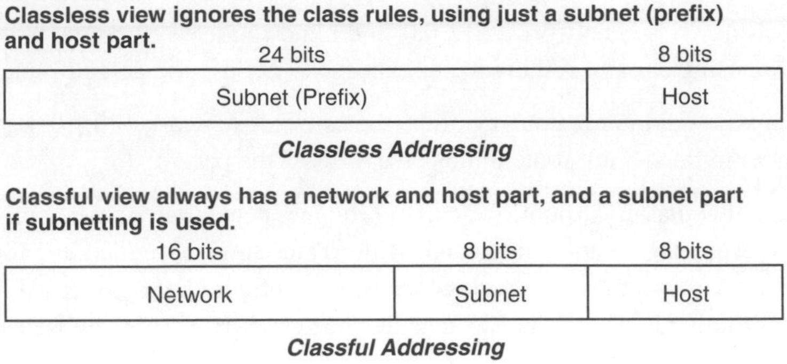

Classless view ignores the class rules, using just a subnet (prefix) and host part.

24 bits	8 bits
Subnet (Prefix)	Host

Classless Addressing

Classful view always has a network and host part, and a subnet part if subnetting is used.

16 bits	8 bits	8 bits
Network	Subnet	Host

Classful Addressing

Summary

Distance vector algorithms call for each router to send its entire routing table, on a periodic basis, to each of its adjacent neighbors. The routing tables include information about each network or subnet, along with the metric associated with each network or subnet.

Distance vector routing protocols use a wide variety of loop-avoidance features. The following table summarizes the commonly used features:

Term	Definition
Poison route	A route that was formerly advertised with a valid metric but is now advertised with an infinite metric. This advertisement means that the route has failed.
Poison reverse	A route that was formerly not advertised due to split horizon rules but is now advertised with an infinite metric. This advertisement means that the route has failed.
Split horizon	A per-interface feature, generally on by default, that limits the routes included in distance vector routing updates sent out each interface. For a given interface, any route whose outgoing interface is that same interface is not included in routing updates sent out that interface.
Infinity	With routing protocols, an actual number that is assigned to routes that have failed. For example, RIP, which has a maximum hop count of 15, uses 16 to mean "infinity."
Holddown	A process that a router applies to a route when the route fails, causing the router to ignore newly-learned alternate routes to reach that subnet. The router uses a timer, called the holddown timer, to determine how long to ignore newly-learned alternate routes. After the holddown timer expires, the router can believe newly-learned alternate routes without the risk of introducing routing loops.
Triggered update	A routing update that is not sent at a regular periodic interval but instead is caused, or triggered, based on some change in routing information.

In particular, the holddown feature helps prevent routing loops in a redundant network. When a route's metric changes to a higher number—for example, when a router hears a poisoned route with RIP, metric 16—the router starts a holddown timer for the route. That router refuses to believe any routes advertised by other neighbors until the timer expires.

RIP Version 2 added many features to RIP Version 1. These enhancements include an authentication mechanism, support of VLSM, and support of discontiguous networks. Like RIP V1, RIP V2 sends full periodic updates every 30 seconds by default, sends triggered partial updates when changes occur, and uses hop count as the metric.

RIP configuration includes many optional features. However, to simply configure RIP V1 to get it working, an engineer needs to configure a **router rip** command, followed by one or more **network** *network-number* commands. The router then enables RIP on every interface whose IP address is a part of one of the classful IP networks listed in the **network** commands.

The two most common commands used to verify that RIP is properly configured are the **show ip route** and **show ip protocols** commands. The **show ip route** command shows the routes that are installed in the routing table and the status of each route. The **show ip protocols** command is used to verify the state of the active routing protocol and the installed routes specific to the protocol. To display RIP routing updates as they are sent and received, use the **debug ip rip** command.

The **passive-interface** command prevents routers from sending routing updates through a router interface. This keeps update messages from being sent through a router interface so that other systems on a network will not learn about routes dynamically.

RIP supports the function of adding multiple equal-cost routes to the same subnet—up to four routes by default, and up to six possible. These equal-cost routes can be seen with the **show ip route** command listing the single subnet, with multiple lines listing different next-hop IP addresses. The load balancing occurs on either a per-packet basis or a per-destination IP address basis.

Classless routing, as enabled with the **ip classless** global configuration command, means that a router always uses its default route (assuming one exists) if a packet's destination address does not match another route. With classful routing enabled (with the **no ip classless** global command), the router may discard some packets even if a default route exists.

Check Your Understanding

Complete all the review questions listed here to test your understanding of the topics and concepts in this chapter. Answers are listed in Appendix A, "Answers to Check Your Understanding and Challenge Questions."

1. What can be determined from the following output?

```
Codes: C - connected, S - static, I - IGRP, R - RIP, M - mobile, B - BGP
       D - EIGRP, EX - EIGRP external, O - OSPF, IA - OSPF inter area
       N1 - OSPF NSSA external type 1, N2 - OSPF NSSA external type 2
       E1 - OSPF external type 1, E2 - OSPF external type 2, E - EGP
       i - IS-IS, L1 - IS-IS level-1
       * - candidate default, U - per-user static route, o - ODR
       P - periodic downloaded static route


Gateway of last resort is not set


C    172.17.0.0/16 is directly connected, Serial0/0
C    172.16.0.0/16 is directly connected, FastEthernet0/0
```

A. The network 172.16.0.0 is directly connected.

B. RIP is configured on the router.

C. The network 172.16.0.0 is a WAN serial connection.

D. The serial 0/0 address is 172.17.0.16 255.255.0.0.

2. Which of the following best describes a static route?

A. A routing table entry that is used to direct frames for which a next hop is not explicitly listed in the routing table

B. A route that is explicitly configured and entered into the routing table and that by default takes precedence over routes chosen by dynamic routing protocols

C. A route that adjusts automatically to network topology or traffic changes

D. A route that adjusts involuntarily to direct frames within a network topology

3. Which of the following options is best defined by the following statement? "When a router sends routing updates to a particular neighbor, the routing updates should not contain any information learned from that neighbor."

A. Route poisoning

B. Poison reverse

C. Holddown timers to prevent routing loops

D. Split horizon to prevent routing loops

4. Which of the following best describes a default route?

    A. A 0.0.0.0/0 routing table entry that is used to direct packets for which a next hop is not explicitly listed in any other route in the routing table

    B. A route that is explicitly configured and entered into the routing table

    C. A route that adjusts automatically to network topology or traffic changes

    D. A route that adjusts involuntarily to direct frames within a network topology

5. Which of the following statements about RIP Version 1 and RIP Version 2 is true?

    A. RIP Version 1 is a classless routing protocol, and RIP Version 2 uses VLSM.

    B. RIP Version 2 is the default version on routers, and RIP Version 1 must be configured.

    C. RIP Version 2 recognizes variable-length subnets, and RIP Version 1 is a classful routing protocol.

    D. RIP Version 1 uses hop count for a routing metric, and RIP Version 2 uses the sum of interface costs for the metric.

6. What metric does RIP use to determine the best path for a message to travel on?

    A. Bandwidth

    B. Hop count

    C. Varies with each packet sent

    D. Administrative distance

7. An engineer suspects that one of the routers connected to her network is sending bad routing information. Which of the answer choices shows the correct command, issued from the correct mode (as implied by the command prompt), that can be used to verify the information her router is sending?

    A. router(config)#**show ip route**

    B. router#**show ip route**

    C. router>**show ip protocols**

    D. router(config-router)#**show ip protocols**

8. What is one reason to display the IP routing table?

    A. To set the router update schedule

    B. To identify the subnets discovered by the router and the routing protocols used to dicover those subnets

    C. To trace where datagrams are coming from

    D. To set the parameters and filters for the router

9. Which of the answer choices shows the correct command, issued from the correct mode (as implied by the command prompt), that produces the following output?

```
00:22:50: RIP: sending v2 update to 224.0.0.9 via FastEthernet0/0 (172.16.0.1)
00:22:50: RIP: build update entries
00:22:50:        172.17.0.0/16 via 0.0.0.0, metric 1, tag 0
00:22:50:        172.18.0.0/16 via 0.0.0.0, metric 2, tag 0
00:22:50: RIP: sending v2 update to 224.0.0.9 via Serial0/0 (172.17.1.1)
00:22:50: RIP: build update entries
00:22:50:        172.16.0.0/16 via 0.0.0.0, metric 1, tag 0
00:23:02: RIP: received v2 update from 172.17.1.2 on Serial0/0
00:23:02:        172.18.0.0/16 via 0.0.0.0 in 1 hops
```

A. router(config)#**show router rip protocol**

B. router#**show router rip events**

C. router#**debug ip rip**

D. router(config)#**debug ip rip**

10. Which of the answer choices shows the correct command, issued from the correct mode (as implied by the command prompt), that should be used to learn which routing protocol a router is configured with?

A. router>**show router protocols**

B. router(config)>**show ip protocols**

C. router(config)#**show router protocols**

D. router#**show ip protocols**

11. In the global configuration command **ip route 2.0.0.0 255.0.0.0 1.0.0.2 5**, what does the last number 5 stand for?

A. The number of hops

B. The number of routes to the destination

C. The administrative distance

D. The destination's reference number in the routing table

12. An administrative distance of 15 indicates which of the following?

A. The IP address is static.

B. The IP address is dynamic.

C. The routing information source is more trustworthy than RIP (assuming RIP uses its default administrative distance).

D. The routing information source is more reliable than a static route (assuming the static route uses its default administrative distance).

13. A router has a single route to network 10.0.0.0 in its routing table. The route shows a metric of 7 and an administrative distance of 120. The router then learns another route to reach network 10.0.0.0, with the details listed in each of the answer choices. Choose the answers that describe a route that the router would choose to add to its IP routing table.

A. A route to 10.0.0.0, metric 9, administrative distance 101

B. A route to 10.0.0.0, metric 2, administrative distance 121

C. A route to 10.0.0.0, metric 7, administrative distance 120

D. A route to 10.0.0.0, metric 1, administrative distance 150

Challenge Questions and Activities

These questions require a deeper application of the concepts covered in this chapter and are similar to the style of questions you might see on a CCNA certification exam. Answers are listed in Appendix A.

Use the following figure to answer the questions in this section:

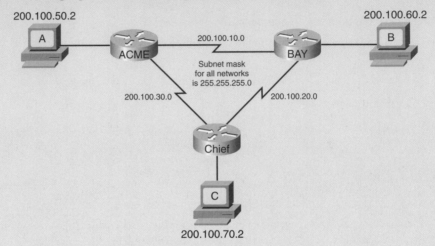

Use the following **show** command output to answer the questions in this section:

```
ACME#show ip route
Codes: C - connected, S - static, I - IGRP, R - RIP, M - mobile, B - BGP
       D - EIGRP, EX - EIGRP external, O - OSPF, IA - OSPF inter area
       N1 - OSPF NSSA external type 1, N2 - OSPF NSSA external type 2
       E1 - OSPF external type 1, E2 - OSPF external type 2, E - EGP
       i - IS-IS, L1 - IS-IS level-1, L2 - IS-IS level-2, ia - IS-IS inter area
       * - candidate default, U - per-user static route, o - ODR
       P - periodic downloaded static route
Gateway of last resort is not set
R    200.100.20.0/24 [120/1] via 200.100.30.2, 00:00:19, Serial0/1
C    200.100.50.0/24 is directly connected, FastEthernet0/0
R    200.100.70.0/24 [120/1] via 200.100.30.2, 00:00:19, Serial0/1
C    200.100.30.0/24 is directly connected, Serial0/1
R    200.100.60.0/24 [120/2] via 200.100.30.2, 00:00:19, Serial0/1
C    200.100.10.0/24 is directly connected, Serial0/0
ACME#show ip protocols
Routing Protocol is "rip"
  Sending updates every 30 seconds, next due in 11 seconds
  Invalid after 180 seconds, hold down 180, flushed after 240
  Outgoing update filter list for all interfaces is not set
  Redistributing: rip
```

```
  Default version control: send version 1, receive any version
    Interface            Send   Recv   Triggered RIP  Key-chain
    FastEthernet0/0      1      1 2
    Serial0/1            1      1 2
  Automatic network summarization is in effect
  Maximum path: 4
  Routing for Networks:
    200.100.30.0
    200.100.50.0
  Routing Information Sources:
    Gateway          Distance     Last Update
    200.100.30.2       120        00:00:13
  Distance: (default is 120)
ACME#
```

```
CHIEF#show ip route
Codes: C - connected, S - static, I - IGRP, R - RIP, M - mobile, B - BGP
       D - EIGRP, EX - EIGRP external, O - OSPF, IA - OSPF inter area
       N1 - OSPF NSSA external type 1, N2 - OSPF NSSA external type 2
       E1 - OSPF external type 1, E2 - OSPF external type 2, E - EGP
       i - IS-IS, L1 - IS-IS level-1, L2 - IS-IS level-2, ia - IS-IS inter area
       * - candidate default, U - per-user static route, o - ODR
       P - periodic downloaded static route
Gateway of last resort is not set
C    200.100.20.0/24 is directly connected, Serial0/1
C    200.100.70.0/24 is directly connected, FastEthernet0/0
C    200.100.30.0/24 is directly connected, Serial0/0
R    200.100.60.0/24 [120/1] via 200.100.20.1, 00:00:07, Serial0/1
R    200.100.10.0/24 [120/1] via 200.100.20.1, 00:00:07, Serial0/1
CHIEF#show ip protocol
Routing Protocol is "rip"
  Sending updates every 30 seconds, next due in 11 seconds
  Invalid after 180 seconds, hold down 180, flushed after 240
  Outgoing update filter list for all interfaces is not set
  Incoming update filter list for all interfaces is not set
  Redistributing: rip
  Default version control: send version 2, receive version 2
    Interface            Send   Recv   Triggered RIP  Key-chain
    FastEthernet0/0      2      2
    Serial0/0            2      2
    Serial 0/1           2      2
  Automatic network summarization is in effect
  Maximum path: 4
  Routing for Networks:
    200.100.20.0
    200.100.30.0
```

continues

```
    200.100.70.0
Routing Information Sources:
  Gateway           Distance      Last Update
  200.100.20.1           120      00:00:13
Distance: (default is 120)
```

1. Refer to the diagram. After studying the ACME routing table and protocol information displayed, what is likely the reason why network 200.100.60.0 is two hops away instead of one?

   A. Network 200.100.10.0 is administratively down.

   B. RIP is not configured on router BAY.

   C. Router ACME is not listening for RIP updates on its serial link connected to router BAY.

   D. A static route is overriding the RIP protocol to 200.100.60.0.

2. Refer to the **show ip protocols** and **show ip route** output from routers ACME and Chief. Why does ACME have one more route in the routing table than Chief?

   A. Chief is not advertising all routes via RIP.

   B. ACME is using a different version routing protocol.

   C. Chief has an interface down.

   D. ACME has the Ethernet interface up, and Chief does not.

   E. ACME can see all the networks on BAY, and Chief cannot.

CHAPTER 8

TCP/IP Suite Error and Control Messages

Objectives

Upon completion of this chapter, you should be able to answer the following questions:

- What is the purpose of ICMP?

- What are some of the ICMP error message types, and how can they be interpreted?

- What are potential causes of specific ICMP error messages?

- What is the ICMP message format?

Additional Topics of Interest

Several chapters contain additional coverage of previous topics or related topics that are secondary to the main goals of this chapter. You can find the additional coverage on the CD-ROM. For this chapter, the following additional topics are covered:

- ICMP messages and encapsulation

- ICMP echo message formats

- Miscellaneous header errors

- ICMP redirect messages

- ICMP timestamp request and reply messages

- ICMP information request/reply messages

- ICMP address mask request/reply messages

- ICMP router advertisements and solicitation messages

- ICMP source quench messages

Key Terms

This chapter uses the following key terms. You can find the definitions in the Glossary.

Internet Control Message Protocol (ICMP)   page 274

ICMP echo request   page 275

ICMP echo reply   page 275

ICMP unreachable message   page 276

maximum transmission unit (MTU)   page 281

fragments   page 281

Time to Live (TTL) field   page 282

By design, the Internet Protocol (IP) is unreliable. However, the term *unreliable* does not mean that IP works badly. It works very well, in fact. In networking, reliable protocols perform error recovery, and unreliable protocols do not. IP does not recover packets that the IP forwarding process cannot deliver; instead, IP simply discards the packets.

When an application wants reliability—in other words, the guaranteed delivery of data to the destination—the application often then uses TCP, which provides that reliability. TCP notices when a packet fails to arrive at the destination host and causes the sending host to resend the packet.

Although IP does not provide error recovery, the TCP/IP network layer does have a mechanism with which hosts can learn of problems with their packets. For example, a router may try to forward a packet, but if the router does not have a route that matches the packet's destination IP address, the router cannot forward the packet—so the router discards the packet. At the same time, it may be useful for the router to send a message to the host that originally sent the packet, telling that host that its packet was discarded, the address of the router that discarded the packet, and why the router discarded the packet.

The TCP/IP standard defines the *Internet Control Message Protocol (ICMP)* to provide this function, as well as several other functions. ICMP defines a set of messages that can be used to control and inform hosts about anything having to do with the operation of the TCP/IP Internet layer. In fact, ICMP itself is one of three key protocols defined as TCP/IP Internet layer protocols, as shown in Figure 8-1.

Figure 8-1   TCP/IP Layers with ICMP, IP, and ARP

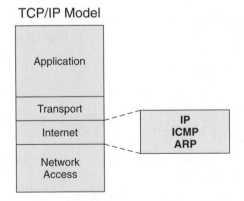

Whereas IP defines how routing occurs in a TCP/IP internetwork, ICMP defines the protocols that control, test, and inform hosts about the behavior of IP. ICMP defines a wide variety of features, all related to some part of the function of IP. So, the best way to understand ICMP is to understand several of its individual features. For example, ICMP defines the messages sent by the **ping** command, with the **ping** command testing how well IP routing is working.

This chapter explains several functions of ICMP so that you can understand the general ideas about ICMP's purpose. The chapter defines the format and encapsulation of ICMP messages and then explains how the **ping** command uses the ICMP echo request and echo reply messages. Next, the chapter covers how routers and hosts can use the ICMP unreachable message to notify the sender of a packet when its packets cannot be delivered. Finally, the last few topics include a method to inform hosts when routing loops have occurred and when packet headers have been incorrectly created.

This chapter's "Additional Topics of Interest" section, which you can find on the CD-ROM, covers additional features of ICMP.

ICMP Echo Messages and the ping Command

The TCP/IP Internet layer defines several features—none more important than routing. The IP routing process defines how hosts and routers forward a packet. Basically, hosts forward packets to their default router (default gateway). The routers forward the packets to other routers. Eventually, the packets arrive at the last router in the end-to-end route, with those routers forwarding the packets directly to the destination hosts.

ICMP focuses on controlling and managing IP, so ICMP rightfully supports the ability to test and verify whether IP can correctly route packets between two hosts. As you have seen many times in the Cisco Networking Academy Program course material, the **ping** command sends an IP packet to another host, with the remote host sending a packet back. While many people refer to these messages as *ping packets*, or simply *pings*, the **ping** command actually sends ICMP messages called *ICMP echo request* and *ICMP echo reply*. For example, when PC1 pings PC2 in Figure 8-2, PC1 sends echo request messages to PC2, and PC2 then sends back echo reply messages.

Figure 8-2   The ping Command Sending and Receiving Echo Messages

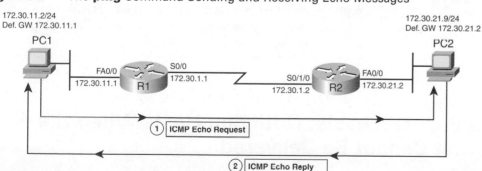

Typically, the **ping** command on a particular OS defaults to send a set number of echo request messages, with the command allowing the user to override the default and specify the number of echo messages sent. The command output lists the number of echo request messages sent, the number of echo replies received, and a percentage of successes (percentage of echo request messages for which an echo reply was received). The **ping** command can also provide feedback about delay in the internetwork, listing the minimum, maximum, and mean response round-trip time for the echo request to be sent, and the corresponding echo reply to be received. Figure 8-3 shows an example from PC1 in Figure 8-2, which is running Windows XP, and uses the Windows XP **ping** command default of sending four ICMP echo request messages.

Figure 8-3   PC1 **ping** Output When Pinging PC2

```
C:\WINDOWS\system32\cmd.exe

C:\Documents and Settings\wodom>ping 172.30.21.2

Pinging 172.30.21.2 with 32 bytes of data:

Reply from 172.30.21.2: bytes=32 time=1ms TTL=254
Reply from 172.30.21.2: bytes=32 time=1ms TTL=254
Reply from 172.30.21.2: bytes=32 time=1ms TTL=254
Reply from 172.30.21.2: bytes=32 time=1ms TTL=254

Ping statistics for 172.30.21.2:
    Packets: Sent = 4, Received = 4, Lost = 0 (0% loss),
Approximate round trip times in milli-seconds:
    Minimum = 1ms, Maximum = 1ms, Average = 1ms

C:\Documents and Settings\wodom>
```

Note that in Figure 8-3, the **ping** command sent four echo requests and got four echo replies. Also, note that the minimum, maximum, and average round-trip times were all 1 millisecond, because no other traffic was flowing through the internetwork at the time.

The **ping** command output also lists a value labeled TTL. Later in the chapter, the section "ICMP TTL Exceeded and Long Routes" explains the meaning of the IP Time to Live (TTL) field. The **ping** command can set the TTL value in packets to test whether routes go through no more than a certain number of routers.

Packet Packet Tracer configuration file NA02-0802 is similar to the topology of Figure
Tracer   8-2. Using real-time mode, by clicking the PC icons, you can issue **ping** com-
                mands from the PC command prompts to test IP. You can also issue **ping**
                commands from the routers.

ICMP Unreachable: Notifying Hosts When the Packet Cannot Be Delivered

IP defines how routing should occur. IP routing includes the end-to-end forwarding of packets through an internetwork, from one host to another host. ICMP provides a means to notify the sender of a packet when the packet could not be delivered to the destination—namely, the *ICMP unreachable message*.

Basically, when any host or router realizes that it cannot forward a packet successfully, the host or router discards the packet, but it can also send an ICMP unreachable message. The host or router sends the message to the source IP address listed in the discarded packet. As a result, the host that sent the original packet finds out when its packets have been discarded.

The first part of this section briefly reviews IP routing, which is helpful when thinking about how ICMP unreachable messages work. Following that review, this section provides a deeper explanation of how hosts use ICMP unreachable messages.

A Review of IP Routing

Routing begins with a host sending a packet either directly to another host on the same subnet or to its default gateway (default router). Following that, the router(s) must forward the packet based on the destination IP address of the packet as compared to each router's IP routing table. Eventually, the packet reaches the last router in the route, with that router forwarding the packet to the destination host.

All of these routing steps require the correct configuration of both hosts and routers. First, consider the configuration required on the origin host, which is the host sending the packet. For proper routing, the host needs to have the following information, either via static configuration or dynamically learned via DHCP:

- A valid IP address

- A correct subnet mask (matching the default router's mask on that same subnet)

- The IP address of its default gateway (default router)

- A working link between itself and the default router

For example, in Figure 8-4, PC1 has an IP address of 172.30.11.2 and a mask of 255.255.255.0, shown in prefix notation as /24. It refers to IP address 172.30.11.1 as its default gateway, which happens to be R1's FA0/0 IP address. Also note in Figure 8-4 that the IP addresses of both PC1 and R1's FA0/0 use a prefix length of /24. (For the purposes of this example, assume that PC1 can forward frames over the Ethernet to and from R1.)

Figure 8-4   Basic Internetwork Used in ICMP Unreachable Examples

R1 IP Routing Table

Source	Subnet	Out Int.	Next-Hop	Metric
RIP	172.30.21.0/24	S0/0	172.30.1.2	1
Conn.	172.30.1.0/24	S0/0	N/A	0
Conn.	172.30.11.0/24	FA0/0	N/A	0

R2 IP Routing Table

Source	Subnet	Out Int.	Next-Hop	Metric
Conn.	172.30.21.0/24	FA0/0	N/A	0
Conn.	172.30.1.0/24	S0/1/0	N/A	0
RIP	172.30.11.0/24	S0/1/0	172.30.1.1	1

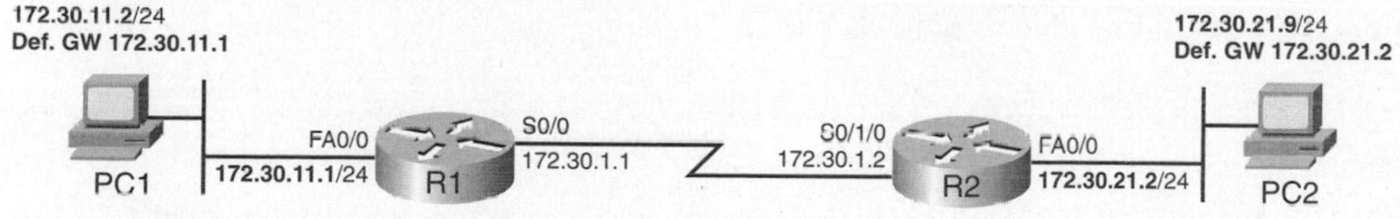

172.30.11.2/24
Def. GW 172.30.11.1

172.30.21.9/24
Def. GW 172.30.21.2

PC1   172.30.11.1/24   R1   FA0/0   S0/0   172.30.1.1   S0/1/0   172.30.1.2   R2   FA0/0   172.30.21.2/24   PC2

Next, the routers need to have IP configured correctly on their interfaces, including the following:

- The routers need to have IP addresses and masks using the **ip address** interface subcommand.

- The interfaces need to be enabled using the **no shutdown** interface subcommand.

- The interface may need additional configuration, depending on other factors.

- At the end of the configuration process, the router interfaces need to be up and working, as can be seen with the **show ip interface brief** command.

Next, the routers need to know routes to all subnets. To learn the necessary routes, static routes can be used, but more typically, each router uses the same routing protocol. Figure 8-4 shows the routing tables on R1 and R2, each with routes to all three subnets in this small internetwork. Regardless of whether the routes have been statically configured or learned via a dynamic routing protocol, the routers need to know how to forward packets to each subnet. After the hosts and routers have been configured correctly, and the interfaces are up and working, IP routing can forward packets back and forth between the two hosts.

Finally, keep in mind that for any useful communication to occur, packets need to flow in both directions. When troubleshooting routing problems, you need to check the routes in both directions. For example, for PC1 to be able to send packets to PC2, the following must be true:

- PC1's IP address, mask, and default router must be correct.

- R1 and R2 need to have a working route that matches address 172.30.21.9 (PC2)—for example, their routes to 172.30.21.0/24.

- All the links need to be up and working.

However, if the IP internetwork can route the packets from PC1 to PC2 but cannot route packets back from PC2 to PC1, PC1 cannot do any useful work with PC2. Also, PC1's ping of PC2 would also fail, because the echo reply messages would not be able to get back to PC1 from PC2. So, when troubleshooting routing problems, make sure to look at the routes in both directions. In this example, you would need to check these details for the route from PC2 back to PC1:

- PC2's IP address, mask, and default router must be correct.

- R1 and R2 need to have a working route that matches address 172.30.11.2 (PC1)—for example, their routes to 172.30.11.0/24.

- All the links need to be up and working.

After both the route for forwarding packets from PC1 to PC2 and the reverse route are working, PC1 and PC2 should be able to ping each other.

Type Codes for ICMP Unreachable Messages

Hosts and routers send ICMP unreachable messages when that host or router cannot forward the packet any further. The host or router sends the unreachable message to the host that originally sent the undeliverable packet. For example, Figure 8-5 shows a common use of the ICMP unreachable message that occurs when a link has failed in an internetwork. In the figure, PC1 tries to send a packet to PC2, but because the serial link between the routers has failed, R1 does not have a matching route with which to forward the packet.

Figure 8-5   ICMP Network Unreachable Message

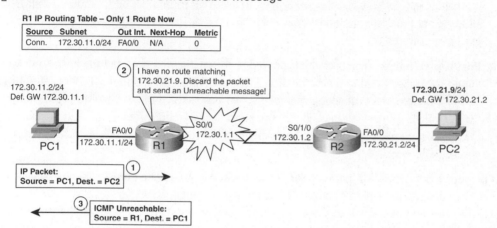

Figure 8-5 begins with the serial link having already failed, so R1 does not have a route to reach host B. The figure shows the following process:

1. PC1 sends a packet to 172.30.21.9 (PC2), sending the packet to PC1's default router (R1).

2. R1 tries to route the packet but does not find a route in its routing table that matches PC2's IP address. So, R1 discards the packet and decides to send an unreachable message back to PC1.

3. R1 sends the unreachable message, destination of 172.30.11.2 (PC1), with source address of one of R1's IP addresses. As a result, PC1 knows the IP address of the device that discarded the packet.

This example shows one reason why a router cannot forward a packet, but a router may have many reasons for not being able to forward a packet. So, the ICMP unreachable message includes several codes that imply the reason why the unreachable message was sent. For example, Figure 8-5 shows an ICMP unreachable message with a code that means network unreachable, which means that the device sending the unreachable message did not have a route to reach the destination.

Rather than use phrases such as "ICMP unreachable with a network unreachable code," most people use a short phrase such as "network unreachable" to refer to the specific ICMP unreachable code. The following list details the three most common ICMP unreachable codes seen in internetworks today and their common names:

- **Network unreachable**—The host or router, typically a router, could not forward a packet because it did not have a valid route.

- **Host unreachable**—The host or router, typically a router, has a route matching the packet's destination address, but the host was not reachable on that subnet. This often occurs on the last router in a route, when the router tries to use ARP to find the destination host's MAC address, but the destination host does not respond. For instance, this may happen if the host has been powered off.

- **Port unreachable**—The packet has arrived at the destination host, but the host is not listening for packets sent to the destination TCP or UDP port listed in the TCP or UDP header. For example, if a host acting as a web server has stopped the web server software for maintenance, but the host itself is still up, packets can be delivered to the host but not to the application port. In this case, the destination host creates and sends an ICMP port unreachable message.

Note

Although the ICMP unreachable message does result in the original sending host learning that its packet has been lost, ICMP does not make the TCP/IP Internet layer reliable. Neither ICMP nor IP attempts to recover the lost packet.

To prevent a flood of ICMP packets, routers and hosts do not create unreachable messages when they discard most ICMP packets. For example, a router could create and send an unreachable message, and that ICMP unreachable packet may not be deliverable. If another router discarded the unreachable message and then created yet another unreachable message, the routers could start flooding the network with ICMP unreachable messages.

ICMP Unreachable Message Formats and Codes

The ICMP unreachable message follows the same general format as the other ICMP messages, as shown in Figure 8-6. Interestingly, besides listing the code that identifies the type of unreachable message, the message also includes a copy of the IP header from the original discarded packet, plus the first 8 bytes of the data following the IP header. Although hosts today do not typically do anything with the information listed in the ICMP unreachable message, an engineer could capture the ICMP unreachable messages with a network analyzer and determine which kinds of packets have been discarded.

Figure 8-6   Format of the ICMP Unreachable Message

0	8	16	31
Type (3)	Code	Checksum	
Unused (Must be Zero)			
Internet Header + First 64 Bits of Datagram			
...			

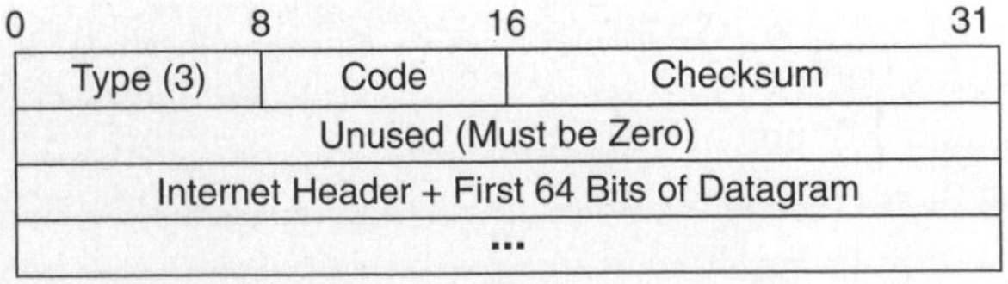

For reference, Table 8-1 lists and describes all the ICMP unreachable codes.

Table 8-1   ICMP Unreachable Code Values

Code Value	Description
0	Network unreachable
1	Host unreachable
2	Protocol unreachable
3	Port unreachable
4	Fragmentation needed and DF set
5	Source route failed
6	Destination network unknown
7	Destination host unknown
8	Source host isolated
9	Communication with data network administratively prohibited
10	Communication with data host administratively prohibited
11	Network unreachable for type of service
12	Host unreachable for type of service

ICMP Unreachable Messages When a Router Cannot Fragment a Packet

The Networking Academy CCNA 2 online curriculum covers some details about one of these unreachable codes: code 4, "fragmentation needed and DF set." To appreciate code 4, you first need to understand the concept of IP fragmentation and the IP header's don't fragment (DF) bit.

Routers and hosts define a limit on the size of IP packets they can both receive and forward on each interface. This configurable limit, typically 1500 bytes, is called the *maximum transmission unit (MTU)* of the interface. If a router needs to forward a packet out an interface, and the packet is larger than the MTU, the router fragments the packet. This means that the router breaks the original packet into smaller packets—called *fragments*—and then forwards the smaller packets. For example, in Figure 8-5, if R1 supported an MTU of only 1000 bytes on its serial interface, and PC1 sent a 1500-byte packet to PC2, R1 would fragment the packet into two packets, of about 750 bytes each, and forward both packets.

Note

The DF bit is often set by hosts that encrypt IP packets when using a Virtual Private Network (VPN).

The unreachable message may be needed when the host sets the DF bit in the IP header. Routers should not fragment packets that have the DF bit set; instead, the routers should discard the packet and send an unreachable message specifically with the "fragmentation needed and DF set" unreachable code.

ICMP TTL Exceeded and Long Routes

As covered in Chapter 7, "Distance Vector Routing Protocols," routing protocols attempt to prevent routing loops. When a routing loop occurs, a packet can be continually forwarded between a small set of routers, never reaching the packet's true destination. Distance vector routing protocols try to prevent routing loops by using such features as split horizon, route poisoning, and holddown. The routing protocols also limit the maximum hop count of routes to help prevent routing loops.

Note

The online curriculum also uses the term *routing cycles* to refer to routing loops.

Although routing protocols attempt to prevent routing loops, they can still occur. Because routing loops can occur, the IP routing process includes a mechanism so that routers discard packets that continually loop around an internetwork. Part of the mechanism uses an IP packet header field called the *Time to Live (TTL) field*, as highlighted in Figure 8-7.

Figure 8-7   IP Header with TTL Field Highlighted

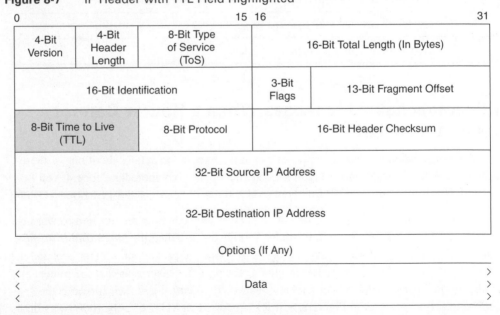

Routers and hosts use the TTL field to limit the number of times a packet can be forwarded by all routers. To begin, the host that creates the packet sets the packet's TTL field to any legal value (from 1 through 255 decimal). When each router forwards the packet, the router decrements the TTL field by 1. Then, if a router decrements the TTL field to 0, the router does two things:

1. The router discards the packet.

2. The router sends an ICMP time exceeded message to the host that originally sent the packet.

When a routing loop occurs, routers keep forwarding the looping packet, decrementing the packet's TTL values. As a result, the packet's TTL eventually decrements to 0, and the router that decrements the TTL to 0 discards the packet. Additionally, that router sends a time exceeded ICMP message to the host that originally sent the packet—in other words, to the IP address listed as the packet's source IP address.

Note

See Chapter 9, "Basic Router Troubleshooting," for more details on how the **traceroute** command uses the TTL field and the ICMP time exceeded message to discover the routers in a particular route.

Summary

ICMP provides control and error-reporting functions for the IP protocol. For example, when an IP packet (IP datagram) cannot be delivered, ICMP uses the ICMP unreachable message to report the error back to the source of the packet. ICMP provides a means to test IP routing via the ICMP echo request and echo reply messages, which are the messages sent and received by the **ping** command.

The ICMP message format starts with the Type, Code, and Checksum fields. The Type field indicates the type of ICMP message being sent. The Code field includes further information specific to the message type. The Checksum field, as in other types of packets, is used to verify the data's integrity. Depending on the particular message, additional fields may define further details related to the function of that message.

IP defines logical addressing and routing. For routing to work properly from one host to another, both the sending and receiving hosts need to have IP configured properly. This configuration may be learned dynamically, typically with DHCP, but it should include each host's IP address, subnet mask, default gateway, and DNS IP addresses. The routers between the two hosts also need to have IP addresses and masks configured correctly on their interfaces and need to have routes to all the required subnets.

One of the more important ICMP functions is the support of the ICMP echo messages. The **ping** command generates ICMP echo request messages and waits on the receipt of ICMP echo reply messages from the other host. The ICMP echo request and reply messages enable network engineers to test whether IP routing is working correctly.

The ICMP unreachable message provides one of ICMP's most useful features. When a router or host cannot deliver a packet, the host or router discards the packet, but it also sends an ICMP unreachable message to the host that originated the packet. The unreachable message includes a code that identifies the reason for the problem. For example, if a router does not have a matching route in its routing table, the router sends a code that means that the destination network is unreachable.

When a routing loop occurs, packets can travel in a loop, repeatedly passing through the same routers and over the same links. The routers continually decrement each packet's TTL field each time a router forwards a packet. After a router decrements the TTL field to 0, the router discards the packet and also sends an ICMP message. In this case, the ICMP message, called the TTL exceeded message, means that the packet has been discarded by a router due to its TTL being decremented to 0.

Check Your Understanding

Complete all the review questions listed here to test your understanding of the topics and concepts in this chapter. Answers are listed in Appendix A, "Answers to Check Your Understanding and Challenge Questions."

1. Which of the following describes ICMP?

   A. It is a reliable error-reporting protocol for TCP.

   B. It is a "best effort" error-reporting protocol for IP.

   C. It is a connectionless-oriented protocol reporting errors for TCP.

   D. It is a connection-oriented protocol reporting errors for IP.

2. What does ICMP stand for?

   A. Internal Control Message Protocol

   B. Internet Control Message Portal

   C. Internal Control Message Portal

   D. Internet Control Message Protocol

3. ICMP has several types of destination unreachable messages, including one that indicates the DF is set. What is meant by DF?

   A. Destination frames are too large.

   B. The discard function is causing bits to drop.

   C. Don't fragment tells the router to discard rather than fragment packets larger than the MTU.

   D. The frames are too small, and the "drop frame" function is on.

4. What two items are true about TTL?

   A. It tells the destination host where to send a reply.

   B. It is a tool to keep packets from looping indefinitely.

   C. Total Traffic Lag indicates delays ICMP can report.

   D. The Time to Live field limits the number of times a packet can be forwarded by routers.

   E. It is a number that is incremented with each router hop up to 256.

5. How is an ICMP echo request generated?

   A. Whenever a packet passes through a router, the echo request is sent to the source host.

   B. When a source host issues an echo reply.

   C. When a **ping** command is entered on a source host.

   D. When a destination host responds to a **ping** command.

6. If a ping is sent to a host on a remote network, what happens if the host is not turned on?

    A. The destination host sends an unreachable reply.

    B. The last router holds the packet in the buffer until the device is powered on again.

    C. The last router sends the source host an ICMP host unreachable message, which indicates that the network was reachable, but not the host.

    D. The default gateway knows the status of the host from the routing table and does not forward the ping.

7. When an ICMP destination unreachable datagram is sent from a router back to the source host, which of the following also happen?

    A. The source host resends the ICMP packet via a different router interface.

    B. The destination host sends an unreachable reply.

    C. That same router discards the original packet.

    D. The ICMP packet is broadcast from the final router to find a possible route.

8. Router R1 has sent an ICMP destination unreachable message to host H1. However, when the ICMP destination unreachable message reached R2, on its way to H1, R2 discarded the ICMP destination unreachable message. Which of the following is true about any other actions taken at this point?

    A. R1 realizes the ICMP unreachable was lost and resends the unreachable to H1.

    B. R2 sends an ICMP destination unreachable message to R1.

    C. R2 generates and sends a new ICMP destination unreachable to H1.

    D. No further ICMP messages will be generated as a result of these events.

Challenge Questions and Activities

These questions require a deeper application of the concepts covered in this chapter and are similar to the style of questions you might see on a CCNA certification exam.

Use the following diagram and the routing table for the ACME router to answer the questions in this section.

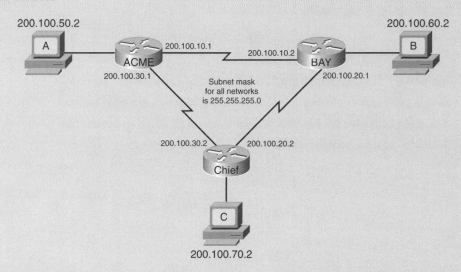

```
ACME#show ip route
Codes: C - connected, S - static, I - IGRP, R - RIP, M - mobile, B - BGP
        D - EIGRP, EX - EIGRP external, O - OSPF, IA - OSPF inter area
        N1 - OSPF NSSA external type 1, N2 - OSPF NSSA external type 2
        E1 - OSPF external type 1, E2 - OSPF external type 2, E - EGP
        i - IS-IS, L1 - IS-IS level-1, L2 - IS-IS level-2,
        ia - IS-IS inter area, * - candidate default, U - per-user static route,
        o - ODR, P - periodic downloaded static route
Gateway of last resort is not set
R    200.100.20.0/24 [120/1] via 200.100.30.2, 00:00:19, Serial0/1
                     [120/1] via 200.100.10.2, 00:00:11, Serial0/0
C    200.100.50.0/24 is directly connected, FastEthernet0/0
R    200.100.70.0/24 [120/1] via 200.100.30.2, 00:00:19, Serial0/1
C    200.100.30.0/24 is directly connected, Serial0/1
R    200.100.60.0/24 [120/2] via 200.100.30.2, 00:00:19, Serial0/1
C    200.100.10.0/24 is directly connected, Serial0/0
```

1. A user on host A issues the **ping 200.100.70.2** command, but the ping is not successful because host C is powered off. What is the likely ICMP message received by host A?

    A. Echo reply from 200.100.70.2

    B. Network unreachable reply from 200.100.30.2

    C. Host unreachable reply from 200.100.30.2

    D. Port unreachable reply from 200.100.30.1

2. Host A sends an echo request to 200.100.60.2. Using information in the diagram and the routing table, select the following statement that is true about the request.

    A. The packets will transit network 200.100.30.0 and network 200.100 20.0.

    B. Host B's network is unreachable, and router ACME will not send the packets.

    C. A host unreachable message will be sent from router Chief to host A.

    D. Host B is only one hop away, and the TTL will not expire.

CHAPTER 9

Basic Router Troubleshooting

Objectives

Upon completion of this chapter, you should be able to answer the following questions:

- How is the **show ip route** command used to gather information about routes understood by the router?

- How is a default route or a default network configured on a router?

- How does a router use both Layer 2 and Layer 3 addressing to move data between networks?

- How is the **ping** command used to test basic network connectivity?

- How is the **telnet** command used to verify application layer communication between hosts?

- How does knowledge of the OSI model assist in troubleshooting and testing of networks?

- How is the **show interface** command used to troubleshoot Layer 1 and Layer 2 problems in a network?

- How are the **show ip route** and **show ip protocol** commands used to identify routing issues?

- How is the **show cdp** command used to verify Layer 2 connectivity?

- How is the **traceroute** command used to identify the path that a packet takes between networks?

- How is the **show controller serial** command used to ensure that the proper cable is attached?

- How are the basic **debug** commands used to show router activity?

Key Terms

This chapter uses the following key terms. You can find the definitions in the Glossary.

Troubleshooting a TCP/IP internetwork requires knowledge, skill, and the self-discipline to use a structured process rather than just doing a bunch of commands. The earlier parts of the Cisco Networking Academy CCNA course (and these *Companion Guide* books) helped provide some of the key bits of knowledge. The labs associated with the course, and those found in the CCNA *Lab and Study Guide* books from Cisco Press, provided an opportunity to build some hands-on skills. This chapter adds the last piece to the puzzle by explaining troubleshooting methods.

This chapter focuses specifically on how to troubleshoot problems that might prevent a TCP/IP application on one host from communicating with a TCP/IP application on another host. Much of the material in this chapter has been covered in other chapters of this book and in the *Networking Basics CCNA 1 Companion Guide*. This chapter collects the explanations about many of the concepts and tools into a single chapter, all explained from the perspective of troubleshooting network problems.

The first major section of this chapter focuses on some of the key knowledge required for troubleshooting routing problems. Engineers should first have a thorough understanding of how an internetwork should work under normal conditions before they attempt to troubleshoot a network that is having problems. This first section reviews the routing and routing protocol processes briefly, focusing on their use of the IP routing table as seen with the **show ip route** command.

The second section of this chapter covers the concept of a structured troubleshooting method. A structured approach or process can help you isolate and solve the problem more quickly. It can also help you organize your thinking so that you can more easily compare the actual (incorrect) operation of the internetwork with the expected correct operation of the internetwork.

Finally, the last major section of this chapter covers a variety of troubleshooting commands on Cisco routers.

Examining the Routing Table

IP defines many important features that together allow TCP/IP internetworks to work properly. Two of the more important features are routing and routing protocols, defined as follows:

- **Routing**—The process by which a router receives a packet, matches the packet's destination IP address to the router's routing table, and then forwards the packet based on that matched entry in the IP routing table. This process is also called *forwarding*.

- **Routing protocols**—The messages and the rules by which routers learn all possible routes, choose the best route to reach each subnet, and add those routes to the routers' routing tables. This process, particularly the part in which the routing protocol chooses the best route, is sometimes called *path selection*.

This section focuses on the IP routing table found in routers. Both routing (the packet forwarding process) and routing protocols (the route discovery and selection process) use the IP routing table. To forward a packet, a router must match the packet to the correct entry in the routing table. To learn all the best routes, routers typically use a routing protocol.

This section first reviews the routing process and then reviews how routers learn routes with routing protocols. Along the way, the text introduces new concepts related to default routes.

IP Routing (Forwarding)

Routers perform a small set of repetitive steps when routing an IP packet. To fully appreciate routing, you need a solid understanding of the contents of a router's IP routing table, as stored in a router's RAM and displayed using the **show ip route** command. This section reviews the output of this command and shows examples of routing—from both a Layer 3 and Layer 2 perspective—comparing the routing process to the contents of the routers' IP routing tables.

The **show ip route** Command

The **show ip route** command displays a router's IP routing table. The table includes all the routes that the router can currently use when forwarding packets. These routes include the following:

- **Connected routes**—Routes to subnets connected to this router's interfaces (assuming the interfaces have been configured with an IP address and are up and working)

- **Static routes**—Routes configured on this router using the **ip route** global configuration command

- **Dynamically learned routes**—Routes learned by using a dynamic routing protocol—for example, RIP

To view the routing table, a user can use the **show ip route** command at the command-line interface (CLI). Additionally, the user can use variations on the **show ip route** command to see subsets of the routing table or to see more specific information. Table 9-1 lists and describes some of the options on the **show ip route** command.

Note

The term CLI refers to the router's user interface.

Table 9-1   Options on the **show ip route** Command

Command	Description
show ip route connected	Displays only connected routes
show ip route rip	Displays only RIP-learned routes
show ip route static	Displays only static routes
show ip route *address*	Displays the route that the router would match when forwarding a packet to the listed address

Figure 9-1 shows an internetwork with three subnets and two routers. Example 9-1 shows three command options taken from R1.

Figure 9-1 Three-Subnet, Two-Router Internetwork Used in the Routing Examples

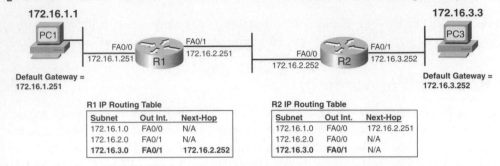

R1 IP Routing Table

Subnet	Out Int.	Next-Hop
172.16.1.0	FA0/0	N/A
172.16.2.0	FA0/1	N/A
172.16.3.0	FA0/1	172.16.2.252

R2 IP Routing Table

Subnet	Out Int.	Next-Hop
172.16.1.0	FA0/0	172.16.2.251
172.16.2.0	FA0/0	N/A
172.16.3.0	FA0/1	N/A

Example 9-1 The R1 **show ip route** Command Options

```
R1#show ip route
Codes: C - connected, S - static, R - RIP, M - mobile, B - BGP
       D - EIGRP, EX - EIGRP external, O - OSPF, IA - OSPF inter area
       N1 - OSPF NSSA external type 1, N2 - OSPF NSSA external type 2
       E1 - OSPF external type 1, E2 - OSPF external type 2
       i - IS-IS, su - IS-IS summary, L1 - IS-IS level-1, L2 - IS-IS level-2
       ia - IS-IS inter area, * - candidate default, U - per-user static route
       o - ODR, P - periodic downloaded static route

Gateway of last resort is not set

     172.16.0.0/24 is subnetted, 3 subnets
C       172.16.1.0 is directly connected, FastEthernet0/0
C       172.16.2.0 is directly connected, FastEthernet0/1
R       172.16.3.0 [120/1] via 172.16.2.252, 00:00:04, FastEthernet0/1
R1#show ip route rip
     172.16.0.0/24 is subnetted, 3 subnets
R       172.16.3.0 [120/1] via 172.16.2.252, 00:00:07, FastEthernet0/1
R1#show ip route 172.16.3.3
Routing entry for 172.16.3.0/24
  Known via "rip", distance 120, metric 1
  Redistributing via rip
  Last update from 172.16.2.252 on FastEthernet0/1, 00:00:23 ago
  Routing Descriptor Blocks:
  * 172.16.2.252, from 172.16.2.252, 00:00:23 ago, via FastEthernet0/1
      Route metric is 1, traffic share count is 1
```

The output of the **show ip route** command at the top of Example 9-1 should be familiar by now, but it is useful to review a few items. The legend at the top of the output lists the possible sources of routing information. The command output lists codes such as C (connected) and R (RIP) beside each individual route; for example, the route to 172.16.3.0 on R1 was learned via RIP, as shown with a code of R. On that same route, the outgoing interface (FastEthernet0/1) and next-hop router (172.16.2.252) are both listed as well.

The **show ip route rip** command lists only RIP-learned routes. As a result, the command does not need to list a legend with codes to specify the source of the routing information.

Finally, the last part of Example 9-1 lists the output of one of the most underappreciated command options in Cisco routers. The **show ip route 172.16.3.3** command lists the route that R1 would use when forwarding a packet sent to 172.16.3.3. The routing table does not list the IP address 172.16.3.3, but subnet 172.16.3.0/24 includes address 172.16.3.3, so R1 considers the route for 172.16.3.0/24 to match packets sent to 172.16.3.3. When troubleshooting routing problems, you can use this command to quickly identify which route that particular router would use when forwarding packets to the listed destination. If the command says no route matches the destination, you learn that the router cannot route the packet properly.

Lab 9.1.1   Using show ip route to Examine Routing Tables

In this lab, you set up an IP addressing scheme using Class B networks.

IP Routing: Layer 3 Perspective

The IP routing process forwards a packet from the source host to the destination host. Figure 9-2 shows an example, with PC1 (172.16.1.1) sending a packet to PC3 (172.16.3.3).

Figure 9-2   Example IP Routing Process

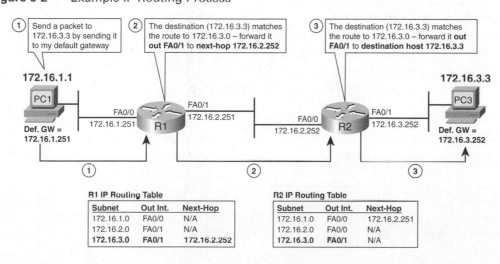

The process in Figure 9-2 shows the following details:

1. The source host (PC1) sends the packet to its default gateway.

2. R1 compares the packet's destination IP address (172.16.3.3) to its routing table, matching an entry that tells R1 to forward the packet out its FA0/1 interface to R2 next.

3. R2 compares the packet's destination IP address (172.16.3.3) to its routing table, matching an entry that tells R2 to forward the packet out its FA0/1 interface directly to PC3.

Note

The **show ip route** *address* command, as shown in Example 9-1, shows the route that the router considers to "match" for the packets sent to a particular destination address.

To route a packet, a router examines the destination IP address and finds a matching entry in that router's IP routing table. For example, R1 looks at the destination—172.16.3.3—and looks at its routing table. R1 has a route for subnet 172.16.3.0/24, and 172.16.3.3 is a member of subnet 172.16.3.0/24. So R1 considers this packet to match the route for 172.16.3.0/24. Then, R1 uses the instruction in that routing table entry—namely, the outgoing interface (FA0/1) and next-hop router (172.16.2.252, or R2) when forwarding the packet.

Most useful communications in an IP network require the use of both the forward route and the reverse route. To understand these terms, reconsider Figure 9-2 from PC1's perspective. The route that delivers its packet to PC3 would be the forward route from PC1 to PC3. However, most useful communications require that PC3 send packets back to PC1. The packets sent by PC3 back to PC1 use a different set of routes—routes that match destination IP address 172.16.1.1 (PC1). So, again thinking from PC1's perspective, the reverse route is the route from PC3 back to PC1. It is easy to forget to test both the forward route and reverse route when troubleshooting IP routing problems, but when a user simply says something like "I can't get to the web server," you need to test both the forward and reverse routes.

IP Routing: Layer 2 Perspective

Note

As a reminder, the term *IP packet* refers to the IP header and encapsulated data, without a data-link header or trailer. The term *frame* refers to the data-link header and trailer and its encapsulated data.

Although Figure 9-2 shows the IP packet being forwarded, the figure and related explanations ignore the Layer 1 (physical layer) and Layer 2 (data link layer) concepts. For the packet to be forwarded, the physical cabling must be installed and working, and the data link protocols must be working. When troubleshooting routing problems, you need to understand and remember how the Layer 3 routing processes use the underlying Layer 1 and Layer 2 technologies such as Ethernet. The key to understanding what happens relates to these two definitions:

■ Routers route Layer 3 IP packets from one host to the other.

■ Routers use Layer 2 data-link frames to move packets to the next router or host in the route; after that next device receives a frame, it discards the data-link header and trailer, leaving the IP packet.

Figure 9-3 shows a Layer 2 perspective of the same packet shown in Figure 9-2. The packet remains mostly unchanged for the entire journey, whereas the Ethernet header and trailer change at each of the three steps to deliver the packet to the next device.

Figure 9-3   Data-Link Encapsulation: Discarding and Building New Ethernet Headers/Trailers

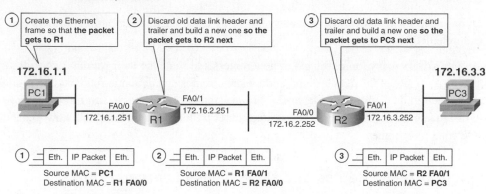

Figure 9-3 shows the logic used by PC1, R1, and R2, as well as the Ethernet frames created by each. Of particular importance, note the Ethernet MAC addresses used. The Ethernet frames serve the purpose of getting the packet to the next device, not all the way across the whole internetwork. So, the destination MAC address in each frame simply identifies the next device. For example, the frame sent by PC1 has a destination MAC address of R1, not PC3, which causes the LAN switch to correctly forward the Ethernet frame to R1.

By loading Packet Tracer configuration file NA02-0903, you can use simulation mode to view PC1's **ping** of PC3 shown in Figure 9-3. Packet Tracer shows details about the headers used at each step in the process, similar to what is shown in the figure.

This concludes this chapter's review of IP routing. The following section reviews the process of filling the routing table with routes.

Filling the IP Routing Table with Routes

Many routing problems result from a router not having a route that matches a particular packet's destination address. So, engineers should be familiar with how routers add routes to their routing table, and the logic routers use to pick which routes to use if they know of multiple routes to the same subnet. This section reviews those rules.

Routers have three types of routes, based on how the routers learn the routes:

- **Connected routes**   Routes to subnets connected to this router's interfaces (assuming the interfaces have been configured with an IP address and are up and working)

- **Static routes**—Routes configured on this route using the **ip route** global configuration command

- **Dynamically learned routes**—Routes learned by using a dynamic routing protocol (for example, RIP)

This section covers many topics related to how routers add routes to their routing tables. It begins with a review of the details about adding static routes and dynamic routes to the routing table. The section then covers a wide variety of other topics, including default routes, administrative distance, metrics, the process of learning routes with routing updates, and how to handle multiple equal-cost routes.

Comparing Static Routes and Dynamically Learned Routes

Every working router learns some connected routes after the router's interfaces have been configured with IP addresses and the interfaces reach a working state. Beyond that, most engineers also configure an IP routing protocol, such as RIP, OSPF, or EIGRP, to dynamically learn IP routes. Additionally, engineers may use static routes in some situations as well, particularly when the engineer needs to use dial backup, when the internetwork rarely changes, or when a router has only one physical path to reach the rest of the internetwork. (See the Chapter 6 section "Static Routes" for more background on the most typical cases for using static routes.)

Generally speaking, routers learn most of their routes using a dynamic routing protocol. However, routing protocols have some disadvantages when compared with static routing. Dynamic routing protocols require ongoing work by the routers, which consumes CPU and memory in the routers and consumes link bandwidth to advertise the routes. Also, because routing protocols advertise the routes by sending messages into the network, a malicious hacker may see the routing updates. The hacker then can take advantage of the information to attack the network. (Cisco routers can be configured to help protect against such attacks, however.) Table 9-2 lists some of the common comparison points for static versus dynamic routes.

Table 9-2   Comparing the Use of Static and Dynamic Routes

Consideration	Static	Dynamic
Adapts to changes in the internetwork by picking and using the currently best routes	No	Yes
Requires additional configuration when subnets are added to the internetwork	Yes	No
Consumes CPU, memory, and link bandwidth	No	Yes
Sends routing information that hackers may overhear	No	Yes

In a given Cisco router, to tell which routes are static and which were learned dynamically, look at the code to the left of each route listed in the output of the **show ip route** command. For example, a code of S means that an **ip route** global configuration command has defined a static route on that router, but a code of R means RIP learned the route dynamically. Also, the top of the output of the **show ip route** command provides a reference list of all the possible codes and the term each represents.

Default Routes and the Gateway of Last Resort

Cisco routers can use a special route called a default route—also called a *gateway of last resort*—to route packets. Without a default route, a router discards packets whose destination address does not match the router's routing table. With a default route, however, a router forwards a packet based on the router's default route when that packet's destination address fails to match any of the other routes.

Chapter 6 already covered the concepts and configuration of static routes, and Chapter 7 covered how an engineer can configure RIP to then advertise a static default route. First, this section reviews the default route configuration discussed in Chapters 6 and 7, which uses the **ip route** global configuration command. Following that, this section focuses on the **show** commands to examine such static routes and introduces another method to configure a default route using the **ip default-network** command.

> **Note**
>
> This chapter describes how routers work with the default configuration that includes the **ip classless** configuration command. See the Chapter 7 section "Classless and Classful Routing" for more information.

Static Default Routes

As covered in the Chapter 7 section "Advertising Default Routes with RIP," a router can configure a static default route and then advertise that default route to other routers by using RIP. To configure the static default route, the engineer configures an **ip route 0.0.0.0 0.0.0.0** *next-hop-router* command. The *next-hop-router* parameter is the IP address of a neighboring router.

This type of static route shows up in a couple of places in the output of the **show ip route** command. To see where, router R-core in Figure 9-4 configures a static default route, using router ISP-edge as the next-hop router. By doing so, R-core intends to forward packets into the Internet if R-core does not know a specific route that matches a packet.

Note

The network topology in Figure 9-4 generally matches Figure 7-15 from Chapter 7, which was used in the discussion of advertising default routes in that chapter.

Figure 9-4   Router R-core Using Default Routing to Forward Packets into the Internet

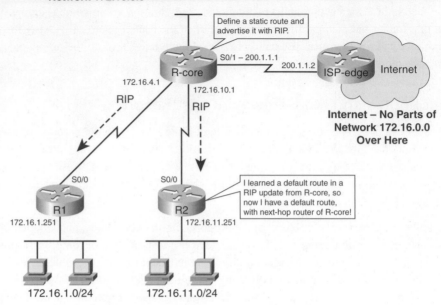

Example 9-2 shows the contents of the IP routing table on router R-core after the engineer has configured the **ip route 0.0.0.0 0.0.0.0 200.1.1.2** command. The comments following the example explain how the routing tables display the default route.

Example 9-2   R-core **show ip route** Command Options

```
R-core#show ip route
Codes: C - connected, S - static, R - RIP, M - mobile, B - BGP
       D - EIGRP, EX - EIGRP external, O - OSPF, IA - OSPF inter area
       N1 - OSPF NSSA external type 1, N2 - OSPF NSSA external type 2
       E1 - OSPF external type 1, E2 - OSPF external type 2
       i - IS-IS, su - IS-IS summary, L1 - IS-IS level-1, L2 - IS-IS level-2
       ia - IS-IS inter area, * - candidate default, U - per-user static route
       o - ODR, P - periodic downloaded static route


Gateway of last resort is 200.1.1.2 to network 0.0.0.0


C    200.1.1.0/24 is directly connected, Serial0/1/0
     172.16.0.0/24 is subnetted, 3 subnets
C       172.16.4.0 is directly connected, Serial0/1/1
R       172.16.1.0 [120/1] via 172.16.4.1, 00:00:06, Serial0/1/1
C       172.16.3.0 is directly connected, FastEthernet0/1
S*   0.0.0.0/0 [1/0] via 200.1.1.2
```

The output of the **show ip route** command lists the default route in two places. The very last line of the example lists the statically defined default route as 0.0.0.0/0 and lists the next-hop address "via 200.1.1.2," which matches the **ip route** command that was configured. The code value of S* on the left side of the last line means the route is both a static route and a candidate default route. Additionally, the router to which packets will be forwarded when using the default route—namely, 200.1.1.2, or router ISP—is also listed about halfway down Example 9-2 as the gateway of last resort. This term simply refers to the next-hop router to which this router will forward packets whose destination addresses do not match any other more specific routes.

For the rest of the routers in R-core's enterprise network to learn of this default route, as described in Chapter 7, R-core would need to redistribute the static default route. Example 9-3 shows R-core's additional configuration, and the resulting routing table on router R1.

```
Example 9-3    Advertising Default Routes with RIP

R-core#configure terminal
Enter configuration commands, one per line.  End with CNTL/Z.
R-core(config)#router rip
R-core(config-router)#redistribute static
R-core(config-router)#^Z
R-core#


! The next command is on Router R1
R1#show ip route
Codes: C - connected, S - static, R - RIP, M - mobile, B - BGP
       D - EIGRP, EX - EIGRP external, O - OSPF, IA - OSPF inter area
       N1 - OSPF NSSA external type 1, N2 - OSPF NSSA external type 2
       E1 - OSPF external type 1, E2 - OSPF external type 2
       i - IS-IS, su - IS-IS summary, l1 - IS-IS level-1, L2 - IS-IS level-2
       ia - IS-IS inter area, * - candidate default, U - per-user static route
       o - ODR, P - periodic downloaded static route

Gateway of last resort is 172.16.4.2 to network 0.0.0.0

     172.16.0.0/24 is subnetted, 3 subnets
C       172.16.4.0 is directly connected, Serial0/1/0
C       172.16.1.0 is directly connected, FastEthernet0/0
R       172.16.3.0 [120/1] via 172.16.4.2, 00:00:03, Serial0/1/0
R*   0.0.0.0/0 [120/1] via 172.16.4.2, 00:00:02, Serial0/1/0
```

Note that R1's **show ip route** command lists the default route information in the same two places as shown in Example 9-2. However, the output lists a different next-hop router. R1's next-hop router for the default route will be R-core, because R1 learned this default route from R-core. Also note the default route lists a code of R, meaning the default route was learned via RIP.

Advertising a Default Route Using the ip default-network Command

Some routing protocols, RIP included, allow a router to advertise a default route by configuring the **ip default-network** *network-number* command. This global configuration command accepts a classful IP network number as a parameter. After it is configured, it tells the router's routing protocols to do the following:

> If this router has a route to any subnet of the listed default network, the routing protocol should advertise a default route to its peers.

Note

The term classful network refers to any Class A, B, or C network. Some people also use the term *major network* instead of classful network.

With this kind of logic, an engineer could cause a router to advertise a default route, but only when the router could reach some other important network. For example, in Figure 9-4 in the preceding section, router R-core could be configured with an **ip default-network 200.1.1.0** command. As long as the link between R-core and ISP-edge was up and working, R-core would have a route to at least one subnet of network 200.1.1.0, and R-core would advertise a default route to the rest of the routers.

Example 9-4 shows the configuration of router R-core and the IP routing table on router R1. Note that R-core has removed the **redistribute static** command (as shown in Example 9-3) before adding the configuration shown in Example 9-4.

Example 9-4   Advertising a Default Route Using the **ip default-network** Command

```
R-core#configure terminal
Enter configuration commands, one per line.  End with CNTL/Z.
R-core(config)#ip default-network 200.1.1.0
R-core(config)#^Z
R-core#
```

```
! The next command is on Router R1
R1#show ip route
Codes: C - connected, S - static, R - RIP, M - mobile, B - BGP
        D - EIGRP, EX - EIGRP external, O - OSPF, IA - OSPF inter area
        N1 - OSPF NSSA external type 1, N2 - OSPF NSSA external type 2
        E1 - OSPF external type 1, E2 - OSPF external type 2
        i - IS-IS, su - IS-IS summary, L1 - IS-IS level-1, L2 - IS-IS level-2
        ia - IS-IS inter area, * - candidate default, U - per-user static route
        o - ODR, P - periodic downloaded static route

Gateway of last resort is 172.16.4.2 to network 0.0.0.0

     172.16.0.0/24 is subnetted, 3 subnets
C       172.16.4.0 is directly connected, Serial0/1/0
C       172.16.1.0 is directly connected, FastEthernet0/0
R       172.16.3.0 [120/1] via 172.16.4.2, 00:00:08, Serial0/1/0
R*   0.0.0.0/0 [120/1] via 172.16.4.2, 00:00:08, Serial0/1/0
```

From the branch routers' perspectives, the default route works exactly the same with both styles of configuration on R-core. Comparing Example 9-4 with Example 9-3, note that R1 does not show any difference in its default route.

Note also that the **ip default-network** command does not do the same thing as a host's configuration for its default gateway. The **ip default-network** command tells a router to advertise a default route to its peers under certain conditions. In fact, routers do not use a default gateway concept at all, because they should know lots of routes and be able to make good routing choices.

Lab 9.1.2   Gateway of Last Resort

In this lab, you configure RIP routing and default routes (gateways) on the routers.

Administrative Distance

A single router may learn routes from many different sources. For example, a router will learn some connected routes; it may have some static routes configured; and it may run multiple routing protocols. When a router learns more than one route to the same subnet, *from different sources* (for instance, using multiple routing protocols), the router needs to decide which route is best and then add that route to the IP routing table.

When choosing between multiple routes to the same destination but learned from different sources, the router picks the route with the lowest administrative distance. For example, when a router has a static route defined for subnet 172.16.1.0/24 and then learns a route to 172.16.1.0/24 using RIP, by default, the router chooses the static route. While that may seem like an obviously good default choice, the router bases its decision on the static route's lower default administrative distance of 1 versus RIP's higher default administrative distance of 120.

Table 9-3 lists the default administrative distances for the various routing sources.

Table 9-3   Default Administrative Distances in Cisco IOS

Protocol or Source of Routing Information	Default Administrative Distance
Connected interface[1]	0
Static route[1]	1
EIGRP summary route	5
External BGP	20
Internal EIGRP	90
IGRP	100
OSPF	110

continues

Table 9-3   Default Administrative Distances in Cisco IOS   *continued*

Protocol or Source of Routing Information	Default Administrative Distance
IS-IS	115
RIP[1]	120
External EIGRP	170
Internal BGP	200
Unknown	255

[1] These routing sources are the sources of routing information that is covered in the most detail in the Networking Academy CCNA 1 and CCNA 2 courses.

The **show ip route** command output lists the administrative distance for most routes, with the notable exception of connected routes, which default to an administrative distance of 0. Example 9-5 shows the **show ip route rip** command. The output highlights the administrative distance for the one RIP route known on router R1, which defaults to RIP's setting of 120.

Example 9-5   The Administrative Distance, Listed in the **show ip route** Command

```
R1#show ip route rip
     172.16.0.0/24 is subnetted, 3 subnets
R       172.16.3.0 [120/1] via 172.16.2.252, 00:00:07, FastEthernet0/1
```

Choosing Routes Based on the Metric

When a router uses a single routing protocol, and that routing protocol learns only one route to reach a particular subnet, the routing protocol simply adds that one route to the routing table. However, when a router's single routing protocol learns multiple routes to the same destination subnet, the routing protocol picks the best route based on the metric. Simply put, the term *metric* refers to an objective measurement, or meter, of how good each route is. The routing protocol adds the route with the best (lowest) metric value to its IP routing table. Table 9-4 highlights the metrics used by RIP, EIGRP, and OSPF.

Table 9-4   Routing Protocol Metrics

Routing Protocol	Metric	Description
RIP	Hop count	The metric represents the number of other routers between a router and the subnet.
OSPF	Cost	Each interface has an associated cost; OSPF adds the costs of each interface out which a packet would have to exit to use a route.
EIGRP[1]	Bandwidth and delay	EIGRP advertises the bandwidth, delay, link reliability, and link loading, applies a mathematical function, and calculates a metric. By default, only bandwidth and delay affect the calculation.

[1] IGRP uses the same metric concept, with minor differences in the formula used to calculate the metric.

Chapter 6 covers the concept of metrics with examples for RIP and OSPF. The Chapter 7 section "Additional Topics of Interest," which you can find on the CD-ROM, covers the IGRP metric calculation in more detail than the coverage listed here. Because Module 9 of the CCNA 2 online curriculum covers the IGRP metric, this section of Chapter 9 also explains the basics of how IGRP and EIGRP calculate the metric.

IGRP advertises each route's constraining link bandwidth, the cumulative delay, the lowest link reliability, and the highest link loading. IGRP then feeds those variables into the following formula:

Metric = [K1 × Bandwidth + (K2 × Bandwidth)/(256 – Load) + K3 × Delay] × [K5/(Reliability + K4)]

The formula includes five constants—K1, K2, K3, K4, and K5—appropriately called *K-values*. These constants can be configured, but Cisco does not recommend changing the K-values. By default, K1 and K3 are 1, and the rest are 0. By leaving these K-values with their default values, the formula reduces to the following:

Metric = bandwidth + delay

Because this formula is simple, it does not tell the whole story. IGRP and EIGRP want the metric to be lower for routes with relatively faster bandwidths and want the metric to be higher for routes with relatively slower bandwidths. So, the bandwidth value in the preceding formula is actually an inverse of the link bandwidth, making the value larger for slower-link bandwidth values.

Note

EIGRP uses the same metric formula as IGRP, except the entire result is multiplied by 256; this chapter uses IGRP's formula to reduce clutter.

Determining the Last Routing Update

Distance vector protocols send periodic routing updates, and each periodic update includes the same full set of routes. When troubleshooting problems with routing protocols, engineers may want to know how long ago a router last heard a periodic update from a neighbor. The following commands list the time since a router last heard a routing update that advertised a route:

- **show ip route**

- **show ip route** *address*

- **show ip protocols**

- **show ip rip database**

Each time a router receives a periodic routing update from a neighbor, the router resets a timer for that neighbor back to 0. Then, the timer increases until it receives the next routing update. With RIP, using its default 30-second update timer, the timer values should vary between 0 and 30 seconds under normal operation. Example 9-6 lists two sample commands that highlight the current timer for each route or neighbor.

Note

The timers in the two commands shown in Example 9-6 differ because the commands were used about 10 seconds apart.

Example 9-6   Examining the Time Since the Last Routing Update

```
R1#show ip route rip
     172.16.0.0/24 is subnetted, 3 subnets
R       172.16.3.0 [120/1] via 172.16.2.252, 00:00:07, FastEthernet0/1
R       172.16.5.0 [120/1] via 172.16.4.2, 00:00:23, S0/1/0
R1#show ip protocols
  Sending updates every 30 seconds, next due in 17 seconds
  Invalid after 180 seconds, hold down 180, flushed after 240
  Outgoing update filter list for all interfaces is not set
  Incoming update filter list for all interfaces is not set
  Redistributing: rip
  Default version control: send version 1, receive any version
    Interface              Send   Recv  Triggered RIP  Key-chain
    Serial0/1/0             1      1 2
  Automatic network summarization is in effect
  Maximum path: 4
  Routing for Networks:
    172.16.0.0
  Routing Information Sources:
    Gateway        Distance      Last Update
    172.16.2.252   120           00:00:17
    172.16.4.2     120           00:00:03
  Distance: (default is 120)
```

As shown in the output of the **show ip route rip** command, each RIP-learned route lists the time that has elapsed since the last routing update about the route. In this case, it has been 7 seconds since this router last heard the update that advertised the route to 172.16.3.0/24. At the bottom of Example 9-6, the **show ip protocols** command lists the time since the last update from each neighbor.

Lab 9.1.8   Last Route Update

In this lab, you gather information about routing updates and routing protocols.

Using Multiple Equal-Cost Routes

As explained in the Chapter 7 section "Load Balancing over Multiple Equal-Cost Routes," a single router may learn several routes to the same subnet, but the metrics may tie. These routes are typically called *equal-cost routes*. When this occurs, the router uses the following logic to choose which route(s) to add to its IP routing table:

- Add up to four of the routes to the routing table (default).

- The number of equal-cost routes added to the routing table can be changed to between one and six by using the **maximum-path** *number* command as a subcommand of the routing protocol.

After routes are added to the routing table, the router then load-balances the traffic over various routes. (Refer to the same section of Chapter 7 for more information about the load-balancing process.)

Example 9-7 shows a router adding two routes to reach the same subnet. In this case, router R1 learns two two-hop routes to subnet 172.30.3.0/24. The **show ip route** command lists the destination subnet once, but with two different lines with two different next-hop addresses and two different outgoing interfaces. The **show ip route 172.30.3.0** command at the end of the example shows the same routes, with the same two different next-hop routers and outgoing interfaces.

Example 9-7   Displaying Multiple Equal-Cost Routes

```
R1#show ip route
! legend omitted for brevity
     172.30.0.0/24 is subnetted, 6 subnets
R       172.30.21.0 [120/1] via 172.30.1.2, 00:00:08, Serial0/0
R       172.30.31.0 [120/1] via 172.30.2.3, 00:00:00, Serial0/1
C       172.30.2.0 is directly connected, Serial0/1
R       172.30.3.0 [120/1] via 172.30.2.3, 00:00:00, Serial0/1
                   [120/1] via 172.30.1.2, 00:00:08, Serial0/0
C       172.30.1.0 is directly connected, Serial0/0
C       172.30.11.0 is directly connected, FastEthernet0/0
R1#show ip route 172.30.3.0
Routing entry for 172.30.3.0/24
```

continues

Example 9-7   Displaying Multiple Equal-Cost Routes   *continued*

```
Known via "rip", distance 120, metric 1
Redistributing via rip
Last update from 172.30.1.2 on Serial0/0, 00:00:26 ago
Routing Descriptor Blocks:
  172.30.2.3, from 172.30.2.3, 00:00:26 ago, via Serial0/1
    Route metric is 1, traffic share count is 1
* 172.30.1.2, from 172.30.1.2, 00:00:26 ago, via Serial0/0
    Route metric is 1, traffic share count is 1
```

Note

This short section about variance may not be covered by some Cisco Networking Academies. You may want to check with your instructor about whether you need to read this section. If not, skip to the next section.

Using Multiple Unequal-Cost Routes Using Variance

RIP's hop-count metric leads to many cases in which metrics tie. However, IGRP and EIGRP use a mathematical formula that leads to almost no cases in which metrics tie but to many cases in which the metrics are relatively close to each other. So, Cisco allows these two routing protocols to add multiple routes to a routing table, for the same destination subnet, when the metrics are unequal. This process is called *unequal-cost load balancing*.

By default, Cisco IOS does not use unequal-cost load balancing, but it can be configured by using the **variance** *multiplier* subcommand inside routing protocol configuration mode. This command defines some integer multiplier, used as follows:

1. Find the best metric among all the routes to reach the same subnet.

2. Multiply the best metric by the variance multiplier.

3. Any routes whose metrics are less than the value calculated at Step 2 may be added to the routing table as if they were equal-cost routes.

For example, imagine that a router has learned three routes to subnet 172.16.1.0/24 using EIGRP. The metrics for the routes are 10,000, 18,000, and 22,000. Now imagine that the router has configured a **variance 2** command under the **router eigrp 1** command. In this case, the router multiplies the lowest metric (10,000) by 2 and finds that two of the routes' metrics are less than 20,000—the original route and the route with metric 18,000—so the router adds two of the three routes to its routing table.

Network Testing Methods and Tips

To troubleshoot a problem in a corporate internetwork, you need to be prepared. You need to know about the many standards and protocols used in the internetwork; you need hands-on skills, including the ability to log on to the routers and switches, use commands, and interpret the output; and you need to know the details of that particular internetwork, including knowledge about the devices, the cable plant, the configuration, and which of the installed devices should be up and working all the time. With these skills and knowledge, you should be able to recognize when problems are occurring, take steps to discover the real cause of those problems, and fix the problems.

Even if you are properly prepared, as just described, the troubleshooting process may still work poorly if you do not also use a *structured troubleshooting method*. Rather than simply trying whatever comes to mind, engineers use a structured method use the same general steps to isolate the problem, discover the root cause of the problem, and then fix the problem. (The term *root cause* simply refers to the reason why the problem is occurring; it is also the issue that must be fixed to make the network operational again.) By using the same structured process each time, engineers can solve problems more consistently, not get lost in the details, and, through experience, troubleshoot in high-pressure situations with confidence.

This second of three major sections of this chapter focuses on the troubleshooting process and reviews a few alternative troubleshooting methods. Additionally, this section covers tips about what to check when troubleshooting a network problem.

Troubleshooting Methods

A *troubleshooting method* is simply a set of general rules about how to attack a network problem, with those rules helping guide you toward the root cause. Engineers who use the same method each time they troubleshoot a problem typically solve the problems more quickly than those who do not use a method. In fact, the specific method may be less important than picking a reasonable method and using it.

The online curriculum suggests two specific troubleshooting methods. The first of these can be easily described as follows:

> Troubleshoot by examining the operation of the network at each layer of the OSI model, starting with Layer 1, up through Layer 7.

For example, when hearing of a problem from an end user, the engineer might start by checking the cables between that end user's PC and a server. Layer 1 troubleshooting includes checks to see whether devices lost power and whether any of the LED lights on networking equipment indicate a failure. Layer 3 troubleshooting includes using the **ping** and **traceroute** commands to verify whether IP packets can be passed between devices.

To troubleshoot by focusing on one layer at a time, it is helpful to remember all the layers. Figure 9-5 shows those layers, along with a list of the most popular tools for testing each layer.

Figure 9-5   TCP/IP and OSI Layers and Typical Testing Items

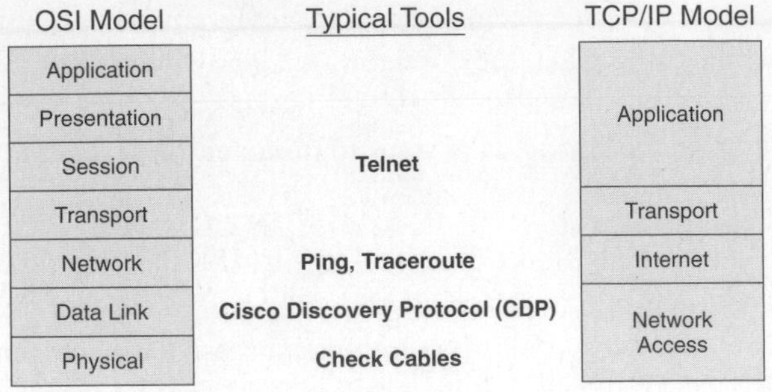

OSI Model	Typical Tools	TCP/IP Model
Application		
Presentation		Application
Session	**Telnet**	
Transport		Transport
Network	**Ping, Traceroute**	Internet
Data Link	**Cisco Discovery Protocol (CDP)**	Network Access
Physical	**Check Cables**	

The other method suggested by the online curriculum defines several general steps in a flowchart, as shown in Figure 9-6. This method may be closer to what most network engineers use.

Figure 9-6   Troubleshooting Flowchart from Online Course

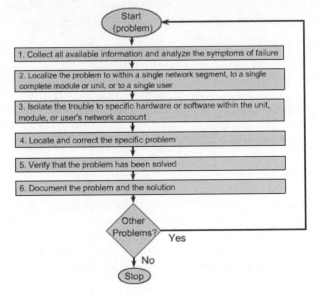

The wording of the steps of Figure 9-6 may be a little too general to teach you how to apply this troubleshooting method. So, to give you a more concrete example of how the method works, consider the following scenario. A user calls the network engineer and says that he cannot "get to the server." At the end of the process, the engineer will discover that the server has been powered off. The following list describes how the method listed in Figure 9-6 could be applied when solving this problem:

1. The engineer asks the user to list the PC's IP address, default gateway, host name, location, and what server the user cannot "get to." The engineer then looks at online documentation and network diagrams that show the PC, server, and all related network devices.

2. The engineer telnets to the router that is the server default gateway. From there, she pings both the PC and the server. (By pinging both, the engineer can test the route in both directions.) The ping of the user's PC works, but the ping of the server fails.

3. From the router attached to the same LAN as the server, the engineer tries to ping the server, and again fails. The engineer also notes that the router's ARP table does not list the PC's IP and MAC addresses, so the server is not even responding to ARP requests. The engineer decides that the problem may exist on the server or in the LAN switches between the router and the server.

4. The engineer walks into the data center and, using the documentation gathered in Step 1, locates the server hardware. Finding it powered off, the engineer turns the server back on.

5. After giving the server a few minutes to boot, the engineer pings the server from the router nearest to the end user (the end user's default gateway), and the **ping** now works. The engineer also calls the user to confirm that the user can again access the server.

6. The engineer documents the problem in a trouble ticket, which identifies the root cause (server powered off), the solution (turn it on), and the basic steps used to solve the problem.

While this scenario had a simple root cause, the general process in Figure 9-6 can be applied to any network problem. Of course, to apply this process, you need to have some ideas about how to isolate the cause of the problem as described in Steps 2 and 3. The next section provides tips about how you can isolate a problem at Steps 2 and 3 of this process.

Troubleshooting Tips

Regardless of whether you use either of the two troubleshooting methods described in this chapter or use another method, it helps to think about the details of troubleshooting by considering one OSI layer at a time. For example, you might first troubleshoot Layer 3, checking IP routing, and determine the router at which the route fails. At that point, you can focus on Layer 1 to ensure that the router's interfaces all work. This section outlines some tips for isolating problems at several OSI layers.

Layer 1 Tips

OSI Layer 1 defines the details of physical connectivity, including cabling and connectors. The following list includes some of the most common items that should be checked when the troubleshooting process examines Layer 1. Following the list, the text further explains some of the more important items.

- Broken cables
- Disconnected cables
- Cables connected to the wrong ports
- Intermittent cable connection
- Wrong cables used for the task at hand

Note

Whereas the speed of a serial interface is typically referenced using the term *clockrate*, the command used to set it on a Cisco router is **clock rate**, with a space between the words.

- Transceiver problems
- Improperly configured clockrate settings on serial interfaces
- Devices turned off
- Wrong choice of DCE or DTE cable
- Devices turned off

The LEDs on switch ports, router interfaces, and PC NICs indicate whether the interface can pass proper signals over the cable. For example, many switch ports have a status LED that, when lit in a solid color, means that the port and cable work. Most PC NICs have a status link, often called a link light, that indicates whether the NIC believes it is attached to a working cable. Some devices have transmit (Tx) and receive (Rx) activity LEDs as well, which light up only when the device is transmitting or receiving bits, respectively. Although it may not be possible to go stand beside the equipment and look at the LEDs, CiscoWorks network management software packages can display graphical views of Cisco equipment located anywhere in the internetwork. These graphical displays include the LEDs, so you can get a quick visual indicator of whether router and switch ports are up or down.

When installing a new Ethernet drop, the troubleshooting process includes many different checks of the cabling. Accurate documentation helps tremendously by spelling out where each wiring drop should connect in wiring panels and to which switch ports the cables should be patched. One of the most overlooked problems with LAN cabling tends to be cables that appear to be connected but are not, so make sure to reseat the connectors. Also, keeping a set of patch cables that is known to be in good working order can help, so you can temporarily swap cables to ensure that the original patch cable does not have a problem.

Engineers may also spend some time testing and troubleshooting LAN cabling when a network is first installed. For example, the engineer should ensure that the cables use the right cable pinouts: a crossover cable when connecting like devices, such as two switches, and a straight-through cable when connecting unlike devices, such as a PC to a switch. The engineer can use cable testing tools to confirm the pinouts of the cables as well. Additionally, testing the cables to confirm that they can support the desired Ethernet speeds has become much more important today as more installations move toward using Gigabit Ethernet to each user PC.

Note

For more information about LAN data link protocols, refer to *Networking Basics CCNA 1 Companion Guide* and *Switching Basics and Intermediate Routing CCNA 3 Companion Guide*. For WAN data links, refer to *WAN Technologies CCNA 4 Companion Guide*.

Layer 2 Tips

OSI Layer 2 defines the protocols that control and manage how the devices use the underlying physical media. The following list includes some of the most common items that should be checked when the troubleshooting process examines Layer 2. Following the list, the text further explains some of the more important items.

- Improperly configured serial interfaces
- Improperly configured Ethernet settings
- Improperly configured encapsulation

Note that the list includes exclusively items that can be configured. Essentially, if you can confirm that the physical links work but the data link does not, the most likely problem relates to some data-link configuration setting. For example, routers typically use either High-Level Data Link Control (HDLC) or Point-to-Point Protocol (PPP) as the WAN data link protocol on a point-to-point serial link. If the engineer mistakenly configures HDLC for one router and PPP for the other, the physical link may work fine but the data link protocol will fail and the link will not be usable.

Layer 3 Troubleshooting Using Ping

As is the case for OSI Layer 2 problems, misconfiguration causes many OSI Layer 3 problems as well. The following list outlines some of the commonly misconfigured Layer 3 settings:

- Routing protocol not configured

- Routing protocol configuration does not enable the routing protocol on all the correct interfaces

- Incorrect static routes

- Wrong routing protocol configured

- Router or PC with incorrect IP addresses

- Router or PC with incorrect subnet masks

- PC with incorrect default gateway

All the items in this list affect the forwarding of IP packets, so the **ping** and **traceroute** commands provide a good means to uncover the location of such problems. This section reviews the **ping** command; the **traceroute** command is covered later in the chapter in the section "Troubleshooting Using the **traceroute** Command."

The **ping** command sends ICMP echo requests, and it expects to receive ICMP echo reply messages in response to each echo request. Each time the **ping** command receives an echo reply, the command measures the round-trip time (RTT), which is the time it took to send the request and receive the reply. The **ping** command can then display an exclamation point (!) for each time a correct echo reply message was received, and display the minimum, average, and maximum RTTs for all echo reply messages.

Example 9-8 shows a working **ping** command on a Cisco router, with router R1 pinging PC3 (172.16.3.3) as shown in Figures 9-1, 9-2, and 9-3.

Example 9-8 Router R1's **ping 172.16.3.3** Command

```
R1#ping 172.16.3.3
Type escape sequence to abort.
Sending 5, 100-byte ICMP Echos to 172.16.3.3, timeout is 2 seconds:
!!!!!
Success rate is 100 percent (5/5), round-trip min/avg/max = 1/2/4 ms
```

The IOS **ping** command sends five ICMP echo requests, waiting up to 2 seconds for the reply (default) in each case, as noted in the first highlighted line in Example 9-8. In this case, a reply was received for each request, as shown with the five exclamation points in the output. The last line states the percentage that succeeded, and the minimum, average, and maximum response times.

When the echo request cannot be delivered for some reason, the router or host that cannot deliver the packet discards the packet. That same router or host may also send an ICMP unreachable message back to the router or host from which the ping was sent. Some **ping** commands may even display some indication that an unreachable message was received. For example, on Microsoft OSs, the **ping** command states "destination unreachable" when it receives an ICMP unreachable message. Although most **ping** commands do not identify the type of ICMP unreachable message they receive, it is occasionally useful to use tools to find out which kind of unreachable message was returned. For reference, Table 9-5 lists the different types of ICMP unreachable messages.

Table 9-5 ICMP Unreachable Code Values

Note

Table 9-5 contains the same information as Table 8-2 in Chapter 8.

Code Value	Description
0	Network unreachable
1	Host unreachable
2	Protocol unreachable
3	Port unreachable
4	Fragmentation needed and DF set
5	Source route failed
6	Destination network unknown
7	Destination host unknown
8	Source host isolated
9	Communication with data network administratively prohibited
10	Communication with data host administratively prohibited
11	Network unreachable for type of service
12	Host unreachable for type of service

Cisco IOS includes a very powerful option for the **ping** command called an extended **ping** command. The extended **ping** command allows the CLI user to specify many different parameters about how the **ping** command works. When in enable mode, the user can simply type **ping** and press Enter. Then the router prompts the user for a wide variety of parameters, such as the number of echo requests to send, the time to wait to receive a reply, and the IP address from which to send the echo request packets. Example 9-9 shows R1 again pinging PC3 (172.16.3.3), but this time using the extended **ping** command.

Example 9-9   An Extended **ping** Command on Router R1

```
R1#ping
Protocol [ip]:
Target IP address: 172.16.3.3
Repeat count [5]: 3
Datagram size [100]: 200
Timeout in seconds [2]: 3
Extended commands [n]: y
Source address or interface: 172.16.1.251
Type of service [0]:
Set DF bit in IP header? [no]:
Validate reply data? [no]:
Data pattern [0xABCD]:
Loose, Strict, Record, Timestamp, Verbose[none]:
Sweep range of sizes [n]:
Type escape sequence to abort.
Sending 3, 200-byte ICMP Echos to 172.16.3.3, timeout is 3 seconds:
Packet sent with a source address of 172.16.1.251
!!!
Success rate is 100 percent (3/3), round-trip min/avg/max = 1/3/4 ms
R1#
```

Example 9-9 shows a series of questions, some answered with defaults (shown with nothing typed after the :), and some with responses (shown in bold) from the engineer. In this case, the engineer used the default setting of IP for the Layer 3 protocol. The engineer chose to send three echo requests, packet size 200, with a 3-second timeout. The highlighted text near the bottom of Example 9-9 reflects the changes made with these options. Looking back up into the questions again, you will see the source IP address specified in the command—namely, R1's 172.16.1.251 IP address. Near the bottom of the output, the last highlighted line shows the **ping** command stating the source address to be used for these packets.

The extended **ping** command gives experienced engineers a wonderful troubleshooting tool. For example, imagine that the user of PC1 claims that he cannot communicate with PC3. You could walk over to the next building where PC1 sits and use **ping** commands to test the problem. You could call the user and ask him to use **ping** commands for you, but sometimes that may take longer than walking to the next building. However, you can telnet to the router on the same LAN and do some testing, which is more accurate when you use the extended **ping** command.

To appreciate why using the extended **ping** command helps in this case, consider Figure 9-7 for a moment. The figure shows parts of what happens with the normal **ping** command in Example 9-8, and the extended **ping** command in Example 9-9. When sending the packet with the echo request messages, the router must use an IP address for the source IP address of the packets, but most routers have several IP addresses. So, the normal **ping** command uses the following logic:

Use a source IP address of the interface out which the echo request will be sent.

In contrast, the extended **ping** command allows the engineer to specify the source IP address. So, with the normal **ping** command in Example 9-8, R1 uses its 172.16.2.251 IP address as the source, but in the extended **ping** command of Example 9-9, R1 uses the listed source IP address of 172.16.1.251.

Figure 9-7   Comparing Normal and Extended **ping** Source IP Addresses

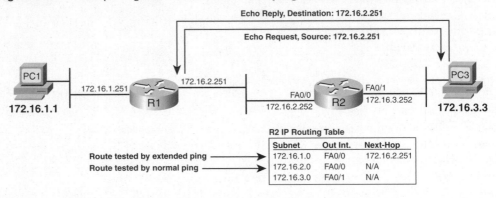

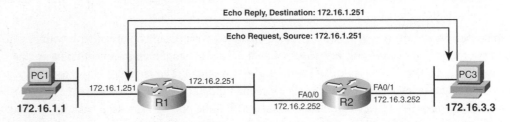

The key difference shown in Figure 9-7 relates to the routes tested by these two different **ping** commands. As a reminder, from R1's perspective, the route from R1 to PC3 is the forward route, and the route from PC3 back to R1 is the reverse route. Both commands test the same forward route from R1 to 172.16.3.3 (PC3), because both commands' echo request messages are destined for PC3. However, the pings test two different reverse routes, because PC3 sends its echo reply messages back to the IP address that was listed as the source IP address in the echo request. So, the following occurs with the echo replies:

- **Normal ping**—PC3 sends the echo reply messages to 172.16.2.251, testing the route from PC3 to subnet 172.16.2.0/24.

- **Extended ping**—PC3 sends the echo reply messages to 172.16.1.251, testing the route from PC3 to subnet 172.16.1.0/24.

By using the extended **ping** command as shown in Example 9-9, the engineer can avoid walking over to PC1 and avoid calling the user of PC1 to ask him to try some **ping** commands, but he can still test both the route from PC1's subnet to PC3's subnet and the route from PC3's subnet back to PC1's subnet. Although the extended **ping** command does not test for all causes of a problem between PC1 and PC3—for instance, it does not test for cases in which PC1's default gateway is incorrect—it does provide a better test than the normal **ping** command provides. As a result, many engineers make it a habit to use the extended **ping** command.

 Packet Tracer The network shown in Figure 9-7 (and Figure 9-3) can be loaded using Packet Tracer configuration file NA02-0903. From real-time mode, you can use both the normal and extended **ping** commands to try different options.

The **ping** commands shown in this section test IP connectivity, but the **ping** command can test other Layer 3 protocols as well. Most Layer 3 protocols define some kind of echo protocol similar to the ICMP echo request and reply messages. The IOS **ping** command will then send the appropriate echo messages to test other Layer 3 protocols, including AppleTalk, ISO Connectionless Network Service (CLNS), IP, Novell, Apollo, VINES, DECnet, or XNS networks.

Layer 7 Troubleshooting Using Telnet

In some companies, the network engineer's troubleshooting job stops when she can prove that all parts of Layer 3 are working and packets can be delivered from one host to another. In those cases, other members of the staff may be responsible for the hardware and software on the client PCs, and possibly others may be responsible for various servers. However, in some companies, the network engineer is responsible for the clients and servers as well.

This book and the related course do not attempt to cover the details of troubleshooting on the hosts. However, it may be helpful to at least test host connectivity, including the application layer, by using Telnet. Telnet provides a virtual terminal service between the client computer and another host computer.

Cisco IOS supports a **telnet** command. Besides being useful for telnetting to another host or router, the **telnet** command can be useful for testing, because a successful Telnet proves that all layers of the TCP/IP model work between the two hosts. To test, the engineer would use the

telnet command, from either a router, a switch, or a host, specifying the remote host's IP address or hostname. If the engineer sees a login prompt, the test worked. In fact, the engineer does not need to log in to the remote host, because when she sees the command prompt, Telnet has created the TCP connection, negotiated Telnet options, and sent a couple of messages.

Unfortunately, a test using the **telnet** command may fail for a large variety of reasons, including reasons that may have nothing to do with the original problem that needs to be solved. So, keep in mind that the **telnet** command may be a good test to confirm that all layers are working between two hosts, but it is not a good test to prove whether a failure has occurred between two hosts. For reference, the following list outlines a few of the common reasons why the **telnet** command might fail:

- If the remote host does not have a Telnet server enabled, which is typically the case on most client computers, the **telnet** command will not work.

- The remote host's Telnet server may not be using the default well-known port 23.

- Telnet requires the negotiation of settings for the terminal emulator before it can send the password prompt to the user. If for some reason the Telnet client and server cannot negotiate a working set of options, the **telnet** command will fail before the user sees the password prompt. (On a Cisco router, this negotiation process can be viewed with the **debug telnet** command.)

You can use other application protocols for testing as well. For example, you can always open a web browser on a host and try to connect to the server. However, as with the **telnet** command, a successful connection to a web server proves that the hosts can communicate through all layers, but a failed attempt may not help isolate the problem, because the web request may fail for many reasons.

 Lab 9.2.6   Troubleshooting Using ping and telnet

In this lab, you gather information about routing updates and routing protocols.

Router and Routing Troubleshooting Tips

When troubleshooting problems in any network today, one of the most important concerns is whether a routing problem exists. To isolate the root cause of the problem and fix it, you need the knowledge and tools discussed in the first major section of this chapter, "Examining the Routing Table"—namely, a good understanding of how IP routing works, how to look at a Cisco router's IP routing table, and knowledge of how routers learn routes using dynamic routing protocols. Additionally, you should apply a consistent troubleshooting method for each problem, as covered in the second major section, "Network Testing Methods and Tips," to solve the problems more efficiently.

This section completes the discussion of troubleshooting by reviewing several other router commands. Although the troubleshooting method is important and understanding routing is important, you need a large set of tools to solve some problems. This section covers a few more of the tools that every engineer needs when troubleshooting a problem in a network that uses Cisco routers.

Troubleshooting Using the show interfaces Command

The **show interfaces** command supplies a lot of important information about interfaces, such as the status of the interfaces, statistics about packets sent and received, and a wide variety of error counters and configuration settings. Any troubleshooting process of a router problem typically includes frequent use of the **show interfaces** command; in fact, it is probably one of the five most frequently used **show** commands on Cisco routers.

Although you can see the many variations of the **show interfaces** command by using the **show interfaces ?** command on a router CLI, this book focuses on the following three main variations:

- **show interfaces**
- **show interfaces** *type number*
- **show interfaces description**

The **show interfaces** command lists a large set of messages for every interface on the router, whereas the **show interfaces** *type number* command lists the same information but only for the interface identified in the command. For example, the **show interfaces serial 0/1/0** command lists information just for serial interface S0/1/0. The **show interfaces description** command lists a single line of output per interface, with only the interface status and interface descriptions listed. Figure 9-8 shows a small internetwork with a serial link connecting two routers. Example 9-10 shows an example of two **show interfaces** commands on router R1.

Figure 9-8   Small Internetwork with Two Routers Connected by a Serial Link

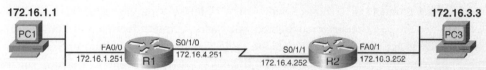

Example 9-10   Example show interfaces Commands on Router R1 from Figure 9-8

```
R1#show interfaces serial 0/1/0
Serial0/1/0 is up, line protocol is up
  Hardware is GT96K Serial
  Description: R1 end of serial link to R2
  Internet address is 172.16.4.251/24
  MTU 1500 bytes, BW 100 Kbit, DLY 1000 usec,
     reliability 255/255, txload 1/255, rxload 1/255
  Encapsulation HDLC, loopback not set
  Keepalive set (10 sec)
  Last input 00:00:02, output 00:00:04, output hang never
  Last clearing of "show interface" counters never
  Input queue: 0/75/0/0 (size/max/drops/flushes); Total output drops: 0
  Queueing strategy: weighted fair
  Output queue: 0/1000/64/0 (size/max total/threshold/drops)
     Conversations  0/1/256 (active/max active/max total)
     Reserved Conversations 0/0 (allocated/max allocated)
     Available Bandwidth 75 kilobits/sec
  5 minute input rate 0 bits/sec, 0 packets/sec
  5 minute output rate 0 bits/sec, 0 packets/sec
     29 packets input, 2600 bytes, 0 no buffer
     Received 29 broadcasts, 0 runts, 0 giants, 0 throttles
     0 input errors, 0 CRC, 0 frame, 0 overrun, 0 ignored, 0 abort
     26 packets output, 1924 bytes, 0 underruns
     0 output errors, 0 collisions, 7 interface resets
     0 output buffer failures, 0 output buffers swapped out
     1 carrier transitions
     DCD=up  DSR=up  DTR=up  RTS=up  CTS=up
R1#show interfaces description
Interface              Status        Protocol   Description
Fa0/0                  up            up
Fa0/1                  admin down    down
Se0/1/0                up            up         R1 end of serial link to R2
Se0/1/1                admin down    down
```

The output from Example 9-10 shows a wide variety of information. For example, it lists the configured interface description (as configured with the **description** interface subcommand) and the IP address and mask (in prefix notation). It lists a large number of statistics. Perhaps the most important information sits in the very first line of output: the interface status. The rest of the discussion about the **show interfaces** command in this chapter relates in some way to the interface status.

Understanding Routing Interface Status

Cisco routers give two indications about whether each interface is working, as listed in the first line of output in the **show interfaces** command. Together, these two indicators are called the *interface status*, and individually, they are called the *line status* and *line protocol status*. Example 9-11 shows the location of the line status and line protocol status. Both the line status and line protocol status are up in this case.

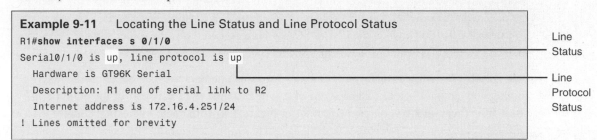

Example 9-11   Locating the Line Status and Line Protocol Status

```
R1#show interfaces s 0/1/0
Serial0/1/0 is up, line protocol is up                          ──── Line
  Hardware is GT96K Serial                                            Status
  Description: R1 end of serial link to R2                       ──── Line
  Internet address is 172.16.4.251/24                                Protocol
! Lines omitted for brevity                                          Status
```

An interface must have both a line status and a line protocol status of "up" to send and receive traffic. All other combinations of status mean that the interface cannot currently be used. Table 9-6 lists the four typical combinations, along with their meanings.

Table 9-6   Interface Status Combinations and Meaning

Line Status	Line Protocol Status	General Meaning
Up	Up	Interface is working
Up	Down	Interface is not working, typically due to a software or data link layer problem
Down	Down	Interface is not working, typically due to a hardware or physical layer problem
Administratively down	Down	Interface is not working due to the **shutdown** subcommand being configured on the interface

After the troubleshooting process has isolated a problem to a small set of routers or switches, the **show interfaces** command can help identify which interfaces are in an "up and up" status, and which are not. The following two sections give a little more background on some reasons why an interface's line status and line protocol status might not be "up."

Note

Many other commands list the same interface status values, including **show interface description** and **show ip interface brief**, which list much briefer output.

Note

A combined status of "down" (line) and "up" (protocol) cannot occur; if the interface cannot physically send and receive bits, the data-link functions cannot possibly be working.

Note

Most network engineers use brief wording such as "Is the interface up and up?" rather than using the terms *line status* and *line protocol status*.

Indications of Typical Layer 1 Problems

The line status—the first of the two status values in the **show interfaces** command output—mainly relates to hardware or Layer 1. As a result, many people refer to this first status value as either the *hardware status* or *Layer 1 status*.

A line status of down means that the interface has some physical problem. To troubleshoot such problems, you can follow some obvious steps, such as checking the cable or checking whether the device on the other end of the cable is powered off. For example, on a serial link that uses an external CSU/DSU, when the CSU/DSU has been powered off, the router's connected serial interface cannot pass any bits and is in a down state.

Additionally, the **show interfaces** commands list some counters that can be helpful in determining why an interface has a line status of down. Example 9-12 lists part of the output of a **show interfaces s0/1/0** command (from R1 in Figure 9-8) with some interesting counter values.

Example 9-12   An Extended ping Command on Router R1

```
R1#show interfaces s 0/1/0
Serial0/1/0 is up, line protocol is up
  Description: R1 end of serial link to R2
  Internet address is 172.16.4.251/24
  MTU 1500 bytes, BW 100 Kbit, DLY 1000 usec,
     reliability 255/255, txload 2/255, rxload 1/255
  Encapsulation HDLC, loopback not set
  Keepalive set (10 sec)
  Last input 00:00:02, output 00:00:02, output hang never
  Last clearing of "show interface" counters never
  Input queue: 0/75/0/0 (size/max/drops/flushes); Total output drops: 0
  Queueing strategy: weighted fair
  Output queue: 0/1000/64/0 (size/max total/threshold/drops)
     Conversations  0/1/256 (active/max active/max total)
     Reserved Conversations 0/0 (allocated/max allocated)
     Available Bandwidth 75 kilobits/sec
  5 minute input rate 0 bits/sec, 0 packets/sec
  5 minute output rate 1000 bits/sec, 0 packets/sec
     427 packets input, 28696 bytes, 0 no buffer
     Received 425 broadcasts, 0 runts, 0 giants, 0 throttles
     0 input errors, 0 CRC, 0 frame, 0 overrun, 0 ignored, 0 abort
     425 packets output, 27982 bytes, 0 underruns
     0 output errors, 0 collisions, 10 interface resets
     0 output buffer failures, 0 output buffers swapped out
     5 carrier transitions
     DCD=up  DSR=up  DTR=up  RTS=up  CTS=up
```

The bottom of Example 9-12 highlights a couple of items that identify whether Layer 1 problems have been occurring. First, the *input errors* counter lists the number of frames that the router received but for which the frame check sequence (FCS) process determined that the frame experienced errors during transmission, meaning that the router had to discard the frame. A high value for the input errors counter could mean that the link has been experiencing a large number of bit errors, possibly due to poor but working cables, bad connectors, or too-long cable lengths. On WAN links, the problems could be happening inside the telco's network as well.

The other highlighted counter, the *carrier transitions* counter, relates to a pin lead on serial cables. The CSU/DSU signals the router serial interface that the link is working by raising the **carrier detect** (also called *data carrier detect*, or DCD) pin lead on the serial cable. The last two lines of the output in Example 9-12 show that the router has seen DCD transition from up to down, or from down to up, a total of five times. The last line of output also lists the current state of the DCD pin. A link on which a large number of carrier transitions occur means that the link has been going up and down a lot.

Both counters mentioned here, as well as many others, have more meaning if you know over what time period the counters have been collected. Look back to Example 9-12 again, to the first highlighted line. This line says that the counters have not been reset since the router was last reloaded. To see how long it has been since the last reload, the **show version** command can be used, as shown in Example 9-13.

Example 9-13   The **show version** Command Listing the Time Since the Last Reload

```
R1#show version
Cisco IOS Software, 1841 Software (C1841-ADVIPSERVICESK9-M), Version 12.3(11)T3,
  RELEASE SOFTWARE (fc4)
Technical Support: http://www.cisco.com/techsupport
Copyright  1986-2005 by Cisco Systems, Inc.
Compiled Tue 25-Jan-05 14:20 by pwade


ROM: System Bootstrap, Version 12.3(8r)T8, RELEASE SOFTWARE (fc1)

R1 uptime is 3 hours, 6 minutes
System returned to ROM by power-on
! lines omitted for brevity
```

At times, it may be useful to reset all the counters that are displayed with the **show interfaces** command. For example, after a problem has been solved, you might want to reset the counters in anticipation of when the next problem occurs so that the counters count only the events since you solved the problem. You can use the **clear counters** command to reset the counters for all interfaces, or use the **clear counters** *type number* command to identify the specific interface for which you want to reset the counters.

Indications of Typical Layer 2 Problems

In most cases, when an interface's line status is up but its line protocol status is down, the problem relates in some way to OSI Layer 2. Many times the problem relates to some configuration problem. This section reviews three such problems:

- Mismatched Layer 2 (data link) protocols configured on the routers on the ends of a serial link

- On a serial link with a back-to-back serial connection in a lab, the absence of a **clock rate** command on the router with the DCE cable

- The failure to receive *keepalive messages*

The first problem, mismatched Layer 2 protocols, is typically just an oversight when configuring a serial link. For example, in Figure 9-8, if R1 configured HDLC as the serial Layer 2 protocol, and R2 configured PPP, the link would not work, and both routers' serial interfaces would be in an up and down status (line status up, line protocol status down).

Next, consider the concept of a back-to-back serial link as created for a lab network, as covered in the Chapter 1 section "Creating Inexpensive Leased Lines in a Lab." After connecting the cables to the routers, the router with the DCE cable connected to it needs to configure the **clock rate** command on the interface. Without the **clock rate** command, neither device provides clocking, and the routers cannot pass any frames to each other. When omitting the **clock rate** command, both routers' serial interfaces settle into an up and down state.

The third cause of an up and down state mentioned here relates to how Cisco routers use a proprietary feature called keepalive messages. By default, Cisco routers send a keepalive message out each interface every 10 seconds. When a router fails to hear a keepalive message on an interface, for a time equal to three keepalive time periods (3×10 seconds by default), the router believes the link has failed and therefore places the link into an up and down state. Figure 9-9 shows the general idea on the link between R1 and R2.

Figure 9-9   Keepalive Process Between R1 and R2 over a Serial Link

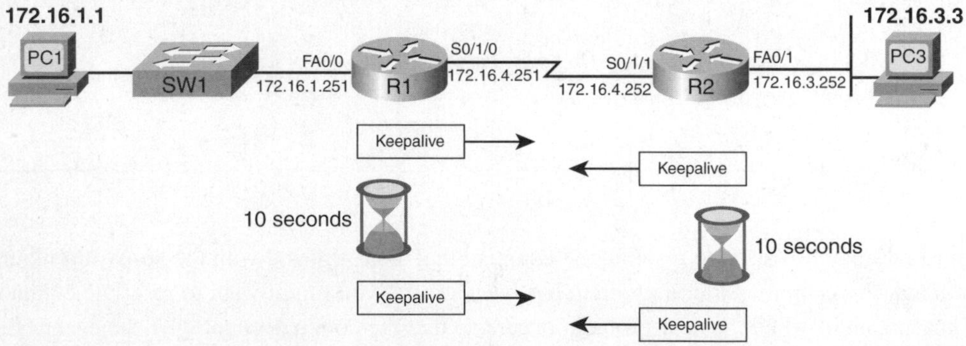

On a point-to-point serial link, each router sends keepalive messages, with the receipt of the other router's keepalive messages keeping the link up and working. For example, if R1 were to

quit sending keepalive messages, R2 would take down its serial interface after not hearing a keepalive for 30 seconds.

When a router ceases to hear keepalive messages for three keepalive time periods, the router puts the interface in an up and down state and increments the *interface reset counter* for that interface. Routers increment this counter for many other reasons as well, but generally this counter increments each time the router software notices some problem that means that the router cannot send traffic. The router resets the interface, which means that the router puts the interface in an up and down state, and then tries to use the interface again after a period of time. Generally speaking, an interface's interface reset counter should not increase frequently unless some type of problem is occurring. So, repeatedly using the **show interfaces** command can be useful so that you can see whether this counter increases.

Troubleshooting Layer 1 Using the show controllers Command

Cisco routers use a ***controller chip,*** which is a small specialized integrated circuit, to control the physical operation of each interface. You can see details about the operation of the controller chip by using the **show controllers** command (which lists information for all interfaces) or the **show controllers** *type number* command (which lists information for a single interface). Example 9-14 shows an example of this command.

Example 9-14   The show controllers S0/1/0 Command Output

```
R1#show controllers S0/1/0
Interface Serial0/1/0
Hardware is GT96K
DCE V.35, clock rate 1536000
idb at 0x6415A2FC, driver data structure at 0x64162110
wic_info 0x64162704
Physical Port 1, SCC Num 1
MPSC Registers:
MMCR_L=0x000304C0, MMCR_H=0x00000000, MPCR=0x00000000
CHR1=0x00FE007E, CHR2=0x00000000, CHR3=0x00000648, CHR4=0x00000000
CHR5=0x00000000, CHR6=0x00000000, CHR7=0x00000000, CHR8=0x00000000
CHR9=0x00000000, CHR10=0x00003008
SDMA Registers:
SDC=0x00002201, SDCM=0x00000080, SGC=0x0000C000
CRDP=0x076BCD90, CTDP=0x076BD1E0, FTDB=0x076BD1E0
Main Routing Register=0x00038FC7 BRG Conf Register=0x00050017
Rx Clk Routing Register=0x76583280 Tx Clk Routing Register=0x76593210
GPP Registers:
Conf=0x43000002, Io=0x46000A50, Data=0x4B7FFD2D, Level=0x8000020
Conf0=0x43000002, Io0=0x46000A50, Data0=0x6B7FFD2D, Level0=0x8000020
! Lines omitted for brevity
```

Even the most experienced router engineers ignore most of the information listed in the output of this command. However, on serial interfaces, the **show controllers** command contains a useful piece of information, as highlighted in the example. This command lists the type of serial cable connected to the interface, in this case a DCE cable with a V.35 connector. If no cable has been connected to the interface, the output lists that fact as well. This command is particularly helpful in real life because most routers are located far away from the network engineers, and this command gives the engineer a way to check the serial cables. Armed with this information, you can ensure that the router connected with a DCE cable has the **clock rate** command configured, as is the case in this example.

Troubleshooting Using the show cdp Command

Note

Chapter 4, "Learning About Other Devices," covers CDP in detail.

Cisco devices can use the Cisco Discovery Protocol (CDP) to exchange basic information with their neighbors. For example, R1 and SW1 in Figure 9-9 could use CDP. R1 would discover the name and software level of SW1, the switch port with which SW1 connects to R1, and other details. Similarly, SW1 would learn R1's host name, Cisco IOS Software version, R1's interface IP address, and other details as well.

Engineers can use CDP to help troubleshoot a network as well. For CDP to work, neighboring devices must be able to send data link layer frames to one another, so both Layer 1 and Layer 2 functions must be working. However, CDP works even if Layer 3 functions, such as IP addressing and routing, do not work. So, when you think some problem might exist at Layer 1 or Layer 2, you can enable router and switch interfaces with a **no shutdown** command and, even before configuring IP, confirm that the underlying physical and data link layer functions work. Essentially, if the devices can learn from each other by using CDP, Layer 1 and Layer 2 functions work between the two devices. (The online curriculum states that CDP should work if Layer 1 works. Because most Layer 2 problems relate to configuration issues, if Layer 1 works, and Layer 2 has been configured correctly [oftentimes using default settings, requiring no effort on the part of the engineer], CDP will work.)

Example 9-15 shows the output from the **show cdp neighbors** and **show cdp neighbors detail** commands for reference.

```
Example 9-15    Example show cdp Commands
R1#show cdp neighbors
Capability Codes: R - Router, T - Trans Bridge, B - Source Route Bridge
                  S - Switch, H - Host, I - IGMP, r - Repeater


Device ID        Local Intrfce     Holdtme    Capability  Platform    Port ID
SW1              Fas 0/0            173            S I     WS-C3550-2  Fas 0/11
R2               Ser 0/1/0         135          R S I     1841        Ser 0/1/1
R1#show cdp neighbors detail
-------------------------
Device ID: SW1
Entry address(es):
```

Example 9-15   Example **show cdp** Commands   *continued*

```
   IP address: 172.16.1.1
Platform: Cisco WS-C3550-24,  Capabilities: Switch IGMP
Interface: FastEthernet0/0,  Port ID (outgoing port): FastEthernet0/11
Holdtime : 168 sec

Version :
Cisco IOS Software, C3550 Software (C3550-I5Q3L2-M), Version 12.2(25)SE, RELEASE
  SOFTWARE (fc)
Copyright  1986-2004 by Cisco Systems, Inc.
Compiled Wed 10-Nov-04 18:07 by yenanh

advertisement version: 2
Protocol Hello:  OUI=0x00000C, Protocol ID=0x0112; payload len=27,
  value=00000000FFFFFFFF010221FF000000000000000AB7DCB780FF0000
VTP Management Domain: ''
Native VLAN: 11
Duplex: full

-------------------------
Device ID: R2
Entry address(es):
  IP address: 172.16.4.252
Platform: Cisco 1841,  Capabilities: Router Switch IGMP
Interface: Serial0/1/0,  Port ID (outgoing port): Serial0/1/1
Holdtime : 128 sec

Version :
Cisco IOS Software, 1841 Software (C1841-ADVIPSERVICESK9-M), Version 12.3(11)T3,
  RELEASE SOFTWARE (fc4)
Technical Support: http://www.cisco.com/techsupport
Copyright  1986-2005 by Cisco Systems, Inc.
Compiled Tue 25-Jan-05 14:20 by pwade

advertisement version: 2
VTP Management Domain: ''
```

Be careful when using CDP. Hackers can use the information learned via CDP to formulate an attack on the network. Cisco suggests disabling CDP on all ports except those known to be connected to some other Cisco device.

Troubleshooting Using the traceroute Command

Although the **ping** command may be more popular, the **traceroute** command provides a powerful testing tool for looking at IP routing problems. This command, sometimes simply called **trace**, provides the following features:

- Like **ping**, it tests both the forward and reverse routes between two IP hosts.

- Unlike **ping**, it lists the IP address and/or host name of each router in the current route to reach a host.

- Similar to **ping**, it lists RTT measurements, but it lists these measurements for each router in the route being tested.

Example 9-16 shows the output of an example **traceroute** command, taken from R1 in Figure 9-10.

Figure 9-10   Sample Internetwork Used for a Sample **traceroute** Command

```
Example 9-16    Sample traceroute Command Output
R1#traceroute 172.16.6.6

Type escape sequence to abort.
Tracing the route to 172.16.6.6

  1 172.16.4.252 4 msec 0 msec 0 msec
  2 172.16.5.253 4 msec 0 msec 4 msec
  3 172.16.6.6 4 msec *  0 msec
```

The **traceroute** command output lists the first two routers in the end-to-end path in the first two lines of output. The last line lists the destination host address of 172.16.6.6.

The **traceroute** command takes advantage of the ICMP TTL exceeded message (abbreviated as "TEM" in this book and in the online curriculum). When a router decrements a packet's Time to Live (TTL) value to 0, the router discards the packet and sends a TEM message back to the sender of the discarded packet. The **traceroute** command makes good use of that logic, as shown in Figure 9-11.

Figure 9-11   The Mechanics of the **traceroute** Command

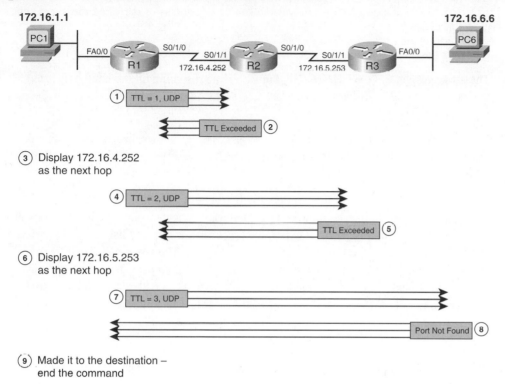

⑨ Made it to the destination –
end the command

The **traceroute** command sends three messages, each with TTL 1, and then sends another three messages with TTL 2, and so on, expecting other routers to discard the packets and send back TEM messages. By doing so, the **traceroute** command can identify the routers in the route. The following steps match Figure 9-11, explaining how the **traceroute** command in Example 9-16 learned the information:

1. The **traceroute** command sends three UDP messages, with a randomly chosen destination UDP port number and a TTL of 1, toward destination address 172.16.6.6.

2. R2 attempts to forward the packets, but when R2 decrements the TTL values to 0, R2 discards the packets and sends back TEMs to R1.

3. R1 displays the line listing 172.16.4.252, R2's IP address. (R1 identified R2 as IP address 172.16.4.252 because 172.16.4.252 was the source IP address of the TEM messages sent by R2 at Step 2.)

4. R1 sends three more messages, just like at Step 1, except these have a TTL of 2.

5. R2 forwards the packets after decrementing the TTL to 1; when R3 attempts to forward the packets, it decrements the TTL to 0, discards the packets, and sends TEM messages back to R1.

6. R1 displays the line listing 172.16.5.253, R3's IP address. (R1 identified R3 as IP address 172.16.5.253 because 172.16.5.253 was the source IP address of the TEM messages sent by R3 at Step 5.)

7. R1 sends three more messages, just like in Steps 1 and 4, except these have a TTL of 3.

8. The messages get to PC6 (172.16.6.6), but PC6 is not listening on the UDP port listed in the message. So, PC6 discards the packets and sends back an ICMP port unreachable message.

9. R1 displays the final line of output, listing 172.16.6.6. R1 knows that the command has finished because R1 received ICMP port unreachable messages in this case instead of ICMP TEMs.

As mentioned at the beginning of this section, the **traceroute** command provides several important functions for troubleshooting. Most importantly, it helps isolate the location of routing problems. When a routing problem exists, the **traceroute** command lists asterisks instead of IP addresses when it can no longer identify the next router. The last router listed by the **traceroute** command is the first router with a problem forwarding packets to the listed destination address. So, an engineer can use the **traceroute** command, see the last IP address listed before the lines of only asterisks, and then telnet to that router to continue the troubleshooting process.

 Packet Tracer You can repeat the tests shown in Figure 9-11 by using Packet Tracer with configuration file NA02-0911.

Using **traceroute** for troubleshooting may be misleading in some cases. Some routers may be configured to filter messages such as ICMP TEM and ICMP port unreachable messages, which means that the **traceroute** command could fail even though the route is perfectly good. Also, the **traceroute** command can become confused when multiple equal-cost routes to the same destination exist, because the ICMP TEMs may be returned from different routers. In that case, the **traceroute** command starts listing only asterisks, making the engineer think the route has a problem when in fact multiple working routes may exist.

 Lab 9.3.4   Troubleshooting Using traceroute

In this lab, you use the **traceroute** or **tracert** command to verify that the network layer between source, destination, and each router along the way is working properly.

Troubleshooting Using the show ip route and show ip protocols Commands

The **ping** and **traceroute** commands test an end-to-end forward and reverse route. A complete end-to-end route consists of a series of routes in many routers' routing tables. So, when an engineer isolates a routing problem to a small set of routers, the engineer may then telnet to the routers and look at the routing tables. At that point, the **show ip route** and **show ip protocols** commands can be very useful.

The **show ip route** command displays all the known routes on the router. If you are having problems sending packets to a particular IP address or subnet, you can then compare the routing table entries to the destination IP address and see if there are any matching entries. Also, you can use the **show ip route** *address* command, which lists the route in that router's IP routing table that would be matched for packets sent to the listed address. Example 9-1 earlier in the chapter shows an example of several options for the **show ip route** command.

In some cases, you may find that the necessary route simply does not exist in a router's routing table. Routers normally learn most routes via a dynamic routing protocol, so the next step in the problem-isolation process would be to determine from which router(s) a given router should be learning the route, and whether that neighboring router is still advertising the routes.

The **show ip protocols** command helps answer such questions by listing the information about the neighboring routers from which routes have been learned, along with a large variety of other information. Example 9-17 shows an example of the command, taken from R2 in Figure 9-10. In this case, R2 has two neighboring routers from which it has learned routes.

Note

The most important parts of the command output are explained with comments inside Example 9-17 in this case for easier reference.

Example 9-17   Sample **show ip protocols** Command Output from Router R2 of Figure 9-10

```
R2#show ip protocols
Routing Protocol is "rip"
!
! The RIP timers are listed next, including when this router will send its next
! periodic RIP update.
!
  Sending updates every 30 seconds, next due in 9 seconds
  Invalid after 180 seconds, hold down 180, flushed after 240
  Outgoing update filter list for all interfaces is not set
  Incoming update filter list for all interfaces is not set
  Redistributing: rip
  Default version control: send version 1, receive any version
!
! Next, the interfaces on which RIP has been enabled are listed.
!
    Interface          Send    Recv  Triggered RIP  Key-chain
    FastEthernet0/1      1       1 2
```

Note

Example 9-17 shows information about RIP only, but if the router were running multiple IP routing protocols, a similar set of messages would be displayed for each routing protocol.

Example 9-17 Sample **show ip protocols** Command Output from Router R2 of Figure 9-10 *continued*

```
    Serial0/1/0                1       1 2
    Serial0/1/1                1       1 2
  Automatic network summarization is in effect
  Maximum path: 4
!
! The following list includes all the classful networks listed in RIP network commands.
!
  Routing for Networks:
    172.16.0.0
!
! The "routing information sources" section at the end lists the IP addresses
! of neighboring routers from which R2 has learned routes in the past.
!
  Routing Information Sources:
    Gateway           Distance      Last Update
    172.16.4.251           120      00:00:13
    172.16.5.253           120      00:00:16
  Distance: (default is 120)
```

Of particular interest is the Last Update column in the very last section of the command output. For each neighbor, this column keeps a timer that increases over time. When this router (R2) receives a routing update from a neighbor, R2 resets this timer to 0. So, under normal operation with RIP, using the default 30-second periodic update timer, this timer should vary between 0 and 30 seconds. If you see a timer over 30 seconds, that neighbor may have failed, RIP may have been disabled, or some other problem may have occurred.

Also, make sure to look for all the neighbors this router should expect to see in the list of routing information sources as well. Having good network documentation helps tremendously in this case, because without good documentation, you may not have any idea which other routers should share a link with a router, and from which neighboring routers a router should be learning routes.

 Lab 9.3.5 Troubleshooting Routing Issues with show ip route and show ip protocols

In this lab, you use the **show ip route** and **show ip protocols** commands to diagnose a routing configuration problem.

Troubleshooting Using the debug Command

The IOS **debug** command tells a router to display messages when certain events happen in a router. Unlike a **show** command, which displays a set of messages about the then-current status of the router, the **debug** command tells the router to watch for certain events. When those events occur, the router then sends a message, called a *log message*, to the console. These messages allow the CLI user to see information about the dynamic operations of the router, instead of the snapshot of information displayed by a **show** command.

For example, the **debug ip rip** command tells the router to generate log messages that describe the contents of each sent and received RIP routing update. Example 9-18 shows an example that uses the following steps:

1. The CLI user types the **debug ip rip** command and presses Enter. The router lists a message that states that the debug has been turned on.

2. The router gives the user a new command prompt so that the user can continue doing **show** or any other commands.

3. The user issues the **show debug** command, which lists information about the currently enabled debug settings.

4. Later, when the next RIP updates are sent and received, the router generates the debug messages shown in Example 9-18.

Note

Routers always send log messages to the console. Users that telnet into a router do not see log messages by default, but the user can see log messages by entering the **terminal monitor** command.

Example 9-18   Sample **debug** Commands for Router R2 in Figure 9-10

```
R2#debug ip rip
RIP protocol debugging is on
R2#show debug
IP routing:
   RIP protocol debugging is on

R2#
*Feb 16 22:20:50.163: RIP: received v1 update from 172.16.5.253 on Serial0/1/0
*Feb 16 22:20:50.163:      172.16.6.0 in 1 hops
*Feb 16 22:20:50.555: RIP: sending v1 update to 255.255.255.255 via Serial0/1/1
  (172.16.4.252)
*Feb 16 22:20:50.555: RIP: build update entries
*Feb 16 22:20:50.555:     subnet 172.16.3.0 metric 1
*Feb 16 22:20:50.555:     subnet 172.16.5.0 metric 1
*Feb 16 22:20:50.555:     subnet 172.16.6.0 metric 2
R2#undebug all
All possible debugging has been turned off
R2#
```

The **debug** command has a large number of options, which can be seen with the **debug ?** command. Each new **debug** command enables another debug option, causing the router to generate more and more log messages. For example:

- The **debug ip rip event** command generates log messages each time a RIP update has been sent or received, but the messages do not list the contents of the routing updates.

- The **debug ip packet detail** command lists detailed information for each IP packet created by the router, and for each packet sent to the router. (This command does not generate messages for each packet forwarded through the router.)

After the **debug** command has been used, the router continues to generate messages based on that **debug** command until that debug option has been disabled using either the **undebug** or **no debug** command. For example, both the **undebug ip rip** command and the **no debug ip rip** command would disable the debug enabled by the **debug ip rip** command in Example 9-18. Alternately, to disable all debug options, use the **undebug all** (as shown in Example 9-18) or **no debug all** command. A reload of the router also disables all debugs.

While many debug options exist, you should be careful when using the **debug** command on routers used in production networks. Cisco optimizes routers to forward packets, not to monitor processes and generate debug messages. Too many debugs, or the wrong debugs, can crash a router. In fact, most every experienced router engineer has a favorite story of when they crashed a router with a **debug** command. In particular, never use the **debug all** command, which enables all debug options, on a production router.

 Lab 9.3.7   Troubleshooting Routing Issues with debug

In this lab, you use a systematic OSI troubleshooting process to diagnose routing problems.

Summary

The **show ip route** command lists the routes in a router's routing table. The router adds connected routes to the routing table for each working interface that has a valid IP address configured. The router also adds static routes based on the configuration of any **ip route** commands on that router. Finally, routers can add routes to their routing tables by learning the routes using a dynamic routing protocol.

Routers can use a special route, called a default route, to forward packets that do not match any other routes in that router's routing table.

When a router learns multiple routes to reach the same network or subnet, the router needs to choose the best route—a process often called path determination. If the routes were learned via different routing protocols, the router chooses the route learned by the routing protocol with the lower administrative distance. If the routes were learned by one routing protocol, the router uses the lowest-metric route. If the routes were learned by one routing protocol, and the metrics tie, the router can add up to six (default four) equal-cost routes to its IP routing table.

Engineers should use a consistent troubleshooting process to more efficiently and more consistently uncover and fix the root cause of the problem. Although hands-on skills and protocol knowledge are both important, the availability of accurate and up-to-date network documentation is a must to solve many network problems. When troubleshooting, a wide variety of items might be examined. For example, when examining Layer 1 functions, the indicator or status lights on routers and switches can be helpful. The **ping** and **traceroute** commands can be very helpful when testing routing and discovering which router might be the cause of a routing problem. Plus, the **telnet** command tests the application layer to some degree.

The **show interfaces** command lists the interface status along with a wide variety of other information. The interface status lists two separate states: the line status, which is related to hardware and Layer 1, and the line protocol status, which is related to software and Layer 2. An interface in an up and up state, meaning the line status and line protocol status are both up, can be used to send and receive packets. If the line status is down, it usually indicates a Layer 1 problem; if the line status is up but the line protocol status is down, it usually indicates a Layer 2 problem, oftentimes a configuration issue.

Many IOS commands can help in the troubleshooting process. For example, the **show controllers** command lists the type of serial cable connected to a serial interface. The **show cdp neighbors** command lists information about neighboring Cisco devices—information that could be learned only if both Layers 1 and 2 are working between the two neighbors. Also, the **show cdp neighbors detail** command lists more information, including the Layer 3 addresses of each neighbor.

The **show ip route**, **show ip protocols**, **ping**, and **traceroute** commands provide the best tools for troubleshooting Layer 3 problems in a router. The **show ip route** command lists a router's current routing table. The **show ip protocols** command lists information about routing protocols, including a list of neighboring routers from which the router has learned routes. The **ping** and **traceroute** commands both test routes, with **traceroute** also identifying the first router at which the routing problem might exist.

Finally, the **debug** command causes the router to display dynamic messages each time an event related to the debug options occurs. Because the **show** commands display only static information, they provide a historical picture of the router operation. The **debug** command output gives you more insight into the router's current events.

Check Your Understanding

Complete all the review questions listed here to test your understanding of the topics and concepts in this chapter. Answers are listed in Appendix A, "Answers to Check Your Understanding and Challenge Questions."

1. If an engineer wants to test network connectivity, which of the following is the best basic command to use?

   A. **telnet**

   B. **ping**

   C. **debug**

   D. **arp -a**

2. An engineer uses the **ping** command from the CLI of one router, trying to ping the IP address of another router that is on the other end of a point-to-point serial link. The ping fails. What command can be used to further test the link?

   A. The **show controllers** serial command, to verify clocking

   B. The **telnet** command, to verify that applications are working

   C. The **show ip protocols** command, to verify information sharing

   D. The **show run** command, to verify network layer connectivity

3. Which is the proper order of the troubleshooting process for network engineers?

   1. Verify that the problem has been solved.

   2. Collect all available information and analyze the symptoms of the failure.

   3. Isolate the trouble to specific hardware or software within the unit, module, or user network account.

   4. Document the problem and the solution.

   5. Localize the problem to a particular network segment, module, unit, or user.

   6. Locate and correct the problem.

   A. 5, 1, 6, 3, 2, 4

   B. 2, 5, 3, 6, 1, 4

   C. 2, 5, 4, 3, 1, 6

   D. 5, 1, 3, 6, 4, 2

4. When an engineer wants to verify the application layer (Layer 7) software between source and destination stations, which of the following commands should be used?

A. **telnet**

B. **ping**

C. **debug**

D. **traceroute**

5. What command-line interface command can be used to check the routing table of a router?

A. **show ip interface brief**

B. **show ip route**

C. **show ip protocols**

D. **show controllers**

6. Why would you display a router's IP routing table?

A. To set the router update schedule

B. To identify known network and subnet numbers

C. To trace where datagrams are coming from

D. To set the parameters and filters for the router

7. Which command allows viewing of RIP routing updates as they are sent and received?

A. **show ip rip**

B. **debug ip protocols**

C. **debug ip rip**

D. **show ip rip update**

8. Which **debug** command has the most impact on processor overhead?

A. **debug ip rip**

B. **debug all**

C. **debug ip icmp**

D. **debug timestamps**

E. **debug ip eigrp**

9. By default, where does the router send the debug output and system messages?

A. The PC

B. The switch

C. The console

D. The Telnet connections

10. The **telnet** command provides what type of terminal?

    A. Physical

    B. Virtual

    C. Cisco IOS Software

    D. HTTP

11. Which of the following is true of the **ip default-network** command?

    A. It has replaced the **ip route** command in recent versions of Cisco IOS.

    B. It can advertise subnets as default route destinations.

    C. It is configured on the interface closest to the default route.

    D. It creates a default route that can be advertised by routing protocols.

12. Most interfaces or network interface cards have what type of lights that show whether there is a valid connection?

    A. Link status indicator lights

    B. Catalyst indicators

    C. Contact Indication Devices (CIDs)

    D. Red and blue link indicators

13. Telnet implements what layer of the OSI reference model?

    A. Layer 1

    B. Layer 5

    C. Layer 6

    D. Layer 7

14. Two routers are directly connected and the **show cdp neighbors** command is successful, but a **ping** command between the two routers is not successful. At which layer of the OSI model will the problem likely be found?

    A. Layer 1

    B. Layer 2

    C. Layer 3

    D. Layer 4

Challenge Questions and Activities

These questions require a deeper application of the concepts covered in this chapter and are similar to the style of questions you might see on a CCNA certification exam.

1. Read the following output from a **show ip interface brief** command and choose three correct statements from the list.

```
Router_Central3>show ip interface brief
Interface       IP-Address      OK?     Method   Status    Protocol
Serial0/0       192.168.2.2     YES     unset    down      down
Serial0/1       192.168.6.2     YES     unset    up        up
Serial0/2       192.168.5.2     YES     unset    down      down
Serial0/3       unassigned      YES     unset    down      down
FastEthernet2/0 192.168.3.1     YES     manual   up        down
```

A. The Serial0/0 interface is working properly.

B. The Serial0/0 interface has a Layer 2 problem.

C. The Serial0/2 interface has a Layer 1 problem.

D. The Fast Ethernet port has a Layer 2 problem.

E. CDP can be used to troubleshoot interface Serial0/3.

F. The **show controllers serial** command could help troubleshoot interface Serial0/0.

2. Referring to the following diagram, which of the following statements are true if host A pings host B? (The LAN switch is a layer-2-only LAN switch.)

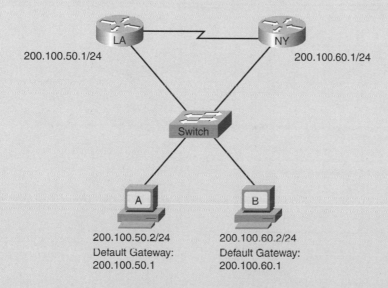

**RIP enabled on both routers.
Both routers show routes to all networks.**

LA   200.100.50.1/24

NY   200.100.60.1/24

Switch

A   200.100.50.2/24
Default Gateway:
200.100.50.1

B   200.100.60.2/24
Default Gateway:
200.100.60.1

A. The packets will travel from A to B but will not involve the routers because the hosts are connected at a switch that holds the host's MAC addresses in the switching table.

B. The switch will drop the packets because the **ping** command is performed at Layer 3, and the switch is a Layer 2 device.

C. The packets will travel from A to B via routers LA and NY.

D. The Ethernet interface on router A will drop the packet because it knows host A can communicate with host B via the switch.

CHAPTER 10

Intermediate TCP/IP

Objectives

Upon completion of this chapter, you should be able to answer the following questions:

- What is the function of the Transmission Control Protocol (TCP)?

- What is TCP synchronization and flow control?

- What is the primary function of the User Datagram Protocol (UDP), and how does it work?

- How does TCP work regarding multiple conversations between hosts?

- What ports are used for services and clients?

- What are the well-known ports and their numbers?

- What is the relationship between MAC addresses, IP addresses, and port numbers?

- What is positive acknowledgment and retransmission (PAR), and what role does TCP play?

Key Terms

This chapter uses the following key terms. You can find the definitions in the Glossary:

This chapter covers the two main transport layer protocols in the TCP/IP protocol model: Transmission Control Protocol (TCP) and User Datagram Protocol (UDP). The first of the two sections introduces the basic operation of TCP and UDP, and the second section focuses on the one feature the two protocols have in common—their use of port numbers to identify application processes.

Note

The only topics included in this chapter that are not included in Chapter 11 of the *CCNA 1 Companion Guide* are in the section "Denial-of-Service Attacks and SYN Floods."

Note that some Cisco Networking Academies may not cover much of this chapter in class. Most of the information in this chapter is covered in Module 11 of the Cisco Networking Academy Program CCNA 1 course (and the corresponding chapter of the Cisco Press *CCNA 1 Companion Guide*). You may want to check with your instructor as to whether you need to read all or parts of this chapter.

TCP and UDP Operation

Note

The name TCP/IP is created by combining the names of the two most popular protocols: TCP and IP.

The TCP/IP transport layer includes several protocols, most notably the *Transmission Control Protocol (TCP)* and *User Datagram Protocol (UDP)*. Although both protocols provide services to applications, TCP provides several more functions. However, those extra functions come at a price—more header overhead and the possibility of a slower data transfer rate due to TCP's features. You can think of TCP as a luxury car and UDP as an economy car. Both types get you where you need to go, but the luxury car has cooler features and is more comfortable, which of course translates to a higher price tag. Similarly, TCP provides many great features not offered by UDP, but it requires more overhead than UDP.

Although TCP in particular provides a wide variety of functions, the main goal of the transport layer can be summarized as follows:

> To provide the function of taking data from one application process on one computer and delivering that data to the correct application process on another computer.

Contrasting the Transport and Internet layers, the Internet layer delivers data (packets) from one computer to another, but it does not think about which application sent the data or which application on the receiving computer needs the data. For example, if you have five web browser windows open, the Internet layer delivers the data to the computer, but the transport layer works to ensure that each browser gets the data destined for it and not for one of the others.

Table 10-1 lists the most important features of both TCP and UDP, noting which features are supported by each transport layer protocol.

Table 10-1 Comparing TCP and UDP

Transport Layer Feature	TCP	UDP
Flow control and windowing	Yes	No
Connection-oriented	Yes	No
Error recovery	Yes	No
Segmentation and reassembly of data	Yes	No
In-order delivery of data	Yes	No
Identifying applications using port numbers	Yes	Yes

This section covers most of the topics shown in Table 10-1 and includes a reference to the contents of the TCP and UDP headers. Note that this section covers all the features supported by TCP, but not UDP, so this section ends with a few comments about UDP.

Flow Control and Windowing

When a host sends data using TCP, the receiving host can control how fast each TCP sender sends the data over time. This process is called *flow control*.

Receivers use flow control for many reasons. First, the receiver needs time to process the received data. The receiving host also has a finite amount of memory, so if data keeps arriving before the receiving host can process the previously received data, it might run out of memory. For example, a receiving host may run out of memory in part because of the speed of today's high-speed LANs, or it could happen if one host receives data from many other TCP senders at the same time. Regardless, a receiving host needs a way to tell the sending host(s) to slow down.

This section describes two forms of flow control: *dynamic sliding windows* and *withholding acknowledgments*.

Flow Control Through Dynamic Sliding Windows

The receiver tells the sending host how many bytes the sending host can send before it receives an acknowledgment—a value called a *window*. When the sending host sends an entire window's worth of data, it must wait on an acknowledgment, thereby slowing its rate of sending data. Figure 10-1 shows an example.

Note

Segments do not have to have 1000 bytes of data; the example shown in Figure 10-1 uses 1000-byte-long segments simply to make the math more obvious.

Figure 10-1 Dynamic Windowing

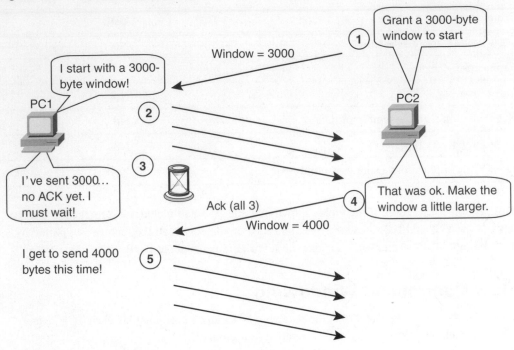

The process illustrated in Figure 10-1 is explained as follows:

1. PC2 sends a segment to PC1 in which the Window field in the header is set to 3000. This means that PC2 grants PC1 the right to send 3000 bytes to PC2.

2. PC1 sends PC2 3000 bytes via three 1000-byte segments.

3. PC1 has sent all 3000 bytes, but it has not received any acknowledgments; therefore, it must wait.

4. PC2 sends PC1 an acknowledgment, and this time it grants a slightly larger 4000-byte window.

5. PC1 now sends four 1000-byte segments.

The example shown in Figure 10-1 is a classic case of dynamic windowing. The receiver, PC2 in this case, grants a window to PC1. PC1 can send the number of bytes in the window before it receives an acknowledgment. The process works well to protect the receiver's memory in particular. For example, if PC2 had 100 KB of memory that it could use for a particular TCP connection, PC2 would know to never increase its window to more than 100 KB, to ensure that it has enough space to store the data.

Note

The window is sometimes called the *granted window* because of the process described in Step 1.

Note

The TCP RFCs use the term *octet* instead of byte. The term octet is a generic reference to 8 bits.

Note

If the receiver can process the data quickly enough, it keeps increasing the window until a state is reached in which the sender keeps sending segments and gets acknowledgments before exhausting the window. As a result, the sending host would not have to slow down.

Flow Control Through Withholding Acknowledgments

After a sending host has sent one window-size worth of bytes, it must wait to send more. Knowing that, the receiver can choose to wait to send acknowledgments, which effectively prevents the sender from sending more data. Figure 10-2 shows an example similar to Figure 10-1.

The first two steps exactly match Figure 10-1. At Step 3, PC2 has received all 3000 bytes but needs more time to process the data. So, instead of immediately acknowledging receipt of the segments, PC2 waits until it can catch up on the work and then sends an acknowledgment at Step 4. Note that PC2 did not increase the window size at Step 4 because it is already having difficulty processing 3000 bytes at a time.

Figure 10-2   Withholding Acknowledgments

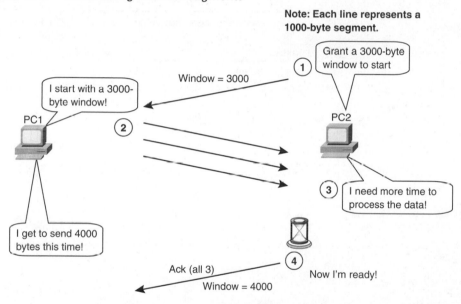

This process of withholding acknowledgments is sometimes referred to as *start/stop flow control*. In effect, the receiver puts up a stop sign for the sender by withholding the acknowledgment. Although simple, this method does not work as well as simply using well-chosen dynamic window sizes.

Note

TCP uses sliding windows for flow control instead of start/stop flow control.

Establishing and Terminating TCP Connections

By definition, connection-oriented protocols use messages, events, or other prearranged settings on the communicating devices before they allow any end-user communication to occur. TCP is a connection-oriented protocol in part so that it can assign initial values to the window and sequence number values shown in Figures 10-1 and 10-2. TCP also allows two computers to

Note

The ACK flag is a single bit that is used to control connection establishment and termination. It differs from the 16-bit TCP Acknowledgment Number field, as covered in the section "Comparing TCP and UDP" later in this chapter.

agree to many other settings before the hosts attempt to send any end-user data. (The term *connectionless protocols* refers to protocols such as UDP that do not establish a connection before communications can occur.)

TCP uses a process called a *three-way handshake* to create a new TCP connection and to initialize the various numbers used to control and manage a TCP connection. The three-way handshake is simply three TCP segments that use two of the TCP flags found in the TCP header. The flags are called synchronize (SYN) (pronounced "sin") and acknowledge (ACK). Figure 10-3 shows an example of the three-way TCP connection-establishment flow.

Figure 10-3   Three-Way TCP Connection Establishment

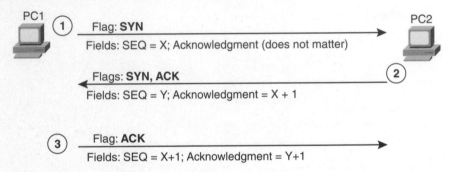

First, note the bold SYN and ACK flags shown in Figure 10-3. The three segments have the following flags set:

1. The first segment has a SYN flag set but does not have the ACK flag set. This means that the SYN bit in the TCP header is set to binary 1, and the ACK flag is set to binary 0.

2. The second segment has both SYN and ACK set.

3. The third and ongoing segments have only the ACK bit set.

Note

Some people think of a TCP connection as a virtual connection, because the connection itself is performed in software.

The first message in a TCP connection is the only segment that can have just the SYN flag set. (Many people think of such segments as meaning that the Sequence Number field is now valid.) The second message is the only segment that can have both SYN and ACK set. The third (and ongoing) segments have the ACK bit set, but not the SYN bit, which essentially means that the Acknowledgment Number field is now valid and the TCP connection was correctly established. After the third segment is sent, data can be sent using this TCP connection.

After a connection is established and the data sent, the application can choose to keep the connection alive or terminate it. For example, after loading a web page, most web browsers terminate the TCP connection. TCP supports several variations on terminating the TCP connection. The most common is a four-way termination flow, which uses another flag called the finished (FIN) flag.

Denial-of-Service Attacks and SYN Floods

Network security may well be the single hottest topic in the world of networking in this first decade of a new century. When hackers attempt to cause problems in a network, they may be looking to steal information. In other cases, they may simply try to cause harm, more like vandalism. A network attack that is primarily intended to do harm is called a *denial-of-service (DoS) attack*.

A *SYN flood* attack is one of the most common types of DoS attacks. To appreciate what happens with a SYN flood, think for a moment about what a server does when it receives the first segment in a three-way TCP connection establishment flow:

1. The server reserves some memory with which to keep track of this new TCP connection.

2. The server sends back the second segment in the three-way connection establishment flow.

3. The server sets a timer, typically a minute or two, waiting for the third segment in the three-way establishment flow.

Beyond these basics steps, a server typically has a setting that limits the number of concurrent TCP connections that it can support. As soon as the server gets the first segment in a new TCP connection request, the server adds 1 to its counter of the number of current TCP connections.

Summarizing, the server consumes memory each time it receives a new TCP connection request (first flow in a TCP three-way connection setup flow), and the server counts that new request against its maximum allowed total of concurrent connections.

A SYN flood occurs when a hacker sends a lot of TCP segments to a server, with each segment looking like a new request for a new TCP connection. However, the attacker never sends the third segment in the connection establishment request. Figure 10-4 shows the general idea.

Figure 10-4   Multiple Uncompleted TCP Connections—SYN Flood

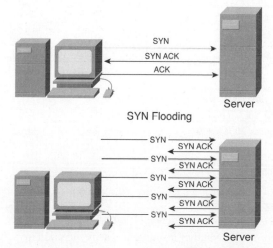

Note

You may also see the term distributed denial-of-service (DDoS) attack, which refers to DoS attacks created by multiple different (distributed) computers.

The SYN flood, whose name comes from the fact that the large number of attacking segments all have the SYN flag set, can cripple the server. SYN floods often include thousands of SYN requests per second, so the server quickly consumes memory. Also, the server may reject legitimate users' requests to connect to it as soon as it believes it has too many connections already.

SYN floods have been around for a while, and network engineers and server administrators can do many things to prevent any harm from such attacks. For example, the server can lower the timeout for waiting on the third TCP segment when setting up a new connection; by doing so, the server can release the memory more quickly. The server can increase the number of allowed concurrent connections as well. Today, however, many tools in routers and firewalls can watch for SYN floods, notice when they occur, and prevent the flood of SYN requests from ever reaching the server.

TCP Error Recovery (Reliability)

TCP is a reliable protocol—at least as far as networking terminology is concerned. In networking, reliable protocols perform error recovery, which means that they ensure that all the data eventually gets to the receiver, even if some data is lost in transit. Figure 10-5 first shows an example of how a TCP receiver tells the TCP sender that all the data was received.

Figure 10-5   TCP Acknowledgments with No Error Recovery Needed

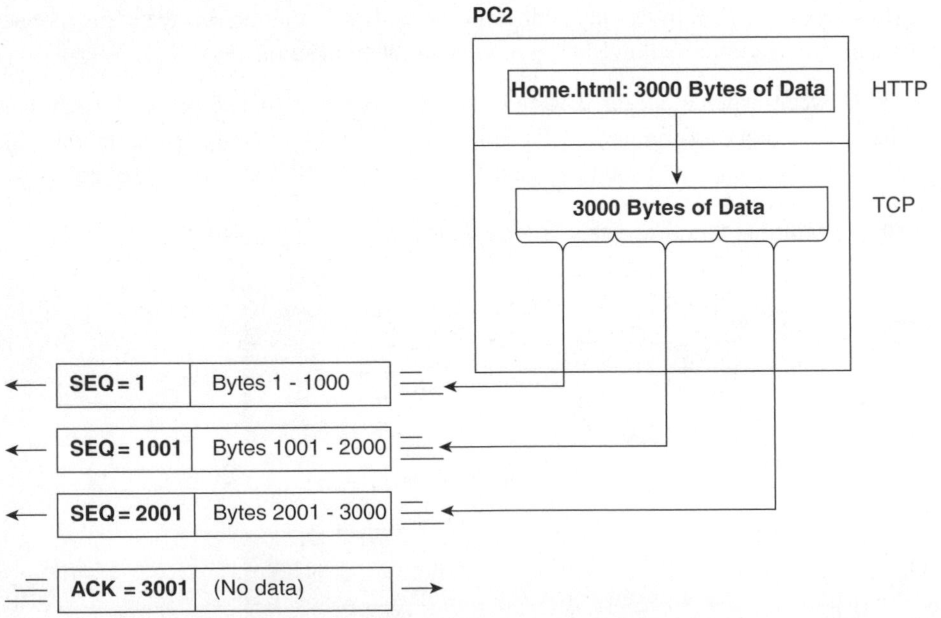

TCP uses two TCP header fields—the Sequence Number and Acknowledgment Number fields—to tell the other computer whether a segment was received. The sequence number keeps track of all the bytes sent over a TCP connection by numbering the first byte of data inside

each segment. For example, the first segment's sequence number of 1 represents the first byte of the 1000 bytes of data in the first segment. The first byte of the second segment is the 1001st byte of data sent by PC2 to PC1; therefore, when PC2 sends its next segment, it sets the sequence number to a value of 1001 because the previous segment's bytes were essentially numbered 1 through 1000.

TCP acknowledges the receipt of data by using the Acknowledgment Number field of the TCP header. The Acknowledgment Number field identifies the next byte a host expects to receive. For example, PC1's Acknowledgment Number field of 3001, set in the next segment sent by PC1 back to PC2, means that PC1 expects PC2 to send it a segment starting with byte number 3001 next. In other words, PC1 expects PC2's next segment to have a sequence number of 3001. The practice of acknowledging data by stating the next byte expected to be received, rather than identifying the last byte received, is called a *forward acknowledgment* or *expectational acknowledgment*.

TCP performs error recovery by having the receiving host send an acknowledgment that implies some data was lost. Figure 10-6 shows an example in which TCP recovers from an error.

Figure 10-6   TCP Error Recovery

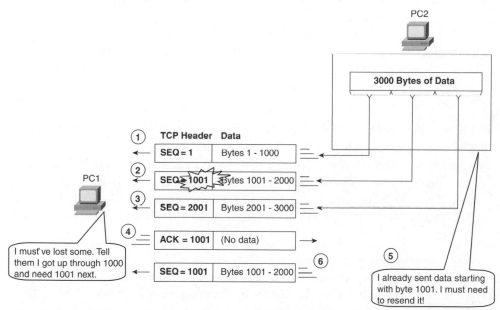

Figure 10-6 shows the process by which the PCs recover some lost data, using a process that the online course calls *Positive Acknowledgment with Retransmission (PAR)*. The key to this example is the logic implied at PC1 and the acknowledgment number in the segment labeled Step 4. The first three steps show the same first three segments shown in Figure 10-5, but in this case, the second segment is lost or destroyed during transmission. PC1 then signals that the segment was lost by sending a segment with the acknowledgment set to 1001. Literally, this setting means that PC1 acknowledges the receipt of the first segment. PC1 knows that PC2 will receive this acknowledgment and decide to resend the lost segment because, as shown in Step 5's logic bubble, PC2 knows that it sent more data—data that apparently, according to the acknowledgment in Step 4, never arrived. Step 6 simply shows PC2 resending the segment.

Several variations of error recovery exist besides this example. For example, to combat losing an acknowledgment in transit, the sending host sets a timer when it sends each segment. If the segment is not acknowledged within a certain amount of time, the sender cannot be sure if the segment made it across the internetwork; therefore, it resends the segment. (The amount of time varies based on how quickly the acknowledgments have been occurring.)

 Lab 10.1.6   Multiple Active Host Sessions

In this lab, you see port usage on a single host attached to a router.

Segmentation, Reassembly, and In-Order Delivery

Figure 10-5 and Figure 10-6 showed another of TCP's many features—*segmentation*. TCP segmentation refers to the process of TCP accepting a large chunk of data from the application protocol and breaking it into pieces that are small enough to be appropriate for transmission through the internetwork. For example, in Figures 10-5 and 10-6, PC2 segments 3000 bytes of application layer data into three parts. PC2 then puts a TCP header in front of each chunk, which creates three different TCP segments. In fact, the term *segment* was chosen to describe the TCP header and its data because of this segmentation process.

As with IP packets, a segment's size or length is limited, typically depending on the types of data link layer protocols used to forward the segment. For example, most end-user hosts reside on Ethernet LANs. Ethernet frames allow 1500 data bytes in a frame's Data field. The Data field of an Ethernet frame holds the IP header and TCP header, followed by the TCP Data field. Because the IP and TCP headers are each 20 bytes long, the data portion of a TCP segment is typically limited to 1460 bytes. The maximum length of the TCP Data field is referred to as the maximum segment size (MSS).

TCP on the receiving computer reassembles the data into its original form. At the same time, the receiver also guarantees that the data will be in order. For example, if a single 3000-byte file is broken into three segments for transmission, but the segments are reassembled in the incorrect order on the receiving side, the file becomes useless. So, TCP provides a guarantee of *in-order delivery*.

Because of IP routing, a TCP receiver can receive data out of order. Figure 10-7 shows a classic case of how TCP segments can be reordered while being forwarded through an IP internetwork and how the receiving TCP software simply puts the data back in its original order. The routing logic hinges on the fact that when multiple routes exist to reach the same subnet, and the routing protocol metrics tie, the routers can load-balance packets over several routes. However, one route might be faster or less congested than the other route, which makes the packets arrive in a different order from the order in which they were sent.

Figure 10-7   TCP Providing In-Order Delivery

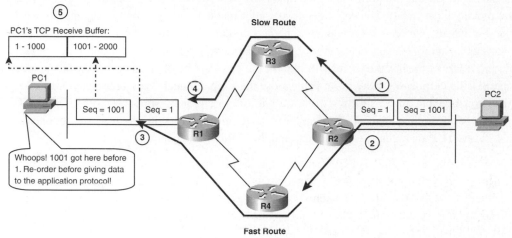

This concept becomes clearer when using the exact steps outlined here, as shown in Figure 10-7:

1. PC2 sends two segments. The first segment (sequence number 1) is routed over the slow high route.

2. Router R2 sends the second segment (sequence number 1001) over the fast low route.

3. The second segment sent arrives before the first segment sent, so PC1 copies the segment into a memory buffer.

4. The first segment sent arrives next.

5. The first segment sent (sequence number 1) should be in front of the segment with sequence number 1001, so PC1's TCP software stores this data in the correct order in its memory buffer.

Comparing TCP and UDP

TCP supports all the rich protocol features covered so far in this chapter, but UDP supports none of those features. The lack of features is not necessarily a bad thing, however, because UDP's lack of features means that it imposes less overhead than TCP. Additionally, UDP can transfer data faster than TCP, because UDP never has to pay attention to any of the constraints of creating connections, using windowing, waiting on acknowledgments, and spending time retransmitting data.

Choosing a new car is a good analogy to choosing between TCP and UDP. Imagine that you are picking a car to buy. You could get a version of that car with just the basics: engine, wheels, steering wheel, and brakes. Or you could get a different version of that car that includes special paint, great stereo, leather seats, sunroof, undercoating to prevent rust, and a lifetime warranty so that if it ever breaks, the dealer will pay for the repairs. The obvious drawback of the second option—the extra cash—may make you choose the simple model. They both get you from place to place, but one in style and comfort, but for more money. Similarly, both UDP and TCP deliver data from one application to another—UDP with speed and little overhead (but some risks), and TCP with guaranteed delivery and the ability to be controlled.

Although comparing TCP and UDP may be interesting, most people never really get to choose which of the two protocols to use. The people who create new application protocols pick whether to use TCP or UDP, so when you pick an application, you use the transport protocol chosen by that application. Table 10-2 lists some of the more common application layer protocols and whether they use TCP or UDP.

Table 10-2   Popular Applications and Transport Layer Protocols

Protocol	Application
TCP	FTP data
TCP	FTP control
TCP	Telnet
TCP	SMTP
TCP, UDP[1]	DNS
UDP	TFTP
TCP	HTTP (Web)
TCP	POP3
UDP	SNMP

[1] A DNS request from your PC to a DNS server uses UDP; DNS messages between DNS servers sometimes use TCP.

Similar to many other networking protocols, TCP and UDP use a header to hold important information for performing their tasks. RFC 768 defines the UDP header, and RFC 793 defines the TCP header. For example, TCP needs the ACK and SYN flags for connection establishment and the Sequence Number and Acknowledgment Number fields to perform error recovery. Figure 10-8 shows the contents of the TCP and UDP headers.

Figure 10-8   TCP and UDP Headers

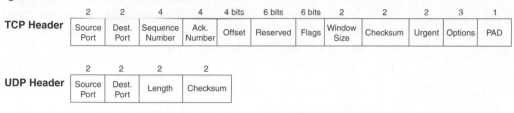

Of particular importance, the first two fields in each header are identical. The one function performed by both TCP and UDP—the use of port numbers to identify application processes—is implemented by using the Source Port and Destination Port fields at each header's beginning. Beyond those fields, TCP has a much longer header (20 bytes versus 8 bytes) so that it has all the fields required to implement the much larger number of features it has compared to UDP.

Table 10-3 describes the TCP header fields.

Note

The term *segment* refers to a TCP header and its encapsulated data, whereas the term *datagram* refers to a UDP header and its encapsulated data.

Table 10-3   TCP Header Fields

Field	Meaning
Source Port	Identifies the application process on the sending computer.
Destination Port	Identifies the application process on the receiving computer for which the data is intended.
Sequence Number	Identifies the first byte of the sent data for the purposes of allowing the receiver to acknowledge receipt of the data and to reorder data as necessary.
Acknowledgment Number	Set in a sent TCP segment, this number notes the sequence number of the next byte the host expects to receive. The Acknowledgment Number field recognizes lost packets and flow control.
Offset (Header Length)	Number of sets of 4 bytes in the TCP header, which allows the receiving host to easily find the end of the TCP header and the data's beginning.

continues

Table 10-3   TCP Header Fields   *continued*

Field	Meaning
Reserved	Reserved for future use.
Flags	Each bit has different meanings to signal some function. For example, connection establishment uses the SYN and ACK flags.
Window Size	As set in a sent segment, the Window Size field signifies the maximum amount of unacknowledged data the host is willing to receive before the other host must wait for an acknowledgment. Used for flow control.
Checksum	Frame Check Sequence (FCS)-like field that can confirm that no errors occurred in the TCP header.
Urgent	Used to point to the sequence number of sent data for which the sender requests an immediate (urgent) acknowledgment from the receiver.
Options and Padding	Additional headers used to expand the protocol in the future. They are seldom used today.

Table 10-4 describes the UDP header fields.

Table 10-4   UDP Header Fields

Field	Meaning
Source Port	Identifies the application process on the sending computer
Destination Port	Identifies the application process on the receiving computer for which the data is intended
Length	Number of octets in the UDP segment, including the data
Checksum	FCS-like field that can confirm that no errors occurred in the UDP header

Now that you have read about all the great features of TCP, and how UDP simply does not provide those same features, the second half of the chapter focuses on the one feature the two protocols share—how they use port numbers to identify the sending and receiving applications.

Operation of Transport Layer Ports

The one function performed by both UDP and TCP is to provide a means to identify the specific application process that sends the data and the application process that needs to receive the data. For example, your PC might simultaneously use two web browsers, an e-mail client, and File Transfer Protocol (FTP) software or an instant-messaging application. Each item is considered to be a different application process.

When your PC receives an IP packet, it must determine to which application process it must give the data. To make this determination, TCP and UDP use *port numbers*. Figure 10-9 shows how two computers use port numbers—in this case, with Keith's PC running four application processes. Each application uses a different local port number, identifying each of the different application processes.

Figure 10-9   Using Port Numbers to Identify the Correct Application Process

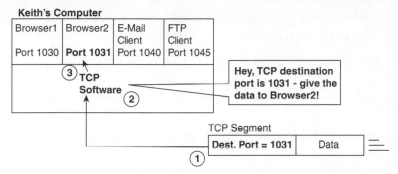

Figure 10-9 shows the steps by which Keith's computer receives a segment and decides to which application process to give the data:

1. An IP packet with a TCP segment inside it arrives at the PC. Because it is a TCP segment, IP gives the segment to the TCP software inside the computer.

2. TCP examines the *destination port number* in the header. The destination port number identifies the application process on the destination (or receiving) computer (Keith).

3. Based on a value of 1031 in the Destination Port Number field, the PC's TCP software gives the data to Browser2.

The port numbers shown in Figure 10-9 are called **dynamic port numbers** because the host computer dynamically picks which port number to use for each application process. A host typically dynamically allocates port numbers of value 1024 (2^{10}) through 65,535 ($2^{16} - 1$), which is the largest possible port number. When the host starts a new application process (for example, the user opens a new browser window), the host allocates a dynamic port number that the computer is not already using for another process. Because each client application on the PC in Figure 10-9 allocated a unique dynamic port number, the PC can easily decide which application process should get any received TCP segments.

Figure 10-9 also provides a good backdrop from which to explain a few variations in terminology related to TCP. First, the procedure shown in the figure is sometimes called *multiplexing TCP connections*, or simply *multiplexing*. The term multiplexing originated in the world of networking, but with TCP, it refers to sending segments from multiple connections to a computer, with the TCP software on that computer choosing the right application based on the port number. Additionally, and as mentioned earlier in the section "Establishing and Terminating TCP Connections," when an application uses TCP to connect to an application on another computer, that application creates a TCP connection. Sometimes, the term *conversation* is used instead of connection.

In some cases, a single application uses multiple ports at the same time. A unique port number is needed for each TCP or UDP connection. For example, when downloading a web page, a browser can open several TCP connections, which use several port numbers.

Connecting to Servers: Well-Known Ports

Most TCP/IP applications use a client/server model for communications. In the client/server model of a computer, a client is software that needs some service, and the server is the software that provides the service. For example, a web browser is a client because it needs to display information for the end user, and the web server is a server because it supplies that information.

Servers cannot use dynamic port numbers because the clients that use the server must know ahead of time what port number the server uses. Servers must wait and listen for segments sent by any and all clients, and the clients need to know the port number that a particular service uses.

To allow servers to work well, TCP/IP defines many **well-known ports**, each reserved for use by a specific application protocol. (Some texts use the term *static port* as a synonym for well-known port.) When a client connects to a server, the client already knows what well-known port the server should be using. Figure 10-10 shows an example of this concept, with a web browser connecting to a server at port 80, the well-known port of the Hypertext Transfer Protocol (HTTP).

Figure 10-10   Client Connecting to Well-Known Port of a Web Server (80)

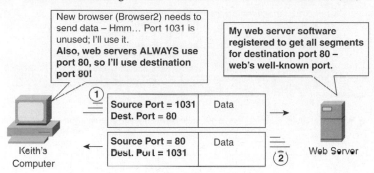

Web browsers know that the well-known port for web servers—more specifically, for the HTTP protocol—is port 80. Figure 10-10 illustrates the following points:

1. Keith's browser sends the segment as shown, with a destination port of 80.

2. The segment has a source port of 80 because it comes from the web server, and the destination port matches the port used on Keith's computer.

Many of the most common application protocols use well-known ports, as listed in Table 10-5.

Table 10-5   Popular Applications and Their Well-Known Port Numbers

Port Number	Protocol	Application
20	TCP	FTP data
21	TCP	FTP control
23	TCP	Telnet
25	TCP	Simple Mail Transfer Protocol (SMTP)
53	TCP, UDP	Domain Name System (DNS)
69	UDP	Trivial FTP (TFTP)
80	TCP	HTTP (Web)
110	TCP	Post Office Protocol version 3 (POP3)
161	UDP	SNMP

Some people prefer a visual reference for some of the key port numbers. Figure 10-11 shows in graphical form many of the same port numbers listed in Table 10-5. Figure 10-11 shows DNS port 53 straddling the line between TCP and UDP because DNS uses UDP in some cases and TCP in others.

Note

The Internet Assigned Numbers Authority (IANA) controls the administrative process for assigning both IP address ranges and well-known ports.

Note

FTP uses a different well-known port for control purposes (port 21) than for the actual transfer of files (port 20).

Figure 10-11   Using Port Numbers to Identify the Correct Application Process

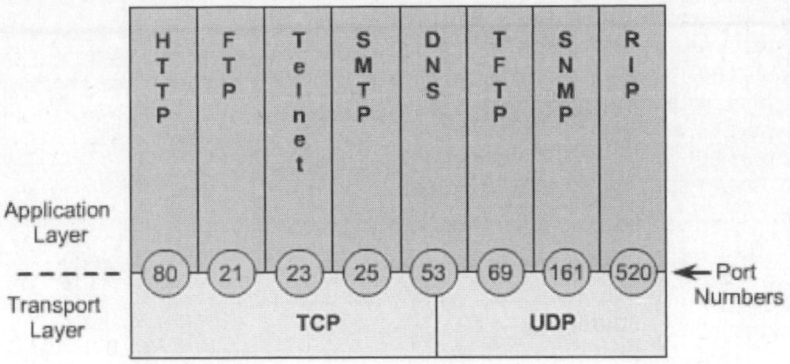

The term *server* can mean "single high-powered computer." In this chapter, server means "TCP/IP software application," one that uses port numbers. An individual physical server might run many TCP/IP servers or services. So, the server hardware, running multiple TCP/IP software services such as web servers (which serve web pages), FTP servers (which serve files), and the like, needs to use port numbers to differentiate the different applications.

Lab 10.2.5   Well-Known Port Numbers and Multiple Sessions

In this lab, you enable HTTP services on a router.

Comparing Well-Known, Dynamic, and Registered Ports

The Internet Assigned Numbers Authority (IANA [www.iana.org]) assigns the values for well-known ports and the values for a similar concept called *registered port numbers*. The difference between well-known and registered ports is that registered ports are assigned to servers that the average end user can start. Well-known ports are used only for applications typically controlled by IT staff. For example, instant-messaging applications, voice applications, and video applications—all of which an average end user can start—technically must have one side of a connection act as a server, so these applications use registered port numbers. However, web services, FTP services, and e-mail services, which are usually controlled by IT staff in a typical company, use well-known port numbers.

Table 10-6 summarizes the three overall categories of uses of port numbers. (Note that the numbers range from 0 through 65,535 because the port number fields are 2 bytes [16 bits] long, which allows for 2^{16} different port numbers.) The table also shows the reserved port number ranges.

Table 10-6   Uses of Port Numbers

Type of Port	Range of Values	Purpose
Dynamic	1024–65,535[1]	Allocated by clients for each new application process
Well-known	0–1023	For high-privilege processes, used so that all clients know the correct port number to connect to
Registered	1025–49,151[2]	Equivalent to well-known ports in concept, but used specifically for nonprivileged application processes

[1] IANA formally suggests that dynamic ports start at 49,152. However, in practice, hosts typically use dynamic port numbers that begin at 1024. The CCNA 1 course also states that they begin at 1024.

[2] The online curriculum states that registered port numbers are simply 1024 and greater, whereas IANA specifically restricts the highest value at 49,151.

Both TCP and UDP use port numbers, as described in this chapter. However, whereas TCP has many features, UDP's only significant feature is its use of port numbers to identify application processes.

Most operating systems (OSs) include commands that display the port numbers used on that computer. For example, Microsoft OSs support the **netstat -an** command to display the currently used TCP and UDP port numbers. To see some useful output from this command, you could create a new TCP connection by opening a web browser and loading a web page. Then, use the **netstat -an** command to view the TCP connection, along with the port number used on your PC and the web server.

Comparing MAC Addresses, IP Addresses, and Port Numbers

MAC addresses, IP addresses, and port numbers all perform some role in addressing, or identifying, the senders and intended recipients of data. Before leaving the topic of port numbers completely, it may be useful to consider all three topics together briefly. The following list summarizes a few key comparison points between these three key concepts:

- **MAC addresses**—Define the physical addressing of LAN NICs, which allows frames to be delivered over a LAN. However, MAC addresses do not define a way to group addresses for easy routing (as does IP), do not define any way to route packets from end to end over an internetwork of routers (as does IP), and do not identify the application processes on the sending and receiving computers (as do port numbers).

- **IP addresses**—Define logical (meaning not physical) addresses that define a way to group addresses (subnets), and define a routing process to allow end-to-end delivery of packets between hosts. IP does not define a means to deliver data over a physical network (as do MAC addresses on LANs), and IP addresses do not identify the application process on the computers (as do port numbers).

- **Port numbers**—Identify the application processes on the sending (source port) and receiving (destination port) computers. Port numbers do not define any methods of sending data over a physical network or any means to deliver data end to end over an internetwork.

In short, data link addresses (such as MAC addresses) allow hosts and routers to deliver data to the next device in an IP route, IP allows routers to forward the packet to the destination host, and port numbers allow the host to determine which application should get the data.

An analogy between these three types of addresses and the postal service can help. Think of the street address on the front of a letter as the IP address. The postal service can deliver the letter to the right house or apartment based on that address, just like routing can deliver IP packets to the right host. When the letter is delivered, the people who live in the house must look to see whose name is on the letter to know which member of the household gets the letter, much like a host looks at the destination port number to decide which application to give the data to. Finally, the postal workers collectively know how to move the letter from post office to post office, using trucks, planes, boats, or whatever to deliver the letter, much like the various data-link protocols know how to move data from one device to the next.

Finally, you should have some understanding of the term *socket* before this chapter about port numbers ends. In the world of TCP and UDP, a socket is a set of three things:

- The computer'sIP address

- The transport protocol (TCP or UDP)

- The port number used by an application

For example, a web server whose IP address is 10.1.1.1, using the well-known port for HTTP, would be using a socket of (10.1.1.1, TCP, 80).

Summary

The primary duty of the transport layer, which is OSI model Layer 4, is to provide the service of taking data from one application process on one computer and delivering the data to the correct application process on another computer. To differentiate between different application processes, the transport layer (both TCP and UDP) identifies data from upper-layer applications based on their port numbers.

UDP essentially provides only the basic delivery and identification of applications using port numbers. TCP provides several additional functions, including reliability (error recovery), flow control, segmentation and reassembly, and in-order data delivery. To do so, TCP uses connection-oriented logic, establishing connections dynamically using a three-way handshake.

TCP numbers the first byte of each segment with a sequence number and acknowledges receipt of data by using an acknowledgment number. This process allows the receiving host to tell the sender to resend data. The sequence numbers allow the receiver to notice when data is received out of order so that the receiver can arrange the data in the correct order before giving it to the application.

Flow control ensures that a transmitting node does not overwhelm a receiving node with data. The simplest method of flow control occurs when the receiving host signals that it is "not ready" by withholding its acknowledgments. TCP also uses dynamic windowing, which is a more efficient process by which the receiver grants the sender the right to send a set amount of data before requiring an acknowledgment.

DoS attacks are designed to deny services to legitimate hosts that attempt to establish connections. They are used by hackers to halt system response. SYN flooding is one type of DoS attack. It exploits the normal three-way TCP handshake and causes targeted devices to send acknowledgments to source hosts that will not complete the handshake. In addition to implementing software specifically created as a defense against these kinds of attacks, an administrator can decrease the connection timeout period and increase the connection queue size.

The term *Positive Acknowledgment with Retransmission (PAR)* refers to the process of explicitly acknowledging received data, with the sender resending any unacknowledged segments. With PAR, the source sends a packet, starts a timer, and waits for an ACK before it sends the next packet. If the timer expires before the source receives an ACK, the source retransmits the packet and resets the timer. TCP uses expectational acknowledgments, in which the Acknowledgment Number field refers to the next octet that is expected.

Connection-oriented TCP provides a wide range of functions, but UDP has some advantages over TCP. The connectionless UDP uses less overhead (an 8-byte header versus TCP's 20 bytes), and UDP does not slow because of flow control.

A port number must be associated with the conversation between hosts to ensure that the packet reaches the appropriate service on the server. Port numbers have the following assigned ranges:

- The well-known ports are those from 0 through 1023.

- The registered ports are those from 1024 through 49,151.

- The dynamic and/or private ports are those from 49,152 through 65,535.

The three methods of addressing include port numbers, which are located at the transport layer. The network layer assigns the logical or IP address, and the data link layer assigns the physical or MAC address.

Check Your Understanding

Complete all the review questions listed here to test your understanding of the topics and concepts in this chapter. Answers are listed in Appendix A, "Answers to Check Your Understanding and Challenge Questions."

1. Which of the following best describes TCP/IP?

   A. It is a suite of protocols that can be used to communicate across any set of interconnected networks.

   B. It is a suite of protocols that allows WANs to communicate.

   C. It is a suite of protocols that allows for data transmission across local-area networks.

   D. It is a suite of protocols that allows different devices to be shared by interconnected networks.

2. At which layer does UDP function?

   A. Layer 2

   B. Layer 3

   C. Layer 4

   D. Layer 5

3. What is the purpose of ports?

   A. To allow hosts to determine which data segments are sent and received by each application process.

   B. Source systems use ports to keep a session organized.

   C. End systems use ports to dynamically assign end users to a particular session, depending on their application use.

   D. Source systems generate ports to predict destination addresses.

4. Which of the following best describes UDP?

   A. A protocol that acknowledges flawed or intact datagrams

   B. A protocol that detects errors and requests retransmissions from the source

   C. A protocol that processes datagrams and requests retransmissions when necessary

   D. A protocol that exchanges datagrams without acknowledgments or guarantee

5. Host A sends three consecutive TCP segments to host B on a single TCP connection. The first segment has a sequence number of 100. Which of the following are correct regarding the other two segments? (Choose two.)

A. The second segment's Sequence Number field must be 101.

B. The second segment's Sequence Number field must be 1100.

C. The third segment's Sequence Number field could be 102.

D. The third segment's Sequence Number field could be 1100.

6. Why is TCP sequence numbering important?

A. To ensure that data is processed in the right order and that data can be recovered if problems occur

B. To determine how much data the receiving station can accept at one time

C. To provide efficient use of bandwidth by users

D. To ensure that data is passed to the correct applications in the upper layers

7. What does a TCP sliding window do?

A. It makes the window larger so that more data can come through in parallel, which results in more efficient use of bandwidth.

B. The window size slides to each section of the datagram to receive data, which results in more efficient use of bandwidth.

C. It is a method of flow control for network data transfers using the receiver's window size.

D. It limits the incoming data so that each segment must be sent one by one, which is an inefficient use of bandwidth.

8. When using UDP, which of the following protocols could provide reliability?

A. Network layer protocols

B. Application layer protocols

C. Internet protocols

D. Transmission Control Protocols

9. Which of the following best describes window size?

A. The maximum size of the window that software can have and still process data rapidly

B. The number of bytes that can be transmitted before waiting for an acknowledgment

C. The size of the window, in picas, that must be set ahead of time so that data can be sent

D. The size of the window opening on a monitor, which is not always equal to the monitor size

10. Which statements best describe SYN flooding? (Choose two.)

A. Flooding occurs when a server sends a stream of data that is larger than allowed by the sliding window.

B. It is a type of denial-of-service attack that attempts to consume a server's available memory.

C. Flooding occurs because the attacking computer initiates a large number of TCP connections but never complete the TCP connection process.

D. Flooding occurs when the client expects the next bit in the sequence but is repeatedly sent the wrong bit, causing TCP to send correction requests.

E. Flooding is a DoS attempt in which the server denies service to hosts by ignoring port numbers on TCP requests.

Challenge Questions and Activities

These questions require a deeper application of the concepts covered in this chapter and are similar to the style of questions you might see on a CCNA certification exam. Appendix A lists the answers.

1. What does it mean when a sending host receives "acknowledgement 20" during a TCP connection?

   A. The sender must repeat the data from the first handshake for verification.

   B. The sender should send byte 19 next.

   C. The receiver is confirming it has received packet 20.

   D. The sender should send byte 20 next.

2. Which services and protocols listed in order below are associated with ports 80, 21, 20, 23, and 25?

   A. HTTP, Telnet, FTP, FTP data, and echo

   B. Telnet, FTP, RIP, SNMP, and FTP data

   C. HTTP, FTP, FTP data, Telnet, and SMTP

   D. Telnet, FTP, RIP, SNMP, and HTTP

CHAPTER 11

Access Control Lists

Objectives

Upon completion of this chapter, you should be able to answer the following questions:

- What is the purpose of an ACL?

- What is the purpose of a wildcard mask?

- What is the difference between standard and extended ACLs?

- How are named ACLs created?

- What factors determine where an ACL should be placed?

Additional Topics of Interest

Several chapters contain additional coverage of previous topics or related topics that are secondary to the main goals of this chapter. You can find the additional coverage on the CD-ROM. For this chapter, the following additional topics are covered:

- Firewalls

- Restricting Telnet access

Key Terms

This chapter uses the following key terms. You can find the definitions in the Glossary.

Access Control Lists (ACLs)   page 366

inbound ACL   page 369

implicit deny all   page 374

wildcard mask   page 380

explicit permit all   page 389

Security may well be the hottest topic in networking today. Most every company in the world connects in some way to the Internet, and the Internet has literally billions of individual users. Beyond that, a large percentage of each company's employees connect to that company's enterprise network. With so many devices and so many people connected to networks today, opportunities exist for people to cause harm by stealing information, money, or identities, or to cause problems to a competitor's network.

This chapter covers one key security feature of Cisco routers: Access Control Lists (ACLs). ACLs filter packets as they pass through a router, allowing only approved packets to pass through, and discarding packets that are not supposed to get through the router.

This chapter contains two major sections that match the major sections of the online curriculum. The first section covers the fundamental ACL concepts, including the basic concepts behind IP ACL configuration. The second half covers the more detailed information about ACL configuration, including standard and extended ACLs and named ACLs.

Access Control List Fundamentals

Like most topics in the second half of this book, in *Switching Basics and Intermediate Routing CCNA 3*, and in *WAN Technologies CCNA 4 Companion Guide*, to understand ACLs, you need to understand some concepts and then understand the configuration. This first section of the chapter introduces the basic principles of both, beginning with the concepts.

ACL Concepts

IP *Access Control Lists (ACLs)* filter packets as they pass through a router. Engineers configure an ACL, including some basic information about which packets to filter (discard), and which packets to allow to keep going through the router. For example, Figure 11-1 shows the results of an ACL on router R1. R1 uses the following ACL logic:

- Look at packets that come in R1's FA0/0 LAN interface.

- Discard packets whose source IP address is 172.16.1.1.

- Allow all other packets to keep going.

In effect, the ACL logic shown in Figure 11-1 uses basic programming logic. Most programming languages allow simple "if-then-else" logic, which is exactly what the router does with the ACL in this case. Using the if-then-else programming terminology, the ACL logic can be summarized as follows: "If the packet is from IP address 172.16.1.1, then discard the packet; else, let the packet keep going."

Figure 11-1   General ACL Logic: Filtering Incoming Packets from 172.16.1.1

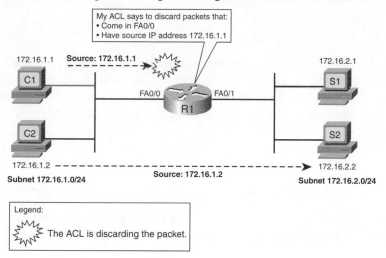

This section covers all the concepts related to how ACLs work. It begins with some discussion of the typical ways engineers use ACLs. Then it examines where ACLs may be used and how a router filters packets either before or after the routing (forwarding) decision. The end of the section examines how routers match packets when processing an ACL, both by looking at several parts of a packet header and by examining multiple lines in a single ACL.

Typical Usage of ACLs

Many people new to networking wonder if filtering packets with ACLs is worth the effort. In practice, the answer is generally yes. Yes, IT departments should protect host computers by requiring logons, with secure passwords. However, most security experts today say that security needs to exist at multiple locations in any network. A simple example can help drive this point home. Imagine that servers S1 and S2 in Figure 11-1 store the payroll records for a company. Without ACLs, any network user could send packets to and from the servers, possibly getting a username and password prompt. At that point, the user could attempt to guess a username and password combination that allows access to the data on the server. ACLs can prevent packets from getting from the users' PCs to the servers, so the malicious user never gets a chance to guess the username and password.

ACLs can be used for a variety of functions inside a router. This chapter focuses on how to use ACLs to provide better security, including the following examples:

- Discard video and audio packets coming from the Internet if the company thinks such traffic is likely to be for personal use instead of business use.

- Allow the IP addresses of people in the payroll department to communicate with the payroll servers, but disallow other hosts from reaching those same servers, helping to protect sensitive payroll information.

- Disallow certain types of e-mail traffic, to reduce spam e-mail.

- Control which areas of the network can be reached from Ethernet ports in the public areas of the building, such as the lobby.

ACLs can be used for many other purposes besides filtering packets. For example, ACLs can be used to filter the contents of routing updates, allowing the routing updates to pass but removing some routes. This allows the network engineer to prevent some parts of the network from even reaching some other subnets. ACLs can also be used to match packets to perform quality of service (QoS) features—for example, to ensure that voice traffic gets good performance to support the ability to send voice traffic over the Internet.

One ACL per Protocol, per Interface, and per Direction

The simple example in Figure 11-1 shows how a router can filter IP packets as they enter one of the router's interfaces. More generally, a single Cisco IOS ACL can filter with the following general rules:

- Filter packets of particular Layer 3 routable protocols (IP, IPX, AppleTalk, and others).

- The filtering logic, as defined in the ACL, is applied to an interface.

- The ACL filters packets that either enter a router's interface (inbound filtering) or exit a router's interface (outbound filtering).

Note

An IP ACL filters only IP packets; likewise, IPX ACLs filter only IPX packets.

Figure 11-2 puts all three points into the context of a single router. In the figure, a single router has two interfaces: one on the left and one on the right. The router has been configured to route three routable protocols—IP, IPX, and AppleTalk. In this case, the router could be configured to enable 12 different ACLs: one for each protocol, for each interface, and for each direction of packet flow.

Figure 11-2   Multiple ACLs per Interface, per Direction

Although this router could have 12 ACLs enabled, you would seldom want to enable an ACL in every case imaginable. For example, back in Figure 11-1, the engineer wants to prevent 172.16.1.1 from sending packets to the subnet where the servers sit on the right. The router could have filtered the packets as they entered the interface on the left or as they exited the router on the right. It would be unnecessary to enable both ACLs.

ACLs happen to be one of the most frequently used IOS tools. The rest of this chapter focuses on IP ACLs, ignoring the other Layer 3 protocols' ACLs for the most part. Specifically, this chapter focuses on the use of IP ACLs to filter packets.

Filtering IP Packets as They Enter and Exit a Router

Cisco IOS software can apply ACL logic to packets as they enter or exit an interface. To appreciate this concept, consider Figure 11-3, which is a more detailed look at the same example in Figure 11-1. The figure shows a bit of the internal logic used on router R1. The R1 router icon has been replaced by a large rectangle to provide room to show R1's internal logic.

Figure 11-3   Using an Inbound ACL

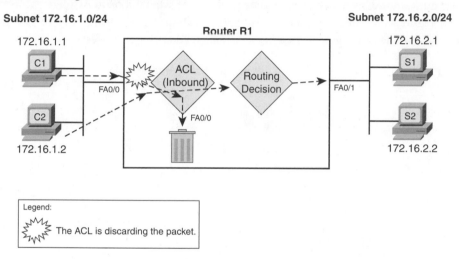

Without ACLs, when a router receives a packet on an interface, the router quickly makes a routing decision, moves the packet to the outgoing interface, and sends the packet out the interface. For instance, for packets sent by 172.16.1.1 (C1) to 172.16.2.1 (S1), the packet would enter R1's FA0/0 interface, R1 would make a routing decision to forward the packet out its FA0/1 interface, and the packet would exit the router.

With an *inbound ACL* enabled on R1, the router applies the logic in the ACL—in this case, to delete all packets whose source IP address is 172.16.1.1—right after receiving the packet on interface FA0/0. Using ACL terminology, this ACL would be considered an *inbound IP ACL on interface FA0/0*, because the router applies the ACL for IP packets that enter interface FA0/0. In fact, because this logic happens before the routing decision, if the router happens to discard the packet, the router does not even have to make a forwarding decision for the packet.

If you're still a little unclear about this, an analogy or two may help. Think of yourself as standing in the center of a router. You can watch packets enter and exit the router. While watching the packets, you can get rid of the packets by stepping on them, and you can step on the packets either as they enter an interface or as they try to exit an interface. Squashing them as they enter the router is analogous to an inbound ACL, and squashing them as they exit a router is analogous to an outbound ACL.

Before creating the ACL, the engineer should write down the requirements for what an ACL should filter. For the example in Figure 11-3, which shows how an inbound ACL filters some packets, the following would be a typical written definition of the requirements for that ACL:

> Prevent packets sent by C1 from getting to all hosts in subnet 172.16.2.0/24, and allow all other packets to continue to be routed as normal.

While the inbound ACL shown in Figures 11-1 and 11-3 accomplished this goal, engineers can also use outbound ACLs to achieve the same goal. To see why outbound ACLs might be useful, consider Figure 11-4, which expands the example shown in Figure 11-3. In Figure 11-4, the *inbound* ACL on R1's FA0/0 interface has some unintended consequences.

Figure 11-4   Problem: Inbound ACL Filters Too Many Packets

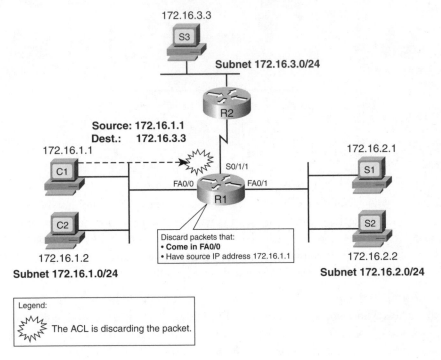

The ACL on R1 filters packets that it should filter, plus packets that it should not filter. In this example, R1 still has its inbound ACL enabled on its FA0/0 (left side) LAN interface. The ACL logic only checks the packet's source IP address. So, when C1 sends a packet to server S3, which is at the top of Figure 11-4, the packet enters R1's FA0/0 interface. R1 applies its ACL logic to the packet, sees the source address of 172.16.1.1, and discards the packet. However, ACL requirements state that only packets from C1, going toward subnet 172.16.2.0/24, should be discarded. As a result, the packet in Figure 11-4, destined for subnet 172.16.3.0/24, should really be allowed to go on its way out the serial link to S3.

Using an outbound ACL provides one solution to this particular problem, as shown in Figure 11-5. In this case, the same ACL logic could be used, but applied to packets going out R1's FA0/1 (right side) LAN interface. The inbound ACL on R1's FA0/0 interface would then be removed. Now, when a packet sent by C1 toward S3 enters R1's FA0/0 interface, there is no inbound ACL, so the packet is not discarded. However, when C1 sends a packet to S2, R1 tries to forward the packet out R1's FA0/1 interface, but R1 checks its outbound ACL logic before allowing the packet to leave the FA0/1 interface. Using the same ACL matching logic, the outbound ACL on R1 notes the source IP address of 172.16.1.1 in the packet header and discards the packet.

Figure 11-5   Solution: Filtering Using Outbound ACLs

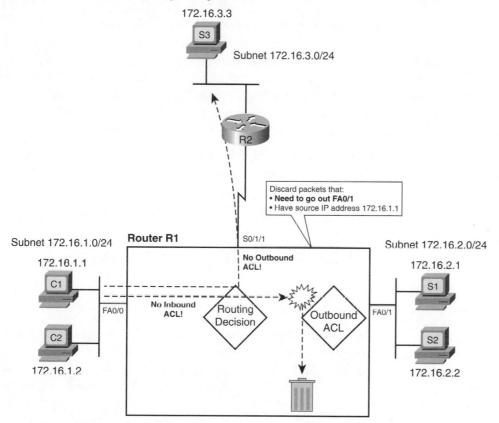

Matching More Header Fields Using Extended IP ACLs

So far, all the figures in this chapter have shown an ACL making its filtering decision based on the packet's source IP address. Cisco IOS software supports two general types of IP ACLs based on what the ACLs can match. *Standard IP ACLs* can examine only a packet's source IP address. Essentially, the figures so far in this chapter have described the matching logic of standard IP ACLs.

Extended IP ACLs differ from standard IP ACLs in one important way: they can look at several fields, with the most popular items listed here:

- The source IP address

- The destination IP address

- The type of transport layer protocol (for example, TCP)

- The source UDP or TCP port

- The destination UDP or TCP port

An extended IP ACL can refer to these fields in a variety of ways. For example, it can just check the source IP address, as in the examples earlier in this chapter. Or, it can check multiple fields, requiring that all must be matched to match and then discard a packet; for example, an ACL could check both the source and destination IP addresses of the same packet. Additionally, the ACL can be used to match just part of a field. For example, an ACL can create logic such as "all addresses whose destination IP address begins with 172.16.2," which allows ACLs to easily match all packets whose source or destination address is in a particular subnet.

In fact, an extended IP ACL can check both the IP header and the TCP (or UDP) header in the same ACL statement. Thus, a single ACL statement could check the source and destination IP addresses and the source and destination TCP port numbers. For example, an engineer could configure an ACL to discard packets that meet *all* of the following requirements:

- Source IP address of 172.16.1.1

- Destination in subnet 172.16.2.0/24 (addresses between 172.16.2.0 and 172.16.2.255)

- Uses the TCP transport layer protocol

- Going to a Telnet server, well-known port 23

With the ability to check for so many things in a packet's headers, the unintended consequence shown in Figure 11-4 can be avoided. (The problem in Figure 11-4 was that the router discarded packets going from C1 to S3.) The solution to this problem, shown in Figure 11-5, is to use an outbound ACL. Next, Figure 11-6 shows an alternate solution with an inbound ACL on router R1's FA0/0 interface. This extended ACL checks a large number of header fields; with the more detailed comparisons in this figure, the packet meant for server S3 makes it through the inbound ACL.

R1 uses an inbound IP ACL on its FA0/0 interface, so it will at least consider discarding both packets shown in Figure 11-6. When the router checks the packet sent by C1 going to S2 (172.16.2.2), the packet meets all four criteria, so R1 discards the packet. However, when the router looks at the packet going from C1 to S3, the destination IP address (172.16.3.3) does not start with 172.16.2, so this packet does match the criteria. As a result, R1 allows this packet through the router and out the serial link.

Figure 11-6 Examining Multiple Fields when Making a Filtering Decision

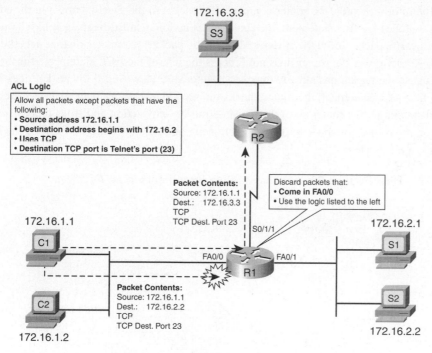

172.16.3.3

ACL Logic

Allow all packets except packets that have the following:
- **Source address 172.16.1.1**
- **Destination address begins with 172.16.2**
- **Uses TCP**
- **Destination TCP port is Telnet's port (23)**

Packet Contents:
Source: 172.16.1.1
Dest.: 172.16.3.3
TCP
TCP Dest. Port 23

Discard packets that:
- **Come in FA0/0**
- Use the logic listed to the left

172.16.1.1

172.16.2.1

S0/1/1

FA0/0   FA0/1

R1

Packet Contents:
Source: 172.16.1.1
Dest.: 172.16.2.2
TCP
TCP Dest. Port 23

172.16.1.2

172.16.2.2

A Single ACL with Multiple Lines

So far in this chapter, the discussion has focused on the most basic ACL concepts. However, ACLs provide programming-like logic with much more complex processing than has been shown so far. This section explains the next step in the complexity of ACLs—namely, the logic that ACLs can create by using multiple lines in a single ACL.

A single Cisco IOS ACL can contain multiple lines—hence the word "list" in the term Access Control List. The **access-list** global configuration command creates each line in an ACL. Each **access-list** command lists a set of criteria for matching the packet, as already described in this chapter. By creating an ACL with multiple statements in it, you can create a sequence of matching logic, something like "If a packet meets these criteria, discard it; if not, if the packet meets a second set of criteria, allow it to keep going; if not, if the packet meets this third set of criteria, discard it;" and so on.

A single **access-list** command contains two main features: the *matching-criteria* and an action to take for packets that match the criteria. The action is configured using one of the following two keywords:

- **permit**—Allow the packet to keep going.
- **deny**—Discard the packet.

When comparing packets to a multiline ACL, the router processes the access list statements sequentially. In other words, the router compares the packet to the first statement in the ACL; if the packet matches the first statement, the router takes action against that packet based on the **permit** (allow the packet through) or **deny** (discard the packet) parameter on that **access-list** command. At that point, the router does not process the rest of the ACL statements for that packet, because the packet has already matched a statement. However, if the packet does not match the first ACL statement, the router checks the second statement. If the packet matches the second statement, the router takes the listed permit or deny action and stops processing the ACL. If not, the router continues to the next statement, and so on. Figure 11-7 shows the idea in the form of a flowchart.

Figure 11-7   How Routers Process the Multiple Statements in an ACL

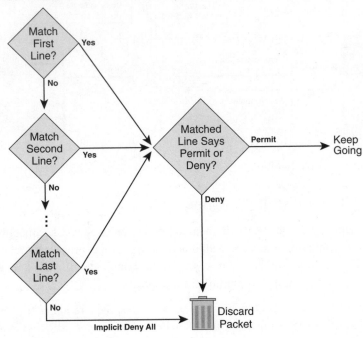

Note

Due to the default action to deny all other packets, each ACL should have at least one explicitly configured **access-list** command that permits some packets; otherwise, the ACL would deny all packets.

Figure 11-7 introduces one additional bit of ACL logic—the *implicit deny all* logic at the end of the ACL. The router discards packets that do not match the criteria in an explicitly configured **access-list** command. You can think of this default action as if a hidden (implicit) **access-list** command exists at the end of every ACL: a command that matches all packets and uses a deny action. All Cisco ACLs use this default implicit deny all behavior.

This completes the explanation of the core concepts behind IP ACLs. The rest of the chapter examines the various access list configuration options more closely.

ACL Configuration Basics

To configure and use an IP ACL on a Cisco router, you need to take a couple of steps:

Step 1 Configure the ACL by using **access-list** global configuration commands.

Step 2 Enable the ACL by doing the following:

    a. Pick the interface by using the **interface** *type number* configuration command.

    b. Enable the ACL and choose the direction by using the **ip access-group** *list-number* {**in|out**} interface subcommand.

The next two sections tackle these two main steps in order.

Configuring the **access-list** Command

Each IP **access-list** command follows the same general structure as the following:

```
access-list number action matching-criteria
```

So far, this chapter has already explained the concepts behind the *action* and *matching-criteria* parts of the **access-list** command. The *action* will be either **permit** or **deny**, with **permit** allowing the packet through, and **deny** discarding the packet. The *matching-criteria* lists the values of different header fields. In effect, these last two major parts of the **access-list** command (*action* and *matching-criteria*) define logic as follows:

    If the packet matches the *matching-criteria*, take the listed deny or permit action.

The matching criteria may be as simple as matching a single host IP address (as in upcoming Example 11-1), or it may include complex matching of multiple items in the packet headers. The section "Access Control List Configuration," later in this chapter, covers the details of how to configure both standard and extended IP ACLs, including how to configure the many matching criteria.

The first of the three parts of an **access-list** command, the ACL's number, tells IOS which **access-list** statements together form a single ACL. For example, to configure the standard ACL described conceptually with Figures 11-1 and 11-3, you need two **access-list** commands, one for each of the following requirements:

- Discard all packets whose source IP address is 172.16.1.1.

- Allow all other packets.

Example 11-1 shows the configuration of the ACL, using access list number 1.

Example 11-1 Configuring Standard IP ACL 1

```
R1#configure terminal
R1(config)#access-list 1 deny host 172.16.1.1
R1(config)#access-list 1 permit any
R1(config)#^Z
R1#
```

In this case, IOS considers both of the **access-list** commands to be a part of the same ACL because both commands use the same ACL number (1). If the engineer needed to create another ACL in the same router, the engineer would need to add access list statements with another number.

The ACL numbers must fit within a particular range of values, depending on the type of ACL being created. IOS supports ACLs for every routable Layer 3 protocol, and IOS uses different ACL number ranges for each different Layer 3 protocol. For example, ACL number 1 sits within a range of numbers reserved for IP ACLs, but to configure an ACL to filter IPX packets, you would have to use a number between 800 and 899 (inclusive).

Additionally, IOS uses different number ranges for standard and extended IP ACLs. Table 11-1 lists a reference of some of the ACL number ranges.

Note

Cisco IOS software originally supported standard ACL numbers 1–99 and extended ACL numbers 100–199; Cisco later added to the ranges as shown in Table 11-1 to support larger numbers of ACLs.

Table 11-1 Numbers Used by Numbered ACLs, per Protocol

Protocol/Type	Number Range
IP Standard	1–99, 1300–1999
IP Extended	100–199, 2000–2699
AppleTalk Standard	600–699
IPX Standard	800–899
IPX Extended	900–999
IPX SAP	1000–1999

Enabling and Disabling IP ACLs per Interface and per Direction

A router does not use an ACL until the ACL has been enabled on an interface, for a particular direction. To enable an ACL on an interface, the engineer must add the following command under the correct interface:

```
ip access-group list-number {in | out}
```

Example 11-2 continues the configuration shown in Example 11-1, with the same criteria. This example repeats the configuration for ACL 1, and also shows how to enable ACL 1 for packets entering R1's FA0/0 interface.

Example 11-2   Configuring and Enabling Standard IP ACL 1

```
R1#configure terminal
R1(config)#access-list 1 deny host 172.16.1.1
R1(config)#access-list 1 permit any
R1(config)#interface fa0/0
R1(config-if)#ip access-group 1 in
R1(config-if)#^Z
R1#
```

The **ip access-group 1 in** command enables ACL 1. This command enables the ACL on interface FA0/0 because of the **interface fa0/0** command that precedes it. The command also references ACL number 1, telling IOS to use the logic defined in ACL 1 on this interface. Finally, by using the **in** parameter, this command tells IOS to process packets coming into the interface.

After it is enabled as shown in the example, the router examines all IP packets entering the interface and filters them appropriately. To disable that ACL, the **access-list** commands do not need to be deleted. Instead, just use the **no ip access-group** *group-number* {**in**|**out**} interface subcommand. In Example 11-2, the **no ip access-group 1 in** command, used from interface FA0/0 configuration mode, would disable the ACL.

Packet Tracer   If you load Packet Tracer configuration file NA02-1101, you will see a network whose IP addresses and topology match Figure 11-1. In topology mode, you can configure the commands shown in Example 11-2. You can then use real-time mode to test the ACL by using PC1 to ping S1 (with the ping failing) and using PC2 to ping S2 (with the ping succeeding).

Configuration Considerations

So far, this chapter's coverage of ACL configuration has focused on the most basic and straightforward parts of ACL configuration. However, ACL configuration includes several small but important details that may seem picky at first but actually do matter when configuring ACLs on routers in production networks. This section covers some of these small but important items.

Enabling One IP ACL per Interface and per Direction

Cisco IOS software supports one ACL, per interface, per direction, and per Layer 3 protocol. Even if you focus only on IP ACLs, a single router with two interfaces could have four ACLs enabled. Example 11-3 shows commands that enable four different ACLs on a router with two Fast Ethernet interfaces, just to show an example of the configuration.

Note

The **access-list** commands used to create ACLs 1, 2, 3, and 4 are omitted in Example 11-3 because their details do not matter for this particular explanation.

Example 11-3   Router R1: Two Interfaces and Four Enabled ACLs

```
R1#show running-config
! lines removed for brevity
interface fa0/0
 ip access-group 1 in
 ip access-group 2 out
!
interface fa0/1
 ip access-group 3 in
 ip access-group 4 out
```

Typically, a router does not need both an inbound and outbound IP ACL on every interface, but Example 11-3 shows the configuration just for reference.

Additionally, IOS does not allow multiple IP ACLs on the same interface for the same direction. For example, if you wanted to add more filtering logic for packets entering R1's FA0/0 interface, you have two basic options:

- Change ACL 1.

- Create a new ACL, disable ACL 1 on FA0/0, and enable the new ACL for packets entering FA0/0.

In particular, you cannot enable multiple IP ACLs on the same interface for the same direction of packet flow. For example, you could not create ACL 5, then configure the **ip access-group 5 in** command under interface FA0/0, and expect IOS to *add* ACL 5's filtering logic to ACL 1's logic. In fact, if you entered the **interface fa0/0** command in configuration mode on R1, followed by the **ip access-group 5 in** command, the router would replace the **ip access-group 1 in** command on the interface. (Even if IOS allowed you to add multiple IP ACLs to an interface for the same direction, all packets would match the implied deny all at the end of the first ACL and would never be processed by the second ACL.)

The Challenge of Changing IP ACL Configuration

When you do need to change the logic of a given ACL—for instance, if you wanted to match and discard additional packets entering R1's FA0/0 interface—you can change the ACL. However, changing the ACL requires attention to a few surprising facts about what IOS does when you try to change an ACL:

Note

This list applies to numbered IP ACLs, but not to named IP ACLs; named IP ACLs will be explained in the section "Named IP ACLs" later in this chapter.

- Cisco IOS software compares a packet to the ACL in the same order as the **access-list** commands in the configuration file.

- You cannot change the order of the statements in an ACL.

- You cannot insert a new **access-list** command into the middle of an ACL.

- When you configure a new **access-list** *list-number* command, the router puts the new command on the end of the ACL.

- The only way to reorder or insert a new **access-list** command into the ACL is to delete the entire ACL and then reconfigure the revised ACL in the correct order.

Essentially, most changes to ACLs require you to delete the ACL and reconfigure the ACL. As a result, most people edit ACLs using a text editor, delete the ACL in configuration mode, and then copy and paste the configuration back into the router.

Before editing an ACL, particularly before deleting an entire ACL, you should first disable the ACL by using the **no ip access-group** *list-number* interface subcommand. There are two main reasons to disable the ACL before changing or deleting it:

- Cisco makes a general suggestion that disabling the ACL before changing it is a good idea.

- In some Cisco IOS software releases, when you delete an ACL that is still referenced by an **ip access-group** *list-number* interface subcommand, IOS acts as if the ACL exists—but with the ACL only using the default action to discard all packets. Essentially, IOS treats the empty ACL as if it contains only the implicit deny all.

By carefully disabling an ACL before changing it, you can avoid cases in which you unintentionally discard packets while changing the ACL.

Caution

If you attempt to delete a single line of an ACL, IOS still deletes the whole ACL. For example, a **no access-list 1 deny host 172.16.1.1** command on R1 in Example 11-2 does not delete that single **access-list** command; it deletes all of ACL 1.

ACL Design Recommendations

Cisco makes a couple of ACL design recommendations that have stayed constant over the years. The first recommendation relates to how to order the statements in an ACL. Cisco suggests that you put more specific statements first and more general statements last. For example, if you want to match packets from host 172.16.1.1 to deny the packets, and match packets from all other hosts in subnet 172.16.1.0/24 to permit the packets, put the more specific statement matching 172.16.1.1 first, and the more general statement matching all hosts in the subnet next. If you put the more general matching criteria first, you may not get the results you want. For example, if an ACL matches all packets from all hosts in subnet 172.16.1.0/24 first, and then tries to match packets from host 172.16.1.1, the ACL will never match the second **access-list** statement, because all the packets from 172.16.1.1 will match the first **access-list** statement.

The other frequent recommendation from Cisco relates to where to locate an ACL in an internetwork. For standard ACLs, Cisco suggests that you locate the ACL as close as possible to the destination host. For extended ACLs, you should locate the ACL as close as possible to the source host. The section "Locating ACLs" later in this chapter discusses some of the reasoning behind this choice.

Additional ACL Configuration Details

This section mentions a few other small points about ACL configuration before the next section moves on to discuss wildcard masks.

First, an outbound ACL on a router does not filter packets created on that same router. For example, imagine that router R1 has an outbound ACL on its interface FA0/1, and the ACL filters all ICMP packets. Then, the engineer uses the **ping 172.16.2.2** command on R1, causing the router to try to send ICMP echo requests out its FA0/1 interface. Because those packets were created by R1, R1 bypasses its own outbound ACL logic for those packets and does not discard the packets.

Finally, whenever a router ACL discards a packet, the router generates an ICMP unreachable message and sends it back to the originating host.

Matching a Range of IP Addresses Using a Wildcard Mask

Both standard and extended IP ACLs allow the user to specify a specific IP address or range of IP addresses. If the packet's address is within the configured range, the packet matches that particular matching criteria. For example, an ACL can check for all source IP addresses that begin with 172.16.2, meaning addresses 172.16.2.0 through 172.16.2.255.

Note

The wildcard mask is not a subnet mask. It is simply a tool used by ACLs to define which parts of the IP address must match for the ACL statement to consider the packet to match the ACL.

The ACL *wildcard mask* defines which part of the packet's address needs to match the address listed in the ACL and which part does not have to match. For example, the following **access-list** command matches source IP addresses that begin with 172.16.2:

```
access-list 1 permit  172.16.2.0  0.0.0.255
```

In this case, the wildcard mask value is 0.0.0.255. The logic defined by this mask is as follows:

Compare the first three octets of 172.16.2.0 to the packet's source IP address; if those three octets match, the packet matches this ACL.

The wildcard mask also tells IOS to ignore the last octet when making the comparison.

Similarly, the next two ACL commands use wildcard masks that tell IOS to look at only the first two octets for ACL 2 and only the first octet for ACL 3:

- **access-list 2 permit 172.16.0.0 0.0.255.255**

- **access-list 3 permit 172.0.0.0 0.255.255.255**

In this case, ACL 2 would match all packets whose source IP address begins with 172.16, and ACL 3 would match all packets whose source IP address begins with 172.

Wildcard Mask: Formal Definition

You may already intuitively know how a wildcard mask works, just from the three example wildcard masks described in the preceding section. Thinking in decimal for a moment, when the wildcard mask's octet is 0, the mask tells IOS that the corresponding octet must be considered when comparing the numbers. Conversely, a wildcard mask octet with a decimal value of 255 means that the corresponding octet can be ignored when making the comparison. This logic does indeed define the logic of wildcard masks that have only 0s and 255s in them.

More specifically, wildcard masks define whether IOS should compare each individual bit position of the two addresses being compared. To do so, the wildcard mask lists a binary 0 in each bit position that must be compared by IOS, and a binary 1 in all bit positions for which IOS does not need to look at the bits to check whether they match. So, a wildcard mask is a dotted-decimal number whose bit values mean the following:

- **Bit value 0**—The corresponding bit positions in the two addresses must be the same value.

- **Bit value 1**—The corresponding bit positions in the two addresses can be anything and do not need to be compared.

For example, imagine a packet whose source IP address is 172.16.1.1. This packet would not match the **access-list 2 permit 172.16.2.0 0.0.0.255** command. The wildcard mask of 0.0.0.255 means that the router must compare the first 24 bits (three octets) of the packet's address (172.16.1.1) with the configured address (172.16.2.0). Because the third octet differs, the packet does not match this ACL. Figure 11-8 shows a graphical view of this same logic.

Figure 11-8   Wildcard Mask Logic for Mask 0.0.0.255

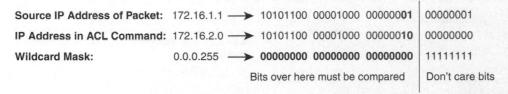

Figure 11-8 shows how the wildcard mask has 24 binary 0s, followed by 8 binary 1s. The vertical line separates the two IP addresses; IOS only looks at the bits to the left of the line, in this case, when deciding if the packet matches this particular **access-list** command.

Next, let's repeat the same example but with a different mask. The packet's source IP address is again 172.16.1.1, but the **access-list** command now uses the **access-list 2 permit 172.16.0.0 0.0.255.255** command. In this case, the packet matches the **access-list** command, because the wildcard mask means "compare the first two octets, and I don't care about the last two octets." Figure 11-9 shows a graphical view of this same logic.

Note

Many people refer to the binary 1s in a wildcard mask as "don't care" bits, because the router does not care whether the corresponding bits in the two addresses match.

Figure 11-9 Wildcard Mask Logic for Mask 0.0.255.255

Source IP Address of Packet:	172.16.1.1	→	10101100 00001000	00000001 00000001
IP Address in ACL Command:	172.16.0.0	→	10101100 00001000	00000000 00000000
Wildcard Mask:	0.0.255.255	→	**00000000 00000000**	11111111 11111111
			Bits over here must be compared	Don't care bits

Complex Wildcard Masks

The examples so far have used the simplest values for wildcard masks. However, wildcard masks represent 32-bit binary numbers. Depending on what you want to accomplish, the wildcard mask may have an octet with some binary 0s and some binary 1s, which makes the decimal value of the wildcard mask look a little funny. For example, imagine that you want to match all IP packets whose source IP addresses fall into the following range:

172.16.32.0–172.16.47.255

As it turns out, the command **access-list 4 permit 172.16.32.0 0.0.15.255** would match the packets. To understand why, first consider Figure 11-10, which shows a visual representation of how a packet from IP address 172.16.40.1, which sits inside the range of source addresses matched by this ACL statement, would be analyzed by the ACL.

Figure 11-10 Wildcard Mask Logic for Mask 0.0.15.255

Source IP Address of Packet:	172.16.40.1	→	10101100 00001000 0001	1000 00000001
IP Address in ACL Command:	172.16.32.0	→	10101100 00001000 0001	0000 00000000
Wildcard Mask:	0.0.15.255	→	**00000000 00000000 0000**	1111 11111111
			Bits over here must be compared	Don't care bits

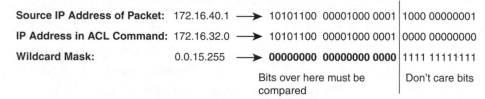

The wildcard mask begins with 20 bits of value 0 and ends with 12 binary 1s (don't care bits). So, as long as the first 20 bits of the source IP address match the first 20 bits of the number 172.16.32.0, the packet's source IP address matches the ACL. As you can see from Figure 11-10, 172.16.40.1's first 20 bits do indeed match.

Although Figure 11-10 may be proof that packets sourced from 172.16.40.1 would be matched by the command **access-list 4 permit 172.16.32.0 0.0.15.255**, the figure does not really show why this command would match the range from 172.16.32.0 through 172.16.47.255. One way to prove that the ACL matches all packets in this range is to write down all the IP addresses in this range, in binary, and compare the first 20 bits to the binary version of 172.16.32.0.

Rather than take all that time, you can look at the first and last address in the range, and if the first and last addresses would match the ACL, those two addresses, and all addresses in between, would match the ACL. In this case, consider the IP addresses of the extreme ends of the range of addresses—172.16.32.0 and 172.16.47.255:

- **172.16.32.0—10101100 00010000 0010**0000 00000000

- **172.16.47.255—10101100 00010000 0010**1111 11111111

The ACL with a wildcard mask of 0.0.15.255 will examine only the first 20 bits of these numbers. You can see that their first 20 bits match. So, the two numbers on the outer edges of the range of IP addresses will match the ACL statement, and all packets in between will also match the ACL statement.

The **any** and **host** Keywords

You can use wildcard masks to tell an ACL to match a specific host address and to match any and all IP addresses. To do so, you would use the masks shown in Table 11-2.

Table 11-2   Matching a Specific Host or Matching Any Host

Goal	Wildcard Mask	Special Keyword
Match a specific host's IP address	0.0.0.0	**host**
Match any and all IP addresses	255.255.255.255	**any**

First, think about the wildcard masks shown in Table 11-2 for a moment. A wildcard mask of 0.0.0.0 tells IOS to compare all four octets, so all parts of the IP addresses must match. A wildcard mask of 255.255.255.255 tells IOS to not bother checking any of the octets—so in this case, the router just assumes the IP addresses match. (This wildcard mask would be useful when using an extended ACL, and either the source or destination IP address does not matter for matching packets.)

You can use the wildcard masks shown in Table 11-2, but IOS prefers the use of special keywords in these two special cases. In fact, if you configure an ACL using either of these wildcard masks, IOS changes the configuration commands to use the keywords listed in the last column of Table 11-2. The two special keywords are **host** and **any**. The **host** keyword, followed by an IP address, tells IOS to match that specific host IP address. The **any** keyword (without an IP address listed) tells IOS to match any and all IP addresses. Example 11-1 and Example 11-2 earlier in this chapter show examples of each of these special keywords.

Finding the Right Wildcard Mask to Match a Subnet

In real life and on some popular Cisco exams, you may want to use an ACL to match all hosts in a single subnet. To do so, you need to figure out what wildcard mask to use. The following short process shows how to quickly find the right wildcard mask:

Step 1   List the subnet mask in dotted-decimal form.

Step 2   Subtract the subnet mask from 255.255.255.255.

For example, consider subnet 172.16.2.0/24. This subnet has a numeric range of 172.16.2.0–172.16.2.255, with the first number being the subnet number and the last being the subnet broadcast address. Intuitively, you may be thinking that this subnet contains all addresses that begin with 172.16.2, which is correct. You also know that wildcard mask 0.0.0.255 can be used to tell the router to just look at the first three octets, so you may already be thinking that wildcard mask 0.0.0.255 is the right answer, and it is. However, using the steps shown here, you would first convert the mask, shown as /24 in prefix notation, to its dotted-decimal equivalent of 255.255.255.0. Then, step 2 subtracts the subnet mask from 255.255.255.255, as shown here:

```
 255.255.255.255
–255.255.255.0
 ─────────────
  0 . 0 . 0 .255
```

So, to match packets whose source IP addresses are in this subnet, you could use the **access-list 5 permit 172.16.2.0 0.0.0.255** command.

This two-step process works very nicely when the subnet mask does not have all 0s and 255s. For example, consider subnet 172.16.32.0/20. This subnet has a range of addresses of 172.16.32.0–172.16.47.255, and the example in the previous section showed how the wildcard mask of 0.0.15.255 could be used to match this range of addresses. However, if a question on an exam instructs you to do something like "Devise an **access-list** command to match all packets whose source IP address is in subnet 172.16.32.0/20," you can use the following short steps to find the right wildcard mask:

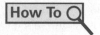

Step 1   Convert /20 to dotted-decimal form: 255.255.240.0.

Step 2   Subtract that number from 255.255.255.255.

For example, at Step 2:

```
 255.255.255.255
–255.255.240.0
 ─────────────
  0 . 0 . 15.255
```

So, to match packets whose source IP addresses are in this subnet, you could use the **access-list 6 permit 172.16.32.0 0.0.15.255** command.

Verifying ACLs

To configure ACLs, you must create them with global configuration commands and then enable them on the desired interfaces. To verify proper configuration of ACLs, you need to also check those same two steps. Table 11-3 lists the three most useful commands for verifying IP ACL configuration. The table also lists whether the command helps verify the ACL configuration and whether the ACL has been enabled.

Table 11-3   Popular **show** Commands to View ACL Details

Command	Shows ACL Configuration	Verifies Interfaces on Which ACLs Are Enabled, and Direction
show running-config	Yes	Yes
show ip interface	No	Yes
show access-lists	Yes	No

The **show running-config** command simply lists the **access-list** commands and the **ip access-group** command on the interfaces. Example 11-4 shows example output from the other two commands.

Example 11-4   The **show ip interface** and **show access-lists** Commands

```
R1#show access-lists
Standard IP access list 1
    10 deny   172.16.1.1 (3 matches)
    20 permit any
Extended IP access list 101
    10 permit tcp 172.16.4.0 0.0.0.255 any
    20 deny tcp any any
    30 permit ip any any
R1#show ip interface fa0/0
FastEthernet0/0 is up, line protocol is up
  Internet address is 172.16.1.251/24
  Broadcast address is 255.255.255.255
  Address determined by non-volatile memory
  MTU is 1500 bytes
  Helper address is not set
  Directed broadcast forwarding is disabled
  Multicast reserved groups joined: 224.0.0.9
  Outgoing access list is not set
  Inbound  access list is 1
! the rest of the output lines were omitted because they do not relate to ACLs.
```

Note

The **show ip access-lists** command displays the same information as the **show access-lists** command, but only for IP ACLs.

Example 11-4 shows a couple of particularly important items. First, note that the **show access-lists** command lists a counter of the number of times a line in the ACL has been matched. In this same command, note that the exact syntax of the **access-list** global configuration command is not listed, but the output does list the details that would be found in each **acccss-list** command. Finally, at the end of the example, note that the **show ip interface fa0/0** command lists whether an inbound or outbound ACL has been enabled and, if so, which ACL.

Access Control List Configuration

This section focuses primarily on the configuration details for ACLs. This section examines the syntax of the standard and extended **access-list** commands and describes how to configure numbered and named IP ACLs. This section ends with a few comments about choosing a location for your ACLs.

IP ACLs differ as to whether the configuration uses numbers or names and how many parts of the packet header can be examined when matching packets. When a single ACL's configuration commands refer to a number, the ACL is called a *numbered ACL*. As you might imagine, if a single ACL's configuration commands refer to a name instead of a number, the ACLs are called *named ACLs*. Additionally, IOS supports a basic type of ACL, called a standard ACL, that can examine only the source IP address of a packet. The more-powerful extended ACLs can examine many parts of an IP header, TCP and UDP header, and other items as well. As a result, IOS supports four general types of IP ACLs:

- **Numbered standard IP ACLs**—Configured using numbers, and can only match packets based on the source IP address

- **Numbered extended IP ACLs**—Configured using numbers, and can match based on more than the source IP address

- **Named standard IP ACLs**—Configured using names, and can only match packets based on the source IP address

- **Named extended IP ACLs**—Configured using names, and can match based on more than the source IP address

This section begins with coverage of numbered standard ACLs, followed by numbered extended ACLs. Following that, the text explains named ACL configuration.

Configuring Numbered Standard ACLs

Before looking at a numbered ACL configuration, a quick review of some of the details of how ACLs work may be helpful. First, a router may use an ACL for packets as they enter an interface (inbound ACLs) and for packets as they exit an interface (outbound ACLs). Figure 11-11 shows just such an example, with a packet moving left to right through a router. The router happens to apply an ACL for inbound packets on the left, and for outbound packets on the right.

Figure 11-11 Locations for Inbound and Outbound ACLs

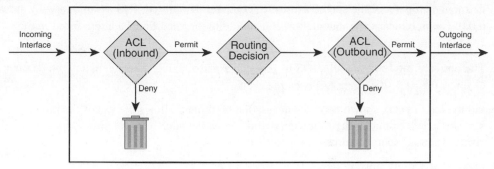

Both the inbound and outbound ACLs could decide to discard a particular packet. When processing both the inbound and outbound ACLs, the router uses the following overall logic:

- The router compares the packet to the criteria in the ACL statements, one at a time, in the order listed in the ACL.

- The router uses first-match logic. In other words, when the router finds the first statement in the ACL whose criteria match the packet, the router quits using the ACL and takes the action (permit or deny) listed in the matched ACL statement.

- If the packet does not match any of the configured statements in the ACL, the router assumes that an implicit deny all statement exists at the end of the ACL, so the router discards the packet.

Syntax Details for Configuring Numbered Standard IP ACLs

The following shows the syntax of the **access-list** command used to configure numbered standard IP ACLs:

```
access-list number {permit¦deny} source-address source-mask [log]
```

Thankfully, the syntax of the command is pretty simple, particularly when compared to the examples earlier in this chapter. The following list points out the key facts about the command:

- All statements with the same number are in the same ACL.

- The numbers for numbered standard IP ACLs are 1–99 and 1300–1999. ACLs with other numbers are not standard IP ACLs.

- A **permit** or **deny** action must be configured.

- The *source-address* parameter must be configured. It refers to an IP address that will be compared to the packet's source IP address.

- The *source-mask* parameter is optional. If configured, it refers to the wildcard mask used to define which parts of the source address to compare. If omitted, IOS assumes a wildcard of 0.0.0.0, which means the statement will match only the specific IP address listed in the command.

- The optional **log** keyword tells IOS to generate a periodic log message listing the number of times the ACL statement has been matched.

Beyond the base syntax shown here, the **access-list** command allows the use of the **host** and **any** keywords. For example, the following two commands match a single host address (172.16.1.1) and all source addresses, respectively:

- **access-list 1 deny host 172.16.1.1**

- **access-list 1 permit any**

Additionally, a remark may be configured for the ACL. A *remark* is descriptive text that remains in the configuration file as a reminder of what the ACL does. The syntax in this case is

```
access-list number remark text
```

Standard ACL Examples

This section provides examples to help you understand ACL configuration options. The ACL examples in this chapter use Figure 11-12.

Figure 11-12   Sample Network for ACL Examples

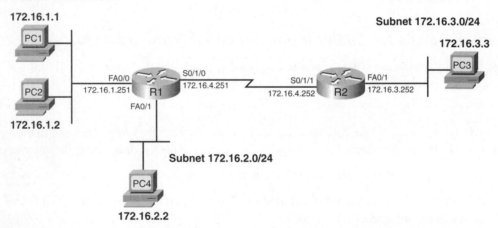

Example 11-5 shows the configuration for Figure 11-12. Example 11-5 shows a standard ACL configuration used to meet the following requirements:

- Discard packets sent by host 172.16.1.1.

- Allow packets sent by other hosts in subnet 172.16.1.0/24.

- Filter packets as they exit router R1's serial link.

Example 11-5   Example ACL to Filter PC1's Packets in Figure 11-12

```
R1#show running-config
! Unrelated configuration statements have been omitted
interface Serial0/1/0
 ip access-group 9 out
!
access-list 9 deny host 172.16.1.1
access-list 9 permit 172.16.1.0 0.0.0.255
```

Example 11-5 shows the key elements of the configuration. The ACL has two statements: the first matches just host 172.16.1.1, and the second uses a wildcard mask that causes the router to match all source addresses whose first three octets are 172.16.1. The **ip access-group 9 out** command under interface S0/1/0 shows that the ACL (ACL 9) has indeed been enabled for packets exiting the serial link.

Although the syntax of Example 11-5 is correct, the requirements and the solution may have some unintended consequences. For example, PC4 may try to send a packet to PC3, but the packet will be discarded. When PC4's packet gets to R1, it will enter R1 and be routed with outgoing interface S0/1/0, but R1 will check its outbound ACL 9. Because the source address of the packet from PC4 will be 172.16.2.2, the packet does not match either statement in ACL 9, so the packet matches the implicit deny all at the end of the ACL, causing the router to discard the packet.

Assuming the real goal is to allow hosts on both LAN subnets on the left (except PC1) to access hosts on the right side of the network, the ACL needs to be changed. Many options exist. Example 11-6 shows three separate new ACLs that each solve the problem.

Example 11-6   Alternative ACLs for Filtering PC1's Packets in Figure 11-12

```
access-list 1 deny host 172.16.1.1
access-list 1 permit any
!
access-list 2 deny host 172.16.1.1
access-list 2 permit 172.16.1.0 0.0.0.255
access-list 2 permit 172.16.2.0 0.0.0.255
!
access-list 3 deny host 172.16.1.1
access-list 3 permit 172.16.0.0 0.0.255.255
```

The three solutions shown in Example 11-6 allow PC4 to send packets to PC3, assuming each ACL would be used for packets going out R1's S0/1/0 interface. ACL 1 uses a concept called an *explicit permit all*. The **access-list 1 permit any** command uses a permit action and matches all source IP addresses. With this ACL, packets will never match the implicit deny all at the end of the ACL, because any packets that do not match the first statement will match the explicit permit all statement at the end of this list.

ACL 2 solves the problem of allowing PC4 to send packets out R1's WAN link by simply including another line in the ACL that matches PC4's subnet. The **access-list 2 permit 172.16.2.0 0.0.0.255** command matches all hosts in the subnet off R1's lower LAN interface. ACL 3 solves the problem by matching all addresses that begin with 172.16, which includes all hosts on both LAN subnets off R1.

Packet Tracer configuration file NA02-1112 mostly matches the network in Figure 11-12. You can add the ACL configuration in Example 11-6 and Example 11-7 and then use real-time mode to test the ACL by using **ping** commands on the PCs.

Lab Exercise 11.2.1a   Configuring Standard Access Lists

In this lab, you configure and apply a standard ACL to permit or deny specific traffic.

Lab Exercise 11.2.b   Standard ACLs

In this lab, you plan, configure, and apply a standard ACL to permit or deny specific traffic. You then test the ACL to determine if the desired results were achieved.

Configuring Numbered Extended ACLs

Note

Rather than repeat "numbered" and "IP" when describing numbered extended IP ACLs, this chapter uses the term "standard ACL" or "extended ACL," assuming the ACLs are both numbered and specific to IP.

Numbered extended IP ACLs work mostly like numbered standard IP ACLs. Both types may be enabled as inbound and outbound ACLs. Cisco IOS software searches both types of ACLs sequentially, using the **permit** or **deny** action defined in the first matched statement. If a packet does not match any configured statements in either type of ACL, the packet is discarded due to the implicit deny all at the end of the list.

Of course, extended ACLs differ from standard ACLs in some ways:

- Extended ACLs can match on a wide range of criteria in the packet's various headers, including the source and destination IP addresses, the type of transport layer protocol, and the source and destination port numbers as included in the TCP and UDP headers.

- Extended ACLs can test multiple criteria in a single **access-list** command. When a command lists multiple criteria, all the criteria must be true for the **access-list** statement to match the packet.

- Extended ACLs use a different range of numbers—namely, 100–199 and 2000–2699.

To see how extended ACLs can match multiple different items in a header, consider the following scenario that shows an extended ACL **access-list** command with as few criteria as can be configured. The extended ACL **access-list** command must list at least the following three criteria for the command to be accepted:

- Protocol type (options include IP, TCP, and UDP)

- Source address (a wildcard mask can be used, as well as the **host** and **any** keywords)

- Destination address (a wildcard mask can be used, as well as the **host** and **any** keywords)

To see a sample of the syntax, look at Example 11-7, which implements the following design:

- Packets from PC1 to PC3 should be discarded.

- All other packets should be allowed to keep going.

- Implement this logic for all packets entering R1's FA0/0 interface (again from Figure 11-12).

Example 11-7   Using as Few Extended ACL Criteria as Possible

```
interface fa 0/0
 ip access-group 101 in
!
access-list 101 deny ip host 172.16.1.1 host 172.16.3.3
access-list 101 permit ip any any
```

The highlighted portions of Example 11-7 focus on the *matching criteria* in the two **access-list** commands. The first command matches all IP packets whose source IP address is 172.16.1.1 and whose destination IP address is 172.16.3.3. Note that this command does not list any keywords like "source" or "destination." The order of the parameters implies what the parameter should be, with the protocol type first (IP), followed by the source IP address, and then the destination IP address.

The second **access-list 101** command shows the extended ACL version of an explicit permit all. The criteria state that this statement matches all IP packets, with any source IP address, and with any destination IP address. As a result, the **access-list 101 permit ip any any** command matches all IP packets, and permits them through the ACL.

Packet Tracer

Packet Tracer configuration file NA02-1112 mostly matches the network in Figure 11-12. You can add the ACL configuration in Example 11-7 and then use real-time mode to test the ACL by using **ping** commands on the PCs.

The Extended ACL Command Syntax

This section lists a relatively complete description of the syntax of the extended ACL **access-list** command. The book includes this information for reference because it is included in the online curriculum. However, the best way to learn about ACLs is to view different examples like the ones that follow this section.

The extended ACL **access-list** command has so many options that it is difficult to show just one version of its generic syntax. The following shows the core options along with several other options. The next section of this chapter includes details about other options of the **access-list** command, including how to match TCP and UDP port numbers.

```
access-list list-number [dynamic dynamic-name [timeout minutes]] {deny | permit | remark}
    protocol source source-wildcard destination destination-wildcard [precedence
    precedence] [tos tos] [log | log-input] [time-range time-range-name] [fragments]
```

Table 11-4 lists the options shown in this command and their meanings.

Note

All parameters listed in Table 11-4 are optional, except as noted.

Table 11-4   Explanations of the Fields in the Extended IP ACL **access-list** Command

Field	Meaning
list-number	(Required) A number between 100 and 199, or between 2000 and 2699, inclusive. Each **access-list** command with the same *list-number* is in the same ACL.
dynamic *dynamic-name*	Used with time-based ACLs that are created and enabled when using Cisco IOS firewall-like features.
timeout *minutes*	When using time-based ACLs, the amount of time to wait before disabling the ACL.
deny | **permit**	(Required) The action taken for packets that match the criteria listed in the command.
remark	Used when the **access-list** command lists descriptive text about the ACL instead of listing criteria for matching packets.
protocol	(Required) Checks the value of the IP header's Protocol field, which identifies the header that follows the IP header. Valid values include **ip**, meaning all IP packets; **tcp**, meaning IP packets with TCP headers; and **udp**, meaning IP packets with UDP headers.
source source-wildcard	(Required) The source IP address and wildcard mask value that will be compared to the packet's source IP address. The **host** and **any** keywords can also be used in this location.

Table 11-4   Explanations of the Fields in the Extended IP ACL
access-list Command   *continued*

Field	Meaning
destination destination-wildcard	(Required) The destination IP address and wildcard mask value that will be compared to the packet's destination IP address. The **host** and **any** keywords can also be used in this location.
precedence *precedence*	Compares the configured value (decimal) to the value in the first 3 bits of the Type of Service (ToS) byte, which are referred to as precedence bits. The precedence bits are also used for QoS features in IP.
tos *tos*	Compares the configured value (decimal) to the value in the ToS byte of the IP header. The ToS byte is used for QoS features in IP.
log	Creates log messages the first time an ACL statement is matched, and every 5 minutes thereafter, listing statistics for the number of packets that have matched each entry in the ACL.
log-input	Does the same thing as the **log** option, except it also includes the incoming interface information about the packets that match the ACL statement.
time-range *time-range-name*	Used to configure time-based ACLs, which IOS enables and disables based on the time of day.
fragments	Matches packets that have been fragmented by IP.

The next section examines two of the most popular options on the extended ACL command—the protocol option and the port number option.

Using the Extended ACL Protocol Option

IP packet headers include a 1-byte field called the Protocol field. This field identifies the type of header that follows the IP header. For example, an IP Protocol field value of decimal 6 means that a TCP header follows the IP header.

Cisco IOS ACLs can match the value of the Protocol field, but rather than make us remember the actual values used in the IP Protocol field, the **access-list** command expects simple text that identifies the protocol. Example 11-8 shows the various options for the Protocol field by using the help option (**?**) in configuration mode. It also shows a simple extended ACL that meets the following criteria, again on router R1 in Figure 11-12:

■ Allow all TCP traffic, with a source IP address in subnet 172.16.1.0/24, with any destination address.

■ Discard all other packets.

■ Apply the ACL to packets exiting R1's serial link.

Example 11-8   Matching the Source and Destination IP Address, and IP Protocol Type, Using Extended ACLs

```
R1(config)#access-list 102 permit ?
  <0-255>  An IP protocol number
  ahp      Authentication Header Protocol
  eigrp    Cisco's EIGRP routing protocol
  esp      Encapsulation Security Payload
  gre      Cisco's GRE tunneling
  icmp     Internet Control Message Protocol
  igmp     Internet Gateway Message Protocol
  ip       Any Internet Protocol
  ipinip   IP in IP tunneling
  nos      KA9Q NOS compatible IP over IP tunneling
  ospf     OSPF routing protocol
  pcp      Payload Compression Protocol
  pim      Protocol Independent Multicast
  tcp      Transmission Control Protocol
  udp      User Datagram Protocol

R1(config)#access-list 102 permit tcp 172.16.1.0 0.0.0.255 any
R1(config)#interface serial 0/1/0
R1(config-if)#ip access-group 102 out
```

Again using Figure 11-12 as a reference, with this ACL, if PC1 were to try to connect to web server PC3, the packet could get through the ACL. In this case, the source would be 172.16.1.1, which matches the source IP address criteria. Also, because web browsers and web servers use HTTP, and HTTP uses TCP, the packet will have a TCP header following the IP header. The Destination IP Address field shows the **any** keyword, so any destination IP address would match.

Conversely, a ping from PC1 to PC3 would fail, as would a TFTP request from PC1 to PC3. For the ping, the source and destination addresses of the packets would match the single command in ACL 102 (**access-list 102 permit tcp 172.16.1.0 0.0.0.255 any**), but the protocol type would not be TCP, because an ICMP header would follow the TCP header. Instead, the protocol type for the ping packets would be ICMP, and for the TFTP application would be UDP.

As you can see, to be ready to use the protocol option on extended ACL commands, you need to remember details about which applications use which transport layer protocols. Table 11-5 lists the most popular TCP/IP applications, their transport layer protocols, and, for reference in the next section, their well-known port numbers.

Table 11-5 Popular Applications and Their Well-Known Port Numbers

Port Number	Protocol	Application
20	TCP	FTP data
21	TCP	FTP control
23	TCP	Telnet
25	TCP	Simple Mail Transfer Protocol (SMTP)
53	TCP, UDP	Domain Name System (DNS)
69	UDP	Trivial FTP (TFTP)
80	TCP	HTTP (Web)
110	TCP	Post Office Protocol version 3 (POP3)
161	UDP	SNMP
520	UDP	RIP

Using the Extended ACL Port Number Option

The ability to match a TCP or UDP port number is one of the most powerful features of extended ACLs. By matching well-known port numbers, an ACL can match packets coming from or going to a particular type of server. To match the port numbers, you must use a different form of the extended ACL command, as follows:

```
access-list list-number [deny | permit] tcp | udp source source-wildcard [source-port-
    operator source-port-operand] destination destination-wildcard [destination-port-
    operator destination-port-operand]
```

Note

This command leaves out many unrelated options, to focus on the port numbers.

Although the generic syntax may be helpful for reference, most people do not understand how to use ports in extended ACLs until after they have seen a few examples. But first, you need to know a few facts about how to use the port numbers in the extended ACL command:

- To match the port number, the **access-list** command must use a Protocol field value of either **tcp** or **udp**, because only TCP and UDP have Port Number fields.

- The **access-list** command can check the source port, the destination port, or both.

- The **access-list** command does not use a **port** keyword; instead, the location of the option shows where the port numbers are listed. Specifically, the source port (if configured) follows the source IP address and source wildcard mask, and the destination port number (if any) follows the destination IP address and destination wildcard mask.

Now, consider a scenario that helps you make sense of ACLs and port numbers. Figure 11-13 shows the same network that has been used frequently in this chapter, but now with notations about the port numbers in a packet. In this case, PC3 has enabled web server software, using well-known port 80. PC1 uses its web browser to connect to PC3's web server. Like all clients, the web browser allocates a dynamic port number of 1024 or larger—in this case, 1050.

Figure 11-13   Port Numbers in a Typical Connection Between Client and Web Server

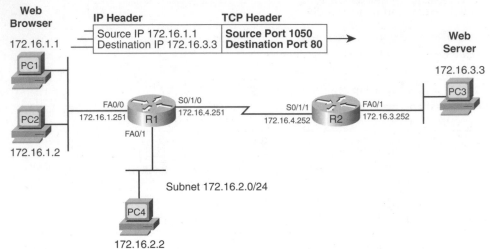

Keep in mind the following requirements for a new ACL on router R1:

- Allow PC1 to connect to the PC3 web server (port 80).

- Discard all other packets.

- Enable the ACL on R1's S0/1/0 interface.

Example 11-9 shows the solution, which includes a check of the destination port for HTTP.

Example 11-9   Matching the Source and Destination Port Numbers Using Extended ACLs

```
R1(config)#access-list 109 permit tcp host 172.16.1.1 host 172.16.3.3 eq 80
R1(config)#interface serial 0/1/0
R1(config-if)#ip access-group 109 out
R1(config-if)#^Z
R1#show ip access-list
Extended IP access list 109
    10 permit tcp any any eq www
R1#
```

First, focus on the single **access-list** command in Example 11-9. This command lists four separate *matching-criteria*, listed here in the same order as in the command:

- A protocol type of **tcp**

- A source IP address of **172.16.1.1**

- A destination IP address of **172.16.3.3**

- A destination port number of **80**

The command configures the destination TCP port number of 80 through the parameters **eq 80** at the end of the command. These parameters follow the destination IP address 172.16.3.3, so IOS knows that these parameters check the destination port number. The **eq** means "equals," so the ACL checks to see if the destination TCP port is equal to 80 in this case. To summarize, this one **access-list** command checks packets to see if they are sourced from PC1, going to PC3, using a TCP header, with TCP destination port 80.

Now, focus on the end of Example 11-9 for a moment. The **access-list** command uses port number 80, but IOS supports a more obvious text keyword for most well-known ports. For port 80, IOS uses a keyword of **www**, meaning World Wide Web. Thus, the command could have ended with **eq www** and achieved the same goal. In fact, if you configure the port number using **eq 80**, IOS will change the port number to the **www** keyword, as shown in Example 11-9.

The formal syntax of the **access-list** command as listed near Figure 11-13 references the port-related parameters as *port-operator* and *port-operand*. These terms come from mathematics, with the operator being the action (such as "equals") and the operand being the value (for instance, the port number itself). Table 11-6 lists the ACL operators and their meanings.

Table 11-6   Operators Used by the Extended **access-list** Command to Process Port Numbers

Operator	Meaning	Example
eq	Equals	**access-list 101 permit tcp any any eq www**
neq	Not equals	**access-list 101 permit tcp any any neq www**
gt	Greater than	**access-list 101 permit tcp any any gt 1023**
lt	Less than	**access-list 101 permit tcp any any lt 1024**
range	Inclusive range of numbers	**access-list 101 permit tcp any any range 20 21**

Packet Tracer configuration file NA02-1112 mostly matches the network in Figure 11-12. The simulation mode has six example packets configured: two from PC1 to PC3, two from PC2 to PC3, and two from PC2 to PC4. In each of these three cases, the two packets are web traffic to a web server and an ICMP echo. You can add the ACL configuration in Example 11-9 and then use simulation mode to see which packets pass through the ACL.

Lab Exercise 11.2.2a   Configuring Extended Access Lists

In this lab, you configure and apply an extended ACL to permit or deny specific traffic.

Lab Exercise 11.2.2b   Simple Extended Access Lists

In this lab, you configure and apply extended access lists to filter network-to-network, host-to-network, and network-to-host traffic.

Named IP ACLs

So far, this chapter has described numbered ACLs, which are characterized by the fact that they use a number to identify the **access-list** commands that make up the same ACL. However, numbered ACLs have a couple of problems. First, the number of different numbered ACLs in one router is limited based on the number ranges defined to IOS. (Refer to Table 11-1 for a list of ranges for numbered ACLs.) Additionally, most people do not remember numbers as well as names, so after you configure ACL 123 and come back to that router 3 months later, you may not remember what ACL 123 is supposed to do.

Cisco added named ACLs as of Cisco IOS Software Release 11.2 to overcome these types of problems. Named IP ACLs provide the following benefits as compared with their numbered cousins:

Note

When Cisco added named ACLs to Cisco IOS Software Release 11.2, IOS only supported numbers 1–99 for standard numbered IP ACLs and 100–199 for extended numbered IP ACLs.

- The engineer makes up the name of the ACL; by choosing a meaningful name, the engineer is more likely to recall the purpose of the ACL when later viewing the configuration.

- The number of allowed ACLs is not limited by a numeric range. The number of possible ACLs on the same router is limited only by the router's memory capacity, so from a practical perspective, you should never run out of named ACLs.

- Named ACLs allow for easier editing than do numbered ACLs. (This concept is explained further in the upcoming section "Editing Named ACLs.")

Besides these differences, numbered and named IP ACLs perform the same functions in the same ways. IOS supports both standard and extended named IP ACLs, with the matching criteria being the same as compared to numbered ACLs. Named and numbered IP ACLs can be enabled in the same places and in the same directions (inbound or outbound). Cisco IOS software also looks at named and numbered IP ACLs sequentially until the first statement is matched, and then the router permits or denies that packet based on the matched entry.

Configuring Named IP ACLs

Named ACLs use a different configuration style than do numbered ACLs. With numbered ACLs, all the **access-list** commands used to create the ACL are global commands. With named ACLs, you first use a global command that both defines the name of the ACL and places the user in named ACL configuration mode. Then, you use a series of **deny** and **permit** commands that list the action along with the matching criteria. To configure named ACLs, follow these steps:

How To

Step 1   Use the **ip access-list** {**standard|extended**} *ACL-name* command to do the following:

   a.   Create an IP ACL with that name.

   b.   Define the type of ACL (standard or extended).

   c.   Move into named ACL configuration mode.

Step 2   Use a series of **permit** and **deny** commands, each of which lists *matching-criteria*.

Step 3   Enable the ACL on an interface with the **ip access-group** *acl-name* {**in|out**} command.

Example 11-10 shows the configuration steps on R1 to enable a named ACL that meets the following requirements for packets exiting R1's WAN link:

- Allow all traffic going to web servers in the 172.16.3.0/24 subnet.

- Allow all IP traffic from subnet 172.16.1.0/24 to get to destination subnet 172.16.3.0/24.

- Discard all other traffic.

Example 11-10   Configuring Named IP ACLs

```
R1#configure terminal
Enter configuration commands, one per line. End with CNTL/Z.
R1(config)#ip access-list extended all-web-all-sub1-to-sub3
R1(config-ext-nacl)#permit tcp any 172.16.3.0 0.0.0.255 eq www
R1(config-ext-nacl)#permit ip 172.16.1.0 0.0.0.255 172.16.3.0 0.0.0.255
R1(config-ext-nacl)#interface s0/1/0
R1(config-if)#ip access-group all-web-all-sub1-to-sub3 out
R1(config-if)#^Z
R1#show running-config
! unrelated lines of output have been omitted
interface Serial0/1/0
 ip access-group all-web-all-sub1-to-sub3 out
!
ip access-list extended all-web-all-sub1-to-sub3
 permit tcp any 172.16.3.0 0.0.0.255 eq www
 permit ip 172.16.1.0 0.0.0.255 172.16.3.0 0.0.0.255
```

Note

Cisco IOS software supports named ACLs for other routable protocols such as IPX. The names must be unique throughout a single router, so you cannot have a named IPX ACL with the same name as a named IP ACL.

■ Use this logic for packets going out R1's S0/1/0 interface.

In Example 11-10, the **ip access-list extended all-web-all-sub1-to-sub3** command creates an extended named IP ACL and puts the user in extended named ACL configuration mode. The name itself could be anything, as long as it has not been used for any other named ACL. In named ACL configuration mode, the two **permit** commands define the two sets of criteria in the ACL. The **ip-access-group** command enables the ACL on the interface just like it does with numbered IP ACLs, except the command references the ACL name instead of the ACL number.

Interestingly, the **permit** and **deny** commands follow the same syntax as the **access-list** command for numbered ACLs, beginning with the **permit** or **deny** keyword in the **access-list** command. For example, the following two lines show a numbered ACL **access-list** command and the first named ACL **permit** command in Example 11-10:

```
access-list 101 permit tcp any 172.16.3.0 0.0.0.255 eq www
                permit tcp any 172.16.3.0 0.0.0.255 eq www
```

Both commands define matching logic for TCP traffic, from any source IP address, destined for any IP addresses that begin with 172.16.3.

Standard named IP ACLs can be configured with the same process, using the **standard** keyword on the **ip access-list** command. However, in named ACL configuration mode, the command prompt would list R1(config-std-nacl), where std means "standard," and the **permit** and **deny** commands would only support the source IP address and source wildcard mask parameters.

Editing Named IP ACLs

Numbered IP ACLs cannot be edited; instead, the entire ACL must be deleted with the **no ip access-list** *acl-number* command, and then entirely reconfigured. Named ACLs allow the removal of individual **permit** and **deny** commands from the ACL, which allows some editing of the ACL without completely removing the ACL. However, when configuring new **permit** and **deny** commands, IOS always adds the commands to the end of the ACL, so you may have to delete several lines in a named ACL, add the new line, and then add back all the deleted lines. In practice, you may still want to make a habit of editing ACL configurations with an editor, deleting the whole ACL, and then pasting the new ACL configuration in from the text editor.

Example 11-11 shows a brief example that changes the named ACL shown in Example 11-10. In this case, the requirements changed such that the new ACL needs one more command, a **deny** command, located between the two existing **permit** commands. Example 11-11 shows how the second line of the existing ACL can be removed, the new **deny** command added to the configuration, and the previously removed **permit** command added back to the configuration.

Example 11-11   Deleting and Adding Lines in Named ACLs

```
R1#show access-lists
Extended IP access list all-web-all-sub1-to-sub3
    10 permit tcp any 172.16.3.0 0.0.0.255 eq www
    20 deny tcp 172.16.1.0 0.0.0.255 172.16.3.0 0.0.0.255 eq telnet
R1#configure terminal
Enter configuration commands, one per line.  End with CNTL/Z.
R1(config)#ip access-list extended all-web-all-sub1-to-sub3
! The next line removes the currently second permit command in the ACL
R1(config-ext-nacl)#no permit ip 172.16.1.0 0.0.0.255 172.16.3.0 0.0.0.255
! The next line adds a new deny command to the end of the ACL
R1(config-ext-nacl)#deny tcp 172.16.1.0 0.0.0.255 172.16.3.0 0.0.0.255 eq telnet
! The next line adds the command removed earlier
R1(config-ext-nacl)#permit ip 172.16.1.0 0.0.0.255 172.16.3.0 0.0.0.255
R1(config-ext-nacl)#^Z
R1#show access-lists
Extended IP access list all-web-all-sub1-to-sub3
    10 permit tcp any 172.16.3.0 0.0.0.255 eq www
    20 deny tcp 172.16.1.0 0.0.0.255 172.16.3.0 0.0.0.255 eq telnet
    30 permit ip 172.16.1.0 0.0.0.255 172.16.3.0 0.0.0.255
```

Lab Exercise 11.2.3a   Configuring a Named Access List

In this lab, you create a named ACL to permit or deny specific traffic.

Lab Exercise 11.2.3b   Simple DMZ Extended Access Lists

In this lab, you use extended access lists to create a simple demilitarized zone (DMZ).

Lab Exercise 11.2.3c   Multiple Access Lists Functions (Challenge Lab)

In this lab, you configure and apply an extended Access Control List to control Internet traffic using one or more routers.

Locating ACLs

Cisco makes a recommendation in most of its introductory courses about where to locate standard and extended ACLs. The recommendation is summarized as follows:

- **Standard ACLs**—Locate the ACL as close as possible to the packet's destination.

- **Extended ACLs**—Locate the ACL as close as possible to the packet's source.

To see why Cisco makes this recommendation, consider the requirement to discard packets sent by PC1 to PC6 but allow all other packets as applied to the network in Figure 11-14.

Figure 11-14   Sample Internetwork for Showing the Best Location for ACLs

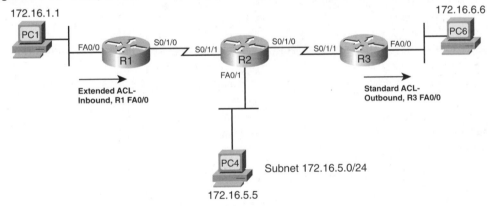

Examine the first place that the packets can be filtered, which is inbound on R1 into R1's FA0/0 interface. A standard ACL can check only the source IP address. So, a standard ACL on R1's FA0/0 interface, for incoming packets, could look for PC1's 172.16.1.1 IP address and filter those packets. However, this ACL would filter all packets sent by PC1, so PC1 would not be able to communicate with other hosts, such as PC4.

To prevent this particular type of problem, the engineer could place the standard ACL near the destination. For example, placing the same standard ACL on R3's FA0/0 interface as an outbound ACL filters the packets that need to be filtered, without filtering any other packets. However, this option allows the packet to be routed across the entire internetwork before being discarded, which wastes bandwidth in the internetwork.

Because extended ACLs can match several fields in one command, including the source and destination IP addresses, they do not have the same location problems as standard ACLs. So, rather than have the packet go all the way to the other end of the internetwork, only to be discarded, placing an extended ACL close to the source can reduce the amount of bandwidth consumed by packets that will end up being discarded anyway. In fact, the ACL on R3 in this example could have been applied as an inbound ACL on R1's FA0/0 interface (as was shown) or on R1's S0/1/0 interface as an outbound ACL. However, using the ACL as an inbound ACL on R1's FA0/0 interface is slightly closer to the packet's source and is marginally better.

Summary

Network engineers create and use ACLs to control the types of packets allowed through the internetwork. ACLs limit network traffic so that only the desired traffic is allowed through the network, thereby increasing network performance and managing security issues.

IOS supports ACLs for each routable protocol. These ACLs may be enabled on interfaces and for a particular direction of packet flow (into or out of the interface). You can enable one ACL per interface, per direction, for each routable protocol.

Each ACL contains a set of **access-list** commands, each of which defines both a set of *matching criteria* and an action to discard (deny) the packet or allow it to keep going (permit). The ACLs can be applied to any router interface, for a particular direction of packet flow. After it is enabled on an interface, an ACL examines all packets (of that particular routable protocol) that flow in the stated direction (into or out of the interface). The router discards packets that match ACL statements that list a deny action, and the router lets the packets keep going when they match an ACL statement that lists a permit action.

Routers use the ACL's **access-list** commands in the same order as listed in the configuration file. In effect, the router uses first-match logic, using the permit or deny action in the first matched statement. For packets that do not match any of the statements, the router discards the packet due to an implicit deny all that exists at the end of every router ACL.

IP ACL configuration includes two steps:

- Create the ACL using **access-list** global configuration commands.

- Enable the ACL on an interface using the **ip access-group** command.

The number of the ACL defines whether the ACL is a standard IP ACL (numbers 1–99 and 1300 1999) or an extended ACL (numbers 100–199 and 2000–2699).

IP ACLs can check for specific IP addresses by using the **host** keyword in the **access-list** command, and match any and all IP addresses by using the **any** keyword of the **access-list** command. Additionally, ACLs can match a range of IP addresses by using a wildcard mask. A wildcard mask is a 32-bit number, written in dotted-decimal form, that tells the router that the bits of the packet's IP address must match the address configured in the **access-list** command. For example, a wildcard mask of 0.0.0.255 represents a number that has 24 bits of value 0 and 8 bits of value 1. So, this wildcard mask means that the first 24 bits of the packet's IP address must match the first 24 bits of the IP address listed in the **access-list** command, and that the last 8 bits can be ignored.

Cisco IOS uses three main commands to check the configuration of IP ACLs. The **show running-config** command shows both the ACL configuration and the commands that enabled the ACL on an interface. The **show access-lists** command lists the configuration along with statistics about how many packets have matched each ACL. The **show ip interface** command lists whether an IP ACL has been enabled on each interface, the direction (inbound or outbound), and the ACL number.

Standard ACLs differ from extended ACLs in the matching criteria they can configure. Standard IP ACLs can only match based on the packet's source IP address, whereas extended ACLs can match a large variety of header fields, including fields for the source and destination IP addresses, protocol type, and source and destination TCP and UDP port numbers. The ability to check port numbers allows the router to identify different application types, such as web traffic that uses HTTP, which typically uses well-known port 80.

Cisco IOS supports named ACLs in addition to numbered ACLs. IP standard and extended named ACLs can match the exact same header fields as their numbered cousins. However, compared to numbered ACLs, named ACLs allow the use of a more descriptive name to identify the ACL, and allow easier editing of the ACL.

Cisco recommends that standard IP ACLs be located as close as possible to the packet's destination, whereas extended ACLs should be placed as close as possible to the packet's source. By discarding packets close to the source, extended ACLs improve overall network performance by discarding packets early in their lives, not allowing the packets to cross network links and waste bandwidth. However, because standard ACLs can examine only a packet's source IP address, placing them close to the packet's source will likely filter more packets than intended, so standard ACLs need to be placed close to the packet's destination.

Check Your Understanding

Complete all the review questions listed here to test your understanding of the topics and concepts in this chapter. Answers are listed in Appendix A, "Answers to Check Your Understanding and Challenge Questions."

1. Which of the following are common ACL functions? (Choose two.)

    A. Verifying routing table functions

    B. Protecting the internal network from illegal Internet access

    C. Rerouting unwanted packets

    D. Filtering packets internally

    E. Assuring user security encryption

2. ACL is an acronym for which of the following?

    A. Accessibility Control List

    B. Accountability Control List

    C. Assessment Control List

    D. Access Control List

3. Which type of ACL works by comparing only the source IP address against the ACL rules?

    A. Extended

    B. Named extended

    C. Standard

    D. Implicit

4. Which type of ACL works by comparing the source IP address, destination IP address, or other parameters against the ACL rules?

    A. Named extended

    B. Named standard

    C. Standard

    D. Explicit

5. When the command **ip access-group 99 in** is applied to an interface, which of the following is true about the referenced Access Control List?

   A. The list is a numbered extended ACL checking packets leaving that interface.

   B. The list is a named extended ACL checking packets entering that interface.

   C. The list is a numbered standard ACL checking packets entering that interface.

   D. The list is a named standard ACL checking packets leaving that interface.

6. According to Cisco, where should you place standard ACLs in the network?

   A. Inbound on the source router's interface

   B. In the core on the interface closest to the source

   C. Closest to the source of the traffic to be controlled as source traffic is checked by the ACL

   D. As close as possible to the destination so that traffic is not restricted in error

7. Which of the following will configure a standard ACL statement?

   A. **access-list 157 permit host 200.5.5.1 63.82.20.0 0.0.0.255**

   B. **access-list 148 permit 201.100.11.2 0.0.0.0**

   C. **access-list 87 permit host 192.5.5.1 0.0.0.255**

   D. **access-list 113 permit any**

8. Which of the following commands can be used to find out whether any ACLs are enabled on an interface?

   A. **show ip interface brief**

   B. **show ip protocols**

   C. **show ip interface**

   D. **show ip network**

9. Which of the following shows a command with valid syntax, used in the correct configuration mode (as implied by the command prompt)?

   A. Router#**access-list 98 deny 193.20.30.0 0.0.0.255**

   B. Router(config)#**access-list 98 deny 193.20.30.0 0.0.0.255**

   C. Router(config-if)#**access-list 98 deny 193.20.30.0 0.0.0.255 eq telnet**

   D. Router(config)#**access-list 98 ip deny 193.20.30.0 0.0.0.255**

10. According to Cisco, which would be the most effective placement of extended ACLs in a network?

    A. Outbound on the destination router's interface

    B. In the core on the interface closest to the source

    C. As close as possible to the source of the traffic to be controlled

    D. As close as possible to the destination so that traffic is not restricted in error

11. Standard Access Control Lists impact network security based on which of the following factors?

    A. The data content of the packets

    B. The destination subnet of the packet

    C. The source of the packets

    D. The media type of the network they are routed through

12. Which command will apply an Access Control List to an interface?

    A. **ip access-group 10 out**

    B. **access-group 10 in**

    C. **access group 10 out**

    D. **ip access-group 10**

13. What impact will the following ACL have on router traffic?

    ```
    access-list 1 deny 192.168.19.162 0.0.0.0
    access-list 1 permit any
    ```

    A. It will permit all traffic from the 192.168.19.0 network.

    B. It will deny traffic from only the host 192.168.19.162.

    C. There will be no impact because the wildcard mask ignores all bits.

    D. The **permit any** statement overrides the **deny** statement.

Challenge Questions and Activities

These questions require a deeper application of the concepts covered in this chapter and are similar to the style of questions you might see on a CCNA certification exam. You can find the answers in Appendix A.

1. Considering the following ACL statement, which of the following statements is correct?

```
access-list 128  deny udp 123.120.230.0 0.0.255.255 any eq 161
access-list 128  permit ip any any
```

A. Web traffic from host 123.120.230.12 will be denied.

B. SNMP traffic from 123.120.210.5 will be allowed.

C. Ping traffic from 65.120.100.10 will be allowed.

D. Web traffic from 172.23.42.1 will be denied.

2. Which ACLs will filter out Telnet traffic but allow web traffic from hosts in network 172.17.0.0?

A. **access-list 199 deny tcp 172.17.0.0 0.0.255.255 any eq 80**

   access-list 199 permit ip any any

B. **access-list 199 deny udp 172.17.0.0 0.0.255.255 any eq 23**

   access-list 199 permit ip any any

C. **access-list 199 deny tcp 172.17.0.0 0.0.255.255 any eq www**

   access-list 199 permit ip any any

D. **access-list 199 deny tcp 172.17.0.0 0.0.255.255 any eq 23**

   access-list 199 permit ip any any

Answers to Check Your Understanding and Challenge Questions

Chapter 1

Check Your Understanding

1. B and D

   WANs can be used by companies to connect remote locations via leased lines from a telco. Only WANs require a CSU/DSU to be used on the ends of the cable. The price of a WAN link is based on speed, and higher speeds are more expensive. This is why most WAN connections are slower than LANs.

2. A, C, D, and F

   UAS-K and OSI-N are fictional acronyms. The others are

   IETF: Internet Engineering Task Force

   ISO: International Organization for Standardization

   EIA: Electronic Industries Alliance

   ITU: International Telecommunication Union

3. A, C, and E

   A router can connect to multiple IP networks and IP subnets using multiple interfaces, for the purpose of forwarding packets between those IP networks and subnets. One of the main functions of a router is to choose the best path for packets to travel between networks. A router's software implements routing protocols that allow the router to dynamically learn routes and determine the best path to reach each subnet. The router CPU executes the routing protocol software and stores the resulting routing table in RAM.

4. A, B, and E

   The items CTG interface and NV-ROM do not exist (although NVRAM is a component). ROM, flash memory, and RAM are components of a router.

5. C and E

   RAM stores the current information such as interface configurations and routing tables. RAM is volatile, so its contents are lost when the router is turned off. NVRAM and RAM have different functions, and both are necessary in a router.

6. C and D

   DTE, or data terminal equipment, is usually located on the customer's premises. DTE can be connected to any serial interface on a router, but it does not provide clocking, which is provided by the DCE.

7. B and C

DCE stands for data circuit-terminating equipment or data communications equipment. Clocking information is configured on the DCE serial interface so that it can provide timing to the DTE.

8. B and D

The term WAN refers to both the physical and data link layers.

9. E

The serial interface with the DCE cable must be configured with a clock rate to operate. None of the others require clocking configuration.

10. C and D

Ethernet interfaces usually use RJ-45 connectors to connect with straight-through or crossover cables. Rollover cables are useful only in the console port, which is different from an interface in that it provides out-of-band router management access. Newer routers have smart serial interfaces, which use smaller connectors than those used by the older serial interfaces.

11. B and D

Console ports provide access to the router for out-of-band management. Management functions include viewing or changing configurations and performing password recovery. Telnet access is "in-band" and is done via an IP connection. The console port cannot function as a serial port. Routing information is stored in RAM.

12. A

The Cisco default is 9600 bps.

13. A, C, and F

Frame Relay, PPP, and HDLC are Layer 2 WAN standards. RIP and OSPF are routing protocols, and IETF is a professional organization.

14. B and C

Routers and modems are used in WANs. Hubs, multiport repeaters, and bridges are used in LANs.

15. A, C, and D

Flash memory holds the Cisco IOS software image for a router and must keep its contents when the power is cycled. If the flash memory is large enough, it can hold multiple versions of Cisco IOS software. The Cisco IOS software is updated without changing the chips. Some of the contents of flash memory are loaded into RAM during startup, but it does not perform RAM's tasks.

16. A, D, and E

Out-of-band management allows administrators to manage a router using communications links besides the links used for sending and receiving packets. Out-of-band access can be gained with a rollover cable using the console port or using the aux port with a modem.

17. A, B, and D

The items in the photo depict ports and interfaces on a router. A points to Ethernet interfaces, which can support management via Telnet. Item C is the console port, and item D is the aux port, both of which provide management access. Item B points to two types of serial interfaces, with the two small interfaces on the left being smart serial interfaces. Only serial interfaces accept DTE and DCE connections, and only DCE connections provide clocking information.

18. B

NVRAM stores the saved startup configuration, and it is loaded into RAM when the router is booted. Changes to the running configuration must be saved to NVRAM, or they will be lost when the power is off. The Cisco IOS software is stored in flash memory. ROM holds the bootstrap program.

Challenge Questions and Activities

1.

A. PC1 to R1: crossover cable

B. R1 to R2: back-to-back serial connection or DTE/DCE serial connection

C. R2 to SW2: straight-through cable

D. R2 to PC2: console or rollover cable

2. A

In the lab, R1 uses a serial DCE cable. When connecting to an external CSU/DSU at the new site, R1 needs to use a DTE cable. So, R1 may be able to use the old DTE cable formerly connected to R2, assuming the cable's connectors match R1's type of serial connector and the CSU/DSU's connector.

For the LAN, R1 formerly used a crossover cable to connect to a PC. To connect to a switch, R1 needs a straight-through cable.

If R1 were upgraded to use an integrated CSU/DSU, R1 would instead connect directly to the cable supplied by the telco, so it would not be able to use either the old DTE cable or the old DCE cable.

Chapter 2

Check Your Understanding

1. C

   CLI stands for command-line interface, the text-based method for accessing a router. Remote management of routers can be performed using CLI via Telnet or using the HTTP protocol with a web browser.

2. B and D

   The --more-- prompt means press the Spacebar for the next page or press the Enter or Return key to see the next line.

3. B, C, and E

   User EXEC mode allows a user to view the router's operation, but not change it. Privileged mode, also known as enable mode, supports the most powerful commands, including those that can change the router's operation. The symbol # at the end of the command prompt, without the word (config), indicates privileged, or enable, mode; the > symbol indicates user EXEC mode.

4. A and D

   The **show ?** and **sh ?** commands have a space between the command and the question mark, so both list possible command syntax. The **sh?** command assists with commands that begin with the letters "sh." The **show help** command is not a valid command.

5. C

   The carat (^) indicates where an error occurs in the typed command syntax. If there is more than one error, only the first error is indicated. In this case, the letter *r* is a typing error of the valid entry **config term**. Both **config** and **configure** will work in the command because **config** is a valid abbreviation of the **configure** command, and the mode is valid for making configuration changes.

6. A, C, and E

   Previous commands can be recalled from the terminal history stored in RAM. The history list can be displayed using the **show history** command. Previous entries can be recalled by using the Up Arrow key or by pressing Ctrl-p.

7. B and E

   Ctrl-z and **end** return to privileged EXEC mode. The **exit** command brings the user back one level to the Router#(config) prompt, indicating global configuration mode. **Ctrl-a** moves the cursor to the beginning of the command line. **exec** is not a valid command.

8. A, C, and D

Setup mode can be accessed using the **setup** command or by rebooting the router when NVRAM is empty. When the router is new, there is no configuration in NVRAM, so setup mode loads by default on the first boot. When the setup dialog is complete, there is an option to ignore the configuration without rebooting.

9. B and D

If both the **enable secret** and **enable password** command are configured, the **enable secret** command is used, and the router does not accept the password defined on the **enable password** command. Passwords are case-sensitive.

10. B and C

The **configure terminal** command puts the router in global configuration mode, and the **router rip** command is available. Interface configuration, such as IP address assignments and Telnet access, requires further mode commands.

11. A

The **router rip** command puts the router into routing protocol configuration mode for RIP, where RIP can be configured using the **network** command. **Ctrl-z** returns the router to privileged mode. The **interface s0/0** command puts the router into interface configuration mode, where the interface IP address can be assigned.

12. C

The four steps for router startup are performing POST, loading bootstrap, loading an IOS image, and then loading the startup configuration.

13. A, C, and D

Boot ROM, ROM Monitor, and IOS are operating environments for a router. IGRP, OSPF, and RIP are routing protocols.

14. A, C, and E

Flash memory and an external TFTP server are common sources for an IOS image. ROM can provide a very limited IOS for troubleshooting. RAM is where the IOS image will reside when loaded. POST is the first step in the boot process, and BIOS is not found on routers.

15. C, D, and E

Router uptime, last restart method, system image file and location, and the configuration register are some of the items displayed with the **show version** command.

16. A, D, and E

The router's CLI can be accessed via Telnet over Ethernet, through the aux port with a modem, or in a terminal session using a console or rollover cable.

Challenge Questions and Activities

1.

1A. No, a routing protocol is not necessary on SW3. Being in the same subnet, PC3 and PC8 would not need a router. Also, routing protocols are applied to routers, not switches.

1B. Telnet can be used to access R1.

1C. Yes, PC1 can connect to R1 via the console. The current configuration shows that PC1 has an Ethernet connection and a console connection to R1.

2.

2A. The **show flash** command produced the output.

2B. The **show version** command can provide the currently used image name.

2C. No. The platform for this image is a 2600 router.

2D. Yes, the router can handle the upgrade. The current image is 5,428,500 bytes, so the new image is 10,857,000 bytes. There is 28,125,932 bytes available. There is room for both images in flash memory.

Chapter 3

Check Your Understanding

1. A and C

   The prompt indicates which mode a user is in. Global configuration mode allows configuration of settings that apply to the whole router. The **exit** command moves the router from a specific mode to global configuration mode, not user mode. Pressing Ctrl-Z returns the router to privileged EXEC mode.

2. B and E

   The **enable password** command is used only if the **enable secret** password has not been configured. The **enable secret** password is encrypted, and the **enable** password is not. Passwords are optional but strongly recommended. To access routers remotely, the vty passwords must be configured. The **login** command is part of the vty configuration, not an access requirement.

3. A, C, and E

The correct commands are

```
Router(config)#line console 0
Router(config-line)#login
Router(config-line)#password cisco
```

4. D

The **show running-config** command displays the current running configuration.

5. D

The **clock rate** command should be configured on the serial interfaces connected to a DCE cable. The configuration is made in interface configuration mode. If DTE cables are connected, no clock rate configuration is necessary.

6. B and D

Enter interface configuration mode by specifying the interface using the **interface** configuration command, and apply the address with a subnet mask. There is no need to shut down the interface or connect a cable.

7. B and D

Design standards allow consistency across a network. With standards in place, changes made by one engineer should be easily understood by another. Thus, network problems can be more easily recognized.

8. C

The **description** command is used to comment on an interface configuration.

9. C

The delimiter indicates the beginning and ending of the free text field.

10. B and C

A host table maps IP addresses to names, which allows a user to ping another device using the name instead of the IP address.

11. B

ip host boston 172.16.27.6 is the correct format.

12. B, C, and E

Configuration backup files can be stored on a TFTP server, a network server, or a disk stored in a safe place.

13. B

After entering the **copy running-config tftp** command, the user is prompted to enter the IP address of the destination host where the file will be stored.

Challenge Questions and Activities

1. C

   The output of the **show controllers serial** command returns output describing the hardware connections, including which cable, DTE or DCE, is connected to the serial interface. The **clock rate** command can then be applied to the interface with the DCE cable.

2. F

   The **description** and **banner** commands simply list text information; they do not have any impact on the actual operation of the router's serial link. The **clock rate** command affects the actual speed used on the interface, assuming a DCE cable has been attached to the interface. However, because the **show running-config** command shows the currently used configuration, and this configuration does not include a **clock rate** command, R1 is not currently supplying clocking, and there is no way to know from the output the speed of the serial link.

Chapter 4

Check Your Understanding

1. B

   The primary use of CDP is to discover all Cisco devices that are directly connected to a local device. CDP does not work on non-Cisco devices. Telnet is the application that provides terminal access to remote devices.

2. A, C, and D

   Device identifiers, address lists, and port identification are three kinds of CDP packet and hold time information that are displayed with the **show cdp** command.

3. A

   The values of the CDP timers are part of the **show cdp interface** output. Interface configuration information can be discovered with the **show cdp neighbors detail** command, along with the value of the CDP holdtime timer.

4. A

   The **show cdp interfaces** command displays line and data link layer protocol status, encapsulation, and CDP packet timer and interval information.

5. A, B, D, and F

   The **show cdp neighbor** command displays the neighboring device ID and the local port or interface ID it is connected to. The output also displays holdtime, remote device capability, neighboring device platform, and neighboring device port/interface ID.

6. A

   The **show cdp entry** [*device-name*] command displays the Layer 3 addresses configured on the interface that the neighbor uses to send CDP updates to the local router.

7. C

   Telnet is the virtual terminal protocol in the Internet suite of protocols that allows users of one host to log in to a remote host and act as normal terminal users of that host.

8. B and C

   Multiple sessions of Telnet are possible when connecting to remote routers. Telnet relies on TCP for reliability. Telnet is the easiest way to test all seven layers of the OSI model; the **ping** command is the basic way to test Layers 1 to 3. The command to suspend a Telnet session is Ctrl-Shift-6 and then *x*.

9. A

   The response to a **ping** command contains the size and quantity of ICMP packets, the timeout duration, and the success rate.

10. A

   The exclamation point (!) indicates the number of successful echo requests, indicating that Layer 3 of the target device is working properly. Hop counts can be determined with the **traceroute** command.

11. C

   The **traceroute** command maps the route that a packet takes to reach the target destination.

Challenge Questions and Activities

1. B and E

   Router#(config-int)**cdp enable** must be used because CDP is running at the global level but not on the interface. After CDP is enabled at the interface level, the Router#**show cdp neighbor detail** command provides IP address information. The **show cdp neighbors** command output does not include IP address information.

2. F

CDP provides information about directly connected neighbors. Because information (in the table) about Router1 is complete, entering **show cdp neighbors detail** on Router3 provides information about both SW1 and Router2. The command **show cdp neighbors detail** must be entered because **show cdp neighbors** does not include IP address information.

Chapter 5

Check Your Understanding

1. D

The boot option entries can specify that a Cisco IOS software image will load from flash memory, a TFTP server, or from ROM. Cisco IOS Software does not automatically boot from a previous IOS image.

2. B and E

The **show version** command lists, among other things, the name of the system image and its location and the router platform and router uptime.

3. C

The **show version** command lists the name of the current configuration register.

4. D

The IOS filename system describes capabilities in the feature set, the platform on which it will run, and the location (RAM or flash memory) where it will run. The image size is not included.

5. C

Before changing the IOS image, it is important to back up a copy of the current image to the TFTP server in case there are problems with the new image. The **copy flash tftp** command is not part of the sequence; this command is used to upload an image to a TFTP server. The command **copy tftp flash** is used to download the image, but it is not the first step.

6. D

When the configuration register hex number ends in 0x*nnn*1 in a newer router, the router boots the first file from flash memory. Older routers (Cisco 2500) with this setting load the RxBoot OS software. Newer routers do not have the RxBoot OS software.

7. A

ROM contains ROMMON, which is a limited version of the IOS that can be used to restore an IOS from a TFTP server after flash memory has been corrupted (see also Chapter 2). Older routers' IOS had the RxBoot ROM software, which resides in the ROM chips and can be loaded even if there is no working IOS in flash memory.

8. D

To have the router use the **boot system** commands in NVRAM, the configuration register should be set to any value from 0x*nnn*2 to 0x*nnnF*.

9. D

Flash memory, TFTP server, ROM is the default boot sequence.

10. A

Statistics for configured interfaces are not part of the **show version** output.

11. C and D

Xmodem is the last-resort method of loading the IOS because it is slower than using an IP connection via Ethernet. Xmodem loads an IOS via the console or aux port on a router.

12. D

It is important to have a backup copy of the IOS before updating the router with a new version; should the transfer fail or the old image be erased, it is essential to be able to return to the old version. When recovery procedures are being performed, it is likely too late to make a backup. It is wise to keep a copy of the IOS image, but copying the image to a new router will not damage the current image.

13. B

The command **copy tftp flash** is used to download a new image from the TFTP server.

Challenge Questions and Activities

1. A

The correct output lists the IP address, subnet mask, default gateway, TFTP server, and TFTP filename. No spaces are allowed in the minimal ROMMON environment, and an equals sign (=) appears between the heading and the data.

2. C

There are 903,848 bytes of flash memory, which is enough to hold a 7.2-MB (7,200,000-byte) image only if the current image is erased.

Chapter 6

Check Your Understanding

1. C

A router determines the best path for traffic to take through a network. Routers do forward traffic between LANs, but the term "reliable" in the answer implies that the routers also perform error recovery—and they do not. Routers use network addresses, not MAC addresses, in their routing tables.

2. B

Path determination occurs when a router evaluates available routes learned by some routing protocol and selects the best choice to a destination according to the protocol used. Setting the administrative distance of a route does directly impact a router's choice of the best route, but it is a secondary part of the path determination process.

3. A

The router uses data in the IP routing table when calculating the best path to the packet's destination.

4. A and C

Routers using distance vector protocols such as RIP exchange complete routing tables every 30 seconds. RIP uses hop counts to determine a path's value in the table. When routers use link-state protocols, such as OSPF, they exchange link-state advertisements (LSAs). LSAs contain route information including path costs but do not use hop counts. The LSAs contain changes in the network since the last update.

5. A

A routed protocol's address provides enough information to allow a packet to be forwarded from host to host. For example, the IP protocol, which is routed, carries address information the routers can use to get the packet delivered. A routing protocol, such as RIP, helps routers communicate paths to each other. Thus, routing protocols (such as RIP) are used by routers to determine the path for routed protocols (such as IP), which are used by hosts.

6. A

Each routing protocol has a distinct algorithm that it uses to build a routing table. The router chooses the best path from the routing table. The protocol that assigns IP addresses as hosts boot up is the Dynamic Host Configuration Protocol (DHCP); it is not a routing protocol. MAC addresses and LANs are not part of the path selection process.

7. D

An advantage of distance vector protocols is that they are comparatively simple to run. Link-state protocols have more variables and thus are more complicated. Counting to infinity is a function of a distance vector protocol.

8. C

Interior Gateway Protocols (IGPs) are used within an autonomous system, and Exterior Gateway Protocols (EGPs) are used between autonomous systems. Both IGPs and EGPs are routing protocols. BGP is the most common EGP; OSPF is one of several common IGPs.

9. C

Routing tables are built by exchanging information from neighbor routers via link-state advertisements (LSAs) and running the protocol's algorithm. The results make up the routing table.

10. D

No routing protocol is necessary for a router to forward packets to directly connected networks. Routing protocols are for exchanging network information between routers, and because there is only one router, there is no need for a routing protocol.

11. A

Static routes are set administratively, and routers do not have to calculate the path. Dynamic routing protocols, including distance vector protocols and link-state protocols such as OSPF, use algorithms to calculate the best route to each subnet.

12. C

A default route is the path used when the packet's destination does not match any valid route in the routing table. If there is no match, the router sends the packet based on the information in the default route.

Challenge Questions and Activities

1. B, D, and E

   From the codes on the bottom left of the output, you can determine that there is a static route and a RIP-learned route. RIP is a distance vector protocol. The numbers [120/1] in the RIP-learned route indicate that the administrative distance for RIP is 120, which is the default, and that network 172.16.0.0/16 is one hop away. The subnet mask for all networks is 255.255.0.0, as indicated by the /16.

2. B and E

   Because PC A appears to be cabled directly to router R1, a crossover cable is required. A router must match an interface with a RIP **network** command for that router to advertise the network or subnet on the matched interface. If R1 does not have a **network 152.16.0.0** command, R1 does not advertise network 152.16.0.0. As a result, R2 does not learn about 152.16.0.0, and R2 cannot send the ICMP echo reply messages back to PC A—making the ping fail. Similarly, if R2 does not have a **network 172.16.0.0** command, R2 does not advertise network 172.16.0.0 to R1, so R1 cannot forward the ICMP echo request packets, destined for PC B, from R1 to R2.

Chapter 7

Check Your Understanding

1. A

   Directly connected routes are indicated by the letter *C* to the left of the interface information. From the command output, you cannot determine the IP address of Serial 0/0. While the network for Serial 0/0 is 172.17.0.0, the IP address can be found with a **show run** or **show ip interface brief** command. Network 172.16.0.0 is a Fast Ethernet connection. RIP may or may not be configured on this router; with no routes learned via RIP in the routing table, it cannot be determined if RIP is configured.

2. B

   A static route is explicitly configured and entered into the routing table. The router prefers static routes by default as compared to routes learned by dynamic routing protocols.

3. D

   Split horizon is used to prevent routing loops by not sending route information back to the router from which the route information was learned.

4. A

A default route is a routing table entry that is used when no other table entry matches the destination network.

5. C

RIP V1 is classful, meaning it does not support VLSM, whereas RIP V2 is classless, meaning it does support VLSM. Cisco routers default to use RIP V1 when configured for RIP. Both versions use hop count as the metric.

6. B

RIP is a distance vector routing protocol, which uses hop count as the metric. Routers use administrative distance to determine the best route when more than one routing protocol learns a route to reach the same subnet.

7. C

The router>**show ip protocols** command verifies routing protocol operations. It can be entered from user or EXEC mode. The **show ip route** command verifies which networks the router has learned and which protocols are being used for the networks, but it does not verify the local router's IP protocol processes.

8. B

The **show ip route** command verifies which networks the router has learned about and which routing protocols are being used on those routes.

9. C

The **debug ip rip** command that was entered from privileged EXEC mode, as implied by the prompt router#.

10. D

The router#**show ip protocols** command verifies routing protocol operations. It can be entered from user or EXEC mode. The **show run** command also displays basic protocol configuration information.

11. C

The 5 at the end of the **ip route** command indicates the administrative distance the engineer wants to use (instead of 1, the default administrative distance for a static route).

12. C

A route with an administrative distance of 15 is more reliable than RIP (default administrative distance 120). It is less reliable than a static route (default administrative distance 1). Both static and dynamic routes can be configured with an administrative distance of 15.

13. A and C

A router always uses a route that has a lower administrative distance over a route to the same destination but learned from a routing source with a higher administrative distance. However, when two routes to the same destination have the same administrative distance, the router assumes the routes were learned from the same routing protocol, so the metrics are meaningful, and the router chooses the route with the best metric. If the administrative distance and the metric tie, the router adds multiple routes to reach the same destination, up to four by default, to its routing table.

Challenge Questions and Activities

1. C

Network 200.100.60.0 is two hops away because router ACME is not listening for RIP updates on the serial link (network 200.100.10.0). The 10.0 network is up and directly connected, but ACME must learn about BAY's Ethernet network via Chief, which adds a second hop. This is possible because Chief is sharing RIP information with both ACME and BAY. No static routes are configured on either router.

2. B

The routing tables show that Chief cannot see ACME's 200.100.50.0 network. RIP is configured on all routers, and ACME is advertising the 200.100.50.0 network. The **show ip protocols** output shows that ACME is using Version 1 of RIP and Chief is using Version 2. ACME can see the 50.0 network because it is directly connected, but neither BAY nor Chief knows about the route. ACME can receive Chief's V2 information, but Chief is not accepting information from RIP V1.

Chapter 8

Check Your Understanding

1. B

IP is unreliable and uses ICMP to send error messages. ICMP does not solve reliability problems and is also considered a "best effort" protocol.

2. D

ICMP stands for Internet Control Message Protocol.

3. C

An unreachable message indicating that the DF bit is set refers to packets that are larger than the interface's maximum transmission unit (MTU) and that need to be broken up. But they can't because the "don't fragment" bit instructs the router to either transmit the entire packet or discard it. This is usually because information in the packet is useless if it is not sent together, such as encryption data or frame information.

4. B and D

The TTL field is used to limit the number of times a packet can be forwarded by all routers. The field can range from 1 to 255. As each router forwards the packet, it decreases the TTL value by 1.

5. C

An echo request is generated by the **ping** command entered at a source host or router. The destination host then replies with an echo reply.

6. C

Although the host is down, the subnet in which it resides may be reachable. So the routers forward the packet to the last router, which then tries to find the destination host using ARP. Once the final router realizes that the host cannot be reached currently, the final router discards the packet and sends an ICMP host unreachable back to the original sending host.

7. C

When an ICMP unreachable message is sent to a source host, the original packet is discarded. No other attempts are made to send or forward the packet.

8. D

When a message fails, the last router sends an ICMP unreachable message back to the source host, but if the ICMP packet is discarded, the discarding device does not generate additional ICMP unreachable messages. Otherwise, the network could be filled with many ICMP unreachable messages, which would slow down the network.

Challenge Questions and Activities

1. C

Because the host is offline, the ping does not succeed. From the ACME routing table, however, you can see that there is a path to network 200.100.70.0, so the ICMP echo request should make it to the router Chief, which would send a host unreachable reply to host A.

2. A

Host B is on the 200.100.60.0 network, which, according to ACME's routing table, is reachable via the 200.100.30 network and is two hops away. The routing table tells you that the packet will travel "via 200.100.30.2," and the diagram shows that the 200.100.20.0 network is the second hop. There is not a route to host B's network via the 200.100.10.0 network, so it is not one hop away.

Chapter 9

Check Your Understanding

1. B

   The **ping** command tests basic network connectivity. The **telnet** command tests network connectivity, but a **telnet** command failure may still occur with good network connectivity. The **arp -a** command helps with local area addresses but does not test connectivity. The **debug** command does not actually test network connectivity.

2. A

   Upon discovering that the network layer connection on a WAN does not work, the technician should attempt to verify lower-layer functions. The **show controllers serial** command verifies the DTE/DCE connection at Layer 1 and whether the clock rate has been configured. **telnet** is an application layer command, and it does not work if the network layer is down. The **show run** command allows verification of configuration but not connectivity. The **show ip protocols** command allows verification of IP protocol performance, but IP protocols operate at the network layer, so this command will not help troubleshoot the Layer 3 problem.

3. B

   The technician should begin by checking all Layer 1 (physical) connections, because problems at this level are common. Then the technician should proceed in sequence from one OSI reference model layer to the next until reaching Layer 7 (application).

4. A

   Because Telnet is an application, the **telnet** command tests all seven layers of the OSI model. The **ping** and **traceroute** commands test up to Layer 3, and the **debug** command lists information, but it does not actually test connectivity.

5. B

   The **show ip route** command lists which routes the router knows, and it must be entered from either user or privileged EXEC mode.

6. B

   Displaying the IP routing table (**show ip route**) identifies known network numbers and how they were learned by the router.

7. C

   The **debug ip rip** command allows for real-time viewing of RIP updates. **show** commands display a snapshot of data about the protocols, but the **debug** commands give live updates.

8. B

   The **debug all** command debugs every process at once. It can bring down a router if used on a production network. The other **debug** commands ask for a log of specific traffic and do not impact a router as much as the **debug all** command.

9. C

   The default output for debugging commands is the console. Telnet output is supported by having the user issue the **terminal monitor** exec command. If a log is viewed on a PC, it is because the PC is viewing activity via the console connection.

10. B

   The **telnet** command provides a vty connection to remote devices.

11. D

   The **ip default-network** command can create a default route by specifying a classful network as the default network. Routing protocols can advertise this route to their neighbors, which can then use it to reach the network or any subnet of the default network. The **ip default-network** command is a global configuration command. Both the **ip route** command and the **ip default-network** command can be used to establish static routes.

12. A

   Most NICs have link status indicator lights, also known as link lights. Cisco link lights are usually green or amber. Catalyst indicators and CIDs are not device names used on NICs.

13. D

   Telnet is an application that operates at Layer 7, which is the application layer.

14. C

   The **ping** command tests whether IP packet forwarding, a Layer 3 function, works. The information gathered by the **show cdp** command relies on a working data link layer. The successful **show cdp** command indicates that Layers 1 and 2 are operational. Layer 4 troubleshooting is not helpful until Layer 3 works, which can be demonstrated with a successful **ping** command.

Challenge Questions and Activities

1. C, D, and F

   Serial interfaces 0/0 and 0/2 have both the status and the protocol down and are not working. The **show controllers** command can help troubleshoot physical connections to the interface.

   The Fast Ethernet port has the interface up but the protocol down, which indicates a Layer 2 problem.

   CDP can help troubleshoot Layer 2 problems, but Serial0/3 is not enabled at Layer 1.

2. C

   A correctly believes that 200.100.60.2 (PC B) is on a different subnet than PC A, so PC A sends the packet with the ICMP Echo request to router LA. Router LA's route to reach 200.100.60.0/24 points to router NY, over the serial link, because router LA does not have an interface connected to 200.100.60.0/24. When router NY receives the packet, the packet can then forwarded directly to PC B.

Chapter 10

Check Your Understanding

1. A

   TCP/IP is a suite of protocols that can be used to communicate across any set of interconnected networks. Other protocols help LANs and WANs communicate, but TCP/IP makes end-to-end communication possible.

2. B

   UDP provides connectionless, unreliable transmission of packets at Layer 4, the transport layer of the OSI model.

3. A

   Ports numbers allow hosts to identify which application processes send and receive the data inside TCP segments and UDP datagrams.

4. D

UDP is a connectionless protocol that exchanges datagrams without acknowledgments or guarantee.

5. C and D

A TCP segment's sequence number identifies the first byte of data in the segment. If the segments had only 1 byte of data each, the sequence numbers of the second and third segments would be 101 and 102, respectively. However, if the first segment had more than 1 byte of data, the next two segments' sequence numbers would be higher. So, the successive sequence numbers must be higher than the previous segment, so the third segment's sequence number could be 102 or 1100—but without knowing how many bytes of data are in each segment, you cannot know for sure what sequence numbers were used.

6. A

Sequence numbering is used to ensure that lost data can be recovered if problems occur later. Data received out of sequence can then be reordered into the original sequence as well. Ports are used to pass data to the correct applications. Windowing is used to determine how much data a receiver can accept.

7. C

Sliding windows is a method of flow control based on the receiver's ability to accept data. When the receiver is not busy, it can take more data between acknowledgments. When the receiver is busy, the "window size" shrinks, and fewer packets are sent between acknowledgments.

8. B

UDP segments are connectionless and contain no way to provide for reliability. Either the application layer must provide reliability, or the application must simply operate well even though lost data may not be recovered.

9. B

When the receiver is not busy, it can take more data between acknowledgments. When the receiver is busy, the "window size" shrinks, and fewer packets are sent between acknowledgments.

10. B and C

SYN flooding is a type of denial-of-service (DoS) attack in which the attacker attempts to consume the server's memory with SYN requests. The server acknowledges the request and holds memory space available for a response, but the attacker does not respond, leaving the memory unavailable for a legitimate TCP request. Sliding windows is not involved in SYN flooding, nor are port numbers ignored.

Challenge Questions and Activities

1. D

   TCP uses "expectational acknowledgments," so a host sends an acknowledgment containing the sequence it expects to receive next.

2. C

   The correct port numbers are HTTP = 80, FTP = 21, FTP data = 20, Telnet = 23, and SMTP = 25.

Chapter 11

Check Your Understanding

1. B and D

   Common ACL functions include filtering packets internally, protecting the internal network from illegal Internet access, and restricting access to virtual terminal ports. Unwanted packets are discarded, and though encryption is in the area of security, it does not apply to ACLs.

2. D

   ACL is short for Access Control List.

3. C

   Both numbered and named standard IP ACLs compare a packet's source address with the source addresses listed in the ACL. Numbered and named extended ACLs compare both source and destination addresses to the rule list.

4. A

   Both numbered and named standard IP ACLs compare a packet's source address with the source addresses listed in the ACL. Numbered and named extended ACLs compare both source and destination addresses to the rule list.

5. C

   Numbered standard IP ACLs are numbered 1–99 and 1300–1999. Extended ACLs are numbered 100–199 and 2000–2699. ACL 99 is in the standard category and is applied to the interface with the **ip access-group in|out** command. The **in** option means that the router checks packets entering the interface from the network.

6. D

As a rule, standard ACLs should be placed as close as possible to the destination to prevent unintended traffic filtering to other networks. Extended ACLs should be placed as close as possible to the source to reduce network traffic.

7. C

Numbered standard IP ACLs are numbered 1–99 and 1300–1999. Extended ACLs are numbered 100–199 and 2000–2699. ACL 87 is the only item in the standard category.

8. C

Output from the **show ip interface** command shows which IP ACLs have been applied to the interfaces. The **show ip interface brief** command displays interface configuration and link status but not ACL information. The **show ip protocols** command displays routing protocol information but not ACL data. The **show ip network** command is not a valid command.

9. B

Router(config)#**access-list 98 deny 193.20.30.0 0.0.0.255** is the correct prompt for an ACL. ACLs are configured globally, and the **access-group** command is applied in interface configuration mode.

10. C

As a rule, extended ACLs should be placed as close as possible to the source to reduce network traffic. Standard ACLs should be placed as close as possible to the destination to prevent unintended traffic filtering to other networks.

11. C

Standard ACLs use the source IP address of the packets to determine if action is necessary.

12. A

The only command with all of the correct syntax is **ip access-group 10 out**.

13. B

The ACL denies traffic only from the host 192.168.19.162. The traffic from the host is discarded at the first statement and is not allowed by the **permit any** statement.

Challenge Questions and Activities

1. C

Ping traffic from 65.120.100.10 is allowed. The ACL denies UDP traffic on port 161 (port 161 is SNMP traffic) from anywhere on the 123.120.0.0 network. Web traffic is TCP and is allowed. ICMP traffic from the 65.0.0.0 network is not filtered by the list and is allowed by the **permit ip any any** statement.

2. D

The correct syntax is

```
access-list 199  deny tcp 172.17.0.0 0.0.255.255 any eq 23
access-list 199  permit ip any any
```

Telnet is TCP and uses port 23. This is the only statement that includes both correct variables.

Decimal to Binary Conversion Table

Decimal Value	Binary Value	Decimal Value	Binary Value
0	0000 0000	23	0001 0111
1	0000 0001	24	0001 1000
2	0000 0010	25	0001 1001
3	0000 0011	26	0001 1010
4	0000 0100	27	0001 1011
5	0000 0101	28	0001 1100
6	0000 0110	29	0001 1101
7	0000 0111	30	0001 1110
8	0000 1000	31	0001 1111
9	0000 1001	32	0010 0000
10	0000 1010	33	0010 0001
11	0000 1011	34	0010 0010
12	0000 1100	35	0010 0011
13	0000 1101	36	0010 0100
14	0000 1110	37	0010 0101
15	0000 1111	38	0010 0110
16	0001 0000	39	0010 0111
17	0001 0001	40	0010 1000
18	0001 0010	41	0010 1001
19	0001 0011	42	0010 1010
20	0001 0100	43	0010 1011
21	0001 0101	44	0010 1100
22	0001 0110	45	0010 1101

Decimal Value	Binary Value	Decimal Value	Binary Value
46	0010 1110	76	0100 1100
47	0010 1111	77	0100 1101
48	0011 0000	78	0100 1110
49	0011 0001	79	0100 1111
50	0011 0010	80	0101 0000
51	0011 0011	81	0101 0001
52	0011 0100	82	0101 0010
53	0011 0101	83	0101 0011
54	0011 0110	84	0101 0100
55	0011 0111	85	0101 0101
56	0011 1000	86	0101 0110
57	0011 1001	87	0101 0111
58	0011 1010	88	0101 1000
59	0011 1011	89	0101 1001
60	0011 1100	90	0101 1010
61	0011 1101	91	0101 1011
62	0011 1110	92	0101 1100
63	0011 1111	93	0101 1101
64	0100 0000	94	0101 1110
65	0100 0001	95	0101 1111
66	0100 0010	96	0110 0000
67	0100 0011	97	0110 0001
68	0100 0100	98	0110 0010
69	0100 0101	99	0110 0011
70	0100 0110	100	0110 0100
71	0100 0111	101	0110 0101
72	0100 1000	102	0110 0110
73	0100 1001	103	0110 0111
74	0100 1010	104	0110 1000
75	0100 1011	105	0110 1001

Decimal Value	Binary Value	Decimal Value	Binary Value
106	0110 1010	136	1000 1000
107	0110 1011	137	1000 1001
108	0110 1100	138	1000 1010
109	0110 1101	139	1000 1011
110	0110 1110	140	1000 1100
111	0110 1111	141	1000 1101
112	0111 0000	142	1000 1110
113	0111 0001	143	1000 1111
114	0111 0010	144	1001 0000
115	0111 0011	145	1001 0001
116	0111 0100	146	1001 0010
117	0111 0101	147	1001 0011
118	0111 0110	148	1001 0100
119	0111 0111	149	1001 0101
120	0111 1000	150	1001 0110
121	0111 1001	151	1001 0111
122	0111 1010	152	1001 1000
123	0111 1011	153	1001 1001
124	0111 1100	154	1001 1010
125	0111 1101	155	1001 1011
126	0111 1110	156	1001 1100
127	0111 1111	157	1001 1101
128	1000 0000	158	1001 1110
129	1000 0001	159	1001 1111
130	1000 0010	160	1010 0000
131	1000 0011	161	1010 0001
132	1000 0100	162	1010 0010
133	1000 0101	163	1010 0011
134	1000 0110	164	1010 0100
135	1000 0111	165	1010 0101

Decimal Value	Binary Value	Decimal Value	Binary Value
166	1010 0110	196	1100 0100
167	1010 0111	197	1100 0101
168	1010 1000	198	1100 0110
169	1010 1001	199	1100 0111
170	1010 1010	200	1100 1000
171	1010 1011	201	1100 1001
172	1010 1100	202	1100 1010
173	1010 1101	203	1100 1011
174	1010 1110	204	1100 1100
175	1010 1111	205	1100 1101
176	1011 0000	206	1100 1110
177	1011 0001	207	1100 1111
178	1011 0010	208	1101 0000
179	1011 0011	209	1101 0001
180	1011 0100	210	1101 0010
181	1011 0101	211	1101 0011
182	1011 0110	212	1101 0100
183	1011 0111	213	1101 0101
184	1011 1000	214	1101 0110
185	1011 1001	215	1101 0111
186	1011 1010	216	1101 1000
187	1011 1011	217	1101 1001
188	1011 1100	218	1101 1010
189	1011 1101	219	1101 1011
190	1011 1110	220	1101 1100
191	1011 1111	221	1101 1101
192	1100 0000	222	1101 1110
193	1100 0001	223	1101 1111
194	1100 0010	224	1110 0000
195	1100 0011	225	1110 0001

Decimal Value	Binary Value
226	1110 0010
227	1110 0011
228	1110 0100
229	1110 0101
230	1110 0110
231	1110 0111
232	1110 1000
233	1110 1001
234	1110 1010
235	1110 1011
236	1110 1100
237	1110 1101
238	1110 1110
239	1110 1111
24	1111 0000
241	1111 0001
242	1111 0010
243	1111 0011
244	1111 0100
245	1111 0101
246	1111 0110
247	1111 0111
248	1111 1000
249	1111 1001
250	1111 1010
251	1111 1011
252	1111 1100
253	1111 1101
254	1111 1110
255	1111 1111

Access Control Entry (ACE)   A single statement in an Access Control List (ACL).

Access Control List (ACL)   A series of **access-list** commands in a Cisco router that collectively defines criteria by which a router can choose which packets to discard and which to allow through the router.

ACK   A flag in the TCP header that signifies whether the Acknowledgment field in the TCP header is meaningful.

acknowledgment   A message sent by one host in reaction to having received some data, with the message meaning that the data was received correctly.

acknowledgment number   Set in a sent TCP segment, this number notes the sequence number of the next byte this host expects to receive. It is used to recognize lost packets and perform flow control.

ACL number   A numeric parameter on the **access-list** command. All **access-list** configuration commands with the same ACL number are in the same ACL.

Address Resolution Protocol (ARP)   A TCP/IP Layer 3 protocol that allows a host that knows another IP address on the same LAN to dynamically discover that other host's MAC address.

administrative distance   A numeric value between 0 and 255 (inclusive) associated with each route based on how the router learned the route. When a router learns more than one route to reach a subnet, using multiple ways to learn routes (for example, multiple routing protocols), the router chooses the route with the lowest administrative distance.

administratively down   One possible interface state on a Cisco router. Interfaces in this state have been configured with a **shutdown** command, which purposefully disables the interface.

algorithm   The logic or process that a computer program uses to make decisions. In networking, many protocols use algorithms, including STP and all IP routing protocols.

American Registry for Internet Numbers (ARIN)   The organization to which IANA assigns the right and responsibility to assign IP addresses to organizations in North America, including the United States.

AppleTalk   A networking model developed by the Apple Computer Corporation. Cisco routers can be configured to route AppleTalk packets.

ARP broadcast   An ARP message sent by a host to request that another host—a host that uses the IP address listed in the ARP broadcast—respond with its MAC address. This message is sent to the LAN broadcast (FFFF.FFFF.FFFF) MAC address.

ARP reply   An ARP message sent in response to an ARP broadcast, which lists the MAC address of the host that sends the ARP reply.

ARP request   *See* ARP broadcast.

ARP table   A list of information learned via ARP—specifically, a list of IP addresses, their corresponding MAC addresses, and the interfaces on which the information was learned with ARP.

assignable IP address   An IP address that can be assigned to an interface. This term specifically excludes reserved IP addresses in a subnet, such as IP subnet numbers and subnet broadcast addresses.

asynchronous communication   A type of communication in which the two endpoints both use the same clock speed but make no attempt to synchronize their clocks. Analog modems typically use asynchronous communications.

asynchronous serial interface   A router interface that uses asynchronous communication.

attachment user interface (AUI)   A 15-pin connector first used with 10BASE5 Ethernet LANs. AUI connectors are sometimes used with older Ethernet NICs and router interfaces as well.

autonomous system (AS)   In the context of routing protocols, an internetwork that is under the control of one company, organization, school, or government division. For example, a single company is typically a single AS, and a school system is typically a single AS.

autonomous system number (ASN)   An integer between 0 and 65,535 that identifies a single autonomous system. Registered ASNs can be obtained by one of the authorized IANA agencies, such as ARIN in North America. Also, IGRP and EIGRP configuration uses a parameter called ASN, but this number can be any valid number and does not have to be registered.

auxiliary port (aux port)   A physical port on most Cisco routers designed to allow out-of-band access to the router. An external modem can be cabled to the aux port and a phone line attached to the modem. Then, the network engineer can use a PC and modem to call the router and log in to that router, even if the IP network is broken.

B channel   In ISDN, bearer (B) channels are separate groups of bandwidth that can transmit data to different sites. For example, a BRI line, with two B channels, can concurrently have connections to two sites, sending and receiving 64 Kbps of data with each remote site.

balanced hybrid routing protocol   The name for the underlying logic of the EIGRP routing protocol. It refers to the fact that EIGRP uses some distance vector concepts and some link-state concepts, making it a hybrid of the two.

bandwidth   In networking, a measurement of the speed of bits that can be transmitted over a particular link. It also refers to a software-based interface setting on Cisco routers that implies the actual bandwidth on the interface, used by the IGRP and EIGRP routing protocols when calculating routing metrics.

Basic Rate Interface (BRI)   A type of ISDN line composed of two 64-Kbps B channels and one 16-Kbps signaling (D) channel.

bit bucket   Jargon referring to where routers (or other devices) put discarded items such as packets.

boot   A verb meaning to initialize a computing device—for example, "Please boot the router now."

boot field   The low-order 4 bits of a Cisco router configuration register. The boot field's setting tells the router which OS to load when the router is initialized.

boot ROM   A ROM chip on a Cisco router that holds the bootstrap program, diagnostics, and, in some router models, a limited-function OS.

boot system   A global configuration command in Cisco routers that tells the router the location from which the router should get a copy of the OS that it should use, typically Cisco IOS, when the router is initialized.

booting   The process of initializing a computing device.

bootstrap   *n.* The program that a computing device loads, using hardware, to initialize enough software to look for and load the fully functional OS. *vb.* The process of loading the bootstrap program.

Border Gateway Protocol (BGP)   A routing protocol designed to exchange routing information between different autonomous systems. As such, BGP is an Exterior Gateway Protocol (EGP).

broadcast   In Ethernet, a frame that is sent to the broadcast MAC address (FFFF.FFFF.FFFF).

broadcast address   In IP addressing, a dotted-decimal address in each subnet for which packets sent to that address are forwarded to all hosts in the subnet.

bus   A collection of circuits through which data is transmitted from one part of a computer to another. The bus connects all the internal computer components to the CPU. The ISA and the PCI are two types of buses on PCs.

Carrier detect   A pin-lead on serial cables that is used by CSU/DSUs and modems to signal when the telco circuit is up and operational. The term refers to the fact that a baseline electrical signal, called the carrier signal, is being sent over the circuit.

carrier transition   On a Cisco router, the process by which a router serial interface senses that the data carrier detect (DCD) pin on the serial cable changes states (up to down, or down to up). The number of carrier transitions, as seen in the output of the **show interfaces** command, identifies the number of times the interface has gone down or come back up.

CDP advertisement   A message sent by a Cisco device, at a periodic interval, that lists important information about the device.

CDP holdtime   The amount of time a Cisco device remembers CDP information learned from a received CDP advertisement before discarding the information. Under normal operations, the neighboring device sends another CDP advertisement before the CDP holdtime expires (the default is 180 seconds).

CDP update interval   The time between CDP advertisements (the default is 30 seconds).

channel service unit/data service unit (CSU/DSU)   A device that connects to a WAN circuit on one side and a serial cable on the other, with the serial cable typically connecting to a router. The CSU/DSU understands how to perform physical (Layer 1) signaling on WAN circuits.

Checksum   An FCS-like field in the TCP header that can confirm that no errors occurred in the TCP header.

circuit   *See* leased line.

circuit switching   A process by which a networking device creates a temporary electrical circuit between two devices, forwards bits over the circuit, and then disconnects the circuit. For example, twentieth-century telephone networks created a circuit between two phones when a phone call was placed; the switching equipment forwarded the binary representation of a voice based on where the circuit was routed when the call was established.

Cisco Discovery Protocol (CDP)   A Cisco-proprietary protocol that defines a set of messages that Cisco devices send. The messages include a basic statement about the device sending the message, such as the device's name, OS level, type of device, and other configuration information. Cisco devices on neighboring data links receive these multicast CDP messages and learn about the neighboring devices.

Cisco Express Forwarding (CEF)   One of several algorithms used internally on a Cisco router for the purpose of routing or forwarding packets. The two other most widely known options are process switching and fast switching. Of these three, CEF is the fastest and lowest-overhead method.

Cisco IOS   The operating system that runs in a Cisco router.

Cisco IOS feature set   A particular subset of IOS features, built into an IOS file by Cisco. Cisco includes different subsets of the possible IOS features in a large set of IOS files. The customer can then pick the IOS with the right set of features, possibly saving money by not licensing the IOS file with the larger set of functions.

Cisco IOS File System (IFS)   The basic file system created by IOS in a Cisco router. Many commands, such as **copy**, can refer to files by using syntax that matches the IOS file system.

Cisco IOS image   A single file that contains a complete copy of the IOS.

Cisco IOS version   An alphameric value that Cisco increments over time each time Cisco changes the IOS software. The value increments when Cisco makes small bug fixes, adds small features, or adds large sets of features.

Cisco Software Advisor   A tool on Cisco.com that guides the user through the process of selecting the correct IOS image based on the needs of that user.

Cisco Technical Assistance Center (TAC)   The name of the technical support group at Cisco Systems.

classful address   A unicast IP address that is considered to have three parts: a network part, a subnet part, and a host part. The term *classful* refers to the fact that the classful network rules are first applied to the address, and then the rest of the address can be separated into a subnet and host part to perform subnetting.

classful network   A Class A, B, or C IP network, as defined by the classful rules that state that Class A networks have a one-octet network part, Class B networks have a two-octet network part, and Class C networks have a three-octet network part.

classful routing   A reference to a router's routing, or forwarding, behavior regarding whether the router uses the default route. With classful routing, if a packet's destination IP address does not match a more specific route in the IP routing table, the router forwards the packet based on the default route, but only if the routing table does not contain any subnets of that packet's classful IP network.

classful routing protocol   A routing protocol that does not send subnet masks in routing updates. Consequently, classful routing protocols cannot support variable-length subnet masking (VLSM).

classless addressing   A unicast IP address that is considered to have two parts: a prefix and a host part. The term *classless* refers to the fact that the classful network rules are not applied to the address.

classless routing   Forwarding behavior of a router whereby if a packet's destination IP address does not match a more specific route in the IP routing table, the router forwards the packet based on the default route.

classless routing protocol   A routing protocol that sends subnet masks in routing updates. Thus, classless routing protocols support variable-length subnet masking (VLSM).

client   In networking, a computer that relies on some other computer to supply a service. For example, a computer that wants to store files on another computer, look at web-based content on another server, or print documents on another computer's printer is a client.

client/server model   A method of networking between computers in which end-user computers are clients that need some services, such as a place to store and print files, and other computers act as servers to provide those services.

clock rate   The serial link function that defines the rate at which electrical signals are encoded onto the link. When using a back-to-back serial link between two routers in a lab, one router must use a DCE cable. That router must also supply clocking, as configured with the **clock rate** interface subcommand. The term clockrate can also refer to the clockrate as set by the **clock rate** command.

clock rate   An interface configuration command that tells the router the speed at which to provide clocking on a serial interface when a DCE cable has been connected to the router.

clocking   On WAN links, the process by which one device on the link is trusted to maintain the timing at which the devices encode and decode bits on the link. In normal cases, the telco provides clocking to the CSU/DSU on each link, and the CSU/DSU provides clocking to the routers.

COM port   A physical connector on a PC that can be used for a wide variety of serial communications functions. The COM port can be used with a rollover cable to connect to a Cisco router or switch console port. Along with a terminal emulator on the PC, the COM port allows a person to log in to the router or switch.

command-line interface (CLI)   The text-based interface on a Cisco router or switch.

command recall   A feature of a Cisco router or switch CLI in which the user can press a key sequence—specifically, the Up Arrow key or Ctrl-p—and the previously entered command appears in the command line. Repeatedly pressing these keys takes you further back into the history of previously entered commands.

configuration mode   An area of a Cisco router or switch CLI in which the user can enter configuration commands.

configuration register   A 16-bit value in every Cisco router that controls a wide variety of low-level functions in the router, including the speed of the console port and instructions about what OS to load when the router is initialized.

connected subnet   From a router's perspective, a subnet to which a router has connected one of its interfaces. Routers learn their initial IP routes based on being connected to these subnets.

connection-oriented   Any communications in which the sender and receiver must prearrange for communications to occur; otherwise, the communication fails.

connectionless protocol   A protocol for which the sender and receiver do not prearrange for communications to occur.

connector   In networking, a reference to a molded plastic and/or metal end to a cable that can be inserted into a socket.

console password   The password required of the user when connecting to a Cisco router or switch through that device's console port.

console port   The physical connector on a Cisco router or switch meant to allow an engineer to connect a cable and a PC, and use a terminal emulator, to gain administrative access to the CLI of the router or switch.

controller chip   A microprocessor (chip) on each Cisco router interface that controls the physical transmission and reception of bits on the interface. The **show controllers** command lists information known by the controller chip, including the type of serial cable connected to Cisco router serial interfaces.

convergence   A process by which routers recognize that something has occurred that changes some routers' routes, react to the event, and find the now currently best routes. At the end of the convergence process, all routers see the most current routing information about the internetwork. The time required for this to occur is called *convergence time*. Rapid convergence is one of the most important features of routing protocols.

copy and paste   A common user interface tool with most user interfaces in which you can select some text, copy it, move to a new window, and paste the copied text into the new window. This function is particularly useful for editing router configurations using a text editor, because the edited configurations can be copied and pasted into configuration mode in a router.

counting to infinity   An undesired process by which routers keep learning seemingly good but actually bad routes to reach a subnet, with a side effect by which the routers keep seeing the metric of the route increase slowly. This unfortunate process stops when the metric value reaches infinity (as defined by that routing protocol).

customer premises equipment (CPE)   From a telco's perspective, any equipment located at the telco's customer site.

data carrier detect (DCD)   A pin on WAN serial cables that signals whether the link is usable (DCD up) or not usable (DCD down).

data circuit-terminating equipment (DCE)   A device that supplies clocking to another device.

data communications equipment (DCE)   *See* data circuit-terminating equipment (DCE).

Data field   The field in a frame, packet, segment, or other data structure defined by some networking protocol that holds the data as supplied by a protocol defined at the next higher layer in the protocol model.

data terminal equipment (DTE)   A device that receives clocking from another device and adjusts its clock as needed.

datagram   Depending on the context, may be synonymous with *IP packet*, or may refer to a UDP header and the data encapsulated after the UDP header.

DB-9 connector   A nine-pin connector, with a shape similar to the capital letter *D*, often used for traditional PC serial ports. Cisco router and switch console cables often have a DB-9 connector to allow the cable to be connected to a PC's serial port.

DCE cable   A serial WAN cable that a router uses when the router is supplying clocking, thereby acting as data communications equipment.

debug   On Cisco routers and switches, a function with which the engineer can tell the router or switch what types of events the engineer would like to monitor. After that, when the router or switch notices one of those events occurring, the router or switch creates a log message (that is sent to the console by default), telling the engineer what happened.

DECnet   A proprietary networking model created by Digital Equipment Corporation (DEC). Cisco routers can be configured to route DECnet packets.

de-encapsulation   A process by which a computer, after it receives data over some transmission medium, examines and removes the headers and trailers at each successive higher layer, eventually handing the data to the correct application.

default gateway   On a computer, a reference to an IP address on the same subnet, with that IP address being the IP address of a router. When the computer needs to send a packet to another subnet, it sends the packet to its default gateway. Also called *default router*.

default network   A mechanism that allows a Cisco router to identify how to forward packets for which none of the routes in the routing table match the destination IP address of the packet. With this mechanism, the router identifies one classful IP network in the routing table as the default network. For packets that do not match any routes in the routing table, the router forwards the packets based on that router's route to reach the default network.

default route   A special route on a Cisco router that matches all packets destined for unicast IP addresses. If a packet's destination IP address does not match any of the other routes in a routing table, the router uses the default route.

denial-of-service (DoS) attack   A type of attack on a network in which the hacker simply tries to inflict harm on the network to the point that legitimate users cannot use the network.

deny   With Cisco ACLs, one of two actions (the other being "permit") that can be taken for packets that match a single **access list** statement. Routers discard packets matching statements with a deny action configured.

Destination Address   Generically, an address field in a header that represents the data's destination. Specifically, it could refer to a destination MAC address, a destination IP address, or any other type of addresses used with other protocols.

Destination Media Access Control (MAC) Address   The field in an Ethernet header that lists the MAC address to which a frame has been sent.

Destination Port   A field in a TCP or UDP header that identifies the application process on the receiving computer for which the data is intended.

destination port number   The value of the Destination Port field in a TCP or UDP segment.

digital signal level 0 (DS0)   The smallest single unit of transmission in the T-carrier system; runs at 64 Kbps.

digital signal level 1 (DS1)   Another member of the T-carrier system, with 24 DS0s plus 8 kbps of overhead for a total bandwidth of 1.544 Mbps. Also called *T1*.

Dijkstra Shortest Path First (SPF) algorithm   One name for the SPF algorithm, with this name giving credit to the creator of the underlying algorithm (Dijkstra). *See also* Shortest Path First (SPF) algorithm.

directly connected network   *See* connected subnet.

directly connected route   From a router's perspective, a route to reach a subnet in which one of the router's interfaces is a member. Cisco routers list these routes in the IP routing table with a *C*, meaning connected, on the left side of the routing table entry.

discontiguous network   A design choice when choosing which subnets to assign to each part of an internetwork. Some subnets of a single classful network are separated from other subnets of that same classful network by subnets of a second classful network. For example, if packets from subnet 10.1.1.0/24 have to pass through subnet

9.1.1.0/24 to reach subnet 10.2.2.0/24, network 10.0.0.0 would be discontiguous.

distance vector (DV)   A type of routing protocol algorithm that advertises each IP subnet along with a numeric metric that describes how far each subnet is from the router sending the route advertisement.

distance vector routing protocol   A routing protocol that uses the distance vector algorithm. RIP and IGRP are the two IP distance vector routing protocols, with some texts suggesting that EIGRP is an advanced distance vector routing protocol.

DNS server   A server that has a list of hostnames and corresponding IP addresses, intended for receiving requests from end-user devices and responding with the IP address that corresponds to the name listed in the DNS request.

domain name   A name, as defined by DNS, that uniquely identifies a computer in the Internet. DNS servers can then respond to DNS requests by supplying the IP address that is used by the computer that has a particular domain name. This term also refers to the part of a domain name that identifies a single company or organization, such as ciscopress.com.

Domain Name System (DNS)   An Internet-wide system by which a hierarchical set of DNS servers collectively holds all the name-IP address mappings, with DNS servers referring users to the correct DNS server to successfully resolve a DNS name.

Don't Fragment (DF) bit   A bit in the IP header of an IP packet that means that routers are not allowed to fragment the packet. If a router needs to fragment a packet that has the DF bit set, the router instead discards the packet and sends back an ICMP message to the packet's source.

dotted decimal   A convention for writing IP addresses, with four decimal numbers, ranging from 0 to 255 (inclusive), with each octet (each decimal number) representing 8 bits of the 32-bit IP address. The term originates from the fact that a dot (period) separates each of the four decimal numbers.

down and down   Jargon used to describe a Cisco router interface whose line status and protocol status are both "down."

DTE cable   A serial WAN cable that routers use to connect to an external CSU/DSU. Routers use DTE cables when, as normal, the router acts as a DTE.

Dynamic Host Configuration Protocol (DHCP)   A protocol used for the purpose of dynamically assigning IP addresses to hosts.

dynamic port numbers   Using values between 1024 and 65,535, port numbers that are allocated by clients for each new application process. Technically, IANA defines a range of 49,152 to 65,535, but in practice hosts use 1024 through 65,535.

dynamic routing protocol   A generic reference to a routing protocol that dynamically learns routes and reacts to changes in the internetwork.

dynamic sliding windows   The method by which many reliable protocols, such as TCP, increase the sequence numbers and acknowledgment numbers used to label and acknowledge data.

echo reply   An ICMP packet sent by any IP host in reaction to the receipt of an echo request. The **ping** command expects to receive this packet from a computer to which it sent an echo request.

echo request   An ICMP packet that the **ping** command sends to test connectivity.

Electronic Industries Alliance (EIA)   An association of companies in the electronics industry that often works in conjunction with the TIA to define the standards for many networking cables, including most electrical and optical LAN cables.

enable mode   An area of a Cisco router or switch CLI in which the user can issue the most powerful EXEC commands, including commands to configure the router, reload the router, and erase the configuration. The name comes from the **enable** command, which moves the router from user mode to enable mode. It is also another name for privileged mode.

enable password   Specifically, the password defined with the **enable password** command; more generally, the password required when the user enters the **enable** command to try to get from user mode to enable mode. *See also* enable secret.

enable secret   The password defined with the **enable secret** command. The **enable** exec command, which moves the user from user mode to enable mode, requires the user to enter this enable secret password. If no **enable secret** command has been configured, the **enable** command expects the enable password. *See also* enable password.

encapsulation   The process by which a computer adds networking headers and trailers to data from an application for the eventual transmission of the data onto a transmission medium.

enhanced distance vector   A term referring to the algorithms used by EIGRP. Some documents state that EIGRP's algorithms use balanced hybrid logic, and others state that EIGRP is simply an advanced version of distance vector logic.

Enhanced Interior Gateway Routing Protocol (EIGRP)
A popular Cisco-proprietary IP routing protocol that uses a robust metric, converges quickly, and is used inside a single organization.

enterprise network   A network created for and owned by a single autonomous entity, such as a corporation, government agency, or school system.

executive mode (EXEC mode)   A term referring to either of the two modes in a Cisco router or switch CLI in which the user can enter EXEC commands—namely, user mode and enable mode.

expectational acknowledgment   With protocols such as TCP that acknowledge data, the process of sending an acknowledgment number that identifies the next byte that the receiver expects to receive, rather than identifying the last byte that the receiver received. Also called *forward acknowledgment*.

explicit permit all   A statement in a Cisco ACL that matches all packets, with the statement listing an action of

permit. Such a statement means that all packets that do not match an earlier ACL statement will match the explicit permit all statement and be allowed to pass through the ACL.

extended ACL   A Cisco ACL that can match a wide variety of criteria in a single **access-list** command. For example, extended IP ACLs can match the source and destination IP addresses, the IP protocol type, and the source and destination TCP or UDP port numbers, all in a single **access-list** command.

extended ping   A **ping** command on a Cisco router in which the command accepts many other parameters in addition to the destination IP address, including the number of ICMP echo messages to send, the timeout value, and the TTL of the packets.

Exterior Gateway Protocol (EGP)   1. An obsolete IP routing protocol that exchanged routes between different autonomous systems. 2. A type of routing protocol used between different autonomous systems, with Border Gateway Protocol (BGP) being the commonly used EGP today.

exterior route   From one routing protocol's perspective, a route that the routing protocol originally learned from some other routing protocol by using route redistribution.

exterior routing protocol   Any routing protocol that is designed to exchange routing information between different autonomous systems.

external modem   A modem located outside a PC, which must be connected to the PC using a cable.

fast switching   One of several algorithms used internally on a Cisco router for the purpose of routing or forwarding packets. The two other most widely known options are process switching and Cisco Express Forwarding (CEF). Of these three, fast switching is the second fastest, with CEF being the fastest.

feature set   *See* Cisco IOS feature set.

field   In networking, a generic reference to a subset of a header or trailer that has been defined for some specific purpose. For example, IP headers include a Source IP

Address field and a Destination IP Address field, as well as other fields.

file   A collection of bits and bytes on a computer, stored together, that comprises a larger cohesive entity (for example, a single document, a single spreadsheet, a single graphics image, a single video, or a single MP3 audio file).

file format   When working with Cisco IOS files, the various types of files available from Cisco. For example, files may be compressed or not.

File Transfer Protocol (FTP)   A robust protocol used to transfer files.

FIN flag   A 1-bit field inside each TCP header that is set to binary 1 in TCP segments that are used to terminate an existing TCP connection.

fixed-function router   A router whose physical interfaces cannot be removed and replaced with other interfaces.

flag   A type of single-bit field in the TCP header, with each bit having a different meaning. For example, TCP connection establishment uses the SYN and ACK flags.

flash memory   A type of permanent computer storage, popular in Cisco routers and switches and in many consumer electronic devices.

floating static route   A static route that is assigned an administrative distance greater than the routing protocol. When the routing protocol learns a route to that same subnet as defined in the static route, the router uses the route learned by the routing protocol due to the smaller administrative distance. When the router loses the dynamically learned route, it then adds the static route to the routing table. In effect, the static route floats into and out of the routing table.

flooding   A process used by a switch or bridge to forward broadcasts and unknown destination unicasts. The switch or bridge forwards these frames out all ports except the port on which the frame was received.

flow control   A process by which computers and networking devices can increase and decrease the rate at which data is being sent; this is done to regulate the flow of traffic, which hopefully improves overall network performance.

flush timer   A timer used by distance vector routing protocols that controls when a router removes a failed route from the routing table. When a router learns that a route has failed, it does not immediately remove the route from the routing table. The flush timer is set when the router learns the route has failed, and after that much time, the router removes the route from the routing table.

forward acknowledgment   *See* expectational acknowledgment.

forwarding (Ethernet)   The process performed by a bridge or switch when it decides that it should forward a frame out another port.

forwarding (IP)   The process by which a router receives an IP packet (encapsulated inside a data-link frame), de-encapsulates the packet, matches the packet's destination to the routing table, discovers the outgoing interface and next-hop router, encapsulates the packet in a new data-link frame, and forwards the packet.

forwarding state   An interface state defined by the IEEE 802.1D STP.

fragment   When a router needs to forward a packet, and the packet is longer than the MTU of the outgoing interface, the router breaks the packet into a number of smaller packets, each of which is smaller than the outgoing interface's MTU.

fragmentation   In IP, the process by which a router breaks a packet into pieces, placing the same original IP header on each piece, and forwards the packets on to the destination host. Fragmentation may be required when a router needs to forward a packet whose length exceeds the MTU of the outgoing interface.

frame   The bits sent over a network, specifically including the data-link header, trailer, and any data encapsulated by the header and trailer.

Frame Check Sequence (FCS)   A field in the trailer of many data link layer protocols, including Ethernet, that determines whether the frame experienced any bit errors during transmission. If it did, the frame is discarded.

Frame Relay   A WAN technology that allows each site to connect to some nearby Frame Relay switch, with logical circuits called permanent virtual circuits (PVCs), allowing a router to directly send data to other sites over the single physical access link.

Frame Relay network   A WAN created using Frame Relay technology.

framing   The process of creating a frame.

gateway   Historically, the original name for a router. Now, a generic reference to any of various kinds of networking devices.

gateway of last resort   In Cisco routers, the next-hop router that a router currently uses for its default route.

global configuration command   In a Cisco router or switch, a command that defines a setting that applies to the entire router or switch.

global configuration mode   An area of a Cisco router or switch CLI in which the user can enter global configuration commands.

hardware flow control   With asynchronous communications, as are used on a Cisco router console connection, a process by which the devices can perform start/stop flow control by using the physical pins on the cable. (Cisco router console ports do not use hardware flow control.)

hardware status   *See* line status.

header   Overhead bytes added to data by some networking protocol so that protocol can interact with other computers and networking devices that implement the same protocol. The header is typically shown to the left of the end-user data so that English-language readers (who read from left to right) see the header first. The header is transmitted on the medium before the end-user data. *See also* trailer.

Header Length   A field in many headers that somehow identifies the header's length. For example, the TCP Header Length field states the number of sets of 4 bytes in the TCP header. This allows the receiving host to easily find the end of the TCP header and the beginning of the data.

High-level Data Link Control (HDLC)   A data link layer protocol used on point-to-point serial links. Cisco uses a proprietary version of HDLC as the default data link layer protocol on Cisco router serial interfaces.

history buffer   In the Cisco router and switch CLI, an area of memory that holds the commands most recently used by that user. The commands are recalled to the command line when the user presses the Up Arrow button or Ctrl-p.

holddown   The process by which a router does not believe any new routing information about a particular route to allow enough time to pass after hearing that the route has failed. Holddown helps prevent routing loops.

holddown timer   A timer that tracks how long a route that is in the holddown state has been that way.

hop count   A popularly used routing protocol metric that represents the number of routers that exist between a router and a particular subnet.

host   In TCP/IP, any computer that has an IP address. In some cases, this term includes only general purpose computers that use IP addresses. This implies that networking devices, such as routers and switches, that have IP addresses are not also hosts.

host address   An IP address used by an IP host.

hostname   A text name, useful for end users, that represents an IP address. DNS servers can be used to resolve the name into the IP address it represents.

hybrid   Generically, a mixture of two or more concepts or techniques. With regard to routing protocols, it refers to hybrid routing algorithms, which are the algorithms used by EIGRP. EIGRP is a combination of some distance vector and link-state routing protocol algorithm concepts.

hyperlink   An icon, graphic, or text on a web page that corresponds to some (hidden) URL. When a user clicks the icon, graphic, or text, the browser retrieves the web page at the hidden URL.

HyperTerminal   A terminal emulator from Hilgraeve, Inc. (http://www.hilgraeve.com) that was formerly shipped as part of most Microsoft operating systems. HyperTerminal is available for free download and can be used to access routers and switches through its console ports.

HyperText Markup Language (HTML)   A convention for how to store text and instructions in a file on a web server so that when it is downloaded to a web browser, the browser displays the correct text, colors, font sizes, and other formatting information. It is the original format used for web content.

Hypertext Transfer Protocol (HTTP)   Defines the commands, headers, and processes by which web servers and web browsers transfer files.

ICMP   *See* Internet Control Message Protocol.

ICMP echo reply   The ICMP message sent by a host when it receives an ICMP echo request message. Also called a *ping response message*.

ICMP echo request   The ICMP message sent by the **ping** command.

ICMP unreachable message   An ICMP message sent by hosts and routers when a packet must be discarded for one reason or another. The packet is sent to the host that sent the discarded packet.

IEEE (Institute of Electrical and Electronics Engineers)   An organization of professionals that does many things, including defining many LAN standards.

IGP   *See* Interior Gateway Protocol.

implicit deny all statement   A term used to describe the default action of an ACL in a Cisco router. When a router uses an ACL, and a packet does not match any of the configured ACL statements, the packet is considered to match the implicit statement at the end of the ACL, with an action of **deny**.

inbound ACL   An ACL in a Cisco router that has been enabled to process packets as they enter a router's interface.

infinite metric   With IP routing protocols, the metric value defined by that routing protocol to mean that the route has failed.

infinity   In the context of routing protocols, a reference to the metric value advertised about a route when the route has failed.

in-order delivery   A feature of TCP in which the TCP receiver reorders any data received out of order so that the receiving application always receives its data in the same order in which the sending application sent the data.

integrated circuit (IC)   A device made of semiconductor material. It contains many transistors and performs a specific task. The primary IC on the motherboard is the CPU. ICs are often called *chips*.

Integrated Services Digital Network (ISDN)   A technology used by telcos to provide digital transmission services over two-wire (one-pair) local telephone circuits to the home, as well as over four-wire circuits. Each single ISDN line has a signaling (D) channel and multiple bearer (B) channels that can be used to send data.

interface   A physical connector on a router that can be connected to a physical network to send and receive packets.

interface configuration command   A Cisco router or switch configuration command that defines some setting that relates to an interface. These commands must be entered in interface configuration mode.

interface configuration mode   An area of a Cisco router or switch CLI in which the user can enter interface configuration commands. This mode is reached by using the **interface** command from global configuration mode.

interface description   A single line of text that can be configured for any router or switch interface for the purpose of documenting any details about the use and purpose of the interface. This description is configured using the **description** interface subcommand.

interface reset counter   A per-interface counter that a router increments for many reasons, but generally the counter increments each time the router software notices some problem that means that the router cannot send traffic. One such reason would be when a router ceases to hear keepalives.

interface status   A pair of indicators that tell you whether a router or switch interface is operational. One indicator, the line status, refers to the status of the interface's physical layer features of the interface. The other indicator, the line protocol status, refers to the status of the interface's Layer 2 features.

Interior Gateway Protocol (IGP)   Any routing protocol designed to be used between routers inside the same AS. RIP, IGRP, EIGRP, and OSPF are all examples of IGPs.

Interior Gateway Routing Protocol (IGRP)   A Cisco-proprietary IP routing protocol that uses a robust metric, distance vector logic, but that has been superseded by the much faster converging EIGRP.

interior route   A route learned by a single routing protocol.

interior routing protocol   *See* Interior Gateway Protocol (IGP).

Intermediate System-to-Intermediate System (IS-IS)   An IGP routing protocol created for Layer 3 of the OSI networking model. It was later expanded to exchange both OSI and IP routes.

International Organization for Standardization (ISO)   An international standards body that defines many networking standards and that created the OSI model.

International Telecommunication Union (ITU)   An international standards body that focuses on the development of standards related to the telecommunications industry. ITU has traditionally focused on standards that affect the interconnection of telcos around the world.

Internet   The network that combines enterprise networks, individual users, and ISPs into a single global IP network.

Internet Architecture Board (IAB)   An organization that oversees the development of the TCP/IP model.

Internet Assigned Numbers Authority (IANA)   An organization that assigns the numbers important to the proper operation of the TCP/IP protocol and the Internet, including assigning globally unique IP addresses.

Internet connection   A network connection that allows bits to pass from a subscriber (which could be an individual or an enterprise) to some ISP.

Internet Control Message Protocol (ICMP)   As part of the TCP/IP Internet layer, defines protocol messages used to inform network engineers of how well an internetwork is working. For example, the **ping** command actually sends ICMP messages to determine whether a host can send packets to another host.

Internet Engineering Task Force (IETF)   The standards body responsible for the development and approval of TCP/IP standards.

Internet layer   A layer of the TCP/IP networking model. This layer includes IP, ARP, and ICMP.

Internet Packet Exchange (IPX)   A proprietary network layer protocol defined by the NetWare protocol.

Internet Protocol (IP)   One of the protocols of the TCP/IP network model. It defines the concepts of logical addressing and routing.

Internet service provider (ISP)   A company that helps create the Internet by providing connectivity to enterprises and individuals, and by interconnecting to other ISPs to create connectivity to all other ISPs.

internetwork   A combination of many IP subnets and networks, as created by building a network using routers. The term internetwork is used to avoid confusion with the term network, because an internetwork can include several IP networks.

IP ACL   An ACL that applies specifically to IP packets. *See also* Access Control List (ACL).

IP address   A 32-bit number, written in dotted-decimal notation, used by the IP to uniquely identify an interface connected to an IP network. It is also used as a destination address in an IP header to allow routing, and as a source address to allow a computer to receive a packet and to know to which IP address to send a response.

IP header   The header defined by the IP. Used to create IP packets by encapsulating data supplied by a higher-layer protocol (such as TCP) behind an IP header.

IP packet   The IP header and the data encapsulated by the IP header as it flows through a network. This term does not include any lower-layer headers or trailers.

IP routing   A process in which a router receives a packet, compares the packet's destination IP address to the router's routing table, finds the best matching route, and forwards the packet based on the instructions in that matched route.

IP routing table   A table held by a router that lists subnet and network numbers, along with details of how that router should forward packets destined for those subnets and networks. The table's entries can include the outgoing interface and the next-hop router's IP address.

IP version 4 (IPv4)   The version of the IP protocol upon which the majority of the TCP/IP internetworks are built.

IP version 6 (IPv6)   A newer version of the IP protocol to which all TCP/IP hosts might eventually migrate; however, the migration might be slow. IPv6 includes a new addressing structure that uses 128-bit-long IP addresses.

keepalive   A proprietary Cisco router function in which a router sends keepalive messages out each interface, and the router expects to receive keepalive messages in each interface. The lack of received keepalive messages for the keepalive timeout period causes the router to think that the interface has failed.

keepalive message   A proprietary Cisco message used by Cisco routers for the purpose of continuously discovering if the router's interfaces can still successfully send and receive packets.

Layer 1 device   A networking device whose main function relates to OSI Layer 1. Ethernet hubs and repeaters are examples of Layer 1 devices.

Layer 1 status   *See* line status.

Layer 2 device   A networking device whose main function relates to OSI Layer 2. Ethernet bridges and switches are examples of Layer 2 devices.

Layer 3 device   A networking device whose main function relates to OSI Layer 3. Routers are examples of Layer 3 devices.

Layer 3 forwarding   *See* routing.

leased line   A WAN service in which a company leases a transmission medium between two points. Also called *leased circuit*.

Length field   A field in many headers in networking protocols that defines the length of the frame, packet, or segment, or part of the frame, packet, or segment.

line configuration command   A Cisco router or switch configuration command that defines some setting that relates to a line, such as the console line or VTY lines. These commands must be entered in line configuration mode.

line configuration mode   In a Cisco router or switch, an area of the CLI from which the user can enter line configuration commands. This mode is reached by using the **line** command from global configuration mode.

line protocol status   The second part of the two-part status code (the first part being the line status) listed by a Cisco router's **show interfaces** command. It indicates the state of the interface's software functions or data link layer functions.

line status   The first part of the two-part status code (the second part being the line protocol status) listed by a Cisco router's **show interfaces** command. It indicates the state of the interface's hardware functions.

link   A generic term, often used for WANs and sometimes LANs, that describes a transmission medium.

link state   A type of routing protocol algorithm in which the routing protocol advertises all the details of each link in the network, each router, and the state (up or down) of each link. The routers can then create a mathematical model of the network, calculate the best path to reach each subnet, and add routes to their routing tables.

link-state advertisement (LSA)   With link-state routing protocols, the format of the information sent in routing updates. Many people use this term to refer to the routing updates themselves.

link-state database (LSDB)   The set of information about a network's topology, held in memory by a router's link state routing protocol.

link-state routing protocol   A routing protocol that uses link-state logic, which includes a process to flood all topology information to all routers so that all routers have the same knowledge of the network in their LSDBs. Additionally, link-state routing protocols process the LSDB using the Shortest Path First (SPF) algorithm to discover the currently best route to reach each subnet.

Linux   A popular operating system for PCs.

load balancing   With routers, the process in which the router first places multiple routes to reach a single subnet into the routing table and then forwards some packets over each route, balancing the bandwidth (load) over the multiple routes.

local host   When describing how Telnet works, refers to the host using the Telnet client. Because Telnet expects a human user to be sitting at a keyboard on the computer running the Telnet client, this host is local to the human user.

log message   Unsolicited informational messages sent by Cisco routers when certain events occur. These messages typically list information about some important event on the router, such as an interface failing. Debug messages are also log messages. By default, log messages go to the router's console port.

major network   Jargon that refers to a classful IP network. *See also* classful network.

maximum transmission unit (MTU)   The largest IP packet size allowed to be sent out a particular interface. Ethernet interfaces default to an MTU of 1500 because of Ethernet's limitation that the Data field of an Ethernet frame should be limited to 1500 bytes, and the IP packet sits inside the Ethernet frame's Data field.

message-of-the-day (MOTD) banner   Text information that a Cisco router or switch is configured to display to CLI users before they see the password prompt. This text is called a banner—specifically, the message-of-the-day banner.

metric   With routing protocols, the objective measurement of how good a particular route is.

microprocessor   A silicon chip that contains a CPU. A typical PC has numerous microprocessors, including the main CPU.

mode   A reference to the different parts of the Cisco IOS CLI. Different modes allow different kinds of commands (EXEC and configuration commands) and different subsets of these commands.

modem   A networking device that modulates an analog electrical signal to encode bits over an analog medium, with the receiving modem demodulating the received signal back into bits. The word modem stems from the combination of the terms modulate and demodulate.

modular router   A router whose physical interfaces can be physically removed from the router and replaced with other interfaces.

name resolution   The process by which a computer sends a DNS request to a DNS server, with a name in the request, and the DNS server replies with the IP address that corresponds to that name.

name resolution request   A message sent by a client computer toward a DNS server to ask the DNS server to supply the IP address that corresponds to a particular name.

named ACL   An ACL that is configured using a name instead of a number.

named extended ACL   A named ACL that can use a large variety of matching criteria—the same matching criteria as numbered extended ACLs.

named standard ACL   A named ACL that can check only the source IP address as the matching criteria—the same matching criteria as numbered standard ACLs.

neighboring router   A somewhat-generic term that refers to a concept in which one router connects to the same data link as another. For example, routers on the ends of a point-to-point link are neighbors, and routers connected to the same Ethernet are neighbors. Neighboring routers can send routing updates to each other.

NetWare   The name of a proprietary networking model defined by the Novell Corporation. Cisco routers can route packets defined by NetWare's Layer 3 protocol, IPX. NetWare is also the name of a server OS from Novell.

network address   A dotted-decimal number used by the IP protocol to identify an entire classful Class A, B, or C network. Also called *network number* and *network ID*.

network analyzer   A type of software and/or hardware tool that can attach to some network medium, capture all frames and packets passing over the medium, and display/interpret the data. Network analyzers help network engineers troubleshoot network problems.

network engineer   A person responsible for planning and implementing a network.

network ID   *See* network address.

network interface   A relatively generic term that refers to any physical interface connected to a network, with that interface also being used to send and receive IP packets. PC NICs and router physical interfaces are examples of network interfaces.

network interface card (NIC)   A computer card, typically used for LANs, that allows the computer to connect to some networking cable. The NIC can then send and receive data over the cable at the direction of the computer.

network layer   Layer 3 of the OSI model.

network layer protocol   Any protocol that performs functions similar to those defined in the OSI network layer (Layer 3).

network management system (NMS)   A collection of software that monitors and troubleshoots internetworks.

network model   A structured definition of protocols and standards, which includes a large variety of different net-working functions, organized into different layers, which when fully implemented allows multiple computers to communicate with each other. The two models covered in this book are the TCP/IP model and the OSI model.

network number   *See* network address.

next-hop router   The next router to which a router should send packets. The next-hop router's IP address is included in the sending router's IP routing table, which allows the sending router to correctly forward the packet.

nonvolatile RAM (NVRAM)   The location inside a Cisco router in which the router stores its initial configuration file. NVRAM's contents are not lost when the router loses power; the router typically copies the contents of NVRAM into RAM when the router boots, using that configuration as its initial configuration.

numbered ACL   An ACL that is configured using numbers instead of a text name to identify the ACL.

Open Shortest Path First (OSPF)   An openly defined IP routing protocol that uses link-state logic.

Open Systems Interconnection (OSI) model   A networking model that was meant to unify the networking world by replacing a multitude of proprietary networking models with a cohesive and comprehensive open-standard net-working model. Today, it is used as a reference for how networking models work and for its many common terms used throughout networking.

operand   Generically, a mathematical term referring to a number or variable against which an operator applies. For instance, in the equation $1 + 2 = 3$, 1 and 2 are operands. In this book, the generic syntax of the **access-list** command's parameters for matching TCP and UDP port numbers refers to the actual port numbers as operands.

operating system (OS)   Software that runs on a computer, controlling the actions taken by the computer hardware. Microsoft Windows XP and Linux are two popular PC OSs.

operator   Generically, a mathematical term referring to a symbol that identifies a mathematical action or concept. For example, the + and = symbols are both operators. In this book, the generic syntax of the **access-list** command's parameters for matching TCP and UDP port numbers uses operators of **eq** (meaning equals), **neq** (meaning not equal to), **lt** (meaning less than), **gt** (meaning greater than), and **range** (referring to a sequential range) to compare the listed TCP or UDP port(s) with the TCP or UDP header field values.

Options and Padding   Additional headers used to expand a protocol in the future.

outbound ACL   An ACL in a Cisco router that has been enabled to process packets as they exit a router's interface.

Outgoing Interface   A field in a router's IP routing table that tells the router that, to send packets to the subnet listed in the routing table entry, the router should forward the packets out this interface.

out-of-band management   A practice of sending information about the status and operations of networking devices over different communications links in comparison to the links used by the networking devices.

packet   Generically, end-user data, along with networking headers and trailers, that is transmitted through a network. Specifically, end-user data, along with the network or Internet layer headers and any higher-layer headers—but no lower-layer headers or trailers—that is transmitted through a network.

packet fragment   *See* fragment.

packet-switched network (PSN)   Any network that uses packet switching.

packet switching   The process by which a networking device forwards a collection of bits, known as a packet, based on an address in a header included in the packet. IP networks use packet switching.

Packet Tracer   A software tool from Cisco Systems, created for use by the Cisco Networking Academy Program, that can demonstrate the basics of how the flow of traffic works in networks.

partial update   With routing protocols, a process by which a routing update does not include all known routes.

Instead, partial updates typically include only information about routes that have changed.

path determination   A feature of routing protocols by which the routing protocol determines all possible routes and then chooses the best route, adding the best route to the IP routing table. Alternatively, and less frequently, it refers to a router's logic by which the router matches its own routing table entries when forwarding a packet.

path selection   The routing protocol function of examining all known routes to reach a single subnet and choosing the best route based on the metric.

periodic full routing update   A periodic routing update that includes all known routing information. *See also* periodic updates.

periodic updates   A feature of some IP routing protocols by which they send routing updates, which contain routing information, at a regular time interval or period.

permit   With Cisco ACLs, one of two actions (the other being **deny**) that can be taken for packets that match a single access-list statement. Routers do not discard packets matching statements with a **permit** action configured.

ping   A command on many computer operating systems and network devices that sends ping requests (ICMP requests) to another IP address, with the host with that IP address (hopefully) sending a response, which verifies whether the network is working properly.

ping packet   Jargon referring to ICMP echo request and echo reply messages that are sent and received by the **ping** command.

point-to-point leased line   A leased line that extends between two points. Routers typically connect to the ends of a leased line.

Point-to-Point Protocol (PPP)   A data link layer protocol used on WAN links between two routers or between any two devices or points.

point-to-point WAN link   A WAN link that connects two devices—and two devices only—essentially connecting two points in a network.

poison reverse   When learning of a failed route, a routing protocol practice by which when a router hears a poison route, it suspends split horizon rules for that route and advertises that route back out the same interface, also using a poisoned route.

port   In networking, this term is used in several ways. With Ethernet hub and switch hardware, port is simply another name for *interface*, which is a physical connector in the switch into which a cable can be connected. With TCP and UDP, a port is a software function that uniquely identifies a software process on a computer that uses TCP or UDP. With PCs, a port may be a physical connector on the PC, such as a parallel or USB port.

port number   The actual values of the 16-bit numbers, typically shown in decimal, used as ports by the TCP and UDP protocols. *See also* port.

positive acknowledgment with retransmission (PAR)
The way in which a reliable protocol, such as TCP, performs error recovery. The receiving host sends an acknowledgment identifying the next byte of data it expects to receive and, by implication, the last byte of data it received correctly. The sender can then identify whether any of its sent data was not received and then resend the data if necessary.

positive voltage   A method to measure voltage and imply the direction of current flow relative to an electrical circuit.

Post Office Protocol version 3 (POP3)   A protocol that allows a computer to retrieve e-mail from a server.

power-on self test (POST)   A term used throughout the world of computing to refer to a basic hardware function that occurs when a computer (or router or switch) is powered on. When a computer's power is first turned on, the hardware performs self-diagnostic testing of the hardware before it can load the OS into memory. This term refers to the power-on process and the self-testing (diagnostics).

prefix   In IP subnetting, the portion of a set of IP addresses whose value must be identical for the addresses to be in the same subnet.

prefix notation   On Cisco products, the style of listing subnet masks as the number of binary 1s in the mask, using a slash followed by the number, such as /24.

privileged EXEC mode   *See* enable mode.

process switching   One of several algorithms used internally on a Cisco router for the purpose of routing or forwarding packets. The two other most widely known options are fast switching and Cisco Express Forwarding (CEF). Of these three, process switching is the slowest.

prompt   The text displayed as the first several characters on the bottom line of the screen when using the Cisco IOS CLI. The cursor sits just after the prompt, so when the user types, the text shows up just to the right of the prompt.

proprietary networking model   A networking model defined by a single networking product vendor, typically without any outside assistance, and with the capability to dictate changes to the model without notifying competitors.

protocol   A written specification that defines how products should perform a certain task, typically in networking, and typically regarding logic or information as it is transmitted through a network. Each protocol defines messages, often in the form of headers, plus the rules and processes by which these messages are used to achieve some stated purpose. A standards body approves and accepts these specifications.

protocol data unit (PDU)   A generic term from OSI that refers to the data, headers, and trailers about which a particular networking layer is concerned.

protocol suite   *See* network model.

Protocol Type field   A field in a header, oftentimes a data-link header, that identifies the type of network layer protocol header that is encapsulated inside a frame.

queuing   The process of holding frames or packets in memory until the interface out which the frame or packet needs to be sent becomes available.

queuing delay   How long a frame or packet sits in a queue in a switch or router waiting for its fair chance to be sent out the interface.

random-access memory (RAM)   A type of computer memory that can have new data written to it and have stored data read from it. RAM is the main working area, or temporary storage, used by the CPU for most processing and operations. A drawback of RAM is that it requires electrical power to maintain data storage. If the computer is turned off or loses power, all data stored in RAM is lost unless the data was previously saved to disk. Memory boards with RAM chips plug into the motherboard. Also known as *read-write memory*.

read-only memory (ROM)   A type of computer memory in which data has been prerecorded. After data has been written onto a ROM chip, it cannot be removed and can only be read. A version of ROM known as EEPROM (electronically erasable programmable read-only memory) can be written to. The basic input/output system (BIOS) in most PCs is stored in EEPROM.

registered port number   Using values between 1024 and 49,151, these numbers are equivalent to well-known ports in concept but are specifically used for nonprivileged application processes.

remote host   When describing how Telnet works, refers to the host using the Telnet server to which the user wants to log on. Because Telnet expects a human user to be sitting at a keyboard on the computer running the Telnet client, this host is remote from the human user.

Request For Comments (RFC)   A document that defines TCP/IP protocols.

Reserved   In networking headers and trailers, fields that have not yet been defined for any specific purpose by any protocol and are available for new protocols to use.

resume   The process by which a user of a router or switch CLI can quickly switch between telnet connections to different routers and switches. On Cisco routers, a user can telnet to many hosts, suspend each Telnet connection, and then easily switch back and forth between connections without having to log in to each host again. Cisco uses the **resume** command to reconnect the user to a suspended Telnet connection.

rollover cable   A UTP cable pinout that specifies that the wire at pin 1 of an RJ-45 connector on one end of the cable connects to pin 8 on the other end; the wire at pin 2 connects to pin 7 on the other end; pin 3 to pin 6; and pin 4 to pin 5. This cable is used for Cisco console cables for routers and switches.

ROM Monitor (ROMMON)   A low-level operating environment or operating system used on Cisco routers for special functions. In particular, ROMMON can be used during the password-recovery process or for low-level debugging as directed by Cisco TAC.

root cause   The reason why a network problem occurs. When a network problem occurs, the users and network engineers may see a variety of symptoms. Many of these symptoms may simply be a result of the one factor that caused the problem in the first place; this one factor is called the root cause.

routable protocol   *See* routing protocol.

route poisoning   A routing protocol process by which a router notices that a route has failed but still advertises the route, but advertises it with an infinite metric.

route redistribution   The process by which on a single router one routing protocol exchanges routing information with another routing protocol. An internetwork can use different routing protocols in different sections of the internetwork. For all routers to learn all routes, some routers must run multiple routing protocols, and take the routes learned by one routing protocol and advertise them with the other routing protocol, and vice versa. This process is called route redistribution.

routed protocol   A protocol that defines a packet that can be forwarded by a router (for example, IP).

router   A network device, typically connected to a variety of LAN and WAN interfaces, that forwards packets based on their destination IP addresses.

router family   *See* router platform.

router mode   A reference to the IOS CLI configuration mode in which a routing protocol is configured. This mode gets its name from the global configuration command used to reach this mode, the **router** command.

router model series   *See* router platform.

router platform   A reference to a set of router products that have the same general physical characteristics and typically share the same set of IOS files that may be loaded and used on those routers. The routers typically have similar product numbers; for example, 2610, 2611, and 2620 are all routers in the same router platform. Also called *router family*, *router model series*, and *router series*.

router series   *See* router platform.

routing   The process by which a router receives an incoming frame, discards the data-link header and trailer, makes a forwarding decision based on the destination IP address, adds a new data-link header and trailer based on the outgoing interface, and forwards the new frame out the outgoing interface.

routing cycle   *See* routing loop.

Routing Information Protocol (RIP)   An old IP routing protocol that uses distance vector logic and hop count as the metric, with relatively slow convergence.

routing loop   An unfortunate problem during which a set of routers forwards packets destined for certain subnets in a loop, with the packets never reaching their destinations. Routing loops waste link bandwidth and cause problems for other packets whose routes do not have problems. Avoiding routing loops is one of the major functions of a routing protocol.

routing protocol   A protocol used between routers so that they can learn routes to add to their routing tables.

routing protocol algorithm   The programming logic, processes, and practices as defined by a routing protocol that specify how a particular routing protocol works.

routing protocol configuration mode   An area of a Cisco router's configuration mode reached by using the **router** global configuration command. This mode is used to configure routing protocols on a Cisco router.

routing table   A list maintained in RAM by a router that lists the best routes to reach each destination subnet. The routes each list a destination, which can be a network, sub-

net, or host, and directions on how the router should forward packets intended to reach that destination. The directions typically include a next-hop router and outgoing interface.

routing update   A message sent by a router, as defined by each routing protocol, that includes various kinds of routing information.

running-config file   The file that contains the configuration commands currently used by a router. This file can be seen by using the **show running-config** command.

segment   *vb.* The work that TCP does when it accepts a large piece of data from an application and breaks it into smaller pieces. *n.* A smaller piece of data resulting from TCP segmenting a large piece of data.

segmentation   In TCP, the process of taking a large chunk of data and breaking it into small-enough pieces to fit within a TCP segment without breaking any rules about the maximum amount of data allowed in a segment.

Sequence Number   A field in the TCP header that lists a number associated with the first byte of the data inside the TCP segment. TCP error recovery uses this number for the receiver to determine if a segment was lost in transit so that the receiver can ask the sender to resend the segment.

serial cable   A cable that routers use when connecting a router serial interface to an external CSU/DSU.

serial interface   A multipurpose physical interface on a router that is used to connect to serial WAN links. Serial interfaces can be configured to use many different data link layer protocols, including HDLC, PPP, and Frame Relay, and can support many types of serial cables.

serial link   *See* leased line.

serial port   A PC interface used for serial communication in which only 1 bit is transmitted at a time. The serial port can connect to an external modem, plotter, or serial printer. It can also connect to networking devices, such as routers and switches, as a console connection.

server   Computer hardware that is to be used by multiple concurrent users. Alternatively, computer software that provides services to many users. For example, a web server consists of web server software running on some computer.

service provider   A somewhat generic term for any company that provides service to another company, particularly some form of network connection. Examples include WAN service providers and Internet service providers.

setup mode   A tool in a Cisco router in which the router prompts the user for basic configuration information via a series of questions. When a router boots with no configuration in the NVRAM startup-config file, the router asks the user if he or she would like to use setup mode to create an initial configuration.

Shortest Path First (SPF) algorithm   The mathematical algorithm applied to a link-state database (LSDB) by a link-state routing protocol for the purpose of finding the best route to reach each subnet. The algorithm organizes the information in the LSDB into a mathematical tree, with the router at the root and the subnets as the leaves. It calculates the shortest path in the tree to reach each subnet—a process that then allows the router to know which routes are the currently best routes.

shutdown state   Jargon regarding a Cisco router or switch that refers to an interface in an "administratively down" state, which is the result of the **shutdown** command being configured on the interface.

Simple Mail Transfer Protocol (SMTP)   Defines the process by which e-mail can be forwarded and then held for later retrieval by the intended recipient.

Simple Network Management Protocol (SNMP)   An application protocol used by the network management software and actual networking devices to allow a network engineer to monitor and troubleshoot network problems.

sliding window   The process used by TCP that allows the receiving host to tell the sending host how many more bytes the sender is allowed to send before receiving an acknowledgment. The receiver tells the sender, over time, sequence numbers that get larger, so the window seems to move or slide along as the numbers increase.

smart serial interface   A type of physical connector on some serial interface cards for Cisco routers.

SMTP client   Software that implements SMTP for the purpose of sending e-mail to an SMTP server.

SMTP server   Software that implements SMTP for the purpose of receiving e-mail sent by an SMTP client.

SNMP agent   Software that responds to an SNMP request from an SNMP management station, supplying information about the device's configuration and status.

socket   In networking, can refer to a physical jack or to a feature relating to how an application program communicates with the TCP or UDP protocol on a computer.

source address   A reference to a field inside several headers in networking, specifically referring to the field that identifies the source address in the header.

Source IP Address   The field inside an IP header that lists the IP address of the host that sent the packet.

Source MAC Address   The field inside an Ethernet frame that lists the MAC address of the device that sent the frame.

Source Port   The field inside a TCP or UDP header that identifies the application process on the sending computer.

split horizon   A loop-avoidance feature used in distance vector routing protocols. Split horizon means that in routing updates sent out interface X, the router does not include routing information about routes that use interface X as the route's outgoing interface.

split horizon with poison reverse   Another term for poison reverse that emphasizes the fact that split horizon rules are suspended for the route so that the routing protocol can advertise a poison route about the failed route.

standard ACL   In a Cisco router, an IP ACL that can check any part of the packet's source IP address, but not other criteria, when deciding which packets to filter. Cisco standard ACLs use a number between 1 and 99 or between 1300 and 1999.

start/stop flow control   A method of controlling how fast data is sent in a network by allowing the receiver to tell the sender to stop and restart.

static-length subnet masking (SLSM)   The practice of using a single subnet mask for all subnets of a single classful IP network.

static route   An entry in an IP routing table that was created because a network engineer entered the routing information into the router's configuration.

structured troubleshooting method   Any organized set of steps with which any networking problem can be attacked.

subconfiguration mode   Any configuration mode besides global configuration mode in a Cisco router or switch CLI. For example, after using the **interface fa0/0** command from global configuration mode, IOS puts the user in a subconfiguration mode for that interface.

subnet   A group of IP addresses that have the same value in the first part of the IP addresses for the purpose of allowing routing to identify the group by that initial part of the addresses. IP addresses in the same subnet typically sit on the same network medium and are not separated from each other by any routers; IP addresses on different subnets are typically separated from one another by at least one router.

subnet broadcast address   The highest numeric value in a subnet. Packets sent to this address are routed to the destination subnet, at which point the packet is sent inside a Layer 2 broadcast frame so that all hosts in the subnet receive the frame. The subnet broadcast address is also useful for finding the range of assignable IP addresses in a subnet.

subnet mask   A dotted-decimal number that helps identify the structure of IP addresses. The mask represents the network and subnet parts of related IP addresses with binary 1s and represents the host part of related IP addresses with binary 0s.

subnet number   A dotted-decimal number that represents a particular IP subnet. Also called *subnet ID* and *subnet address*.

subnet zero (zero subnet)   The numerically smallest subnet number in any subnetting scheme, characterized by a value of all binary 0s in the subnet portion of the subnet number. With classful IP addressing, this subnet is one of the two reserved subnets that should not be used.

subnetting   The process of taking a classful IP network and subdividing it into smaller groups called subnets. It is the process of creating subnets.

suspending a Telnet connection   On Cisco routers, after telnetting from a router's CLI to some other host, the process of switching back to the original router's CLI by pressing Ctrl-Shift-6 and then *x*. The user can repeat this process, leaving many suspended Telnet connections open, easily connecting back to each suspended Telnet connection.

SYN   A flag in the TCP header used only in the first two segments of the three-way TCP connection establishment sequence.

SYN flood   A type of DoS attack in which the attacker sends the first of the three segments in a TCP connection request to a server but never completes the TCP connection with the third message in the TCP three-way connection setup flow. The server consumes memory and may reach its limit of the number of client connections, eventually refusing service to legitimate users. The term comes from the fact that the first of the three TCP segments has only the SYN flag set.

synchronization   A process used by two devices on either end of a transmission medium by which one end watches the incoming signal and continuously adjusts its clock based on the changes in the incoming signal. This process allows the devices to communicate even if one device's clock runs slightly slower or faster than the other device's clock.

synchronous   In networking, any communications link in which one device adjusts its timing based on signals from another device.

T/1 circuit   See digital signal level 1 (DS1).

TCP/IP *See* Transmission Control Protocol/Internet Protocol (TCP/IP).

Technical Assistance Center (TAC) The name of the technical support group at Cisco Systems.

telecommunications carrier (T-carrier) A WAN specification in the United States and some other parts of the world that defines the structure and speeds of many typical WAN transmission media.

Telecommunications Industry Association (TIA) An electrical standards body that defines the standards for many networking cables, including most electrical and optical LAN cables.

telephone company (telco) A company that traditionally provided voice services to home and businesses, but today offers voice, video, data, and other services.

Telnet Defines the protocols that allow a user on one computer to remotely access another computer, enter commands, and have those commands execute on the other computer. It is commonly used by network engineers to remotely access routers and switches.

Telnet client Software that provides a terminal emulator, with the emulator using Telnet protocols to communicate with a Telnet server, so that the user of the Telnet client can log in and issue commands on the Telnet server.

Telnet password The password that is required from the user when the user telnets to a Cisco router or switch.

Telnet server A TCP software service that can run on most any computer and allows a user on another computer to use a Telnet client to connect to the Telnet server. The commands entered on the Telnet client are sent to the Telnet server and used as commands on the Telnet server host.

Telnet session The communication that occurs between a particular Telnet client and a Telnet server.

terminal A simple old computing device that had a video screen, a keyboard, and very little processing logic.

terminal emulator Software that makes the computer act like a terminal. When a PC is connected to a router's con-sole port, the PC must use a terminal emulator so that the commands typed on the PC are sent to the router, and the messages generated by the router can be returned to the PC and displayed in the terminal emulator's window.

terminal history A list of the last several commands entered in a Cisco router or switch EXEC and configuration modes. These commands can be recalled to the command line by using the Up Arrow key or Ctrl-p, which saves typing effort when using the same commands repeatedly.

TFTP server Software, running on any computer, that implements the Trivial File Transfer Protocol (TFTP) server functions, as defined in RFC 1350. It supplies file transfer services with minimal overhead.

tftpdnld The name of a command used on Cisco routers to use TFTP to download a Cisco IOS image.

three-way handshake The three TCP segments that must flow between two hosts to create a TCP connection.

time exceeded message An ICMP message sent by a router when the router discards a packet because the router decremented the packet's Time to Live (TTL) field to 0. The router sends this message to the IP address listed as the packet's source IP address.

Time to Live (TTL) field A field in the IP header that prevents a packet from indefinitely looping around an IP internetwork. Routers decrement the TTL field each time they forward a packet, and if they decrement the TTL to 0, the router discards the packet, which prevents it from looping forever.

traceroute (tracert) A command on many computer operating systems that discovers the IP addresses, and possibly host names, of the routers used by the network when sending a packet from one computer to another.

trailer Overhead bytes added to data by some networking protocols to help the protocol perform its work by interacting with other computers and networking devices that implement that same protocol. The trailer is typically shown to the right of the end-user data so that English-language readers (who read from left to right) see the trailer last.

The trailer is transmitted on the medium after the end-user data. *See also* header.

Transmission Control Protocol (TCP) Part of the TCP/IP model. Lets applications guarantee delivery of data across a network.

Transmission Control Protocol/Internet Protocol (TCP/IP) A network model defined by the IETF that has been implemented on most computers and network devices in the world.

transport layer Layer 4 of the OSI model or Layer 3 of the TCP/IP model. Both the OSI and TCP/IP transport layer protocols perform the same kinds of functions. This layer focuses on protocols to deliver data from an application process on one computer to the correct application process on the other computer.

triggered update A routing protocol update message that is specifically sent by a router in reaction to some event in the internetwork (typically, the loss of a route).

Trivial File Transfer Protocol (TFTP) A simple protocol, which can be implemented by using a small amount of software, that allows file transfer.

Type field *See* Protocol Type field.

Type Length Value (TLV) A somewhat generic data structure, used throughout the world of computers, that allows for easy expansion of a set of consecutive fields inside a packet. The type refers to a number that identifies the type of information, the length lists the number of bytes in that TLV, and the value lists the information described by the TLV.

unicast IP address An IP address that represents a single host IP address.

Universal Resource Locator (URL) A formatted string of text that identifies any computing resource to a web browser. It includes the protocol, the name of another computer, and some information that identifies the location of the resource on the other computer. For example, http://www.cisco.com/univercd describes the HTTP protocol, a computer with hostname www.cisco.com, and a

resource (it happens to be a web page) located in a directory or file called univercd on that server.

Universal Serial Bus (USB) A type of interface found on most modern PCs that allows serial communications to occur with devices external to the PC.

Universal Serial Bus (USB) connector A PC interface that enables peripheral devices, such as mice, modems, keyboards, scanners, and printers, to be plugged in and unplugged without resetting the system. USB connectors, also called ports, eventually might replace serial and parallel ports.

unreliable protocol A protocol that does not perform error recovery.

up and down Jargon used to describe a Cisco router interface whose line status is up but whose protocol status is down.

up and up Jargon used to describe a Cisco router interface whose line status and protocol status are both up.

Urgent A field in a TCP header used to point to the sequence number of sent data for which the sender requests an immediate (urgent) acknowledgment from the receiver.

User Datagram Protocol (UDP) A major protocol in the TCP/IP networking model, an alternative to TCP at the transport layer, providing very few functions but with the benefit of less overhead.

user EXEC mode Another term for user mode, with specific emphasis on the fact that this mode allows the user to enter EXEC commands instead of configuration commands.

user mode An area of the Cisco router CLI in which the user can enter some EXEC commands but cannot use any EXEC commands that could harm the router or change how it operates.

variable-length subnet mask (VLSM) A condition in which more than one subnet mask is used in different subnets of the same Class A, B, or C network.

VINES   A proprietary networking model from the Banyan company. Cisco routers can route packets defined as part of the VINES networking model.

vty lines   Used by Cisco routers to track different Telnet users telnetted into the router at the same time. Any configuration related to Telnet, such as Telnet passwords, is configured under the vty lines.

WAN circuit   *See* leased line.

WAN interface card (WIC)   A removable card that can be installed into modular Cisco routers. WICs have different types of physical connectors that are useful for WAN connections.

web address   *See* Universal Resource Locator (URL).

web browser   A type of software product that has a graphical window to display the contents of a website. Today, Microsoft Internet Explorer, Mozilla Firefox, and Netscape are the most popular web browsers.

well-known port   Used by TCP and UDP, with a value between 0 and 1023, this port is allocated by high-privilege processes. It is used so that all clients know the correct port number to connect to.

wide-area network (WAN)   A network that connects devices in a wide geographic area that requires the use of transmission services from a WAN service provider. The service provider has the right-of-way to install cables over wide geographic areas.

wildcard mask   A 32-bit number, written in dotted decimal, used by Cisco ACLs. This mask tells IOS which bits of a source or destination IP address must match for that ACL criteria to match. Wildcard mask bits of value 0 mean that the corresponding bit positions in the addresses must be compared and must match.

window   As set in a sent segment, signifies the maximum amount of unacknowledged data the host is willing to receive before the other sending host must wait for an acknowledgment. Used for flow control.

Window field   A field in the TCP header that allows a host to tell another host how large a window the first host will grant. *See also* window.

windowing   A protocol process used by protocols (such as TCP) that perform error recovery, with the receiving host telling the sending host how much data the sending host is allowed to send before receiving an acknowledgment. Windowing implements flow control, because it enables the receiver to dictate when the sender must wait before sending more data.

withholding acknowledgments   A flow control mechanism in which the receiving host could send an acknowledgment but instead waits, thereby making the sender wait before sending any more data.

Xmodem   A serial communications protocol supported by most terminal emulators. On Cisco routers, Xmodem can be used to load a new IOS into the router, although this process is seldom used.

XNS (Xerox Network Systems)   A proprietary networking model defined by Xerox. Cisco routers can route packets defined by the XNS protocol.

zero subnet   *See* subnet zero (zero subnet).

Register this Book for
Exclusive Content

Gain access to the following benefits when you register *Routers and Routing Basics CCNA 2 Companion Guide* on ciscopress.com.

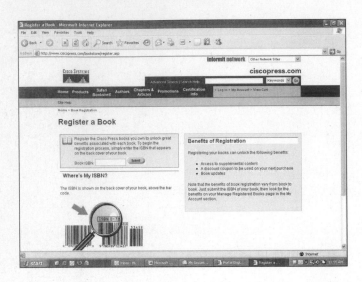

- **Packet Tracer** configuration files for activities described in the book

- PDF of chapter 5, "Managing Cisco IOS Software", from *CCNA Command Quick Reference*

- PDF of chapter 10, "Virtual LANs and Trunking", from *CCNA INTRO Exam Certification Guide*

- Coupon code for **35% off** most Cisco Press titles

To register this book, go to **www.ciscopress.com/bookstore/register.asp** and enter the book's ISBN located on the back cover. You'll then be prompted to log in or join ciscopress.com to continue registration.

After you register the book, a link to the supplemental content will be listed on your My Registered Books page.

ciscopress.com

Learning is serious business.   **Invest wisely.**

CISCO SYSTEMS